finding your roots

finding your roots

HENRY LOUIS GATES JR.

THE OFFICIAL COMPANION TO THE PBS SERIES

FOREWORD BY David Altshuler

The University of North Carolina Press • Chapel Hill

Designed and set in Miller and Myriad types by Rebecca Evans
Manufactured in the United States of America

The paper in this book meets the guidelines for permanence and
durability of the Committee on Production Guidelines for Book
Longevity of the Council on Library Resources.

The University of North Carolina Press has been a member of the
Green Press Initiative since 2003.

Jacket illustrations: photograph of Henry Louis Gates Jr. by
Bloomberg/Getty Images; background photograph courtesy of
Kunhardt McGee Productions.

Complete cataloging information for this title is available from the
Library of Congress.
ISBN 978-1-4696-1800-5 (cloth: alk. paper)
ISBN 978-1-4696-1801-2 (ebook)

18 17 16 15 14   5 4 3 2 1

FOR MARIAL IGLESIAS UTSET

CONTENTS

FOREWORD

Few questions are as universal as "where did I come from?" We ask out of native curiosity about our forebears, to understand how their choices, journeys, opportunities, and misfortunes set the stage on which we act. We ask because we want to know ourselves and to learn from clues found in the culture, ancestry, and traditions of our past. We ask because ancestors are family, even if we didn't have the chance to know them.

As children, we watch our family and surroundings, and we may be lucky enough to hear at the family dinner table stories told by parents, aunts, uncles, and grandparents. But the answers provided by such stories go back only so far in time, and they are colored by family lore. For many of us, the twists and turns of migrations and social change block our view—the record stops at Ellis Island, or behind the veil of slavery, or with a family member whose story, secrets and all, died when he or she did. Even if we are able to trace one thread or a few back into the past, the record is incomplete, for we each have many ancestors, and their stories are distinct and diverse.

Henry Louis Gates Jr. taps into this universal human desire in *Finding Your Roots*. He has gathered participants whose remarkable accomplishments and public profiles make them compelling and accessible. Gates combines the novelist's ability to craft a narrative that provides insight, the historian's rigor in exploring the documentary record, and the scientist's newfound ability to trace human history through the mapping of our genes. He combines these different ways of knowing to illustrate the varied and interacting paths of American history and American lives.

While we each may have heard a family story or examined a birth certificate, the analysis of DNA as a key to unlocking our past may be less familiar. What is DNA, how is it analyzed, and what can it tell us about our ancestors?

Each copy of the human genome contains twenty-three chromosomes, twenty-five thousand genes, and 3 billion letters of DNA. Each chromosome can be thought of as a volume in an encyclopedia, with each gene corresponding to an entry in the volume, and each chemical letter of DNA corresponding to the letters printed on the page. One of these chromosomes is involved in determining the sex of the child and is called the "sex chromosome." The other twenty-two chromosomes are present in both boys and girls, and are known as "autosomes." Like an encyclopedia, the full complement of twenty-three chromosomes contains a complete set of information—in this case, the information needed to determine the structure and regulation of proteins in our cells.

Each cell is endowed with two paired copies of this encyclopedia—one from the mother, one from the father. The only exceptions are the sperm and egg, which contain a single copy of the genome. Moreover, the sperm and egg contain not a replica of the entire genome passed on from one or the other parent, but rather a mix of the two: each chromosome is independently selected at random from among the parent's pair, resulting in a chimera. When the sperm and egg fuse at conception, the embryo receives a new and unique pair of genomes, with 50 percent having come from each parent, so that 25 percent came from each grandparent, and so on into the past.

Because all humans are the descendants of a small population that lived in Africa tens of thousands of years ago, the sequence of any two copies of the human genome is remarkably similar, differing at only one in a thousand letters. These differences in spelling exist because in each generation, in the course of copying the DNA, a very small number of errors is inadvertently introduced. These spelling differences are mostly silent at the level of our biology, but they can be passed on to offspring and then faithfully preserved through the generations. Today, scientists use these spelling differences to trace ancestry across the generations, much as Hansel and Gretel's breadcrumbs were used to trace their journey through the forest.

Because of remarkable advances in the technology for studying DNA, it is now possible to catalog the spelling differences that are common in the human population and to routinely and inexpensively measure these variations in our DNA. Statistical methods have been invented to interpret patterns of DNA variation with regard to ancestry. (These technologies, data, and methods were developed to study human disease but have been appropriated to inform studies of human history.) Because every cell in our bodies carries the entire genome sequence, almost any cell sample will do: common sources include saliva (containing cells sloughed off from the inside of the cheeks) and blood. Such samples are sent to a laboratory, where the sequence of some or all of the DNA letters can be determined. In *Finding Your Roots*, technologies were used that test only a subset of the DNA letters—a subset specifically chosen because it provides information about certain aspects of ancestry among human populations.

The simplest case of tracing ancestry with DNA limits the search to two special portions of the genome—the mitochondria and the Y chromosome. From the perspective of biology, the mitochondria are the power plant of the cell, turning the food we eat into energy that can be used by our cells, and the Y chromosome contains a gene that determines that the sex of the child will be male. From the point of view of ancestry, what makes the mitochondria and Y special is that each is passed down from only a single parent: the mitochondria are passed via the egg from the mother to her offspring (received by both boys and girls), whereas the Y chromosome is passed only from the father to his sons. The mitochondria and Y make up only a tiny portion of the genome and, as described below, trace only a tiny portion of a person's ancestry. But, because they are relatively simple to measure and easy to interpret, they were for many years a mainstay of genetic ancestry studies.

If the goal is to go back only a single generation, then the combination of mitochondrial and Y chromosomal DNA can be sufficient to trace the mother and father. But, looking any further into the past, the limits of mitochondria and Y become clear. The mitochondria trace a strictly maternal lineage: from your mother to her mother to her mother (and so on). Similarly, the Y chromosome traces only the paternal lineage: from your father to his father to his father (and so on). Ignored in such an analysis is information about the rest of your ancestors, such as your father's mother or your mother's father. That is, mitochondrial and Y chromosome analysis systematically excludes information about all your ancestors who don't trace back in a strictly maternal or paternal line.

In recent years, the field of genetic research has progressed from studying only the mitochondria and Y to studying the entire genome (that is, the twenty-two autosomes as well). Such analysis is more complete, as it captures information about the many ancestors who are not in the strict maternal and paternal lineages. But, whole-genome analysis is also more complex, because your genome is in fact a patchwork quilt made up of stretches of DNA inherited from each of many different ancestors, and whole-genome analysis needs to capture, integrate, and communicate this varied information.

Such whole-genome analysis can be particularly informative when two people are close relatives. At the level of parents and children, and all the way to third or fourth cousins, modern DNA analysis is very good at spotting stretches of DNA they share, and thereby making a definitive link. As the relationship becomes more distant, the ability of a DNA test to make the connection decreases. This is because only occasionally do distant relatives happen to inherit the same stretch of DNA from the ancestor they share. In other words, although our genomes are patchwork quilts made up of fabrics passed down from distant ancestors, not all ancestors are represented in each person's quilt.

DNA testing can also be used to estimate the proportion of a person's ancestors who lived long ago in different regions of the world—Europe, Asia, Africa, and the Americas. Such analyses exploit the fact that whereas most DNA variations are shared by all human populations, deriving from our shared ancestry in Africa, a subset of DNA variations arose or changed in frequency during the tens of thousands of years that our ancestors were migrating and living across the globe. Differences in the frequencies of these DNA variants can be used to estimate the proportion of a person's ancestors who lived in each region thousands of years ago.

Such DNA-based analyses are informative, but they face challenges of at least three types. First, the statistical methods for ancestry estimation are rapidly evolving, and different methods can give different answers even when applied to the same DNA sample. Each method depends on assumptions that color the results obtained. Just as different methods exist for evaluating baseball players based on combinations of batting average, on-base percentage, slugging and fielding statistics, etc., different methods for determining ancestry exist and are debated among researchers. While the underlying data and calculations may be "objective," the statistics and interpretation are subjective in that they weigh different factors. This state of affairs will likely continue for some time, as there are at present no generally agreed upon standards for calibrating such analyses.

A second challenge is posed by the fact that each of our genomes includes DNA from only a subset of our distant ancestors. Whereas the legacy of our parents and grandparents is well represented in our genomes, that of more distant relatives is incompletely represented. Only ten generations ago (250 years), each of us had over a thousand ancestors; twenty generations ago (500 years), over a million. Of that vast array of ancestors, only a subset has passed along DNA that lives in our genome today. This is because in each generation, the sperm or egg selects at random one of the two parental chromosomes, leaving the other behind; if an ancestor's DNA was represented only on the chromosome left behind, then it can't be detected with any DNA test regardless of the test's power or precision. For this reason, a DNA test can never prove that a distant ancestor was *not* in the family tree.

Third, estimates of ancestry are only as reliable as the population databases to which a person's DNA is compared. If a DNA test provides a highly specific origin for a person's DNA, that likely says more about the DNA database that was used for comparison, which contains that highly specific population, than it says about another population next door or across the continent that might, if included, be an even better match. There is and must be a mismatch between the question being asked—where did my ancestors live in the distant past?—and the DNA databases available for comparison, which are based on samples collected from populations that are alive today. Moreover, current human population samples remain incomplete and biased, leaving out entire groups or oversampling others.

Despite these limitations, existing DNA tests already add considerable value in genealogical research by reliably detecting close relatives and estimating the legacy of ancestors who lived in different parts of the world. Studies of DNA are of unique and particular value where traditional information is limited—because of adoption, immigration, or gaps in the records that were kept in the past or are available today. DNA tests show that many Americans have mixed ancestry, in ways both expected and not. This speaks to the cosmopolitan nature of American society and the inadequacies of labels based on racial and ethnic categories.

In combining family history, genealogical documentation, and DNA research, *Finding Your Roots* shows that a mix of many types of evidence is more illuminating and penetrating than any one type alone. Stories of families and communities, things that are personal and tangible, are of greatest interest to most of us: holding a newly found family photo or reading the announcement of an ancestor's marriage, birth, or death gives us a sense of connection. Such moments will likely always remain more powerful than anything DNA has to offer. But, where distant relatives have been lost and now can be found, or where our ancestors' stories have been obscured by the twists and turns of history, DNA offers a new light to illuminate our path back in time. Thanks to Henry Louis Gates Jr. for showing us the rich tapestry of American lives and the varied and powerful ways we now have at hand to probe our shared past.

David Altshuler, M.D., Ph.D.
Deputy Director and Chief Academic Officer,
Broad Institute of Harvard and MIT

finding
your
roots

CHAPTER ONE

Genetic Gumbo

It's often been said that people in New Orleans don't just tell history; they *do* history. You can see it everywhere in the Big Easy. The streets seem to vibrate with tradition, from the second-line parades originating in Tremé, the oldest African American neighborhood in the country, to the brass bands and twenty-four-seven parties on Bourbon Street in the French Quarter, to the dazzling array of Cajun and Creole cooking that continues to make the Crescent City one of the most exciting laboratories for culinary fusion in the world. The diversity of the people of New Orleans, a trading post that changed hands twice between the French and Spanish before joining the United States via the Louisiana Purchase, is as striking as their resilience, especially in the weeks and months following Katrina, among the most devastating hurricanes in memory. Capturing New Orleans's personality and pride—its exuberance and defiance—is the cheer emanating from any open-air bar when the city's beloved Saints score a touchdown: "Who Dat?"

Pulsating through this port city along the Mississippi River are the rhythms of jazz. A fusion of African and European musical influences, these intimate cultural and personal exchanges have characterized New Orleans since slavery. It is the city's musical form of gumbo, and in the venerable old jazz clubs that fill the Vieux Carré (French Quarter), musicians tell the story of New Orleans through their songs, solos—and improvisations.

Native sons Branford Marsalis and Harry Connick Jr. share an enduring connection to New Orleans, and to each other, as well as a passion for the marvelous music that was born there. Taken together, the stories we found about their pasts illuminate the complicated history of race in one of America's most beloved cities.

Talking with these exceptional musicians who have been immersed in New Orleans jazz for their whole lives, I began to wonder where musical gifts come from. Some people believe musical talent is part of the cultural DNA, something you pick up on the streets. Others believe musical talent is genetic: like perfect pitch and rhythm, it's passed down through generations.

Perhaps we will be able to find some answers on the branches of each musician's family tree. How have Branford's and Harry's ancestors, both known and unknown, influenced who they are today?

Branford Marsalis (b. 1960)

Born in Breaux Bridge, Louisiana, on August 26, 1960, Branford Marsalis is perhaps best known as the original bandleader for Jay Leno's *Tonight Show*. But he's also one of the most respected musicians of his generation. He is the eldest son of the so-called first family of jazz. Father Ellis is both a pianist and a gifted teacher—among his students was Harry Connick Jr.—while younger brothers Wynton, Delfeayo, and Jason are all acclaimed jazz musicians themselves. I had heard that Branford Marsalis had deep musical roots in New Orleans stretching back generations. I assumed, because his father is such an accomplished jazz musician himself, that those roots were all on his father's side. A visit to Ellis and Dolores Marsalis's New Orleans home shed light on some surprising information about the origins of their sons' musical talent.

"A lot of people think it came from my side, which it did not," Ellis told us. "There was nobody on my side of the family that I even heard of that performed, even sang. Didn't even sing in the church. . . . Now, on Dolores's side, there's several musicians, lots of them."

Dolores Ferdinand was born in 1937 in New Orleans into a family that Branford described as Creole. After spending the day in New Orleans and asking three or four different people to define Creole for me, and coming up with at least as many different answers, I asked Branford what he meant by Creole. Where did the culture first arise? He gave me a less-than-objective, thoroughly enjoyable, and essentially true history lesson:

"What it really is, quite simply, is that because France was a really cool place to live and England wasn't, when they said, 'We want to put all you on a boat and go for two months on the seas and you might die; we're going to send you somewhere and give you a piece of land,' they're like, 'Anything's better than this; I'm in.' The French were like, 'Why would I give this up to go on a boat?' So the English colonies were swelling with people. And militarily that was a problem for France, because they didn't have enough soldiers, and they couldn't get people to come to New Orleans or to the Louisiana Territory. Napoleon solves the problem by developing the Napoleonic Codes. Whereas in the English system one drop of blood meant you were black, the French version was one drop of blood meant you were French, much like in South Africa, where there was a middle culture that was established. In South Africa they call them the Coloreds, and in Louisiana they were called the Creoles."

Originally the term "Creole" was actually used to describe a white person of European descent born in the New World—white, not mixed race. After a time, in New Orleans, it came to mean a person was French and Spanish. Finally, the mulattoes—people with black and white ancestry—appropriated the term as "Creoles of color," and this is the meaning that has remained. The color line in Creole society was severe. To put this in a musical context, Creoles were not inviting the very dark-skinned Louis Armstrong to play in their parlors. Race has always been socially constructed in a very complex way in New Orleans.

French society, Branford said, was benevolent toward the Creoles. "There were schools, orchestras, which is one of the reasons why, when you hear the early New Orleans music, almost all of the clarinet players are light-skinned blacks. They're Creoles with names like Sidney Bechet and Barney Bigard and Alphonse Picou. My mother's people are part of that culture."

Branford calls his mother the "quintessential New Orleans woman. They tell you what they're thinking right off the bat." The same was true of her approach to her sons' playing. "She doesn't play music, but she has a great ear for music," Branford said. "She knows when we're playing good—and she definitely knows when we're playing bad." And, like the New Orleans woman Branford described, she has never hesitated to tell her son the truth. "She came to one of my gigs about ten years ago.

She said, 'Did y'all rehearse before y'all played?' I said, 'No, we didn't rehearse.' She goes, 'This is a damn shame. You all got paid to rehearse. Y'all should be ashamed of yourselves.' I mean, we were raggedy that night, too. Whereas a lot of people would say, 'It's just so great to see my children on stage,' she was like, 'Y'all sucked.' She knows when she hears it." That no doubt comes from being a part of a family steeped in music.

Dolores's relatives were no ordinary musicians. Some were jazz innovators, part of New Orleans musical royalty. Wellman Braud, a pioneering jazz bassist famous for playing with Duke Ellington, was the younger brother of Branford's maternal great-grandmother, Helen Braud, born in June 1881 in St. James Parish, Louisiana. In the 1900 census for the parish, Helen, described as black, is listed alongside her eight siblings.

Wellman brought a sound to music that hadn't existed before. "He was probably the first guy to employ the walking bass line, because before him, the acoustic bass was just taking the place of the tuba. The tuba was the instrument that kept the rhythm in those military bands that went bump, bump, bump, bump, bump, bump, bump, bump, bump, bump, bump, bump. And then the bass players were doing it." Branford paused and continued: "I think he's the first one that started, when the music started to subtly shift, started walking, boong, doong, doong, doong, the walking bass line. I think Wellman was the first."

Interestingly, some members of the Braud family retained the French spelling Breaux (as in the name of Branford's birthplace, Breaux Bridge), although the family was almost entirely English speaking. While members of Branford's mother's family considered themselves Creole, they would not describe the Marsalises that way. As has so often been the case in African American culture, skin color was a determining factor in status. The lighter the skin, the higher the social standing. Branford described one of his mother's brothers as a "proud Creole." "They just thought they were the bee's knees," he said, "and they would not have included us, and I felt no real desire to join that crew."

Branford is also related on his mother's side to the Dejean and Eugene families, two New Orleans music dynasties. Harold Dejean was a great saxophonist who re-formed the Olympia Brass Band in 1958. A half century before, the Olympia Brass Band had been incredibly popular, but it disbanded around World War I. Other members of the Olympia Brass Band included Wendell Eugene and Leroy Braud, no doubt distant cousins on Branford's mother's line.

In addition to the Dejeans and Eugenes, Branford's mother had said that her Braud family was related to the great New Orleans clarinetist Alphonse Picou. We couldn't find an actual blood link to him, but, ironically, our search for Picou turned up an astonishing piece of Branford's personal history that allowed us to take him deep into his mother's family tree. In this case the crucial clue was a court document that dated from 1894, two years before *Plessy v. Ferguson* made "separate but equal" the law of the land. The document details the assault and battery complaint that the colored cigar maker Alfred Picou filed against John Joseph Learson. "In his affidavit," the file read, "Alfred Picou says that he saw John Joseph Learson on Bayou Road and Villere Street and asked to introduce him to some of his friends. In response to this invitation, John Joseph called Alfred Picou an old rascal. Alfred seemed to be offended by this remark and words were exchanged. The two men continued on their way until a few minutes later, John Joseph Learson struck Alfred Picou with some sort of object from behind in the back of the head of the Plaintiff."

In our quest to find a link between Dolores Marsalis and Alphonse Picou, we had discovered Branford's great-great-grandfather was the man at the other end of the stick, so to speak: John Joseph Learson. His was a life history that would lead us to a time before the Civil War.

■ Searching for genealogical records that predate the Civil War can be profoundly difficult for African American people. This was a time when most African Americans were slaves, a people without names, identified only as "Negro" on slave rolls. For most of us, it's a black hole, and we have to rely on the paper record after emancipation and work backward to piece together our family history.

The most valuable document in this kind of research is the 1870 census, the first census where all African Americans were listed as people, not property, with both a first name and last. There, in the 1870 census for the Seventh Ward in New Orleans, is John Joseph Learson, born on May 13, 1851. The description of Learson's color is intriguing: "John, 19, male, color, Mulatto." Either John himself or the census taker assumed that he was of mixed race because of the way he looked.

This was not particularly surprising to Branford, who had long suspected that he had white ancestry. In his mother's family, there was a widely talked-about white, French great-great-grandmother. No one knew her name, but they suspected she was in their family tree somewhere.

Branford always felt the mixed ancestry of his mother's family was written on their faces.

"The Brauds, man, they could pass for high society in Cuba—light-skinned, gray eyes, straight hair," Branford said. Branford has a darker complexion than do these relatives, but he saw that ancestry in himself as well. "When the sun would come up, when I was fifteen or sixteen, in the middle of all the Black Power stuff, all these little blond hairs would come out on my arm. It was clear," he said. "They don't show up by mistake. I mean, there's some stuff there."

Most African Americans have some European ancestry somewhere on their family tree, but almost none of us can identify our white ancestors by name. To try and discover why Branford's great-great-grandfather was described as a mulatto, we searched for the name of Learson's father in the 1850 census. Astonishingly, we found it.

Most black people can get back only as far as the 1870 census—and only if they're very lucky. Here was another generation of Branford's family: John Reinhardt Learson. His race was left blank—blank in America means white—but next to his name it says "Germany."

It is something of a miracle to have such clear documentation of the name of a black person's white ancestor. For example, I know I'm descended from a black slave named Jane Gates, my great-great-grandmother. Jane had five children with the same white man, but she took the secret of his identity to her grave. I am still searching for his name today.

But in this case, we had found the white ancestor's name; that left us the task of finding the black ancestor's name—a woman we assumed was a slave. The thought of this relationship didn't shock Branford at all. "I always knew that we are descendants of slaves. There's no way to deny it. That's how we got here."

Still, finding Branford's third great-grandmother was no small undertaking. Before emancipation in 1865, the birth, death, and marriages of slaves were not part of any official record. So if Learson did father a child with a slave, finding the identity of that woman would be virtually impossible. Greg Osborn, a researcher at the New Orleans Public Library, helped us pore over historical documents left behind by Branford's relatives, systematically searching through the archives and visiting cemeteries all over New Orleans to record names from old gravestones.

The document we needed was buried deep, but Osborn found it. It was an 1851 birth certificate of John Reinhardt Learson's son, John Joseph Learson. On it was the name of the child's mother, the very woman for whom we were searching: Branford's third great-grandmother. Alongside her name—Myrte Valentin—was the unexpected description, "Free woman of color."

Branford's third great-grandmother Myrte, who had a son with the white immigrant from Germany, wasn't a slave at all. Nor did this appear to be a coercive relationship in any way. John Reinhardt Learson (original spelling Lurson) owned no slaves and fathered each of Myrte's seven children. Each one bore his surname. Someone much closer to Branford bears his name as well: his brother Wynton's middle name is Learson. Branford had known it was a name from his mother's side of the family, but never the story behind it.

Branford is one of the very few African Americans descended from black people who were free before the Civil War. Fewer than 10 percent of us can make that claim. On his mother's family tree are two generations of free Negroes before the Civil War even starts.

"It certainly allows for a head start," Branford said, struck by the information about his ancestors. "He was a noble man, clearly, to do that in those times. But if it was going to happen in America, it would happen in Louisiana, and New Orleans specifically. This was one of those places where, if that's what you wanted to do, that's what you would do."

That is the popular image of old New Orleans anyway: a freewheeling place where colorblindness and creativity reigned and differences were celebrated instead of condemned. For a time, free people of color shared some of the same freedoms as white people. They could own land; they published their own newspapers; they attended their own schools. My colleague at Harvard, Walter Johnson, has studied and written about New Orleans history extensively. I asked him: how free was free? Were there degrees of freedom, or were these free people of color as free as white people in New Orleans? "I think 'degrees of freedom' is a good phrase," Johnson replied. "It would be a mistake to imagine the city of New Orleans as a multicultural paradise. And over time, there are limitations placed on free people of color in New Orleans. After 1830 it's officially illegal for free people of color to move to the state of Louisiana."

Whatever rights free people of color had, they were continually being chipped away. "Free people of color have to carry their papers," Johnson continued. "They can be stopped on the street and made to prove out their identity. A lot of these are working class. They're what today we might call the working poor."

While the free people of color in New Orleans were freer than slaves, legally they were anything but the white man's equal, and this carried heavier burdens than their designation implied. Perhaps a more apt phrase would have been the "somewhat free people of color."

■ For all of our amazing discoveries on Branford's mother's side, we wanted to look into his father's past as well. To most Americans, the name Marsalis is practically synonymous with both jazz and New Orleans. But where does it come from? The stories that Branford had heard—that Marsalis is a Dutch name and comes from a plantation in Summit, Mississippi—are absolutely true. Any black person born with the name Marsalis around Summit, Mississippi, was most likely a former slave of a Dutch plantation owner named Peter Marsalis.

Ellis Marsalis Sr., Branford's grandfather, was a descendant of one of these slaves. Born in Summit on April 16, 1908, he looms large in Branford's memories of his childhood. As a young man, Ellis Sr. left Mississippi for New Orleans, unlike many African Americans of his generation who had chosen to move North. "Most people never leave the place where they live," Branford said. "So the only places he could have logically gone were Memphis or New Orleans. New Orleans was certainly a lot more attractive at that time than Memphis was." New Orleans, Branford explained, had an established mercantile class that didn't really exist in other places, and where it did exist—in a place like Tulsa, Oklahoma, for example—it was often put down violently. "New Orleans was a place where they could get their slice of the American pie and not have to worry about people who are embittered by their success burning their stuff down," Branford said.

After working as a hearse driver for the Duplain Rhodes Funeral Home, in 1936 Ellis Sr. became one of the first black owner-managers of an Esso gas station in the entire country. (Esso is now Exxon.) To be a business owner in the Deep South during Jim Crow could not have been easy, but Ellis Sr. didn't talk to Branford much about his past. "My paternal grandfather was a very unsentimental fellow," Branford said. "I think that was his coping mechanism for living in the segregated South. He just went from day to day and didn't look back."

In 1943 the United States was involved in two wars overseas, while at home Jim Crow laws were still strictly enforced. As a result, virtually all of the hotels and motels in the South *and* the North were for whites only. Ellis Marsalis Sr. was a man of vision, renovating a barn on his property into a place for prominent black people to stay when they were passing through New Orleans. That was the first version of the Marsalis Motel, which later became the Marsalis Mansion. The list of luminaries who spent the night there is mind-boggling: Martin Luther King Jr., Malcolm X, Count Basie, Thurgood Marshall. Mostly, though, Branford heard about the sports figures. "He was proud of the fact that Jackie Robinson stayed there. Buck O'Neil, who used to play for the Kansas City Monarchs, stayed there. Hank Aaron stayed there."

Branford said his grandfather had a lot of opinions he kept to himself. "He was an entrepreneur. It's like, should we be able to stay in the other motels? Yeah, we should. But we can't, so what do we do now? And he looked at the barn, and he said, 'There's an opportunity.' There's an opportunity here, and he took advantage of the opportunity."

Ellis Marsalis Sr.'s business savvy should not be mistaken for apathy toward civil rights. Between 1951 and 1966 he worked to register black voters in Jefferson Parish. Because of today's political climate, it may come as a surprise to younger readers that Ellis Sr. was a Republican, because, as Branford said, "The Democrats did not want a black person anywhere near a voting booth." The shift in party affiliation for blacks came largely in the 1960s, when Lyndon Johnson assumed office after John F. Kennedy's assassination. Ironically, it was the civil rights movement that led to the dismantling of all-black institutions, which of course included the Marsalis Mansion. After years of declining business, it closed in 1986 and was demolished in 1993.

Our inquiry into Branford's family history took us back to Peter Marsalis's plantation. According to Marsalis's will, the Mississippi landowner owned more than forty slaves, one of whom, Sam Marsalis, was Branford's third great-grandfather. He was born around 1825. To find a slave ancestor by name is an incredible achievement; to find the slave's owner's name is equally remarkable.

Something unusual caught our eye in the following generation. Sam's son Joseph Marsalis married Elizabeth Montgomery—Branford's great-great-grandparents—in 1886; according to birth records, though, their son Simeon had been born three years earlier, in 1883.

It wouldn't have been unusual to discover that a child was born out of wedlock. But Branford's aunt Yvette had told us that Sime, as he was known, looked slightly different from the rest of the family. In reference to his color, she called him "bricky." The fact that he didn't resemble anyone in his household made us curious about his father. Was it actually Joe? We found a document that we thought would help us unravel the mystery of Sime's paternity, if there was one: Branford's great-great-grandmother's marriage record from December 12, 1882—to a man named Ben Carter. Turns out, before Elizabeth married Joseph Marsalis, she had been married to an African American man named Ben Carter—except the certificate wasn't signed, which means the marriage never took place. We found a second document, dated a mere four days later in Amite County, Mississippi, authorizing the marriage of Lizzie Montgomery and Isaac Black. This one, however, *was* signed. Just what was Lizzie up to?

Neither the Carter name nor the Black name was known to Branford. No stories had ever been told about them. We did the math and figured out that Simeon was born ten months minus four days after Lizzie married Isaac Black, so it seems highly likely that Isaac Black was Simeon's actual father. The fate of that marriage is unknown, but when she and Joseph Marsalis married in 1886, Simeon was already three, and Joseph raised him as his own.

In other words, the Marsalis family does not actually come by its name through blood. Branford's family bears the last name of a kindhearted African American man who was willing to give his wife's son—not his own biological child—his name, a name he had adopted from the white man who owned him. Those who keep up with the Bible, or look for rhymes in history, will find it interesting that Sime's stepfather's name was Joseph.

When I passed this information along to Branford, he took a moment to absorb the news before responding. "It's OK. It's really OK," he said. "It's the whole nature-nurture thing. I am who I am because of my parents. And even though as teenagers Wynton and I did have a wonderful time going to Summit, Mississippi, and knocking on the homes of the white Marsalises and saying, 'I think we're related,' and then watching the horror on their faces, that still happened. It will still last. It's part of life." Joseph Marsalis had a history, and by marrying Lizzie and raising her son, that history became the family's history, too.

■ The paper trail tells us that Branford Marsalis has deep roots in the Deep South on both sides of his family. We rely on DNA to tell us the rest of the story. We can trace Branford's father's line back to his great-great-grandfather, Isaac Black, the husband before the husband who gave Lizzie Montgomery's son the Marsalis name. A test of Branford's Y-DNA takes us back to Africa; in other words, Isaac Black had no white ancestors on his father's line. The Y-DNA corresponds to the haplogroup E1b1a, a branch of haplogroup E, which originated about twenty thousand years ago in the pockets of western Africa. Today it is most common among the speakers of the Bantu language, reaching levels of up to 90 percent among the Mandinka and Yoruba people. Its distribution throughout Africa can be used to trace the great Bantu Migration of four thousand years ago, which started out near present-day Cameroon. This was one of the greatest migrations in human history. Spurred by the development of agriculture and iron working in the region, the migration spread haplogroup E1b throughout much of sub-Saharan Africa. It is the most common haplogroup among African American men, with about 60 percent of us falling into it because of the transatlantic slave trade. We asked AfricanAncestry.com, a company specializing in identifying the tribal origins of African American people, to examine the results to determine just where Branford's ancestors originated. Branford guessed that they were from one of the Francophone countries in Africa—maybe Benin or Sierra Leone. Our analysis reveals that it is Gabon—indeed once part of Francophone Africa—with matches to the Shaka, Tsogo, and Kota tribes.

We also tested Branford's mitochondrial DNA, which comes from his mother. He said he never thought about where his mother's line came from. "My mother reminds me so much of just being from here, not beyond here." His maternal haplogroup, we learn, is L3f1b. Between twenty thousand and thirty thousand years ago, the L3f haplogroup diversified into two subgroups called L3f1 and L3f2. L3f1 appears to have risen in East Africa and moved westward before the peak of the Ice Age, which was about twenty thousand years ago. That's when the Sahara Desert expanded and rendered much of the northern part of the continent uninhabitable. Today the haplogroup is found all across Africa, but it is relatively common among one group in Sierra Leone, the Limba. So Branford's ancestors *are* from Sierra Leone—just not on the side he had guessed.

The admixture test is the last one we administer. It calculates an individual's percentages of African, European, and Native American ancestry over the past five hundred years, since the time of Columbus. Like almost every African American person I've ever spoken to, Branford describes a grandmother who looked Native American. "I was always kind of thrown, because in her eighties, she started having braids, and goodness, she looks incredibly Indian—high cheekbones, straight black hair, olive complexion, long nose," he said. "But I think we're more European than Indian. I think it's romantic for black people to say they're Indian because they've got problems with their white ancestry."

We used two testing services for Branford's admixture. The first, Family Tree DNA, breaks his ancestry down as 71 percent African and 29 percent European. This rules out the Native American ancestor with certainty. Now, 23andMe shows very similar results, but it says 62 percent African, 31 percent European, and 7 percent Asian, which is the Native American designation. Only 5 percent of African Americans have any significant amount of Native American ancestry, and if Branford does, it is not on a direct line.

We had gone back generations on both sides of Branford's family. He had embarked on this journey with us with very few preconceived notions about his ancestry and was willing to part with them when necessary. The grandmother from long ago who he'd always thought was white turned out to be a free person of color. He wasn't related to the musician Alphonse Picou, but that misconception allowed us to find his white great-great-great-grandfather. I asked Branford what he thought were the most important factors in forming our sense of self: our experiences, our family, our societies, our genes, or some combination of those?

"It's a combination," Branford answered. "But I think that my DNA, as you explained it to me, makes me receptive, a lot more receptive to differences in people as opposed to the people who cling to similarities." He paused. "I'm fortunate to not be one of those."

If you think about it, Branford's genome is the embodiment of jazz itself, a patchwork of segments that trace ultimately to Africa and Europe. Like jazz, chromosomal quilting can transmute centuries of often painful history into beautiful art. Geneticists call this recombination; musicians call it riffing.

Harry Connick Jr. (b. 1967)

Harry Connick Jr.'s multiplatinum-selling albums have helped bring jazz standards back into the mainstream. His 1989 Grammy Award–winning soundtrack for the hit movie *When Harry Met Sally* thrust him into the spotlight at the age of twenty-two. Since then, Harry has found great success as an actor, winning praise for his role on the hit TV show *Will and Grace* and garnering a Tony Award nomination for his performance in *The Pajama Game* on Broadway.

Joseph Harry Fowler Connick Jr. was born in New Orleans on September 11, 1967, to a distinguished family. His father, Harry Connick Sr., was the district attorney of New Orleans for more than three decades, and his mother, Anita Livingston (née Levy), was one of the city's first female judges. Anita played the flute, and her brother was a musician, but no one before Harry had pursued music to the extent that he did. "I wasn't good at sports; I wasn't good in school," Harry recalled. "I just felt very, very comfortable, and I couldn't understand why everybody didn't understand the concepts of key signatures and time signatures and melody. It just seemed very easy to me." His parents encouraged Harry to start playing the piano at the age of three. It was clear he was a prodigy, mastering intricate classical pieces by Bach and Beethoven. But Harry's heart was with jazz.

New Orleans, he said, was "an unbelievable school." He absorbed all the styles of music that saturated the air. "Just solely from the musical perspective New Orleans is so diverse. The entire spectrum is represented here," he said, "from classical music to R&B. Some nights I would play at some hotel bar room playing background music. Some nights I would show up and play, and Walter Washington and George Porter and Zigaboo Modeliste would be there. And some nights I'd play modern jazz." He credits his hometown more than anything else with allowing him to hone his talent and mature as a musician. "Had I been born anywhere else, I don't think I would have been interesting to anyone. Anything that I have of any worth is because of my history here."

Harry cut his first jazz record when he was only ten. It wasn't his age that made him feel like an outsider in the milieu he loved, but his race. "It frustrated me to not be black," he said straightforwardly. "I did everything I could to get as close as I could. I tried to dress black, whatever that meant. I tried to talk black." Harry actually sought to model his look on that of Sherman Hemsley's iconic television character George Jefferson. "I was real skinny. I used to save up all my money and go to this fancy store called Rubenstein Brothers, and I would buy clothes and pull the front of my pants down and try to let my stomach hang over because I liked the way he looked on that show. I wanted to be fat and black, because all of my heroes were fat and black. Or not. Some of them weren't fat—people like Miles weren't fat, and Duke. But they were all black."

Comments from friends didn't help. "The only comments I heard about being white, and not in a mean way, but guys like Wynton and Branford would say, 'Man, you sound white, man. You need to be more negroidal.' I didn't know what that meant. I don't even know if that's a word. But those kind of things, when you're fifteen or sixteen, you go home and you look at yourself, and you say, 'I'm not part of the club.'" New Orleans history is littered with black people wanting to be white, and I may have met the only white man who wanted to be black!

Looking through Harry's family history turned out to be an experience fraught with a certain amount of apprehension. For many white people who grew up in places in the Deep South, uncovering secrets about ancestors who lived during the Civil War can be very, very difficult.

Harry told me that he's thought a lot about these roots. "My whole life I've had this sense of guilt that I really shouldn't have. But I think it's because of my association with so many black people growing up that didn't know their history primarily because things got so mixed up with slavery and identity that it was impossible for any black people to trace their roots back as far as a white person could." Harry said his guilt prevented him from looking too deeply into his family's past. "I've always felt like, you know what? They're not able to find that out, I don't really want to find it out either." Fortunately for us, though, he's changed his mind.

■ We started our journey on his father's side. Joseph Harry Fowler Connick Sr. was born in 1926 in Mobile, Alabama. The longtime district attorney of New Orleans, Harry Sr. shared a deep commitment to the city with his son. In 1993 they formed the Krewe of Orpheus, the first multicultural Krewe in the history of Mardi Gras. Krewes are historically homogeneous organizations that put on parades during Mardi Gras each year.

Before settling in New Orleans, Harry Sr.'s family had been in Mobile for three generations. His grandfather, James Paul Connick, was born there in 1902, as was Harry's great-grandfather, John Joseph Connick, in 1873. Harry was very close with his grandfather, but they never talked about how their family got to Alabama in the first place. Harry had heard that his last name might derive from Connacht in Ireland, but he's never known for sure.

The name was indeed from Ireland. Harry's first Irish immigrant ancestor, James Connick, his great-great-grandfather, arrived in America in 1853. James Connick had left County Wexford, Ireland, to escape devastating famine and religious oppression in his homeland. Once he arrived in Mobile, Alabama, he would be forced to confront the issue of slavery and racial subjugation that was threatening to tear apart his adopted country. Harry hoped that his ancestor, although living in the Deep South, would have had a critical view of slavery. "If they came from Ireland," he speculated, "they knew what it was like to be oppressed."

Harry's Irish ancestors came to this country during the nineteenth century, a time for which no national records survive. Not only were many records destroyed under British rule, but penal laws restricting the civil rights of Catholics from the late 1500s until well into the 1800s served as a powerful disincentive to keeping records in the first place. As we know, James Paul Connick came to America in 1853, a crucial moment in Irish history. It was the time of the Irish potato famine, what the Irish to this day call the Great Hunger.

On the eve of James's departure, the population of Ireland had dropped by an astonishing 20 to 25 percent. About a million died of starvation and disease, and nearly a million more left Ireland for good. James Connick was one of the multitudes looking for a better life in America. We often think of Irish immigrants as going to cities like New York, but many went to the Deep South to work as farmers, either independently or on large cotton plantations.

To learn more about James Connick and the life he led, we met with Art Green, a local Civil War historian, in Mobile, Alabama. Digging through the church registry, Green found the Connick family burial site, where today James Connick lies in an unmarked grave.

James Connick, we learn, worked on the docks as a cotton bayman or stevedore. He performed a backbreaking job loading bales of cotton onto ships—likely side by side with slaves—at the busy port of Mobile on the Mississippi River. In 1862 he married Margaret White, also an Irish immigrant, untraceable beyond her marriage certificate.

Green described what James's circumstances were probably like. "This would not have been a skilled laboring job, and probably relatively poor pay. They were like day laborers hired on the site as needed. And there would be days you simply didn't get chosen, so it would have been a day-to-day thing and probably a rather hard life." With the coming of the Civil War, that life most likely was about to get even harder.

In 1861 Confederate troops fired on Fort Sumter, South Carolina, and North and South took up arms. James Connick would have been twenty-six years old when the fighting began. And while the origins of the Civil War have been debated for generations, it was inevitably a referendum on slavery.

Harry was relieved when we informed him that his great-great-grandfather never owned slaves. But that didn't mean he favored their freedom. We found a muster roll from Company 5, 15th Confederate Cavalry, with James Connick's name on it. James joined the Confederate army in October 1861 and served for three years.

Harry was crushed. I reminded him that he wasn't responsible for his ancestors' actions, but still he felt ashamed. "To hear it for the first time, you would hope that your ancestor would have been working with Harriet Tubman or something, trying to help as many people. The fact that he's a private in the Confederacy—it's not like he tried it for six months and said, 'You know what, man? This isn't for me.'"

Wrestling with this news, Harry tried to make sense of it all. "The fact that he didn't own slaves, does that mean he just didn't have any money and he was too young? I'm grasping to try to rationalize. Maybe there were other reasons. I know that's the reason the war was fought, but was he getting paid better than working as a bayman? Was it like, 'I'm going to sign up to feed my family'?"

There are many reasons men enlisted in the Confederate army. We may never know exactly why James did, but we can imagine that life for him and his new family got a whole lot harder once the war was under way. For a bayman like Harry's great-great-grandfather, work on the docks dried up as Union troops tightened their grip on trade routes into the Port of Mobile.

Art Green, our historian in Mobile, speculated that James was probably motivated to join the army for economic reasons. "I assume that he came from Ireland under duress, looking for a better life for him and his family, and hoped he had found it, and he saw that threatened," Green said. "It was a terrible time for the South. The South had been embargoed by the federal fleet, so there was no coal for fires, there was no oil for lights. There was a bread riot in this town because there was no flour for bread. It was just a destitute time."

We found Confederate pension records that show that James received a pension from 1907 until his death in 1914. The only way to receive a pension as a Confederate soldier was if you were wounded or indigent. Still grappling with the choice his ancestor made, Harry joked that maybe his great-great-grandfather enlisted for his own nefarious reasons. "It was all a master plan to get the pension."

■ Harry's mother's background adds a new dimension to his family story. For the most part, Harry's personal experiences were firmly rooted in the South, but his mother was born into a Jewish family in New York. "I was taught to think I was this Southern Irish Catholic kid," Harry said of his upbringing. "But we were kept abreast of my mother's heritage. It wasn't a hidden thing. My mother would make us matzoball soup and things like that. She was very proud of it."

His mother loved music. She and Harry's father owned a record store while they were pursuing their law degrees. She was a flute player and a dedicated listener and supporter of her son's musical pursuits. After she became sick with ovarian cancer, the eleven-year-old Harry tried his best to make her dream of seeing him play at Carnegie Hall come true. "I called Carnegie Hall and got the number from the operator. It was a box office. I said, 'My name's Harry Connick. I'm a piano player. I'd like to play there. My mother wants me to play there.' They said, 'Well, this is the box office.' I said, 'Well, what can I do to play there? Because my mother really wants me to play.' They said, 'Well, do you have an agent? Do you have anything?' I said, 'No, I don't.' They said, 'Well . . . ' I think they understood it was a kid calling. But I told her, 'I tried, I tried.' But I still haven't played there because I'm waiting for a year to line up on her birthday where I can play. In fact, I've never even been in there because I'm waiting for that day."

Anita Frances Livingston was born in 1926 in New York City. Her surname at birth was Levy, but the family changed it. I asked Harry if he knew why. "I think Levy was a little bit too Jewish at the time," he said, "so they went for more of an Anglo-sounding name like Livingston." Unfortunately, the obstacles in tracing Jewish family histories—as with African American histories and, as we learned with Harry's paternal ancestors, Irish histories—are often insurmountable, and while we sometimes get lucky, this was not the case with Harry's grandparents. Anita's father, Gershon Levy, was from a part of Russia now in Belarus. Her mother, Mary Rothstein, was born in an area of Hungary called Uzghorod, which today is part of Ukraine. In both places, because of the persecution of Jews and the forced migrations that sent them out of Eastern Europe, records are scattered and hard to access, if they exist at all. We were able to go back three more generations on Harry's mother's side, to Germany, and Harry's second great-grandparents, Ben Zion Rothstein and Toba Fanny Hurtz. That's where the paper trail ends.

We had hoped to find some evidence of musical talent in Harry's genealogy. In addition to his mother being a flautist, he had heard that his grandmother Mary liked to sing, but there was nothing documented. That doesn't mean the talent wasn't there, just the evidence. And although the paper trail is very short on his mother's side, we can use DNA science to look further into the past.

Harry's maternal haplogroup is K1a1b1a. A few branches of haplogroup K are specific to Jewish populations, especially the Ashkenazi Jews whose roots lie in Central and Eastern Europe. These branches of haplogroup K are found at levels of 30 percent among the Ashkenazi people, but they are also found at lower levels in Jewish populations from the Near East in Africa and among those who trace their roots to medieval Spain. This indicates that the origin of the K haplogroup is in the Near East before A.D. 70, when the Roman destruction of Jerusalem scattered the Jewish people around the Mediterranean and beyond. About 1.7 million Ashkenazi Jews living today share a single branch of the K haplogroup: K1a1b1a, Harry's branch. This one branch of haplogroup K ties more than a million and a half people to a single maternal ancestor. Most people who share this haplogroup are in Belarus, Poland, Hungary, Ukraine, and Lithuania, which corresponds to what we know about Harry's family tree. Robert Downey Jr., Kyra Sedgwick, and Barbara Walters are all distant relations. In fact, Harry and Robert share so much genetic material that we were able to establish that they are fourth cousins.

On Harry's father's side, we traced his ancestry back to his great-great-grandparents James Paul Connick and Margaret White on one line, and on another to his fifth great-grandparents, David McCullough and Phoebe Boyd. Harry's paternal haplogroup is R1b, which was confined to pockets of territory in Mediterranean Europe, most notably the Iberian Peninsula, during the Ice Age. After the Ice Age, the haplogroup expanded rapidly and today is by far the most common haplogroup in Western Europe, reaching levels of about 40 percent in Great Britain, the Netherlands, Germany, Italy, and Switzerland. Harry and I share the same haplogroup, with a slight variation, but it definitely goes back to Ireland. We are genetic cousins.

The final test we administer is the admixture test, which tests African, European, and Native American ancestry over the past five hundred years. One company, 23andMe, specializes in Jewish ancestry, which provides a slightly different read of the results. Harry guessed that his admixture would be "50/50." His results actually come back 80 percent European and 20 percent Middle Eastern. Although his mother's side of the family was entirely Jewish, this means that most of her Jewish ancestors came from Europe and not Israel; in other words, she was not purely Ashkenazi herself. There had been mixing somewhere in her family's history.

Like the town that is so dear to him, Harry's background has borrowed from many parts to make a whole. He believes that what has made him who he is is a blend of his experiences, his family, his culture, and, finally, his genes. "I'm sure genetics has an umbrella effect over everything."

If the first thing that comes to mind when most Americans think of New Orleans is music or culture, a close second has to be Hurricane Katrina, which has seared our collective image of the city in the years since 2005. The horrific events following Katrina revealed the racial and economic fault lines that still exist in New Orleans today. Images of African Americans, left desperately to fend for themselves, shocked the country.

For Branford and Harry, as for many other New Orleanians, Katrina was a call to action. Harry recalled the devastation of Katrina like it was yesterday. The destruction in some parts of the city is still evident, a painful reminder of what was lost. "I'm telling you, it blows my mind," said Harry. "Every time we come home and see the markings on the doors, the x's showing the inhabitants and stuff, you can still see it, but the real inception of it was both of us were trying to say, 'God, we're about to lose our city. What can we do?'"

Together, Branford and Harry helped raise millions of dollars to rebuild homes in the severely damaged Upper Ninth Ward. The Musicians' Village provides housing for more than seventy families that lost everything in the floods. In 2011 the Ellis Marsalis Center for Music opened its doors in the Musicians' Village, a state-of-the-art performance space and music school named in honor or Branford's father and Harry's mentor.

For generations of New Orleans musicians to come, the name Marsalis will live on. But, Branford said, none of this is about the Marsalis name; it's about using your short time on this earth to do the right thing. "It's not about the media attention," Branford said. "My parents passed the idea down to us that you use your position to do things for people, but don't do it to garner more attention for yourself. You do it because it's the right thing to do. I reject the idea of calling it 'giving back to the community.' I can't give back enough to a community that made me what I am." Clearly, for Branford and Harry, inheritance isn't just about music, or names, or history, or ethnicity—it's also about community.

Like the mantra of New Orleans Saints fans, "Who Dat?" propelled our journey into the lives of the Marsalis and Connick families. The answers we found—about race, color, family, and the complex reasons immigrants came to these shores and fought for them—were as surprising as a jazz musician's improvisational lines in a song we thought we knew by heart. Thanks to jazz greats like Branford Marsalis and Harry Connick Jr., the sounds of New Orleans not only continue to be heard in the French Quarter today. They are clearer for what those playing them know and what those listening believe is possible for a city damaged but never defeated by the storm.

CHAPTER TWO

The Long Arc of Freedom

As politicians, Congressman John Lewis of Georgia and Senator Cory Booker of New Jersey have always kept their eyes fixed firmly on the future. As African Americans, they know that there is a good deal in their past that connects them. Last year, both served for the first time together in the Capitol: Lewis, the lone surviving keynote speaker from the first March on Washington in 1963 and a lion of the House since 1987; Booker, the former mayor of Newark, who, upon winning a special election in his state in 2013, became only the second African American to serve concurrently with another in the Senate. (The other, Tim Scott of South Carolina, had been the first to do so when he joined William "Mo" Cowan of Massachusetts earlier in the year before Cowan departed following a special election in his state.)

When John Lewis and Cory Booker met in 2011 at the King Center in Atlanta, where John is honored with a footprint on the Civil Rights Walk of Fame, Cory was noticeably moved. "They're my shoes," Lewis told Booker, who wasn't yet born when John Lewis took his early steps into history. "Step in them." Booker demurred. "I don't know if I want to step in the shoes, but I'll tell you what: I'm standing on your shoulders." For African Americans especially, it is often impossible to learn whose shoulders we are actually standing on. Both John and Cory knew little about their family histories—their genealogical and genetic backgrounds presented intriguing challenges and great mysteries to be solved. Our research uncovered many answers. In one man's background, we found a story of stable family relationships and quiet victories; in the other's, secrets and reconciliations that stretched back into history.

For both John Lewis and Cory Booker, we discovered a story of family lost and found.

John Lewis (b. 1940)

John Lewis is a living legend and one of my personal heroes.

The last living member of the "Big Six"—Martin Luther King, Whitney Young, A. Philip Randolph, James Farmer, and Roy Wilkins rounding out the list—John Lewis was the youngest of the leaders of the civil rights movement who transformed American race relations in the 1960s. He risked life and limb in his pursuit of equality that African Americans had been promised but denied. During the 1960s and 1970s John canvassed the South door-to-door, encouraging black people to register and vote. At sit-ins, he was dragged from lunch counters, jailed, and savagely beaten. At the March on Selma, he was hosed and brutalized along with thousands of other supporters, most of whom to this day remain anonymous but no less courageous.

Yet from his beginnings in Pike County, Alabama, it might not seem that John Lewis was destined for the front lines of a movement or a life in the political spotlight. John Robert Lewis was born in Troy, Alabama, on February 21, 1940. He and his nine siblings grew up on land that their family had farmed for generations. Early on he wanted to be a preacher, and he was baptized in the Macedonian Baptist Church when he was about nine years old. "I felt and believed as a young child I heard the trumpets sound, the voice saying go and preach," he said. The chickens that he took care of, he joked, comprised his congregation. "They never quite said amen, but I'm convinced that some of those chickens that I preached to in the '40s and the '50s tended to listen to me much better than some of my colleagues listen to me today in the Congress. And when the chicks would grow up, my mother and father wanted to kill the chicken for lunch or dinner, and that became my first nonviolent protest."

The town of Troy, where Lewis grew up, was typical of many small southern towns of the time: the white people lived predominantly in the town, and black people lived in their own communities, farther out, where the farms were. Because Lewis lived with his large family among only African Americans, he didn't really think about the concept of race until his family went into town. On a trip to Montgomery some fifty miles away, he saw the signs that said "Colored, White; White Men, Colored Men; White Women, Colored Women; White Waiting, Black Waiting." Suddenly the entire world was stratified, and young John wanted to know why.

John's world changed irrevocably in the summer of 1951, when he went to visit relatives in Buffalo, New York. "I saw another world, a different world," he remembered. "I saw black and white people living together, eating together in restaurants, at lunch counters. I rode an elevator for the first time, went in a very large department store for the first time. And I knew that it was different. It's better."

John's family told him to avoid trouble. His parents were hardworking farmers, earning a living, providing for their large family, but certainly not challenging the status quo. "They were just wonderful, beautiful people," he said of his beloved parents. "They worked so hard. They looked out for us; they took care of us. They wanted us to do better." For John, doing better meant getting an education. He had grown up with no books in his home—just a set of encyclopedias and the Sears Roebuck catalog, which he and his siblings called the "wish book"—but he was encouraged by teachers and an uncle to pursue an education.

John burned to get involved in the early civil rights movement, but the reality of activism was dangerous, and even he hung back when he first met Martin Luther King in 1958. King was eager to have the "boy from Troy," as he called him, join his fledgling movement, but he warned John, "If you pursue this, your folks can lose their home, the land. It could be bombed or burned." To spare his parents, John chose to get an education in Nashville, at the American Baptist Theological Seminary, now called American Baptist College.

While at college, John studied the philosophy and discipline of nonviolence, as well as the great religions of the world. In 1959 he and other students, black and white, convened near Fisk University—the alma mater of the incomparable W.E.B. Du Bois—for what they called test sit-ins, with discussions and activities led by a young man named Jim Lawson, a conscientious objector to the Korean War who had spent time in jail. After a year of practice, the scenarios the group acted out—a white person blowing smoke in a black person's face, maybe putting a lighted cigarette out on his or her back—ceased to be rehearsals.

After years of fighting for civil rights, in 1986 John Lewis was elected to the United States Congress, the Democratic representative from the state of Georgia. Sadly, his father didn't live to see his son's victory, but his mother did (although, being an Alabama resident, she was unable to cast a vote for her own son). John Lewis's humble beginnings might have crushed someone else, or at least kept them out of the halls of power—but now the "boy from Troy" has been a voice in Congress for nearly three decades. I couldn't help but wonder what was in John's background—whom we might meet on his family tree—that may have paved the way for this remarkable man.

■ Our journey began unpromisingly, limited by a lack of paperwork documenting the history of John's father's family. We did learn that Edward Lewis and his twin sister, Edna, were born on April 23, 1909, in Roberta, Georgia—this was news to John, who had had no idea that his father had been born outside of Alabama. We tried to trace his Georgia roots, to see what had made his family move. In our search, we started out with the 1930 census for Pike County, Alabama, which was the Lewises' home for all of John's childhood. It shows Eddie Lewis, age twenty-one, living with his mother, Lula Murphy. We knew Lula died sometime between 1930 and 1940, but we couldn't locate her—or any woman named Lula—in any of the death records filed in Alabama after 1930. Just because registering a death was legally required by law doesn't mean that it necessarily happened, especially when the deceased was a poor black person in the Deep South.

We hit a similar roadblock in tracing John's grandfather, Lula's first husband, Henry Lewis. We looked for men born in Georgia with ties to Covington or Pike County in Alabama, but there was not one record of anyone named Henry Lewis who died before 1930 who seemed to fit his description. Unfortunately, this kind of dead end is all too common when searching for information on African American families.

John was disappointed to see his paper trail on his father's side end so quickly, at his paternal grandfather. His own father, however, left his mark for generations to come—and not only in the person of his famous son. Eddie Lewis, called by the nicknames Buddy and Shortie, was the first person in his family to own land. In 1944 he bought a 110-acre parcel of land for three hundred dollars. "My father, with limited resources, limited education, he was very proud. And he wanted to be independent,"

John said, speaking with emotion. "My mother and father, they wanted to break the cycle." John credits his father with instilling in him the desire to make things better.

John would learn a great deal more about the roots of his activism when we turned to the family tree of his mother, which contained wonderful surprises.

■ John was the third generation on his mother's side born in Troy. His mother, Willie Mae Carter, was born there on June 13, 1914, as were her parents, Dink Carter, on April 25, 1884, and Della Etheridge, in October 1878. John grew up around his Carter family. Of all the subjects I have interviewed in my work tracing family histories, John is the only one who has actually known his slave ancestors personally. His great-grandfather, Frank Carter, was born a slave in Pike County, Alabama, in 1862. Frank's wife, Betsy Shipman, was born there a year later. Both were just toddlers when the Civil War ended. John says he didn't know much about his great-grandmother, Grandma Betsy. "I've heard she was part Indian," he said, citing the usual claim of African American families. "And I know she had a mean streak. We would go to visit, she would give us bread or cake, and sometimes there would be mold on it, and she would say things like, 'Just cut it off. Break it off and eat it.'" Grandma Betsy was a somewhat fearsome figure, but John recalled his great-grandfather with great warmth. "He was a wonderful man. He would sit in his rocking chair on his porch, and he acted like he was the king."

John said that the Carters, particularly his grandfather Dink and his great-grandfather Frank, had a superior attitude. "My grandfather, Dink Carter, did present the attitude or feeling that he was a step up; that he was somewhat better than others in the community." Just looking at pictures of the two men tells us the reason why. "I believe my grandfather in particular, and some of his children, because they were of a different hue. They were light, very fair, and their hair was different, what we could call good hair." As a teenager, John assumed that his great-grandfather's father was white, but it was never discussed. "I would ask my mother, my older sister. I asked my first cousin and others," John recalled. "And they would say he was our great-grandfather and we don't talk about it."

To learn more about the Shipman family, we looked back to the 1870 census, the first census in American history in which freed slaves appeared with a first and last name. The record shows his great-grandmother living with her parents, Thomas and Caroline Shipman, and her siblings. Incredibly, we had found John's second generation of slave ancestors, his great-great-grandparents. Thomas and Caroline were both born in North Carolina, in 1822 and 1824 respectively. John's North Carolina roots were a surprise. So the "boy from Troy," who thought his family was from Alabama through and through, had discovered roots in both Georgia on his father's side and North Carolina on his mother's.

Since Thomas and Caroline had lived most of their lives to this point under slavery, we guessed that they had taken their surname, Shipman, from their white master, so we looked for white men named Shipman living in the vicinity of where Thomas and Caroline lived. We obviously couldn't look for Thomas and Caroline by name, because slaves' names were not recorded in federal censuses prior to 1870. There was a separate census for slaves, called the Slave Schedule, on which individuals were listed by age, color, and gender.

According to the Slave Schedule of 1850, a man named James Shipman owned nine slaves. We looked for a male slave who was around the age of twenty-eight, on the basis of Thomas's birth year. Remember that ages were approximate, and in the record is a twenty-six-year-old black male slave who we believe is John's great-great-grandfather. This is close, but so far the evidence is circumstantial.

The key to searching for African American relatives from this era is to look in property inventories. Slaves were, of course, property, and upon the death of a slave owner, his property needed to be inventoried and distributed among his heirs. Only at this point would a slave be identified by name. In the inventory and appraisal of the estate of James Shipman, late of Barbour County, Alabama, dated September 1, 1853, we found exactly what we were looking for: "Thomas, a negro man, aged 32," valued at $1,000. Tears came to John's eyes when we showed him his ancestor's name in writing, "along with the cattle, oxen, sheep, and the tools."

John was curious to know how his ancestors got from North Carolina to Alabama. "I've always thought that somehow my entire family came from Alabama," John said. "But I guess during slavery they had to make it someplace across the way to get there." Alabama had been Indian territory, and the land the Native Americans sat on was some of the richest cotton-growing soil in the world. After Eli Whitney invented the cotton gin in 1793, the federal government wanted that soil. In 1830 Andrew Jackson signed the Indian Removal Act, sending the Five Civilized Tribes—Creek,

Choctaw, Chickasaw, Cherokee, and Seminole—on the Trail of Tears to the Indian Territory, which would become the state of Oklahoma in 1907. White settlers poured in from the Upper South to take advantage of this fertile soil that was being parceled out, and they took their slaves with them. James Shipman and his wife, Elizabeth, both born in North Carolina, were part of this influx, as were John's slave ancestors. (Condoleezza Rice's slave ancestor arrived in Alabama as part of the same migration.)

As slaves, African Americans had no choice but to go where their masters brought them. But even in freedom, they lacked the financial resources to stray very far from where they had been enslaved. Barbour County, where James Shipman held his thousand-plus acres of land—and which, incidentally, was the childhood home of Governor George Wallace—was adjacent to Pike County. In a century and a half, John's family had essentially moved one county over.

Yet, as much as we had found already, another pair of great-great-grandparents, the Carters, awaited us, complete with an inspiring and unexpected life story.

■ Tobias and Elizabeth Carter lived most of their lives as slaves not far from John's birthplace in Pike County. Tobias was born around 1825 in Georgia, Elizabeth around 1831. Though not public figures or firebrands, Tobias and Elizabeth took advantage of their freedom and their rights in a most personal, incredibly significant way: they got married.

Legal marriage was one of the many rights denied to enslaved African Americans. During slavery, many African American couples held ceremonies called "jumping the broom," rituals of marriage that were not recognized by the law. Of the many dehumanizing practices of slavery, one of the most brutal and heart wrenching was the willful destruction of families by slave owners, where children and lovers were separated and sold to the highest bidder.

Almost as soon as they were freed—ten days later, to be precise—Betty and Tobias made their union legal. The Thirteenth Amendment, which ended slavery and granted those in bondage their freedom, was ratified on December 6, 1865; the marriage license of Tobias and Betty Carter is dated December 16. A week and a half after they became free, they claimed their right to marry legally.

Tobias and Betty Carter left behind a legal paper trail very unusual for former slaves. Exactly four years after they married, on December 16, 1869,

Tobias Carter purchased a piece of property for four hundred dollars. We uncovered five deeds that show Tobias and Betty buying and selling land in the twenty years following their emancipation. At one point they owned more than two hundred acres. We had no idea how two former slaves could have amassed enough money to buy one piece of property, let alone several, in such a short period of time.

A similar mystery sits at the heart of my own family tree. My great-great-grandmother, Jane Gates, purchased a house in Cumberland, Maryland, in 1871, after living her life as a slave. She was a single woman. How could she have been able to pay for her own home in a white neighborhood? We suspect that it was given to her by her slave owner, but we've never found proof of a white plantation owner named Gates in the area. If this was true of Jane Gates, it was quite possibly true of the Carters as well. With no documentation, though, we feared this might remain an unsolved mystery for John as it has for me.

As it turns out, after emancipation, Betty and Tobias lived near a white man named Joel Carter. Because many freed slaves took their master's surnames, we suspected that Joel might have been their owner. Sure enough, Joel Carter's granddaughter had written a memoir that actually mentions Betty and Tobias by name. I visited Joel Carter's third great-grandson, Tom Buchanan, in Atlanta to view this incredible document firsthand.

About twenty years ago, when Tom was twenty-three, he found a memoir written by his great-grandaunt Sarah Abernathy in his parents' closet. He had read the document repeatedly and recognized the names Betty and Tobias Carter as soon as I asked him about them—but he had had no idea that they were any relation to John Lewis. Around 1940, Sarah Abernathy began to write down all the family stories that had been passed down to her orally over the years. It seems that Sarah's grandfather, at least in her view, was not a diehard Confederate. John read from the book. "Grandfather had about one hundred slaves, plantations, shops, and a mill. Grandfather Carter was not a secessionist, and he didn't answer Jefferson Davis' call for cotton. He had expected his wealth to be grown in slaves, and was too anxious for their health to allow his overseer to drive them. His Negroes were loyal to the Old Master."

This romantic view of the slave owner is not uncommon. After all, *Gone with the Wind* shaped many Americans' idea of what slavery was like. But Sarah followed up her description of her grandfather with a remarkable story that gives us an amazing image of Tobias and Betty Carter—and insight into life with their master: "Betts, the cook armed with an ax, stood at the door and defied the Yanks to pester old master or to enter the home. For her loyalty, she and her husband were given a piece of land, a cabin, and supplies. My grandfather said, 'They have grown old in my service. I share with them what they have helped produce. My children are young and able to get for themselves what Toby and Betts are too old and feeble to earn.'"

When conjuring up images of master-slave relations, that of a female slave wielding an ax to protect her slave master isn't one that often comes to mind. I asked John if it bothered him to learn that his ancestors were loyal to their master during the Civil War. "No, it doesn't disturb me. There's relationships," he said thoughtfully. "You be around people, you become family."

■ Before we embarked on our journey through his family tree, though, John Lewis had no idea how deeply ingrained his family's bonds were, or how closely their achievements mirrored his own, albeit in less public ways. As a civil rights hero, John Lewis is most closely associated with voting rights for African Americans. By the 1960s, in a country where African Americans had been freed and granted the right to vote one hundred years before, blacks had become increasingly disenfranchised. What we uncovered in our research of the Lewis family tree made his long-fought battles personal.

We had learned that Tobias Carter had gotten married as soon as he was legally able, bought and sold land at a rate that was often unheard of among recently freed slaves—but he exercised his rights as a free citizen after emancipation in another way that came as a shock to John Lewis and me. In 1867 the U.S. Congress—of which John Lewis is now a member—passed a statute saying that it was unconstitutional to deprive anyone of the right to vote because of his or her race. Theoretically, black people could now make their voices heard as members of the electorate. On the voter registration rolls for Alabama in the year 1867, one name stood out to us from all the others: Tobias Carter.

John became very emotional at this discovery. "I don't think my parents or grandparents ever voted before 1965," he said, overwhelmed. "They weren't allowed to register to vote, as far as I know." Between 1867 and 1965, Tobias Carter and John Lewis were quite possibly the only two members of their family to cast a vote.

Tobias's right was short-lived. Harvard Law professor Ken Mack explained that in 1874, the Democrats won the majority in the Alabama legislature. Simply put, they did not want African Americans to vote. "There was rampant violence throughout Alabama, throughout the 1860s and '70s. Voters were intimidated at the polls," Professor Mack said. To put this history into perspective, it is interesting to compare numbers. In 1867, the year that Tobias Carter registered to vote, 41 percent of black men in Alabama did the same. In the 1940s, only 3 percent of black people in the entire South were registered. The unprecedented degree of freedom experienced by Tobias Carter and other blacks across the post–Civil War South had disappeared within a decade, only to be brought back by John Lewis. "Yes," Mack said, "to be brought back by John Lewis and people like him, who got beaten and some of them got killed in order that we can vote today as equal citizens."

Just shy of a century after John's great-great-grandfather registered to vote for the first time in his life, John would take part in what has gone down as one of the most egregious abuses of American citizens by American citizens in the painful history of this country. John describes that day, March 7, 1965, whose images have been seared into the national consciousness and would become a rallying cry for the civil rights movement and human rights. "About six hundred of us had gathered at a little church, Brown Chapel AME Church in Selma, to dramatize to the nation and to the world that people of color wanted to register to vote. In Selma, Alabama," Lewis explained, "only 2.1 percent of blacks of voting age were registered." He recounted some of the indignities blacks were subject to when attempting to register to vote: "You had to pass a so-called literacy test. On one occasion a man was asked to count the number of bubbles on a bar of soap. On another occasion, a man was asked to count the number of jellybeans in a jar."

Before the march, John and the others participated in a nonviolent workshop during which they prayed and planned their peaceful protest. "I was wearing a backpack. In this backpack, I had two books. I had an apple, and I had an orange and toothpaste and toothbrush. I thought that we were going to be arrested and that we were going to go to jail," John recalled. "We came to the highest point on the bridge. Down below we saw a sea of blue—Alabama state troopers. The sheriff's name was Jim Clark. He was a very big man. He had a lapel button that said, 'Never.' He said, 'This is an unlawful march, and it will not be allowed to continue. I give you three minutes to disperse and return to your church.' And Hosea Williams from Dr. King's organization spoke up and said, 'Give us a moment to kneel and pray,' and the major said, 'Troopers, advance.' They came toward us, beating us with nightsticks and bullwhips, trampling us with horses, releasing the tear gas. I was hit in the head by a state trooper with a nightstick. I had a concussion at the bridge. My legs went from under me. I thought I was going to die." Amazingly, John told me he wasn't afraid. "Many of us were prepared to give our very lives to what we believed in."

It was the courage of John Lewis and so many others who sacrificed their own safety—and sometimes their lives—for the rights of others that allowed changes to take place in the 1960s. President Lyndon Johnson signed into law two great pieces of legislation: the Civil Rights Act of 1964 and the Voting Rights Act of 1965. John said that the Voting Rights Act was significant not only for African Americans but for all Americans, whether they realized it or not.

"The Voting Rights Act helped liberate America. It's not just to liberate the South, the eleven states of the old Confederacy from Virginia to Texas. But it liberated America in making it possible for people of color to be able to register to vote," John said, still passionate about the legislation that was enacted almost fifty years ago. "It freed the whole of America, freed white America, freed would-be white politicians, and made it possible for people of color to run for office and get elected in the heart of the Deep South." The effects of the act can be seen in the highest offices of America today. "If it weren't for the Voting Rights Act, I wouldn't be a member of Congress. If it weren't for the Voting Rights Act, Barack Obama wouldn't be president of the United States of America."

Recently, the Supreme Court has begun chipping away at the Voting Rights Act, for many a dangerous sign that history is being forgotten. One man who cannot forget it is John Lewis. He lived it, and he cried at the thought of his great-great-grandfather registering to vote for the first time only two years after he had been freed. "The vote is the most powerful instrument, the most powerful nonviolent tool in a democratic society," Lewis said. "Knowing that a member of my family registered and voted in Alabama one hundred years before I did, before my mother and my father, my grandparents, it's amazing. Maybe it's part of my DNA, my bloodline."

■ As far as we know, there is no gene for ambition or bravery, but we wanted to trace John's ancestry back much farther than the paper trail would allow. On John's father's line, we were able to trace his direct paternal ancestors back only as far as his grandfather, Henry Lewis, who was born in Georgia in the 1880s. John's paternal haplogroup is E1b1a81a, which means that he descends directly from the Mother Continent. This is a subgroup of haplogroup E1b1a, which originated in Africa about twenty thousand years ago and today is found predominantly south of the Sahara, where it spread all over Africa about four thousand years ago in the Bantu Migration. Sixty percent of all African American men share it because of the transatlantic slave trade.

On his mother's side, we were able to trace his ancestors all the way back to a woman named Celie Ann Henderson, who was born in Alabama in 1852. John's maternal haplogroup, L1b1a, also goes directly back to Africa. This haplogroup arose and expanded to northeast Africa about fifteen thousand years ago. Today it is found broadly across the Sahara Desert on the coast of Senegambia, where many of our ancestors came from. It is also found in populations in Sierra Leone and Ghana, as well as in the Fulani people farther east in Ethiopia and Sudan. But none of our ancestors came from there. All of our ancestors—in other words, 98 percent of the people who were brought here as slaves—came from the area between Senegal and Angola. Only 2 percent came from Mozambique. In the 1960s John traveled to Africa. He visited Senegal, Guinea, Liberia, Ghana, Ethiopia, Kenya, and Zambia. In Kenya he bumped into Malcolm X; in Zambia he had the privilege of attending the Independence Day ceremony, witnessing the British flag being lowered and the Zambian flag raised. "I didn't have any idea where I came from," John said of his journey, "but I saw people who I thought looked something like me."

A company called AfricanAncestry.com specializes in determining the present-day African country and ethnic group or tribe that we are most similar to in our DNA. On his father's side, John is related to the Lyela people from the country of Burkina Faso, which used to be called Upper Volta and borders Ghana on the north. On his mother's side, his tribe is Mende, from Sierra Leone, which sits just northwest of Liberia. His mitochondrial DNA sequence is 100 percent the same as the Mende. The brilliant Maya Angelou descends from the Mende. Cinque and the brave Africans of the *Amistad* were Mende as well.

The admixture test measures an individual's African, European, and Native American ancestry. John guessed that he was a composite of all three. He was right, although Native American registered at only 3 percent. His other percentages, however, were very significant: 76 percent African and 21 percent European. I have never tested an African American before who doesn't have some white ancestry, and this is not an uncommon amount. John said that because of his great-grandfather's complexion, he had already guessed at his white ancestry. But that he was almost a quarter white came as something of a shock. "It doesn't bother me, no," he said. "I truly believe that we are one people, one family. We're a human family."

I asked John one last question: after learning so much about his ancestry, if he could ask his fairy godmother to take him back in time and meet an ancestor, who would it be? John said unhesitatingly that it would be Tobias and Henry—Tobias, who registered to vote as soon as he could, who married his wife Betty as soon as he could, and Henry, his grandfather who had vanished from the historical record without a trace. "In order to know something about where you're going, where you're headed," John said, "it's good to know something about the beginning. Without the beginning, you're lost." He believes that our path is laid out for us by the people who came before us. "We are who we are because of kinship, blood, DNA. Call it what you may. It's part of your makeup, part of your being. You cannot destroy it; you cannot erase it. Even if you wanted to move in a different direction or go down another road, the spirit of history has already ordered it."

The history that we share makes us who we are and connects us all as Americans, from the big events that shaped history to the smallest details of our ancestors' lives. As Congressman Lewis reminded me of Dr. King's old saying, while our ancestors came to this land in different ships, we're all in the same boat now.

Cory Booker (b. 1969)

Senator Cory Booker came into the world after the Selma march, after President Johnson signed into law the Voting Rights Act, after the assassination of Martin Luther King. Born on April 27, 1969, in Washington, D.C., he was too young to experience the tensions and conflict of the turbulent 1960s personally, but the legacy of that era shaped him. "I grew up around a kitchen table with stories of the civil rights movement really present, and it was a generation my brother and I came to see as legends."

Booker also grew up in a world of privilege. His parents, among the first black executives at IBM, settled their family in the suburb of Harrington Park, New Jersey, the only black family in the affluent town. "My father used to affectionately call us 'the four raisins in a tub of vanilla ice cream.'"

Cory's parents never let him and his brother take their privilege for granted. "My parents would reinforce to me that you drink deeply from wells of freedom and liberty that you did not dig. Boy, don't grow dumb, fat, and happy on all this that you have. Use your blessings to make a difference in this country that's given you so much."

Harrington Park, he says, was in many ways an idyllic environment; nonetheless, his parents faced terrible but typical discrimination when they moved in. They needed a white couple to pose as them in order to buy the house from a real estate agent who had refused to sell property to African Americans. On the day of their closing, Cory's father was escorted by a lawyer from the Fair Housing Council. The agent and the lawyer actually came to blows. "My dad is holding back a dog," Cory said, recounting the story he'd heard. "Then the real estate agent breaks down crying at the end of the fight, begging my father not to move in the town, thinking that we were going to start a white flight in the town. Fast-forward twenty-two years, and the mayor declares a Cory Booker Day when I won the Rhodes Scholarship."

Cory acknowledges that while he felt loved and accepted by the town as a whole, he experienced subtle forms of racism. "You endure what become subtle pricks—everyone wanting to touch your hair and see what it feels like, people coming back from vacations and running over to you to compare their tan right away."

As always, though, Cory was careful to emphasize the positive, stressing that his environment also gave him a "launching pad" for the rest of his life. The real inspiration, though, came from home. The Stanford football star, Rhodes Scholar, and Yale Law School graduate had his choice of lucrative career paths, but he listened to his parents and directed his talents where they were needed most: the tough streets of Newark, New Jersey. The young upstart from the suburbs first ran for mayor of the crime-ridden city in 2002 and lost, ridiculed for his elite background. But Cory refused to give up, and in 2006 he was elected mayor by a landslide. He is the third African American mayor of Newark. Newark, as it happens, was the first major northeastern city to elect a black mayor at all. That was

Ken Gibson, the candidate for whom I did voter registration drives when I was a student at Yale. As Cory said to John Lewis upon their meeting in Atlanta, we are all standing on each other's shoulders.

Cory felt that to represent Newark he had to be part of it. As mayor, instead of retreating to a leafy suburb or gated community at the end of the day, Cory rented an apartment in Newark's Brick Towers Housing Project, where he lived for eight years. I told him that when I first read about that, I thought he was crazy to live there. "This may sound strange, but when I came home there, I felt home, and I felt love," Cory recalled. "I would not trade the eight years I lived in these high-rises for anything, because if you want to find American heroes, find them in the communities that are still fighting for their American dream."

But Cory worries that that dream is slipping out of the reach of too many. In 2004, on his thirty-fifth birthday, Cory witnessed the death of a young man who had been shot on the street in Newark. With his own father, Cary, by his side, they were powerless to save him. "My father turns to me and looks anguished and says, 'I worry that a child born under my circumstances—black, poor, to a single mother, in a segregated environment—in 1936, would have better life chances than a child born under those same circumstances now.' It was really a moment for me to check myself," said Cory, "because it was a reminder that we have come so far, but as a nation, we have so much further to go."

As surely as the civil rights movement has propelled him forward, his own history—or the holes in it—has haunted him. On his father's side, Cory knows nothing about the origin of his last name, Booker; on his mother's, rumors and questions about his ancestors, black and white, have swirled unanswered for decades. One look at Cory, with his blue eyes and fair complexion, and it is obvious that he has white ancestry. Where it's from, or when, Cory has no idea. It was our mission to find answers to Cory's questions.

■ Cory knew well that his experiences of growing up were nothing like his father's. "My father, from the South, always had this nostalgic love for farms. In fact, he bought an apple orchard and a farm in North Carolina that I think he still owns." I questioned Cory about what seems to me an incongruity. So many of our people fled rural areas in the South to come north because we had so many negative memories associated with farming, sharecropping, slavery. What did he think was driving his father's nostalgia? "He had some unfinished roots, I think, that still draw him back to North Carolina."

Cory clearly adores his father. He likes to think that he has inherited his father's ability to see the humanity in everyone. "I love that quality, that my father could have not only affirmed the humanity of everybody, but see within them something worthy of bringing out and enjoying in celebration." Yet in spite of his loquaciousness and infectious spirit, Cory says his father has spoken very little of his childhood.

Cory's father, Cary Booker, was born in Hendersonville, North Carolina, on December 10, 1936, to a single woman at a time when illegitimacy was still a stigma. Cory explained to me that his father was essentially raised by the community, so specific details about his family roots were few and far between. "My father has this wonderful story about an African American community, a segregated community," Cory said. "I always believed I was the result of a grand conspiracy of love, because there's all these nameless people that I don't know that sustained my dad, got him on track, literally gave him money so he could pay for his first semester at North Carolina Central so he wouldn't put off school."

Not all of the people were nameless. Cary Booker was adopted—officially or unofficially, we're not sure—by James and Eva Pilgrim, funeral home operators in Hendersonville. Cory grew up calling them Grandma and Pop Pilgrim. The names of those other generous people who stepped in may have been lost to time, but it was our intention to rescue at least the names of Cory's own ancestors from the same fate.

Through a 1975 obituary that ran in the *Asheville Citizen Times*, we learned the name of Cary's biological father: Wathia Clarence (W.C.) Allen. Alongside his other survivors was listed "a son, Cary A. Booker of Harrington Park, New Jersey, [and] two grandchildren." As is newspaper policy, the obituary had to be approved by kin. Someone—whether it was W.C. before he died or his wife or other children—chose to acknowledge Cary.

Cary used the last name Booker, not Allen, his biological father's name, and not Pilgrim, the name of the couple who raised him. He had always maintained that he didn't know where the Booker name came from, and when we showed Cory a photograph of three generations of African American women—notable for its absence of men—they were strangers to him. In fact, these were the women, we had confirmed, who had passed the name down through generations: Cory's grandmother, Jesse Lucille Booker, born on September 14, 1909, already twenty-seven by the time Cary was born; his great-grandmother, Mary Willie Booker, born on March 31, 1892; and his great-great-grandmother, Nannie Bailey (not a Booker), born in July 1871. All three women were born in Stanford, Kentucky, Cory's great-great-great-grandmother Nannie just six years after the Civil War ended.

Researcher Phillip Smith in Knoxville, Tennessee, was able to fill in more blanks for us. The 1920 census for the Eighth Ward of the city of Knoxville lists a twelve-year-old girl named Jesse Lucille Booker, who lived there with her parents, Frank and Mary Booker. On the census, Frank is listed as black; Mary and their daughter Jesse are both categorized as mulatto. Frank and Mary didn't marry until Jesse was about six years old, so Frank may not have been her biological father. Regardless, Lucille, as she appears to have been called, bore his surname, and she lived in a nuclear, two-parent family that resembled Cory's own—and the idealized American nuclear family in general. Further research, however, would reveal that it didn't stay intact for long. Frank Booker's occupation, listed in Knoxville city directories throughout the 1920s, offers a clue as to why the family didn't stay together. Literally, they couldn't.

Cory's great-grandfather was a fireman for the Southern Railway. Not to be confused with firefighters, firemen tended the steam engines on the train. This was a promising occupation for a black man of that era, as many African Americans were still working the fields as sharecroppers. It gave Cory's great-grandfather his first chance at upward mobility, but at a steep cost. The railroad kept Frank constantly on the move and away from his family. Frank Booker shows up consistently in public records for Asheville, North Carolina; Knoxville and Chattanooga, Tennessee; and Cincinnati, Ohio—all stops on the Southern Railway. Mary and Lucille Booker remained at home in Knoxville.

At some point Mary Booker decided she had had enough. In the divorce proceedings that researcher Phillip Smith discovered, the reasons for the dissolution of the Booker marriage are laid out in plain English. Cory read to his father from the document: "'The defendant willfully and maliciously deserted and abandoned' your grandmother. So your grandmother was raising your mother alone." From his grandparents' divorce to his own fatherless childhood, Cary Booker's past is a sad pattern of broken domestic relationships. It is an emotional experience for him to see this theme reflected in his family tree. For too many African Americans, economic mobility in the 1920s came at the cost of family stability.

Yet in spite of this instability, perhaps somewhat ironically, we discovered that the Booker line has been unbroken since the early 1800s. Frank Booker's father, Harrison Booker, was born a slave in South Carolina around 1841 (Frank's mother, Selena Suttles, was born around 1859), and his father, Joseph Booker, was born around 1820 in North Carolina (his wife was Mary Foster). With these blanks filled in, Cory and his father have gone from knowing nothing about the Booker name to having the entire line restored.

The origin of the name Booker was solved for Cory and his father, but another mystery involving Cory's mother's line lingered on—the mystery of her father's paternity.

■ Carolyn Rose Jordan was born in Detroit on December 29, 1939. "The older I get," Cory said, looking at a picture of his mother, "the more in awe I am of her." A high-ranking professional at IBM, she worked with the Urban League, helped organize a march in Washington, and ran a homeless shelter in Atlanta. "Every time I turned around, she was doing something extraordinary," Cory said. "She could fill a room with her voice and really inspire people."

His mother, Cory says, has always been much more forthcoming about her family than his father ever was. Yet her history was obscured by questions surrounding her father's birth. For nearly a century, rumors swirled around Carolyn's father—Cory's grandfather—Limuary Jordan. Limuary was born in Columbia, Louisiana, on September 27, 1916, at the height of Jim Crow. Although raised as the child of black parents, he looked so unlike his brother that his actual biological father's identity was always in question. Cory's blue eyes and his mother's white complexion are testimony to the fact that they have white ancestry, even though they have no proof.

"It was painful for him," Cory recalled. "He was a larger-than-life figure who played such a seminal role in raising me." Cory's grandfather Limuary was one of the first African Americans in the United Auto Workers union in Detroit, and he was proud of his political consciousness. "He bragged till the day he died that he had converted so many districts in Michigan from Republican to Democrat." What he hadn't told Cory was that during

World War II, he documented cases of discrimination at Ford and exposed the company to local newspapers. Cory's grandfather walked a very dangerous line, especially for a black man. His grandmother Adeline Jordan, an IRS employee, also worked for the betterment of African Americans. In her job, she was able to help other African American families make their way in the northern community of Detroit, which had seemed to hold such promise for southern blacks but which constantly erected obstacles to their success. Limuary and Adeline Jordan were essentially civil rights activists before there was even a civil rights movement.

Limuary recorded his life story in a fifty-eight-page handwritten memoir that Cory had never seen. "I heard later in life," Cory said, "that he was trying to write down a lot of his incredible Horatio Alger–like story." Now Cory read his grandfather's words, written in his own hand, for the first time: "I was told later that a lot of hell was raised when I was born," Limuary wrote. "A fourteen-pound baby boy, white with red hair and freckles. Needless to say, I was different from my brothers and my mother's husband. There was a lot of white blood in my ancestors, and this sort of quieted some of the gossip."

Although so much went unspoken in African American families of the post–Civil War generations, Cory's grandfather had actually confided in his grandson about this painful secret. "There's a powerful moment that I remember him telling me, choking up, that he was—he used the word 'illegitimate.' He said to me that my great-grandmother, whom I got to know, Big Mama, took him one day to a white doctor, and then when they left, she said to him, 'By the way, that was your father.'"

Big Mama, as Cory knew her, was Alzenia Jordan, just a teenager when she gave birth to Limuary in 1916. She was married at the time to John Jordan, an African American. Like most towns in the Deep South, Columbia, Louisiana, had a sharply drawn color line. In 1908, several years before Limuary was born, Louisiana had passed a law that made interracial relationships a felony. It is impossible to determine the nature of the relationship between Alzenia and the white town doctor whom she'd identified to her son. But whether it was coercive or consensual, it would have been a dangerous thing for Alzenia to make public. Limuary died never knowing his biological father's name, a painful secret that haunted him throughout his life.

There were three white doctors in Columbia around the time of Limuary's birth. The first was a veterinarian, but since the story went that

Alzenia had taken her son to see the doctor for an appointment, this didn't seem right. The second was a man who died too early for Limuary to have met him at age thirteen or thereabouts. That left the third: Stephen H. Brown, who at the time of the 1920 census was forty-six years old. Dr. Brown seemed like the most logical lead to pursue.

In the past, the only tools we had to prove paternity were oral history or printed records. Fortunately, today DNA testing is available to us to help uncover the truth, and we also had a cooperative direct descendant of Dr. Brown: his great-grandson, the fifty-year-old Louisiana lawyer Michael Hislop. Michael agreed to take the DNA test, administered by the company Family Tree DNA, that would determine if he and Cory were cousins.

Virtually all pairs of second cousins share long segments of DNA that are matching, usually several of those segments. If the two men were to share significant segments of identical DNA, they would indeed be second cousins.

The results were conclusive: Cory and Michael Hislop shared segments of DNA on their first, fourth, and tenth chromosomes. They are descendants of the same man, Dr. Stephen H. Brown. Furthermore, Cory's admixture test reveals that he is 45 percent European. In DNA testing, European is synonymous with white.

Cory was thrilled to learn the truth about his mother's family once and for all. "This to me is the fulfillment of a dream that was spawned by my grandfather's desire to bring closure to his life. I wish my grandfather knew this. I wish my grandfather knew it for sure."

Limuary had such a longing to know who his biological father was, but he penned a beautiful passage that said his true father was the man who raised him, not the man who created him. "John Jordan was my father, and never once did he even refer to me that I was not his," Cory read from Limuary's memoir. "My philosophy causes me to believe that the man that puts food on the table, a roof over your head and clothes on your back is really your father."

On one level Cory agrees. "I have strong feelings that it's not always about biology." In fact, his own father was devastated when the man who raised him as his son, James Pilgrim, referred to him in writing as a "good friend." At the same time, though, Cory believes biology has a claim on us as well. "If this man, Mr. Brown, and my great-grandmother, who I met and knew as Big Mama, if they did not come together, I would not be. And so that connection, whatever the circumstances of it was, life was created that led to my life."

■ For a black person, a direct white ancestor in the South leads to a rather complicated family tree. On Cory's father side we learned that he is, like 90 percent of African Americans, descended from slaves. Now, on Cory's mother's side, we learn that Stephen E. Brown, Stephen H.'s grandfather—so Limuary's great-grandfather and Cory's great-great-great-grandfather—fought with the Louisiana state militia to drive the Native Americans westward in the Creek War of 1836. The Creek War was fought after Andrew Jackson signed the Indian Removal Act in 1830, sending the Creek, Chickasaw, Choctaw, Seminole, and Cherokee from their home in Alabama, on the richest cotton-growing soil in the world, to resettle in the Indian Territory.

Stephen E. Brown eventually bought land in Louisiana, and the family had settled there by the year 1850, with several slaves in its possession. In 1862 the son of Stephen E. Brown, Cory's great-great-grandfather, Fielding Brown, enlisted as a corporal in the 12th Louisiana Infantry of the Confederate army. His regiment fought several brutal battles in Mississippi, and after the surrender of Vicksburg on July 4, 1863, his regiment was ordered to retreat. Fielding didn't get out quickly enough, and he was captured and held as a prisoner of war. He somehow escaped and never returned to the army, instead returning home to Columbia, Louisiana, where he and wife, Eliza Hair, had their only child, Cory's great-grandfather, Stephen H. Brown.

Much as we had learned about Cory's white family, we were also interested in learning about Cory's black ancestors on his mother's side. Our investigation added yet another twist to his story. Limuary's mother, Alzenia Collins, was born on November 25, 1891, in Grayson, Louisiana. Her father, Windsor Collins, was born on August 7, 1873, in Louisiana, eight years after the Thirteenth Amendment ended slavery. Once again, we turned to the federal census to see if we would be able to find slave ancestors on this branch of Cory's tree as well. In the 1880 census, Windsor was shown to be living with his parents, Alfred H. Collins, black and age thirty, and Henrietta Collins, a twenty-five-year-old mulatto. Both were born in North Carolina, in slavery. These are Cory's third great-grandparents.

We have enough information—first and last names and ages—to press our luck and see if we can go back another generation. Locating the marriage license for Alfred and Henrietta, we learned that her maiden name was Stamper. While the name Henrietta Stamper was not known to Cory, it was to his grandfather Limuary, who wrote about her in his memoir. "Mama said that her folks came from Raleigh, North Carolina, and that somehow they had half-sisters that were passing for white that resided in Raleigh, North Carolina," Limuary wrote. "My great-great-grandmother or my mother's great-grandmother, Grandma Rett, was in slavery and had several sons by different men that were sold into different plantations." Grandma Rett, as in Henrietta.

As so often happens in African American genealogy, the 1870 census once again proves invaluable. In it we find Henrietta Stamper, also known as Harriett, black, seventeen years old, living alone and working on a farm in Sandy Creek Township, Franklin County, North Carolina. Because she was living alone—highly unusual for a young woman of that time—we don't have her parents' names, but we might have her slave owner's name: Stamper. It's a relatively unusual name, and freed slaves often took the last names of their masters. In a court petition from Warren County, North Carolina, dated 1855, a slave named "Eda" is listed as one of thirteen slaves to be divided in equal lots among James Stamper, Briton Harris, Solomon Sutherland, and Jordan Jones. Spelling was often a phonetic exercise, so the similarity of "Eda" to "Etta" leads us to believe that this is Cory's great-great-great-grandmother, known to his grandfather through oral history and now found in the paper trail of the slave owner James Stamper. Seeing these people divided up as if they were cows or pigs was emotional for Cory. "You feel the pain and the insult, or the compassion toward them for the pain and the insult."

Now comes the twist: Henrietta Stamper was her master's daughter. The proof is on her death certificate, which describes her as "yellow"—often written at the time as mulatto—and lists her father's name as none other than James Stamper. Her mother's name is unknown, tragically listed only as the anonymous "Slave Mother."

Frederick Douglass famously wrote: "My father was my master. My master was my father." Cory Booker's fourth great-grandfather is the white man who owned his third great-grandmother. "That to me is the painful story, where the master took a slave and had sex with her. That's a different kind of story," he said, referring to the presumed relationship between Limuary's parents. "But out of that painful, brutal pairing—potentially so—came part of my family tree and my lineage." Amazingly, this has all come to us through a complicated tangle of legal documents and death certificates, which are corroborated by Limuary's memoir.

Cory's history reaches back into many corners of the Civil War and post–Civil War. In a beautiful bit of closure, on another line of his mother's family, we found John Reeves, Cory's great-great-great-grandfather and his oldest slave ancestor. He was born in Elmore County, Alabama, around 1832. The same John Reeves name appears on the 1867 voter registration rolls for the state of Alabama, which came to be as a direct result of the Reconstruction Acts passed by the United States Congress on March 23, 1867. In the pages of this same chapter we introduced John Lewis to his ancestor, Tobias Carter, who registered to vote at the same time, in the same state, as soon as he was legally able.

John Reeves: Cory's oldest slave ancestor and his first ancestor to become a registered voter. Learning of his existence, Cory was awestruck. "It makes me feel the complicated, painful, amazing, wondrous stories of America, how they all mix to produce us," Cory said, "a history of endurance, resiliency, of love, of persistence. It's amazing. I just wish America knew how interdependent and interwoven we really were."

■ DNA revealed to Cory the true paternity of his grandfather Limuary, and the name and relations of his white ancestor. There was more we could learn through DNA, which would tell Cory about his most distant ancestors and where they originated. We were able to trace Cory's oldest direct paternal ancestor back to Charles A. Allen, Cory's great-grandfather, who was born in May 1840 or 1850, depending on the record, in North Carolina. Through his Y-DNA, we determine that his paternal haplogroup is E1b1a7a—which, as we know, originated in western Africa twenty thousand years ago. In spite of the fact that it's evident that Cory has a great deal of white ancestry, we now know that on his father's side, he is not descended from a white man. The company AfricanAncestry.com determined that on his father's side, Cory shares ancestry with the Bamileke people in modern-day Cameroon.

Cory's oldest direct maternal ancestor was his third great-grandmother, Louisa Reeves. Louisa was born into slavery between 1838 and 1841 in Alabama. His maternal haplogroup is L2a1t, a subgroup of the larger haplogroup called L2a that originated fifty-five thousand years ago in East Africa and spread throughout Africa in the Bantu Migration. Twenty percent of both Africans and African Americans on their mother's side are in the broad maternal haplogroup called L2. Like his hero John Lewis, Cory descends from the Mende people of Sierra Leone.

We have been on an amazing journey with Cory. I wanted to know, if he had a fairy godmother who could take him back through history, which of his ancestors would he choose to talk to. "I would definitely want to go back and sit with the slaves," Cory said. "There's so many people I think in our day and age that are giving in to cynicism and hopelessness about their circumstances, and nobody had more right to do that than the slaves that were deep into slavery and didn't see a change coming. Their determination to keep living, keep fighting, keep struggling, keep being, I'd love to let them see that their love would one day bring about a free African American man who is living and enjoying the same liberties and freedoms as others."

This is what our work is all about: finding the threads that tie us to the people whose ancestry we share, whatever their color, whenever they lived. Sometimes we observe these connections in a physical trait, or prove them with genetics, or discover clues buried deep in the pages of a family memoir.

In John Lewis and Cory Booker both we found a common thread. Witnessing them take their respective oaths of office at the Capitol in Washington, it is easy to think of the shoulders we know they stand on—of Douglass, Tubman, King, and other famous leaders of the antislavery and civil rights movements who made freedom, citizenship, and voting possible for African Americans and their descendants. Yet, in searching the hidden transcript of history, of family lore and found science, we see others come into view: men and women, black and white, who, in all too human lives, spawned generations whose heroic deeds could scarcely have been imagined possible. Given the gridlock that exists in Washington today and, as important, the new precedents being made at the Supreme Court, it would do all of our leaders well to remember the shoulders they stand on, including those in the Lewis and Booker lines who voted decades before the nation secured that right at the apex of the civil rights movement.

CHAPTER THREE

What's in a Name?

"What's in a name?" The question famously posed by Shakespeare in *Romeo and Juliet* is at the root of many family stories. Countless inquiries into genealogical records turn on a name change, and many dead ends result from a previous generation's reinvention. But more often than not, last names are both the biggest mysteries and the best clues we have to a larger story.

This certainly holds true for the stories of television pioneer Barbara Walters and education reformer Geoffrey Canada. Neither had a clue about their family's original name. Barbara suspected that the nonethnic Walters couldn't be her Jewish family's original surname, and Geoffrey never learned how his Bronx-centered African American family had acquired the name of our nation's neighbor to the north. Any efforts they had made to find out the truth were fruitless. It took a concerted effort, the expertise of numerous researchers, and the aid of archivists and librarians to find even provisional answers.

Yet changed names are only the tip of the genealogical iceberg. While this is a story about lost names, it is also a tale of two fathers and the mysteries surrounding the origins of their lines. Both Walters and Canada were influenced tremendously by their fathers: in Barbara's case, by his larger-than-life presence; in Geoffrey's, by his unrelenting absence. And each was driven on by some combination of genetics and experience to the successes they have achieved in their own lives.

When I contacted Barbara Walters to ask if we could research her family history, she had a one-word answer for me: No! Someone had done her family tree already; she knew it all. What more could we possibly offer? This shouldn't have surprised me: Barbara is famous for getting to the bottom of other people's stories. Still, we wanted to do the same for her—and, as it turned out, we found a great deal more than she expected.

Barbara Jill Walters was born on September 25, 1929, in Boston, Massachusetts, the daughter of Dena and Lou Walters. Her childhood was, by her own account, glamorous. Her father's chain of nightclubs, the Latin Quarter, was an East Coast sensation, a draw for the rich and famous in Boston, Miami, and New York. Barbara was the youngest of three children: her brother, Burton, had died before she was even born (in fact, Barbara was named for him); and her sister Jackie, three years her senior, was developmentally challenged.

Barbara's father, Lou Walters, was an entertainment visionary, but his genius didn't always extend to the bottom line. "My father was an impresario. My father was like Ziegfeld. He did beautiful shows, great costumes, but he had no head for business," she recalled. "He always spent too much money. Everything had to be perfect, and it was a huge success." The highs were very high, but the lows were extremely low. In the 1950s, Lou Walters's elegant and expensive tastes could no longer compete with the newest entertainment craze: television. Changing tastes and rising costs drove his club into bankruptcy. In 1958 his significantly reduced circumstances—financial, professional, and social—led Lou Walters to attempt suicide.

This was a devastating blow to the Walters family, and everyone turned to Barbara for emotional and financial support. Barbara grew up in a time when women were expected to marry and raise children, with little attention to their own ambition. Her mother, however, never placed limitations on her. Nor did she particularly push her in one direction. "I don't remember my mother encouraging me in my career or saying, as I hear some mothers do, 'You can do anything.' Again, it was a different generation." Marriage, not a career, was the expectation for a daughter, but even there Barbara's mother was reticent. "My mother probably thought I'd get married, although she never pushed that. She was not a mother who said, when I was twenty or twenty-one, 'Why aren't you married?' Thank God. I wasn't very good at marriage, so it's just as well."

Just as television helped bring her father's career to a halt, it proved to be the vehicle for launching Barbara's. In 1961 she landed a job on the *Today* show as a "Today Girl." "Today Girls" were young women hired to deliver weather reports and the like—lighter fare. "I wasn't beautiful, I didn't sing, I didn't dance," Barbara said. "Most of the 'Today Girls' did." Barbara quickly caught the public's attention with her impish wit and quick intelligence—but the rising star crashed squarely into the glass ceiling of the network newsroom. Her co-anchor, Frank McGee, came close to sabotaging her career. "He was a newsman who had been on at night. He thought being on the *Today* show was a comedown. And it was very much a comedown working with me." Barbara said this was one of the hardest times for her professionally. "This was the man who went all the way up to the president of NBC and said, 'She can't do the hard-news interviews.' The compromise was that I could come in after he asked three questions."

Barbara wouldn't accept that sort of treatment. "I fought that. One of the things I say to young people, especially young women, I say, fight the big battles. Don't fight the little ones."

The battle was over, but the war was not won. Her time as the co-anchor of the ABC nightly news with Harry Reasoner was even worse. "Harry Reasoner was a decent man, but he was terrible to me, and I was a failure, total failure," she said, recalling this dark period. "I had a seven-year-old child, I was divorced, I was supporting my family, and my career was over. I was drowning, and there was no life preserver."

She worked her way back up, paving the way for the female news anchors who now routinely sit behind the desk on local and network news programs.

She is aware of her role as a pioneer for women in television news reporting, but she says her fight was practical more than political. "I wasn't burning my bra as a feminist. I wasn't raising a flag. I worked because I had to, and I worked because I was ambitious and I had drive. Who knows where that comes from?"

Barbara acknowledged that it was her gender far more than her religion—Judaism—that was an obstacle for her in the early years of her career. Although many Jews had found a place for themselves in Hollywood's film studios, Barbara says that she wasn't aware of many others in television during the early years. But Judaism wasn't something that she was preoccupied with. Barbara came from a family of Jewish immigrants who had drifted away from their religion and culture as they became more and more American. Her grandmother spoke Yiddish, but beyond that, Judaism didn't have much of a presence in her home. "We never said a prayer. We never celebrated the Jewish holidays. We didn't then; I don't now. Being Jewish had nothing to do with my career."

Barbara describes herself as "culturally Jewish," with no attachment to the religious aspects of Judaism. "There's been this discussion for thousands of years: Is it a religion? Is it a race? What does it mean to be Semitic? What does it mean to be anti-Semitic? Am I Jewish? Yes. Does it govern my life in any way? No."

But it did govern the lives of her ancestors, if not in terms of religious practice, then in terms of their decision to come to America in the first place and to leave parts of their past behind. To learn who these ancestors were, we turned to Barbara's father's family.

■ Lou Walters was born on August 22, 1894, in Whitechapel, London, England. Barbara's father was larger than life, but in many ways he was also an enigma. "He was an elegant man. People would have thought he was a lawyer or an accountant." His appearance, according to Barbara, wasn't that of the typical nightclub owner, who tended to be more flamboyant, nor was his personality. "He was soft-spoken. He was quiet. He was a voracious reader. I never saw him without a book in his hand. And this was a man who created these enormously popular nightclubs."

Yet the true story of where he came from, and therefore where *she* comes from, remained a mystery to Barbara. She was able to provide us a rough outline. Her father, she told us, came to America from England as a teenager. Not all of his family came over at once. Many Jewish immigrants, upon arriving in New York, took jobs as shoemakers, tailors, or other similar professions. Not Lou Walters. Barbara's father went into show business. He booked acts and shows here and there, and soon Lou opened his own place in Boston, which is where he met Barbara's mother.

Lou had a card that said "Stop, look, and listen," which sounds very much like a slogan Barbara could borrow in her professional life. For several years he met with amazing success, but then the end came. Just as television changed the environment and put Lou out of business in the

1950s, talkies did him in in the 1920s. "When talkies came in," Barbara explained, "that was the end of all these different shows that they used to do all over the country. So suddenly it was over. And that's when I was born."

Barbara was born one month before the stock market crash in 1929 that triggered the depression that would paralyze the country for the next decade. But Lou was determined to succeed, and he bought an abandoned church in Boston and turned it into a nightclub. Riding on the success of the Boston Latin Quarter, he opened Latin Quarter clubs in New York and Palm Island, Florida, as well. The clubs attracted a very elite clientele. Barbara heard stories that Joseph P. Kennedy Sr. was a frequent visitor when he was in Palm Beach.

Before we started our research into Barbara's family history, she had graciously given us the thick family history research that professional genealogists had previously compiled. But as we examined the documents, we noticed inconsistencies. It seemed like the researchers might not have discovered the whole story.

■ Starting in the 1880s, Jewish people filled boat after boat crossing the Atlantic. They were fleeing the violent anti-Semitism that was sweeping across Eastern Europe. In 1909 Lou Walters joined his parents in this exodus, following a well-worn path to New York's Lower East Side, where a half-million Jewish people had already put down new roots. For many Jews, new roots meant a new name.

Barbara always knew that her grandfather's name was Abraham Walters and that he had emigrated to London from Poland. However, the genealogy report she received years earlier contained almost no information about his family back in its homeland. Unable to find his original surname, the first group of researchers had been stymied.

We consulted with Jim Yarin, a Boston-based paralegal who spends his weekends researching Jewish genealogy, to help us get over this stumbling block. For Jewish immigrant ancestors from Eastern Europe, Jim explained, name changes can wreak genealogical havoc. A paper trail is often impossible to follow for long because if records were kept at all, they were often destroyed in pogroms and forced migrations. Further, no legal status—the case for both Eastern European Jews and enslaved African Americans—meant no legal surname; by the time these two groups had adopted legal surnames, they often changed them in an effort to reinvent themselves and put distance between them and their painful past. But the term "carved in stone" and all the permanence it implies has special meaning for those researching Jewish roots.

Traditional Jewish tombstones are unique. They contain not only the Hebrew name of the deceased but also the Hebrew name of the person's father: two generations, chiseled in stone. Yarin had a hunch that Abraham Walters's tombstone might provide the key to unlocking the mystery of Barbara's past. Barbara's grandparents were buried in Newark, New Jersey, an ocean away from their country of origin, but Abraham's tombstone gave us exactly what we needed to get us closer to Barbara's family's homeland. According to the tombstone, Abraham Isaac Walters was the son of the respected Tzvi Getzel.

In the State Archives in Lodz, Poland, our researcher looked for any document from the late nineteenth century that listed a man named Tzvi Getzel who had a son named Abraham Isaac. If we found a father and son with this combination of names, they would most likely be Barbara's grandfather and great-grandfather.

Poring over the records, we found a match: a birth certificate dated April 14, 1866. The baby boy was named Abraham Isaac. But Getzel, it turned out, was not a last name. Tzvi and Getzel were both first names. Barbara read the document that contained the family name she had never before seen. "Getzel Waremwasser, a coachman, 36 years old, showed us a male child born in the city of Zgierz on the fifth of April of this year. The son of himself and his wife, Bina, nee Simkowitz, 30 years old, to whom was given the name Abraham Isaac." Barbara's grandfather was Abraham Waremwasser. Her great-grandparents would become Bina and Harry (the English equivalent of Tzvi) Walters in America.

At the time Abraham was born, Zgierz, near Lodz, was part of Russia. It had a large Jewish population—about thirty-five hundred out of a total population of nineteen thousand. Nineteenth-century Poland was a very dangerous place to be a Jew. Poverty was common, and anti-Semitism increasingly erupted into violent pogroms. By the 1890s, Jewish families across Eastern Europe were abandoning their homelands to save themselves, the Waremwassers among them. Their first stop: London, England.

Barbara had always known her father was born in England. We'd found the World War I draft registration confirming the fact. But the trail went cold again when we looked for Waremwassers in London. Somewhere in between Waremwasser and Walters, we suspected that there existed another name. Jewish history scholars Antony Polonsky and Jonathan Sarna explained to us that Jews in Europe often got their surnames through an exchange of money; the more money they could pay, the nicer the name. "*Schoen* names, beauty names," explained Sarna, "were more expensive. If you didn't give them money, you were stingy, or *karger*." Polonsky offered another example: "Some of these names, like Wieseltier means 'weasel'—it's not really an animal you want to name yourself after."

W*aremwasser* in English translates to "warm water." Sarna postulated that they might have been among the first families in their village to have warm water in their home. We found Barbara's father's birth certificate the very morning we were scheduled to meet with her, and only because of Jonathan Sarna's hunch about the family's last name. The man who would become known as Lou Walters, whose name would be immortalized on Lou Walters Way in New York, was born under the legal name of Louis Warmwater on August 22, 1894, in Whitechapel, London, England.

Barbara was stunned. "So I'm Barbara Waremwasser. Barbara Warmwater. I like Barbara Warmwater."

The name Warmwater breathed new life into our search for Barbara's ancestors. It turns out that Barbara's family did not go directly to New York from England, as Barbara had always believed. A passenger list from a ship departing London and destined for the United States in the late 1890s reveals that Abraham Warmwater left behind his wife, Lily, and their children to embark on a journey not to New York City but to San Francisco.

Today we don't think of San Francisco as a major destination for Jewish immigrants, but in the late 1800s San Francisco was home to the second-largest Jewish community in the United States. Stories of the Gold Rush and overnight fortunes lured waves of all sorts of ambitious newcomers looking to strike it rich. Records reveal that Abraham Warmwater got work as a tailor in the city by the bay. A passenger list from the year 1899 shows us that Lily Warmwater, at the age of thirty-eight, and her three oldest children (including Barbara's father) made the journey to San Francisco as well. They would stay only a few years.

The London census of 1901 places the Warmwaters back in London—except that they were no longer the Warmwaters. According to this document, Lily and Isaac Abrahams were now living with their children in the Mile End Old Town neighborhood in the East End of London. Mile End was one of the main hubs for the Jewish immigrant community in London. In the wake of Russia's violent anti-Jewish pogroms of 1881 and

1882, somewhere between 120,000 and 150,000 Eastern European Jews fled to the United Kingdom, and most of them settled there.

We consulted with Jonathan Sarna again to make sense out of the Warmwater/Abrahams family's journey. To spend all this money to get from Poland to London, London to New York, and New York to San Francisco, only to turn around again to return to London was less unusual than we might think. "In this period, 15 to 20 percent of the Jews who immigrate to the United States return," Sarna explained. "They find that America's streets are not paved with gold, that it's tougher than they imagined. Some of them find that religious life in the United States is not what they hoped it would be. It's harder to be a religious Jew."

Ironically, people who fled their country of origin to escape religious persecution, presumably to practice that religion more freely, were now confronted with another option: to assimilate and possibly choose not to practice that religion at all. That is essentially what Barbara's family did. The Abrahams remained in London for nearly another decade, but in 1909, when Barbara's father was fifteen years old, they made the journey to America again, this time to stay—and to once and for all adopt a surname that would stick. According to the passenger list of the SS *Cedric*, Isaac and Louis Abraham (no "s"), with their race listed as Hebrew, left Liverpool on August 1, 1909, on a ship bound for Ellis Island. The following year, in New York, they adopted the name Walters, and it has remained so since.

Finding the name Waremwasser allowed us not only to follow her grandfather on his journeys back and forth from Europe to America but also to find the names of all eight of her paternal great-grandparents. This is an achievement for anyone tracing his or her genealogy, but for an Eastern European Jew it is nearly impossible. Barbara's oldest ancestor was born in 1786, just two years after the American Revolution ended.

Barbara's father had never told her why his family changed its name. In fact, he never even told her they had. "I never knew until very recently that their name hadn't been Walters. I thought that when they left, I don't know what it was then but today would be Poland, when they came to England, the name was Walters," Barbara explained. In little more than a decade, the Waremwasser/Warmwater/Abrahams/Abraham/Walters family had gone through five name changes and multiple journeys across the ocean. These intrepid travelers brought Barbara Walters where she is today.

■ We also wanted to look at Barbara's mother's side. Dena Seletsky was born in Boston on January 31, 1897. Barbara's mother was one of seven children. Her father, who worked in the shoe business, died relatively young, Barbara thought in his fifties or sixties, and Dena Seletsky had to go to work to help support the family. This recalls her own daughter's experience. According to Barbara, her mother's family was quite dismayed when she decided to marry Lou Walters. Show business was not a real business. "When she married my father, why didn't she marry someone in the dress business? Why don't you marry someone in the shoe business? This is a dangerous business," Barbara said, quoting her mother's family. She added quietly, "It was, it was."

I asked Barbara if she had a sense of what her mother would have become if she had been born during her daughter's generation. "Oh, who knows? It's a different time. First of all, she had to help support her family. She didn't go to college. I'm not sure that any of those sons and daughters went to college. They all went to work," Barbara said. "In those days the man worked, and the mother stayed home, and worked if she had to. My mother would have continued to work if she had to, but they were not very interesting jobs."

Barbara grew up surrounded by her mother's family. Her maternal grandparents were Jacob Seletsky and Celia Sacovich. Barbara's grandfather died before she was born, but she was extremely close with her grandmother. "In those days children didn't say, 'Tell me about Grandpa,'" Barbara reflected. "Now I'd be enormously interested, but we never talked about any of that." Celia was born in Vilna—then part of the Russian Empire, now a region split between Lithuania and Belarus, on the Lithuania side—in 1875. This information triggered a memory for Barbara. "My father and mother used to joke about the fact that my mother was a Russian and my father was Polish," she laughed. "And Russian was considered better."

Celia arrived in America in 1893, and two years later, she married Barbara's great-grandfather, Jacob Seletsky. He worked in a shoe store owned by his older brother, Joseph, who, in 1888, became the first member of the Seletsky family to arrive in America. We couldn't find a similar record of arrival for Jacob, but we found his gravestone, and, as we learned on Barbara's father's side of the family, Jewish tombstones can be very useful in tracing genealogy. From Jacob's headstone we learned that his Hebrew name was Selig, a name that still appears in Barbara's family.

Much as the name Waremwasser had done in Barbara's father's family, the name Selig opened doors for us. Selig Seletsky, we learned, landed in Boston in 1890. The record documents the arrival of a twenty-two-year-old laborer from Russia, bound for Boston, with only one piece of luggage. Selig is Barbara's original immigrant ancestor. We don't know why he changed his first name to Jacob. Perhaps he thought the Old Testament name sounded less Jewish.

Jacob's journey to America was the last leg of a longer trip from Russia through Germany and, again, the United Kingdom. The form he filled out in Hamburg was actually more detailed than his arrival record; on it, under "Former Residence," he wrote the name of his shtetl, Benyakoni, Russia. Benyakoni was a small town in the Vilna district, the site of a border crossing between Belarus and Lithuania. Unlike his future wife's hometown, Jacob's was on the Belarus side. Again, Barbara had never heard much about this part of her family history. Tracing Barbara's mother's genealogy didn't present the same challenges as her father's, simply because the last names remained the same. Getting from Selig to Jacob was just a momentary delay.

■ When Barbara originally turned down my request to trace her family roots, I had used the promise of DNA analysis as the bait to lure Barbara in. "I want to find out if I was a Persian princess or an Egyptian serf," Barbara proclaimed. "What was I?"

In Jewish people, DNA reveals more than migration. It reveals a history of Jewish oppression and ghettoization as well as self-imposed isolation. Translated, this means that Ashkenazi, or Eastern European, Jews have more cousins than anybody else in the world, because they all had unwittingly and inadvertently been intermarrying with distant relations for generations.

On Barbara's mother's side, we were able to trace her oldest maternal ancestor to her great-grandmother, Jenny Sakowitz, the wife of Daniel Sakowitz, who was probably born in Russia in the middle of the nineteenth century. Barbara's mitochondrial DNA revealed that her maternal haplogroup is J1b1a. Haplogroup J arose in the Near East seven thousand years ago, when agriculture developed in the region. From there it extended out to Lithuania, Belarus, and other points in Eastern Europe. About 7 percent of all the Jewish women in the world today have this haplogroup root J1. In other words, it is a very common Jewish maternal haplogroup. The genealogical evidence backs up this finding, because we learned that on her mother's side, her recent ancestors came from the border area of Lithuania and Belarus. Barbara is probably descended on this side from people who farmed and then moved into the trades.

Barbara predicted the outcome of her admixture test, which measures our African, Native American, and European ancestry. "Oh, I'm sure it's all Jewish, isn't it?" She then lowered her guess to 99.9 percent. That was closer. Her admixture results, according to Family Tree DNA, which specializes in Jewish DNA analysis, are 91.2 percent Middle Eastern and 8.9 percent European. Middle Eastern could mean Bedouin, Druze, Iranian, Palestinian, or Jewish, but Barbara's DNA shows matches only with Semitic or Jewish populations in its database. European refers to non-Jewish people. There was a bit of mixing outside of those self-contained Ashkenazi communities—but not much. Amazingly, about 3.5 million of today's Ashkenazi Jews—or 40 percent of the Ashkenazi population—are descended from just four women.

I reminded Barbara of the second thing she told me after I asked her to participate in the series—after "No." She said there was nothing we could tell her that she didn't already know, because the Mormon genealogy center had traced her roots already. I lured Barbara in with the DNA, but I also promised her we would find information she'd never heard. When she gave us her family history, it went back only as far as her grandparents on her father's side. (And, incidentally, her grandfather, Abraham Walters, had been wrongly identified as Icek Ibramovich.) We managed not only to uncover Barbara's original surname—Waremwasser—and its many iterations but also to add two generations to her family tree going back to the eighteenth century.

I asked Barbara my usual question: if she had a fairy godmother who could take her back in time to meet any of the relatives she learned about today, who would it be? "I don't know," Barbara said, after pondering the question, "because we know so much about him, but probably my grandfather and my grandmother, because from what I'd heard from cousins who knew her, she was a very elegant lady and a kind of funny lady." Barbara was, of course, referring to her father's parents, Abraham and Lily Walters, who tried on several last names and two different American cities before finally settling into their new identities as Americans. "There is a story that I tell in my book about my grandmother. My grandmother supposedly, on her deathbed, said to her children, my father and so forth, 'You know I'm a virgin.' And they said, 'How could this be, Mama? You have seven children.' She said, 'I know, but I never participated.'"

If there are genes for sense of humor and tenacity, I think I know through which relative Barbara came by hers.

Geoffrey Canada (b. 1952)

Education superstar Geoffrey Canada is featured in the award-winning 2010 documentary *Waiting for Superman*. When it comes to the film's subject, public school reform, he is a bona fide revolutionary. In 1997 he founded the Harlem Children's Zone, a cradle-to-college pipeline that is dramatically transforming the lives of severely disadvantaged children of color, children the system had long given up on. Growing out of a one-block pilot program to a project that encompasses one hundred city blocks and serves ten thousand children, the HCZ provides not only high-quality education for its students but also after-school programs that keep kids safe and engaged and outreach programs that teach parents and caregivers how to take part in their children's education and school lives. "We get the kids in kindergarten," Geoffrey explained. "They will stay with us through elementary, through middle, into high school, and then the mission is to get these kids into college and help them get through college."

Despite all of his success, Geoffrey has never felt complete. His life has always been haunted by a single question: Where did his father and his father's people come from? His father abandoned his family when Geoffrey was only four years old. Raised by his mother, Geoffrey knows nothing about his father's side of the family—where they were from or the origin of their unusual last name.

Geoffrey was born in the South Bronx on January 13, 1952, less than ten miles north of Barbara Walters's home. It may as well have been on the other side of the world. Knowing where you're from begins with your own parents, but Geoffrey was completely cut off from his deeper roots on his father's side when his father walked out on the family. His father's name was McAllister Canada. Everyone, including his children, called him Mac. Geoffrey said he had two keen childhood recollections of his father. The first was from the day he left.

"I remember him leaving, and I began to cry," Geoffrey said. "The crying was not because I had such a warm and fuzzy relationship with him, because our mother was the main part. The crying was because I was like, well, who's going to protect us? How are we going to make it in this place if the only guy who could fight is out and he's not coming back?"

The second memory was from a few years later, when Geoffrey was about nine or ten. He and his brother Dan tracked down their father. "I was convinced that my father really loved us, and he just didn't get to see us, so he kind of forgot how wonderful we were as kids," Geoffrey said, recalling his naiveté. "My brother Dan and I went to Harlem to find him. He was a super in a building. He had a drinking problem. We showed up, and I walked up to him, and he said, 'Hi.' And I was like, 'Hi! How you doing?' and I was talking to him. He looked at me, and he said, 'Uh, are you John?' He didn't even know my name. And when I said, 'I'm Geoff,' nothing. I thought he would say, 'Oh, Geoff! Oh, I remember!' And it was just nothing." The fact that his father felt no connection, no sense of responsibility or ownership toward his sons made an impression on Geoffrey that never left him.

But early on, Geoffrey knew there was a different world out there, the one that he learned of through books. "I read about a world," he said, "where kids had fathers who played baseball with them, and they went to the park, and they went to cookouts." This was not the world Geoffrey saw when he ventured out into the street. "I could not reconcile how people could allow one group of kids to have what would be considered this nice, idyllic childhood, *Leave It to Beaver*, and this other group—that was not the world we were growing up in."

Schools weren't much safer than the streets. "It was a safe haven until the bell rung," he said. "The fact that you could be terrorized from school to home is something that I never understood. Where were the adults? It's one of the things that I've never forgotten; that our responsibility for young people does not end when they walk outside of whatever building; that if you can't create an environment of safety for young people, they figure out how to keep themselves safe."

Today Geoffrey believes that education is the one sure path out of poverty. It is a path he took himself. At age fifteen, Geoffrey found his environment of safety outside of the South Bronx, at his grandparents' home in Wyandanch on Long Island. Because he didn't pass the academic entrance exams to get into one of New York's three specialized high schools—Bronx Science, Stuyvesant, and Brooklyn Tech—he was going to have to attend one of his neighborhood schools, and he was terrified. "I knew if I went to Morris High School my academic career was over." He and his brothers all moved in with their grandparents to attend high school. "What a difference that made in our lives," Geoffrey said plainly. Voted Most Likely to Succeed as a senior, Geoffrey had found his *Leave It to Beaver* world in the small suburban black community, one of "three or four exclusively black places" on Long Island where black people were welcome (and encouraged by realtors) to buy their homes.

A strong and engaged student, Geoffrey won a scholarship to Bowdoin College in Maine. He enrolled in 1970, at a time when affirmative action opened the doors of previously white institutions to people of color. There were more than thirty African American men in his class. Although he had come to Bowdoin from Long Island, he felt isolated from many of the black students there. One of his brothers told him it was because he hadn't yet lost his Bronx "edge," and he greeted people with hostility instead of warmth. After he had been there for two years, his brother Reuben came to visit him and said to him, "They got you, didn't they? Look at you. You're sitting on the floor. You're talking all this stuff. You could never walk around the Bronx like this."

When Geoffrey was a junior, his girlfriend became pregnant, and they got married. "Anyone with any sense would have probably figured out, well, this is not going to last over the long haul," Geoffrey said, looking back at himself as a twenty-year-old father. "But that didn't even matter to me. This idea of being married and being a family and making a go of it was, to me, paramount." That his own experience was driving him was obvious. "I was determined, no matter what, I would not be an absent father in my kids' life." His wife, Joyce, gave birth to twin boys, Jerry and Geoff. Tragically, Geoff died from sudden infant death syndrome. At the time SIDS had not yet been recognized, and no one knew that it was dangerous to let babies sleep on their stomachs. This was a terrible time in the young couple's lives. "To have a kid die from no reason that you could figure out makes you so paranoid as a parent. I used to just watch Jerry in the night just to see his chest go up and down to make sure he was breathing."

His years with his grandparents, Leonard and Lydia Williams, in a nurturing home and high-performing school, made him realize that the vulnerabilities he had experienced growing up were not inevitable. The system could be changed, and he could play a role in changing it. After graduating from Bowdoin and earning his master's degree in education at Harvard, Geoffrey returned to New York and founded the Harlem Children's Zone. "When I got to places like Harvard, the possibilities were always much more overpowering than the imminent failure." In the Bronx, it was failure that children were taught to prepare for and accept. "That was one of the first things they taught you: give up that theory that in the end this is going to have a happy ending." The Harlem Children's Zone works under the premise that there are happy endings waiting out there for everyone; it's the beginnings that need nurturing to get there.

Geoffrey considered his own beginnings and admitted that had his father stayed in his family's life, he would not have been the idyllic, tossing-the-ball dad that he saw depicted on TV and in books. "The men I knew on Union Avenue were not the Cleaver family-type men," Geoffrey noted. "These were men that the kids were terrified of. We never saw men playing games with their kids, teaching them how to do anything. We just never saw it in our neighborhood at all." He and his brothers, like so many others in their community, were missing a positive model of manhood and fatherhood.

Geoffrey's father died in the mid-1970s. They had reconnected after not having any contact for about fifteen years when both men were living in Boston. Geoffrey had finished at the Ed School at Harvard, and his father was living with his second family and working as a custodian. His lifelong struggle with alcoholism eventually killed him. Geoffrey and his brothers attended the funeral. It was a confusing time for all of them. "We tried to make sense out of how we felt. I think what we really felt, in the end, was the absence of any possibilities for things being better in the future," Geoffrey reflected. "Even at that late point now in life, we all hoped that he was going to say, 'Guys, you know what? I messed up.' When he died we knew that was it. Whatever we had was all we're ever going to have."

Geoffrey is well aware that his career has been largely driven by his fatherless life. He has spent much of his adult life trying to piece his lost roots back together, even searching for people in the phone book who happen to share his last name. The only connection Geoffrey had to his Canada side was his father's sister, Pearl. Pearl lived nearby in the South Bronx with her twins, Bernice and Frances, and their brother Jimmy. One of the twins (Geoffrey said no one ever learned to tell them apart) always knew where his father was. Neither Pearl nor her twins were sources of any family history or information, only occasionally Mac's whereabouts.

When Mac Canada died, so, it seemed, did whatever history he had.

■ We started our search for Geoffrey's father in the most logical place. Everyone has a Social Security card, and Social Security card applications contain a great deal of information necessary to tracing someone's genealogy. Luckily, our search yielded results. "Mack Canada" was born on October 5, 1929, in Cleveland, Ohio, to Henry Canada and Winifred Jackson—names that were unknown to Geoffrey until now.

Now that we had the name of Geoffrey's grandfather, we took a chance and tried to go back another generation using Henry Canada's death certificate—and we succeeded. Born in Montgomery, Virginia, on January 7, 1888, Henry was a longshoreman. He died in the Bronx in 1950, two years before Geoffrey was born, just a few blocks from where Geoffrey lived as a child. How is it no one had ever spoken of him? I joked with Geoff about his family's proclivity for the Bronx. We had discovered something unusual in his DNA: the Bronx gene, the twenty-fourth chromosome. The borough—apparently just a few blocks of it—was certainly a constant in Geoff's family's history.

The death certificate contained still more valuable information: the names of Henry Canada's parents, or Geoffrey's great-grandparents, Peter Canada and Sarah Smothers. Both were born in Virginia, Peter in 1856 and Sarah in 1867, just two years after the Thirteenth Amendment abolished slavery. Born nine years before the end of the Civil War, Peter is Geoffrey's original slave ancestor.

Geoff was stunned by the number of discoveries we had made. There had always been family rumors that they had ancestors in West Virginia, so it seemed likely that this Virginia connection was at the root of that. The discovery of his great-grandfather, a slave, was poignant. "It seems terrible to say I'm so glad to find out my great-grandfather was a slave," he said. "You don't mean it in that way, but you want to know where you're from."

Our research had turned up much more information than most African Americans were privy to about their slave ancestors: an actual name. Because we had a name and a birthplace for Peter Canada, there was a chance that Peter's father's name—that would be Geoffrey's great-great-grandfather—could be found. To find this slave ancestor's name, though, another player would have to enter the picture: the white slave master who owned Peter's father, and possibly Peter himself. To learn precisely where Geoffrey's ancestors were held as slaves in Virginia, we would have to trace the Canada family, in reverse, through every census conducted in the United States every decade for as far as we could. We called this, not unintentionally, the Canada Family Migration.

Because we were working in reverse chronological order, we returned to the Bronx, where Henry and Winifred Jackson were living from 1942 to 1947. Prior to that, Henry and Winifred had lived in Baltimore, where Henry worked as a hod carrier, or brick hauler.

At this point, Geoffrey's great-grandfather Peter vanished from the paper trail. There is no evidence of him on the 1940 census. Fair enough. It was possible that by this time Peter might have passed away, so we went back ten years. But now, in the 1930 census, neither Henry *nor* Peter Canada was anywhere to be found.

As it does with Eastern European Jews, the trail for African Americans often disintegrates before their genealogy can be traced very far. But researcher Rhonda McClure of the New England Historic Genealogical Society in Boston had an idea about how to look for Geoff's great-grandfather: ignore the last name and focus on his own first name coupled with those whom we know from other research would be in his household. If there was a sixty-seven-year-old black man living with people named Sarah (his wife) and Elizabeth (their daughter) in one of the states in which they made their home, it might be possible to pick up the paper trail again.

Rhonda's hunch panned out, and suddenly Geoffrey's great-grandfather resurfaced, but with a different name: Peter Kennedy. Geoffrey laughed. "Maybe I could use that every now and then: 'you know, I'm descended from the Kennedys.'"

All we have to do is say each name aloud to recognize the similarities between "Canada" and "Kennedy." While Geoffrey himself has never been mistaken for a Kennedy, he acknowledged that his name has often been mangled by others: they put the accent in the wrong place when saying "Canada" or spell it with a "K." In the past, confusion often arose in transcribing people's surnames because of varying levels of literacy and unfamiliar accents. In the case of African Americans, both issues could have been at play. If the census taker were white, a black southern accent might have been unfamiliar and therefore difficult to understand. This is a problem that existed not only among blacks but among vast numbers of immigrants arriving in America in the early twentieth century. Scientists have tackled this problem, which can bring genealogical research to a screeching halt, by developing a system called Soundex. Soundex uses phonics to search for the many phonetic variations possible in a name.

Between 1926 and 1942, the Canada/Kennedy family lived in Baltimore, where Peter worked as a laborer in a junkyard. It was during this period that Mac was born in Cleveland, so apparently there was some movement back and forth. In the 1920 census, Henry Kennedy, Geoffrey's grandfather (identified on his death certificate as Henry Canada), was listed as a fireman and the head of the household in Harrisburg, Pennsylvania; Peter and Sarah, his parents, were members of the household.

The Canada family's names were as ever changing as their residences. The 1910 census places Peter and Sarah Kennedy in Washington County, Maryland (Henry, once again, could not be located); but 1900 shows them at home in Montgomery County, Virginia—where, according to his death certificate, Henry, Geoffrey's grandfather, was born in 1888. In the census, the twelve-year-old Henry is listed as Richard, a railroad laborer. Cross-referencing of documents—in this case Henry Canada's draft registration from World War I, on which he signed his name "Henry Richard"—allowed us to determine that the twelve-year-old Richard and Henry were one and the same.

The Canada Family Migration mirrors precisely what has come to be called the Great Migration for African Americans. By the turn of the twentieth century, millions of blacks were leaving the South for the North, trading rural life for urban. As both the Kennedys and the Canadas, the family trekked northward, from Virginia to Maryland to Pennsylvania (and back to Maryland, with a side trip at some point to Ohio for the birth of Geoffrey's grandfather) to New York, in a matter of decades.

Now we wanted to know where the Canada/Kennedy family was in the nineteenth century. There was no trace of Peter or Henry, with either surname, in the 1880 census. We turned back to Rhonda McClure of the New England Historical Genealogical Society and Soundex. We knew Geoffrey's ancestors were alive and included somewhere, but we had to expand our phonetic search to find them. As she had done before, she dropped the last name and searched for a man named Peter in his early twenties whose name sounded like "Canada," who was living with the men we knew to be his brothers: Charles and Thomas.

On a page of the 1880 census for Franklin County, Virginia, we found exactly whom we were looking for: Thomas Cannaday, a farm laborer, age forty-seven, and his wife, Julia Cannaday, a housekeeper, age forty-five, living with their sons Charles, Thomas, Benjamin, and Peter, all laborers, in a remote corner of Virginia.

In one fell swoop, we found Geoffrey's great-grandparents—and his family's original name! "It's so fascinating, because if I've been asking people where did the name Canada come from, at least you can assume it came from folks maybe trying to get to Canada," Geoffrey said. "The name Cannaday, I can see why someone would just say, 'Well, that doesn't mean anything, Cannaday. Why not be Canada?' At least that's a place, and people know it."

We know the family's name changed, but we don't know why. It could have been a homonymic substitution (the different way of rendering two names that sound the same); it could have been a census taker mishearing or misrepresenting; or it could have been an act of naming. Naming is a very important tradition in African American culture. Whatever the cause, these long-lost names are the link to distant relatives, the keys to piecing together a particular branch of a family tree. Thomas and Julia Cannaday bore the surname they had had while they were in slavery, the name they used among themselves, and the name they declared to be their legal name as soon as they were freed.

For African Americans, it's virtually impossible to trace their roots back across the Atlantic. Even to trace two generations of slave ancestors in America, with first and last names, is extremely rare. Twelve and a half million men, women, and children were ripped from their homelands in Africa and packed onto ships like cargo, bound for the New World. Fifteen percent would die en route. Those who managed to survive were stripped of their names and treated like chattel property. These long-forgotten anonymous ancestors are the very people Geoffrey longed to find.

"It's part of a hunger I have, that I think many African Americans have," he said, "to fill in the blanks of life, to know that you were more than just a slave, you were more than just somebody who accidentally ended up somewhere. And for a lot of folks like myself, that's missing."

■ Our discovery of Geoffrey's original family name was the essential breakthrough we needed to restore branches of his family tree. Using the name Cannaday, we were able to find Geoffrey's great-great-grandfather listed in the 1880 census. Thomas was born in Virginia in 1833. Since his name didn't appear in any of the federal censuses before 1870, we knew he must have been a slave.

Now that we had found the family's ancestral name, we made a journey to the ancestral home of Franklin County, Virginia, where Thomas

Cannaday lived after the Civil War. There we met Alta Cannaday, an amateur genealogist and African American descendant of the Franklin County Cannaday slaves herself. Alta is probably Geoffrey's cousin. She told us that most of the slaves who took the name Cannaday were owned by one white Cannaday family that lived in this area. If Geoffrey's great-great-grandfather had been the slave property of the white Cannadays, then his name might be recorded in one of their wills.

According to the 1840 census, the white man Charles Cannaday from Franklin County owned nineteen slaves, eight of whom were males under the age of ten. Geoffrey's great-great-grandfather would have been seven in 1840, so it's quite possible that he was one of these boys. Eight years later, Charles Cannaday died. His will was a gold mine for us. Inventoried among the furniture, pigs, and cows were also the slaves, listed by name, age, and value. Three years old at the time the will was written, Thomas Cannaday was assigned a value of $250. Geoffrey read from the will of the man who owned his great-great-grandfather: "'Ben valued at $850, Charlotte valued at $600, Stephen valued at $700, Suzy valued at $500, and Thomas valued at $250.' And they gave Thomas to Asa. I'm a little worried that he was worth so much less than everybody else!"

Geoffrey greeted this latest amazing discovery with levity, but he was awestruck at what he had learned about his family. "I didn't know who my grandfather was, what his last name was," Geoffrey said. "And now I'm finding out that my great-great-grandfather was not just a slave. I now where he lived, where he grew up, who owned him. This is something you've heard about. I never thought I would see the day. The assignment of a dollar value on someone's life who was your relative, your great-great-grandfather, it just brings this era that we all thought somehow we were connected to to life."

It seemed that many descendants of Charles Cannaday had stayed close to home. A few miles from the five-hundred-acre farm where Geoffrey's great-great-grandfather had been enslaved, we met Ola Wagner, another Cannaday descendant dedicated to preserving her family's history. "Our Cannaday family had plenty of slaves," Ola told us. "They're like everybody else. The slaves was worth the most money, so they had more slaves without having to buy them." In other words, Ola had heard that the white Cannadays frequently added to their labor force by impregnating their slaves, a practice called "growing slaves."

We couldn't help but wonder who Thomas's father was. The paper trail had run out. Could it be the slave master, Charles Cannaday, himself? Before we could answer that question, we had to examine Geoffrey's mother's side of the family.

◼ As we've learned, Mary Elizabeth Williams raised four boys on her own. This would be no small feat anywhere, but the South Bronx presented a single woman with special challenges. "I think as a lot of mothers, she really felt like her boys had to be prepared to go out and be independent," Geoffrey said, "and she didn't want us, as she would say, up her skirts all the time." She knew that fighting was par for the course on the streets of their neighborhood, and she taught her boys to stand up for themselves. Geoffrey and his brothers would look down at the street from the safety of their apartment, terrified that the boys outside planned to beat them up. (They weren't misreading the signals.) Their mother offered them no safe harbor; she felt it was her job to make them able to protect themselves, and if it meant getting beaten to a pulp a few times, so be it. "It was like gladiator schools on the block," Geoffrey said. "I had determined I wasn't ever going outside."

Geoffrey's mother attended elementary school in Harlem, but then in junior high, based on a photograph we found, she appeared to be the only African American student in her class. Never at any point had she mentioned this to Geoffrey. In 1946 she enrolled in Johnson C. Smith University, a historically black school in Charlotte, North Carolina, but was unable to graduate because her parents couldn't afford the tuition. She would go back to finish college many years later.

Mary's parents, Leonard and Lydia Williams, were both born in North Carolina in the early 1900s. They moved to Harlem before settling on Long Island, part of the Great Migration like the Canada family and millions of other African Americans. One of the many different jobs Leonard worked at was as a hat blocker. "I remember that he said that Kennedy put him out of work," Geoffrey said, "because when President Kennedy became president, he didn't wear hats. And suddenly the fashion of wearing hats disappeared, and so did my grandfather's job." Geoffrey said his grandfather, who had served as the pastor of Mount Pleasant Baptist Church in Harlem, was always working at some occupation or another. "He drove a bus for a while. He did odds and ends. He sold vegetables and flowers and other things. My grandfather was the only man in our life who was a working man and a very pious and religious man."

Geoffrey was very close to his grandmother. "My grandmother, whom I loved more than anybody, treated me, even as a kid, like I had a brain. She would talk to me about serious things, and we would have the deepest conversations, because she was very religious, and I was a kid who was looking for the facts and the logic of things." As a child, Geoffrey openly questioned whether there was a God. "Why did the good people have to suffer?" he would ask. "And she didn't smack me. She knew that somewhere along the line she was saving my soul. She would sit there and explain to me, 'I know what you believe, but let me tell you why there really is a God.'"

Geoffrey's question about why the good people suffer was never answered satisfactorily. His grandmother died of cancer, "the slow, wasting-away, painful cancer. This woman who never lied, never smoked, didn't drink, didn't do anything wrong, and here she's dying this horrible, horrible death. And I just couldn't help myself, because we had had these conversations. I said to her, 'Do you still believe in God?' And she looked at me, and she said, 'Now more than ever.'"

Geoffrey said his grandmother's faith, which he questioned and challenged, buoyed him after her death. "Because I had this experience growing up of knowing what faith looked like, what people who really believed were like, it strengthened me," he said, "and it kept me not doubting that this was going to end up somehow OK."

Although his relationship with his grandparents was very close, he didn't know much about his mother's side of the family other than that they were from North Carolina. One of his earliest childhood memories is of a trip to Kinston, North Carolina, to visit his great-grandmother, Lillian Foy Williams. "I remember moving to the back of the bus, and I remember asking my mother why. And she said, 'No, no, you're too young. You can't understand.'" Geoffrey said he was probably only three years old at the time. The native New Yorker got his first taste of the segregated South at a very early age, and the memory never left him. When the family decided to go into town, Geoffrey's southern family members laid down the law to their northern relatives. "Family members were telling us how we could not look white people in the face. They said, 'No, no, no,' because they knew we were New Yorkers. They said, 'Now, when you go in the stores, don't be looking up at white people. You keep your eyes down.'" And I just thought, I've got to get out of here. I'm three years old, and I'm thinking, this is a terrible place."

He was happy to leave North Carolina behind, but he has always known it is a part of his history, yet in only the most vague way. Geoffrey's great-grandmother Lillian Foy was his connection to the Old South, although when he was a young child he dismissed her talk as the cranky ranting of an elderly woman. Her husband was John Harvey Williams, whom Geoffrey didn't know. On occasion Lillian would come up from North Carolina to visit her son, Geoffrey's grandfather Leonard, on Long Island. "She was from the real old school and just didn't understand. She used to just fuss at us because we were like the worst example of disruptive kids. We didn't sit; we didn't listen; we had all the questions." He paused before continuing: "But she did tell me that she knew in her direct family slaves, and that she was trying to impress on me that you don't understand what's going on and why this is so important. And the concept was just so foreign to me that she could personally say, 'I knew slavery personally.' And that was just like, 'Oh, please. Come on. Right. The olden days.' It's hard to believe that it was that close."

But it *was* that close. Lillian's parents, George Foy and Mary Wittfield, were born into slavery. George was born in 1859, the year of John Brown's raid, and Mary was born in 1862, one year before Abraham Lincoln issued the Emancipation Proclamation. They were extremely young when slavery ended, but the fact is, they were born in bondage.

The 1870 census introduced us to Geoffrey's third great-grandparents. This is astonishing. Henry Foy and Lucy Hatch lived in Jones County, North Carolina. Henry, forty-five, was a farm laborer, and Lucy, thirty-one, was "keeping house." This means that Henry was born in 1825 and Lucy in 1839. Both spent many of their adult years enslaved.

As we did with the Canada family, once the slaves' paper trail ran out, we investigated their owner. Henry Foy was born forty years before the end of slavery. We searched Jones County for white men who owned slaves and white men named Foy in an effort to find his owner. The 1840 census provides us with the information we were seeking. A man named Enoch Foy owned seven male slaves between the ages of ten and twenty-four; Geoffrey's third great-grandfather would have been fifteen in 1840, so it seems very likely that we had found his owner.

Enoch Foy died in 1842, and, like Charles Cannaday, he left a will detailing all his property. At the end of the list of twenty-seven slaves, all identified by name, is Henry's name. For Geoffrey, the anonymity of slavery has been erased.

From a contemporary newspaper advertisement in the *New Bern Spec-*

tator, we learned that Enoch Foy may have been an upstanding citizen and pillar of the community, a member of the state senate and a state judge, but he was also fiercely protective of his slave property. The slave referred to in the ad is not Henry but Sampson. "Fifty dollar reward," the ad reads. "Ran away from the subscriber on Sunday the 26th, a negro man named Sampson. The above reward will be given for the delivery of him to me or his confinement in any jail so that I get him, and all reasonable expenses paid. And should he resist in being taken so that violence is necessary to arrest him, I will not hold any person liable for damages should the slave be killed. Enoch Foy, Jones County, November 28, 1837."

This was not *Gone with the Wind*. Enoch Foy was not the benevolent master of lore. He did not treat his slaves like family. Here was written proof, from his own pen, that a slave's life was expendable. Geoffrey is understandably, momentarily speechless. "This is real slavery and what it was really like."

Geoffrey's paternal and maternal family trees go deep into slavery, with paper trails that allow us to identify slave ancestors by name. All these names belonged to people who had been lost—not spoken of by relatives who remembered them, not known at all from one generation to the next. "They'll never be lost again," Geoffrey said, grateful for the chance to meet them.

"This has filled in a picture that's been a blank wall for me forever," said Geoffrey. "At fifty-nine, to put these pieces together and to understand how I ended up where I am today has just been quite a revelation."

■ The paper trail took us further back in time than we could have dreamed, but DNA science could reveal still more about Geoffrey's origins. On his mother's side, we were able to trace his oldest ancestor to Sarah Skinner, who was born in North Carolina in the late 1800s. His maternal haplogroup is X2b, a relatively uncommon signature found in Europe and the Near East—not Africa. Ninety-nine percent of African American people can trace their mitochondrial DNA back to Africa; 1 percent descend from a white woman who was impregnated by a black man during the colonial period. As a matter of comparison, 35 percent of black men in the United States can trace their paternal ancestry back to Europe because of rape or coercive sexual activity. In all likelihood, this white female ancestor was an indentured servant from England or Ireland who chose to have sexual relations with black men. We've done four of these series, and Geoff Canada is only the second African American with mitochondrial DNA that goes back to Europe. I am the other one.

In spite of the many names and places we were able to confirm in Geoffrey's paternal line, one big mystery still remained: Was the plantation owner Charles Cannaday the father of his slave, Thomas? Was he Geoffrey's great-great-grandfather? Legal documents prove that Cannaday owned Thomas, and oral history suggested that the white Cannadays were known for "growing slaves," adding to their labor force as cheaply as possible by impregnating their slaves.

Geoffrey's Y-DNA can't prove actual paternity. Only a test taken by other direct descendants of Charles Cannaday could determine whether Charles Cannaday was Thomas's father, and therefore Geoffrey's ancestor. We tracked down two such descendants, Charles Cannaday's great-grandchildren. Unfortunately, as of this writing, neither had agreed to take the test. "I just think it's about the science of understanding who we are and how we got here, so I'm disappointed they wouldn't do it," Geoffrey said. "I thought actually that they would."

DNA doesn't keep secrets, though. And while it may not be sufficient to prove paternity, Geoffrey's paternal haplogroup, R1b1b2, proves beyond a doubt that he is descended from a white man on his father's side. R1b1b2 is the most popular haplogroup not in Africa, but in Europe, most commonly found on the fringes of the North Sea, England, Germany, and the Netherlands. In the group of people we studied for this series, Geoffrey shares this haplogroup with three of our other guests, but they are all white: Kevin Bacon, Robert Downey Jr., and Harry Connick Jr. "This is not the crew I was expecting it to be," Geoffrey laughed. He also has DNA in his other chromosomes that leads back to recent black African ancestors, but on the basis of his mitochondrial DNA and his Y-DNA—those two out of twenty-three chromosomes—his genome tells a different story from what his own life does: Geoffrey Canada is, like me, a white man.

Geoffrey's admixture test—which was conducted by two different companies, 23andMe and Family Tree DNA—tells us a bit more about why Geoffrey looks like he does, why he is black when his genome tells us he could just as easily be white. Both admixture tests reveal that his admixture is between 80 and 85 percent African and between 15 and 17 percent European, with only 3 percent coding for Asian, or Native American. "Sometimes you feel part of something," Geoffrey says. "I never felt part of anything that preceded slavery in this country. So to think that my ancestors could have been here as Europeans was never in my consciousness; that some of my ancestors were free."

The family that Geoffrey lived with was never far from his mind. He told us numerous stories about his brothers, and their closeness was evident. When we learned of a new relative, he frequently commented before saying anything else that he couldn't wait to share this information with his family. He wondered aloud how they would react to the news of their white origins.

"I don't know whether or not my family is prepared to hear all of this," Geoffrey said, "because we're going to have to redefine what we thought would be the roots. I think everybody is looking for their roots to take them back to Africa. . . . But it's part of the American story. And it's a much more complicated story than most of us have been led to believe. So much of it we closed the book on never to look at again, because it's tough. It's about rape and brutality, and who wants to revisit that kind of stuff? But somehow we have to take the good with the bad, or else we wouldn't be here."

Geoffrey and I took one final look at his family tree, and I asked him if a fairy godmother touched down and told him he could pick one ancestor to meet, who would it be? "I want to meet Thomas," he answered. Thomas is his paternal great-great-grandfather. "When he was twenty-two years old, what was it about him that made them depreciate him so much? I'd really like to understand what that was, . . . and just to hear what his life was like, and what it was like after his master died, and then he became the property of someone else. Now, I'm hoping he would say, 'Because I just refused to do what these people tell me to do.' I'm one those kind of folk. Hopefully that's the answer, but I would love to know more about that."

When I first asked Geoffrey Canada about what he knew about his origins, his response was frank. "Look, the most I can say is, 'I'm from the South Bronx,' right? Where do you belong? Short of that, I know nothing about the history of belonging to this country, and I have wondered, 'Where am I from?'" As we learned from Barbara Walters's family's peregrinations and changing name, Geoffrey isn't alone in asking this question.

For Geoffrey, this feeling of rootlessness manifests itself very practically in the children he teaches at Harlem Children's Zone. Geoffrey believes that the inability to connect with the past has had a devastating effect on many of the at-risk children he has dedicated his life to helping. "This issue that you're a part of belonging somewhere that has a history allows you to feel that you're connected in some way to more than just what is happening right now," Geoffrey reflected. "I know so many young people who think they're part of the Bloods. That's what they really think, that that's who they really are. And if you ask them, 'Well, what else do you belong to?' they couldn't tell you anything, because as far as they know, their life began right here in Harlem, and that's what they know, and these are the connections. And if you were to go to them and say, 'Let me tell you a little bit about your people and what your people have done,' it would give them a place to see themselves in a larger context."

Geoffrey Canada has spent so much of his life looking for answers to his questions about his last name and about his father's family, and now they have been answered beyond his wildest imagination. "It's not that it brings closure in a sense of finality," he said. "But boy, does it answer some questions we've had forever. And to be able to say to my sons and my grandchildren, 'Guess what? Let me tell you a little bit about who we are, where we came from,' that's a story that I just can't wait to begin to tell."

What's in a name? Between every letter, it seems, is a saga, the Walters and Canada lines have revealed. And the only way to be sure you're spelling it correctly is to go back.

CHAPTER FOUR

Redemption

Kyra Sedgwick and Kevin Bacon are two of the most popular actors in Hollywood, notable not only for their accomplished careers but for their unusually long and happy partnership. Profiling them was a first for our team. We'd never researched the family histories of a married couple.

Amazingly, both have ancestors who participated in the founding of America and in the shaping of African American history, in courtrooms and classrooms. Kevin had no idea that his roots in this country ran so deep, and Kyra, whose family history was passed down proudly to her and her siblings while they were growing up, was astonished at what we unearthed about her family's hero, the Revolutionary-era judge who built the house they continue to gather in for reunions. To our surprise—and theirs—the stories contained in Kyra's and Kevin's past shed new light on the issue of slavery in colonial America, and though their ancestors played a role in this sad history, theirs is ultimately a story of redemption, within and across generations, worthy of a different kind of star on the walk of fame.

Kyra Sedgwick has been acting for three decades, but she is best known for her Emmy Award–winning role as Deputy Chief Brenda Leigh Johnson on the hit TV crime drama *The Closer*. Johnson, a homicide detective known for solving crimes in an unconventional manner, asks all the right questions in a soft southern purr—and ultimately gets the answers she's looking for. As we began our investigation of Kyra's roots, we hoped we would, too.

Kyra Minturn Sedgwick was born in New York City on August 19, 1965, to Henry Dwight "Harry" Sedgwick V and Patricia Rosenwald. Her father, Harry, was the privileged son of a prominent New England family, while her mother, Patricia, was the daughter of prosperous Jewish immigrants—two lineages from two different worlds. When Kyra was only two or three years old (by her recollection), her parents' marriage dissolved, and though her mother eventually remarried, it was a difficult period in Kyra's life. As a child, she says, she bounced aimlessly between private schools until, at twelve, she discovered a passion for acting. Four years later, she landed her first television role, on the soap opera *Another World*.

Kyra herself seems to be from two different worlds—the worlds of the American establishment and the affluent immigrant. To get a sense of how these two worlds shaped Kyra, we started by looking at her mother's family. Patricia Rosenwald was born on May 27, 1932, in New York City. Kyra's mother rarely spoke of her Jewish heritage, and the family never observed Jewish traditions or holidays in their home. Kyra credits her stepfather, Ben Heller, for opening the door on this part of her past. "My Jewish awakening was through my stepfather, as we started having Passover and talking about what it means to be Jewish and what the Jewish religion is all about." Since then, "being Jewish" for Kyra is, as it is for so many American Jews, rooted in the cultural and the metaphysical rather than in the observance of religious traditions. Today Jews can choose to identify with or celebrate their heritage (or not) in a variety of ways, but the deeper we delved into Kyra's roots, the more evidence we found of the daily humiliations visited on people purely because of such a heritage.

Kyra's grandfather, James Benno Rosenwald, born in New York City on November 27, 1905, was the son of incredible privilege. In fact, in the 1920 census his family is listed with more servants in the home than family members. There were Kyra's great-grandparents, Bernard and Mae

Rosenwald; Mae's mother; James and his brother Edward; and six servants. Kyra's mother described her grandfather James as a "poor little rich boy"—raised more by the servants than his parents. Kyra thinks her mother's experience growing up may have been similar.

There was a massive influx of Jewish immigrants from Eastern Europe into the United States at the turn on the twentieth century. But Kyra's grandparents *and* great-grandparents were born in this country. How—and why—did Kyra's ancestors come to the United States earlier than so many other Jews? We found a passport application for Edward Rosenwald, Kyra's great-great-great-grandfather, dated 1859. This is nearly thirty years before the Statue of Liberty was dedicated in New York Harbor and nearly forty years before Ellis Island opened its doors.

Edward Rosenwald was Kyra's first immigrant ancestor, born in the then-kingdom of Bavaria in 1833. Once in America, Edward and his three younger brothers, Isaac, Henry, and Sigmund, built the very successful E.J. Rosenwald and Brothers Tobacco Company. Edward's children and his grandchildren, including Kyra's grandfather, grew up with every material advantage. This is a true immigrant success story, but how did it happen? If the Rosenwalds left Germany, we can assume they were looking for a better life elsewhere. They certainly found that better life, but what did they leave behind?

■ As we've already seen, Jewish ancestry, like African American ancestry, is astonishingly difficult to trace. But because we already had Bavaria as the starting place for our search, we knew there was a chance we could go back farther—and we did. Using Edward's death certificate, from 1892, we then obtained the name of his parents, Kyra's third great-grandparents, Carolina Berg Rosenwald and Moritz Rosenwald.

Between 1813 and 1860, Jews in Bavaria had to conform to an edict that dictated the conditions of their people in the kingdom. One such rule, the *Matrikelgesetz*, or registration law, required Jewish men to purchase a *Matrikel*, or license, essentially a letter of protection allowing them to live freely, much like the papers free African Americans had to carry in the United States to ward off (re)enslavement. The Bavarian registry also kept track of Jewish property and verified that license holders were engaged in an accepted Jewish profession. Kyra's third great-grandfather, Moritz Rosenwald, as it happens, was learning the trade of bookbinding.

"The Land Registry of Israelite People of Jewish Faith in the Town of Burgebrach" was an incredible discovery for us—opening a window onto the world in which the Rosenwald family lived. It contains Moritz's *Matrikel* and lists information about not only him but his family: his siblings' names and those of his parents, Barukh and Gertrude Rosenwald, Kyra's *fourth* great-grandparents.

Although Jews were granted citizenship in Bavaria in 1813, it was really in name only. They were restricted to living in certain areas, and only ten Jewish families were allowed to live in each community. The *Matrikels* were available to only one son at a time. The *Matrikel* system hearkened back to the old pharaonic law from Egypt, designed to prevent population growth among Jews. In Bavaria, there was little incentive for Jews to have large families, because a man without a *Matrikel* could not get permission to marry or work. Jewish people in Bavaria at that time had a saying that the path to the wedding canopy led only over the grave of someone who had already been registered with the *Matrikel*, because the *Matrikel* holder had to die to free it up. This was systematic, institutionalized oppression verging on torture.

Yet the opulent lives Kyra's mother and grandfather lived in America may have had their roots in Bavaria, for local historians there told us Barukh Rosenwald was not only a prominent person but one of two presidents of Burgebrach's Jewish community. With a thriving spice and textile business, he was also the wealthiest person in the community.

This did not keep his grandson, Edward Rosenwald, from sailing for America in 1859, however. We will never know the full reason behind his leaving, but we do know that around this time, approximately one-half of the Jewish youth of Bavaria emigrated to the United States.

To go back two hundred years into a Jewish person's ancestry is very, very rare. "I figured a lot of them were killed," Kyra marveled. "At least my closest relatives made it out before the Nazis came."

But not all did. At least two of Moritz's nieces perished in the Holocaust. Olga Caroline Rosenwald Reichmann died in Treblinka in 1942, and her sister, Lili Clara Rosenwald Sack, died in Auschwitz the following year.

Kyra was saddened but not surprised. "I figured someone had to be connected." Kyra told me about one of her early films, *War and Love*, in which she played a girl who ended up in one of the death camps. "We actually shot in Auschwitz/Birkenau. I had an intense connection with that time. It almost felt genetic on some level, honestly," she recalled. "For years every book I picked up had to do with the Holocaust. I was trying to search for meaning and read a lot of Elie Wiesel. I think that was where a lot of my connection to my Jewish heritage came from, the persecution of them."

■ Kyra's father's family needs little introduction. The Sedgwicks are one of the most prominent and most chronicled families in all of New England. Since their ancestors arrived here more than three centuries ago, they've played a vital role in the creation of the new republic. The Sedgwicks have been congressmen, senators, elder statesmen, judges, writers, and witnesses to many of the most important events in American history.

Kyra's father, Henry Dwight Sedgwick V, was born in 1928 in Boston. You know you're dealing with serious history when you come across someone with a "V" after his name. In many ways, though, he defied the stereotype of the well-established, staid New England WASP. "He has an artist's personality and soul," Kyra said. "He is passionate and loving, and he loves history." His family history is extremely important to him. "I would say he feels like he's part of a lineage," Kyra explained, "and he is very smart and in equal parts heart-driven and head-driven."

The Sedgwick family built its stately colonial home in Stockbridge, Massachusetts, well west of Boston in the Berkshires more than two hundred years ago. It both stands as a monument to the family's collective past and acts as a locus for its gatherings today.

Kyra's fond memories of the summers she spent in Stockbridge were evident as she described the home to us. "It's a beautiful old colonial. You can just feel the history walking around. It's got a wing that was probably used for the servants' quarters back in the day. It reeks of history," she said. Even as a child, Kyra understood she was privileged to be part of such a distinguished family. "It was a big deal, the Sedgwick line. I think everyone probably has a rich family history when you go back. But I knew so much about my dad's because it was a celebrated story."

The Sedgwick ancestors came from England in the year 1636 (the year my own Harvard University was founded) and quickly established themselves in a colony known as Charlestown, not far from Plymouth Rock.

Three generations later, the family name was made famous by Kyra's fourth great-grandfather, Judge Theodore Sedgwick. It was Judge Sedgwick who built the house in Stockbridge in 1785, and his descendants have occupied it ever since. Kyra's father, Harry, kindly gave me a tour.

The son of farmers, Theodore Sedgwick was the first Sedgwick to go to college, attending my undergraduate alma mater, Yale University, in 1761.

Determined to make a name for himself, Theodore moved to western Massachusetts to establish a law practice.

Kyra's uncle, John Sedgwick, filled me in on the judge. "He had an unbelievably forceful personality. I think he could probably win any case, whether the facts were for or against him, whether the law was for him or against him. It really didn't matter. The power of his personality was such that he would just be able to push through."

By the early 1770s, Theodore Sedgwick's home colony was boiling over with resentment toward the British crown. From the streets and taverns of Massachusetts to parlors and places of worship, revolution was in the air, and Sedgwick was determined to use his mind and influence to aid the cause.

"He believed very much in democracy," John explained, "and what the English were imposing on the colonists was more of a tyranny."

In January 1773 Theodore Sedgwick and other prominent Berkshires men wrote a manifesto demanding liberation. Known as the Sheffield Declaration, or Sheffield Resolves, the document served as a road map for colonial independence, insisting that all men have a right to happiness, property, and liberty. When the thirteen colonies formally demanded separation from the crown three years later, Thomas Jefferson would echo Sedgwick's words in the language of the Declaration of Independence.

Theodore's role in the revolution launched his career as a leading American statesman. First, he was elected to the state legislature, then to the state senate, and then to the Continental Congress. He eventually served as the fifth Speaker of the U.S. House of Representatives, from 1799 to 1801.

"I can remember at such a young age, hearing about how great Judge Theodore Sedgwick was. I was very proud," said Kyra.

How are family stories passed down? Some are recounted over and over at the dinner table, on holidays, or at family reunions—and there's always one person in most families who becomes the unofficial record keeper, the family historian. I can still remember the day in 1960 when my father showed my brother and me my great-great-grandmother's photograph and obituary from the year 1888. It ignited in me a passion for genealogy, to find out where she had come from, and how she and I were connected. What's unusual about the Sedgwicks is that most of what we know about Kyra's family, and especially her fourth great-grandfather Theodore, comes directly from books written by generations of Sedgwicks themselves. The walls of the house in Stockbridge are lined with leather-bound volumes of family history. Her uncle John is this generation's storyteller.

"You realized that, in a family like mine anyway, the past is not past," John Sedgwick said. "The past remains present. In looking at history, you're really looking into yourself, because every bit of history that I have uncovered in my family has some remnant in my own self."

But how reliable are the stories we tell ourselves about our families? As we sifted through Kyra's past, we discovered a surprising story, a story about Theodore Sedgwick that has never been part of any written family history—and one that seemed to contradict the ideals he struggled for during the revolution. Peter Drummey, the head researcher at the Massachusetts Historical Society, uncovered a shocking document in a folder marked "Real Estate" in the Theodore Sedgwick papers: a bill of sale for a slave.

"The author of the Sheffield Resolves," Drummey explained, "in 1777, during the heart of the Revolution, is buying a slave named Ton from another Revolutionary soldier named John Fellows." Maybe, I said, he was buying the slave to free her? "No," Drummey confirmed, "buying a slave to act as a servant in his household."

The fact is Ton was not the first slave Theodore Sedgwick had owned. The earlier 1771 census lists him as owning another servant for life. Drummey was as flabbergasted as I was. In all of the written material about the judge, the outspoken advocate of independence, there is not a single reference to his status as a slave owner. "I honestly thought it must be another Sedgwick, that it must be a coincidence of name," Drummey said. "But it's clearly Theodore Sedgwick."

When I showed Kyra and her father the bill of sale, it was the first time either of them had seen or heard anything about this. Dated July 1, 1777, it reads: "Know all Men by these Presents that I, John Fellows of Sheffield, in consideration of the sum of sixty pounds to me in hand well and truly paid by Theodore Sedgwick. Bargain, sell, and convey unto him one Negro woman named Ton, about 30 years old, to have and to hold said Negro for and during the term of her natural life."

Though often overlooked, slavery in the North was widespread. In 1775 one in ten adults in Rhode Island—the colony founded as a haven for those seeking political and religious tolerance—was a black slave. And, according to Peter Drummey's records at the Massachusetts Historical Society, there were more than two thousand slaves in Massachusetts alone.

"It's everywhere," Drummey said, reviewing the files. "And I think people today are not aware of that, not aware of slavery in Massachusetts. And even the people who are aware of slavery in New England—early slavery in New England—don't understand it to be everywhere in the landscape."

How different the story would be if it ended there. Instead, almost a century before Abraham Lincoln—a man born in a slave state possessing conventional racist views, who evolved to the point of penning the Emancipation Proclamation and arming black soldiers to win the Civil War—Theodore Sedgwick embarked on a similar journey of enlightenment that began one day in 1781 when a black woman known only as Mum Bett walked into his law office in Sheffield, Massachusetts. I have long known the name Mum Bett. Hers is a seminal story of African American history, a female slave who demanded her own freedom and hastened the end of slavery in Massachusetts. But I had absolutely no idea that an ancestor of Kyra Sedgwick had played any part in her fascinating story.

Kyra's father Harry said that Mum Bett was very much a part of their family history. Her portrait even hangs in the foyer of the old Stockbridge mansion. "She was a very strong woman, at least from everything that I can determine," Harry said. "In terms of history, she was a lot more interesting than any of the Sedgwick family, which is fine with us."

The story of Mum Bett comes down to us from Theodore's daughter Catharine, who wrote about her in 1853. Catharine described the night that Mum Bett's master's wife threatened to beat another slave, a girl named Lizzy, who many believe was Mum Bett's daughter.

Kyra read from her ancestor's account: "She seized a large, iron shovel, red hot from cleaning the oven, and raised it over the terrified girl. Bett interposed her brawny arm and took the blow. It cut quite across the arm to the bone. But she would say afterwards in concluding the story of the frightful scar she carried to her grave, Madam never again laid her hand on Lizzy."

Catharine also tells the story of the day Mum Bett heard a reading of the new Declaration of Independence at the Sheffield Town Hall. Kyra again: "She went the next day to the office of Mr. Theodore Sedgwick, then in the beginning of his honorable political career. 'Sire,' said she, 'I heard that paper read yesterday that says all men are born equal and that every man has a right to freedom. I am not a dumb critter. Won't the law give me my freedom?'"

Despite his close friendship with Mum Bett's owner, John Ashley, Theodore decided to take her case. Kyra's uncle John reasoned why. "He was impressed, I think, with her argument. He had to have been impressed by her personality, and that trial was, in that part of the world, the trial of the century."

Many slaves in Massachusetts had petitioned for their freedom and lost. But Theodore Sedgwick tried a novel approach: challenging the institution of slavery itself. What is remarkable about the argument he crafted is that he didn't look for a loophole or some special circumstance that would oblige John Ashley to set Mum Bett free. Rather, he acted on the assumption that since all men were born free and equal, as stated on the state's brand-new constitution, then nobody in Massachusetts could be held in slavery. This was a radical position. While many at the time believed slaves should be freed, they thought it could only be done gradually, over time. But there was nothing gradual about Theodore's approach—or the result.

On August 21, 1781, a jury of twelve local farmers—all white, all male—granted Mum Bett her freedom. The first thing she did was change her name. Now a free woman, she became Elizabeth Freeman and came to work for Theodore in the old house in Stockbridge, helping to raise his seven children. So special was her place in the family that, to this day, she remains the only non-Sedgwick buried in the family cemetery, referred to as the Sedgwick Pie. The inscription on her headstone reads: "Elizabeth Freeman, known by the name of Mum Bett, died December 28, 1829. Her supposed age was 85 years. She was born a slave and remained a slave for nearly thirty years. She could neither read nor write, yet in her own sphere she had no superior nor equal. She neither wasted time nor property. She never violated a trust nor failed to perform a duty. Good mother, farewell."

Mum Bett's case ended slavery in Massachusetts and by extension New England. For Kyra, her father, and the entire Sedgwick clan, the story of Mum Bett has always been a symbol of their family's decency and liberal sensibilities. But now, having learned that Theodore, their patriarch, once owned a slave himself, Mum Bett's legacy is also powerfully redemptive.

■ Long and distinguished as the paper trail may be on Kyra's father's side, DNA allowed us to go even farther back. We were able to trace her direct paternal ancestors to a Major General Robert Sedgwick, born in England when Shakespeare was still alive, in 1613. We tested her brother Rob's DNA to determine her paternal haplogroup. It is R1a1a1, a branch of haplogroup R. Haplogroup R originated in southwestern Asia thirty thousand years ago and then split into two branches, R1 and R2. Kyra's branch, R1, spread widely across Eurasia from Iceland to Japan. Her particular haplogroup is found in about one-third of Norwegian men and a quarter of the men from the far northern British Isles. Groups that carried this haplogroup to the British Isles over the past two thousand years include Anglo-Saxons and Vikings. She has living distant relations today in England, Germany, Hungary, Russia, and Sweden. Out of all the guests I have profiled in these four series, there is only one other person besides Kyra with this haplogroup: Dr. Ben Carson, chief of pediatric neurosurgery at Johns Hopkins and the most famous black surgeon in history. Kyra and Ben share a patrilineal line that goes back ten or fifteen thousand years. "Smart and good-looking," Kyra said, studying his picture. "Not bad. And a doctor!"

Now we turned to Kyra's mother's side, which we discovered had a surprisingly long and documented paper trail for an Eastern European Jewish family. Kyra's oldest direct ancestors on her mother's side are Barukh and Gertrude Rosenwald, born in 1779 and 1789, respectively, in the kingdom of Bavaria, now Germany. Kyra's maternal haplogroup is H1. Haplogroup H originated in the Near East forty thousand years ago, and it expanded after the peak of the Ice Age into Europe. It's the most prevalent haplogroup in Europe today. H1, which developed out of H when genes mutated, originated thirteen thousand years ago, when people migrated to southern France, to the Iberian Peninsula, and to Italy. The H1 mutation likely arose in a woman living on the Iberian Peninsula and was then carried into the British Isles by hunter-gatherers as far as Scandinavia. The maternal haplogroup H1 reaches levels of 15 percent in Britain today, and in Ireland that number is up to 40 percent. Thirteen percent of all people in Europe trace their maternal ancestry to the H1 haplogroup.

But here's the kicker: those people are not Ashkenazi Jews. H1 is not one of the Ashkenazi haplogroups. This means that Kyra is *not* genetically Jewish. This was certainly an unusual result, but one that can be explained historically. Because for centuries Jews were confined to small areas where they could live, they had the highest level of cousins of any database genetically; in other words, Ashkenazi Jews have been marrying each other, extended cousins, for a very long time. Because Jews were marrying Jews, they had the same gene pool. The traditional Ashkenazi haplogroups are K and N. Somewhere along the way—we don't know exactly when—there was a new influx of Jewish women into Kyra's Jewish ancestors' community, women with different mitochondrial DNA. They may have been Christians who converted to Judaism. After 1096, Jews in the Middle East were under deadly attack during the First Crusade. Four hundred years later, at the time of Columbus, the Spanish Inquisition was well under way, and King Ferdinand gave all the Jews from Spain a painful choice: convert or leave. Many chose to leave, fleeing Spain for Germany. We know that Kyra's haplogroup, HI, arose in the Iberian Peninsula. With this information, we can surmise that Kyra most likely descends from one of those women who was kicked out of Spain and settled in Germany.

Kyra was crushed by this new knowledge. I assured her that we could analyze other parts of her DNA to find genetic Jewish ancestry. According to one of the companies we use, Family Tree DNA, 30 to 40 percent of all Ashkenazi Jews probably descend from a non-Semitic mother for the same reason. This information consoled Kyra. "So I'm not alone."

A different analysis of her DNA, however, where we examine all of her twenty-three chromosomes, tells us that she has recent ancestry from Ukraine, Russia, and Poland—Ashkenazi territory. This test shows us that half of all of Kyra's genetic material traces back to Ashkenazi Jews.

Kyra breathed a sigh of relief. "Thank you," she said. "I want to be half Jewish. I'm proud of my Jewish heritage."

Because Kyra is Jewish, we have two ways of analyzing her admixture, which is her percentage of African, European, and Native American ancestry. The first reading, from 23andMe, dovetails with her genealogical history: 99 percent European and 1 percent Asian. Anything of such a low percentage is not considered significant. Family Tree DNA looks specifically at Jewish, or Middle Eastern, percentages, and from that company Kyra gets a result of 72 percent European and 28 percent Jewish. Those numbers add up also, in terms of what we have just learned about her maternal haplogroup. Because she is genetically not Jewish on her mother's line, she has more non-Semitic ancestors than Semitic ones.

Kyra's DNA is a reflection of Jewish history itself. Most Eastern European Jews are descendants from the Pale of Settlement, a region of imperial Russia to which Jewish residency was confined. Today that region covers parts of Poland, Belarus, and Ukraine. From our genealogy research, we also know that Kyra is a German Jew. Both of these geographic regions correspond to what we have learned about Kyra's DNA.

I asked Kyra the same thing I ask all of my guests at the end of our journey: if she had a fairy godmother who could take her back in time, which of her ancestors would she choose to meet? Maybe because she was so well versed in her Sedgwick ancestors already, she chooses one of the Jewish relatives she'd known nothing about: her immigrant ancestor and great-great-grandfather Edward Rosenwald. "I'd like to meet the person who at sixteen wanted to leave the bosom of his family and everything that he knew to make it big in New York City," Kyra said. "Who gave him the gumption and chutzpah to leave cozy little Bavaria? As hard as it was, it was something he knew."

Of course, Kyra began working in New York City when she was sixteen also. There just might be some things that truly do run in the family.

Kevin Bacon (b. 1958)

"Kevin Bacon" has become a metaphor for human connectedness. Because he has appeared in more than sixty films, his prolific career placed him at the center of a pop culture phenomenon, the game Six Degrees of Kevin Bacon. The conceit is that Kevin Bacon can, through his films, be linked to every actor in Hollywood, of any time period, within six steps. With acclaimed ensemble films like *Mystic River*, *JFK*, *Apollo 13*, and *A Few Good Men* on his résumé, it's no surprise how far his reach into Hollywood history is. He and his wife, Kyra Sedgwick, are linked by one step, having acted together in the films *Lemon Sky*, *Pyrates*, *Murder in the First*, and *The Woodsman*. But their true connection is far more enduring and deep, and they have long kept their off-screen life just that—off-screen—working hard to raise their children, Travis and Sosie, away from the spotlight.

Unlike those playing the Six Degrees game, we were interested only in Kevin Bacon's connections to his actual ancestors. Born on July 8, 1958, he grew up in Philadelphia, the youngest of six kids. Even as a child, Kevin enjoyed dressing up in costumes and acting. "My brothers and sisters were my first audience," he recalled. "I can absolutely remember, as a little kid, thinking to myself, if I walk into a room, I want people to look at me."

Kevin's father, Edmund Bacon, was a man people looked at—for his vision. An urban planner known as the father of modern Philadelphia, he served as city planner for more than two decades. Edmund Bacon was so celebrated he even made the cover of *Time* magazine, an honor, Kevin admits ruefully, he has yet to achieve.

"I remember when he was on his last years, and we'd go down to Philly, and I'd take off for walks with him, a lot of times people would say, 'Mr. Bacon, Mr. Bacon!' And I'd turn around and say, 'Oh, here they come. I'm going to have to sign an autograph.' And it was always for him."

Kevin makes no bones about what was driving him as a child, beyond his esteemed father. "Probably by the time I was twelve or thirteen, I knew that I wanted to do something to become rich and famous and get girls and be in magazines," he said candidly. "I was really into rock 'n' roll and into the kind of stardom that rock 'n' roll would give you, if you were a Beatle or a Monkee or a Rolling Stone."

Although they took different paths, Kevin certainly seems to have inherited his father's drive and confidence. We wanted to learn who came before him. Did Kevin's family history contain any secrets, as Kyra's did? And at any point in the larger American story did their trees overlap?

■ Kevin's mother, Ruth Hilda Holmes, was born in New York City on May 5, 1916. Her upbringing was strangely similar to his mother-in-law's. Both women grew up very wealthy, surrounded by fine things and lots of household help. In Ruth's case, her parents and two siblings were tended to by no fewer than five live-in servants. "They would kind of get rolled out to see their parents," Kevin explained. "They didn't eat with them. I think the parents would have dinner, and they'd get all cleaned up, and they'd say, 'Good night, Mommy. Good night, Daddy,' and they would take them out. It was almost like royalty, the way they grew up."

As adults, Hilda and her identical twin sister, Prudence, who later changed her name to Anne, lived lives that bore no resemblance to the one they had known as children. Ruth was an educator, opening preschools in the projects of Philadelphia and initiating a program at Graterford Prison in nearby Montgomery County for families visiting incarcerated men. She was passionately antiwar, going so far as to forbid Kevin to play with G.I. Joes when he was little, and when Kevin was ten, she brought him to the Poor People's Campaign march in Washington. "She would never make quite enough food for everybody," Kevin recalled. "It was a strange thing, I think probably as a reaction to the opulence she grew up with, where she'd sit down to dinner and they'd have a giant roast for two people, and she didn't believe in that kind of waste."

Ruth's twin sister became a writer. Under the name of Anne Near, she published *A Dubious Journey from Class to Class*. In it, she wrote that she really envied the "normal people," the working-class people, because they were inspired to live different kinds of lives from those in which they were raised. Her point was clear, if not slightly patronizing: the trappings of wealth could be limiting and stifling.

"Both of the girls rejected this lifestyle," Kevin said of his mother and his aunt, "one in one way by marrying my father and coming to Philadelphia and working with poor people, and the other by going as far away from a northeastern kind of life as possible, living on a ranch in California, marrying a cowboy."

Kevin speculated that part of their disdain for their own background came from their relationships to their nannies. As we learned in the 1920 census for Ruth Holmes's childhood household, all the servants were immigrants from Denmark, Finland, Holland, and Ireland. In fact, Ruth and Prudence were so close to one of their nannies in particular, a working-class Irish immigrant named Katherine, that before his mother died, the sisters took a trip to Ireland to see where Katherine had come from. "Kind of amazing when you think about finding your roots through your nanny," he remarked.

■ A family tree like Kevin's reveals endless stories worth retelling. His father, Edmund Norwood Bacon, was born on May 2, 1910, in Philadelphia. Kevin described him as brilliant and eccentric and ahead of his time. "He believed that our natural resources were going to dry up, and people were like, 'You're out of your mind. There's no reason we'll ever run out of oil.' His life's work," Kevin said, "was to try to make cities, starting with Philadelphia, habitable, safe, with pieces of green in them."

This was during an era when people were leaving cities in droves for the suburbs. "That was the kind of fifties' dream, probably to get away from black people," Kevin said bluntly. "You can go out and you can get a white picket fence, and you can have a split-level home, and you get a nice big car, the biggest car you can get, and that's going to be the American dream.

"My father just felt that it was wrong," he continued. "He said, 'We've got to come back. We've got to walk. We've got to take buses, and people have to live in these cities.'" From 1949 until 1970, Edmund was the director of Philadelphia's City Planning Commission.

Edmund's ideas for the city were sometimes lauded but just as often were met with opposition. Independent in his professional life, he was also very much of an outsider in his Quaker family.

As a child, the religion seemed entirely foreign to Kevin. "I don't re-member my dad talking all that much about what being a Quaker meant, but to me, I had a difficult time with it, because the very few times that we ever went to a meeting, I was a little boy, and it's that thing where you've got to sit still in silence. That's torture for a kid." Visits to his grandparents were equally trying. "The house was old, and it was dark, and they were old, and there were no toys."

It was his parents' way of speaking to his grandparents that upset Kevin the most. "My mother and father would start saying 'Thee' and 'Thy,' and it freaked me out, because my parents never talked like that," he recalled. "And they never gave me a heads-up, like 'When we get to your grandpar-ents' house, we're going to refer to them as 'Thee' and 'Thy.'"

Edmund broke with his Quaker faith when he decided to serve in World War II. Whether his grandparents were disappointed, Kevin didn't know. "I think the disappointment probably had started a bit before the war," he said.

Was this streak of independence something new to Kevin's father, or was it in his ancestry? We were able to trace Kevin's father's line on his mother's side back twelve generations, to a Quaker named Henry Comly, who was living in Bristol, England, in 1663. At that time, Quakers like Henry Comly were considered heretics and could be jailed or even beaten simply for holding their own religious meetings, for not attending the Church of England, or for refusing to take an oath of allegiance to the king. Naturally, many looked for a way out.

We found a document that explains what was waiting for Henry Comly when he joined his fellow Quakers in America. "William Penn, proprietary governor of province of Pennsylvania and territories thereunto belonging," Kevin read, "at the request of Henry Comly, purchaser of five hundred acres, I would grant him take up a lot in the city of Philadelphia."

Kevin's ancestor was given two plots of land, three hundred acres in Bucks County and two hundred acres in Philadelphia, the city for which his father eventually served as planner. Henry Comly was the first member of Kevin's family to own land in America. His family is part of the founding fathers of the most important colony in America at that time, Pennsylva-nia. "In a strange kind of way, knowing this brings me closer to that time period," said Kevin. It wasn't the only abstract time in American history we would make personal for Kevin.

■ As we learned through Kyra's family history, slavery was part of the landscape in the North as well as in the South. In Kevin's line, we met a man who, early on, struggled with its morality: the devout Quaker Samuel Atkinson, a New Jersey farmer born on May 17, 1685, in Bristol, England. Atkinson is Kevin's paternal sixth great-grandfather.

Most associate Quakers with abolitionism, but Christopher Densmore, curator of the Friends Historical Library at Swarthmore College in Pennsylvania, shared with us some surprising facts that helped us understand more deeply Quakers' shifting views.

"When Quakers arrived in America in the 1650s, slavery already existed, and Quakers did own slaves in New York and Philadelphia and New Jersey," Densmore explained. "By the 1680s, Quakers clearly are unhappy with some of the aspects of slavery, but it really takes them until the 1750s before they come forth with a clear position that it's not just treatment of slaves, it's not just the African slave trade, but it's a system that we can't make better, we can't make humane, and it's fundamentally wrong."

Densmore showed us the minutes from Quaker meetings that describe these debates on the issue of slavery and their eventual decision to call for its abolition. "They will include one of the questions at every meeting asked, and that's whether Friends are clear of owning slaves, and the expectation is that you're going to be able to answer that question, 'Yes.'"

According to Densmore, by 1775, the year before the Declaration of Independence was signed, about 10 percent of Quakers still owned slaves, Kevin's sixth great-grandfather among them. Samuel's wife, Ruth Stacey, was from a wealthy, well-known family in Burlington County, New Jersey, and she and Samuel lived quite comfortably on her family's land. An ad he ran in the *Pennsylvania Gazette* in 1746—a newspaper Benjamin Franklin wrote for—was our first clue that Samuel was still holding on to the Quakers' old ways. "Runaway, 30th of October last from Samuel Atkinson of Chester Township, a servant man named Michael Clarke about 40 years of age, middle stature, pale complexion, black eyebrows, he has much of the brogue on his tongue." In the ad, Atkinson offered a reward for the man's return.

Based on his "brogue," we can assume that Michael Clarke was an Irish immigrant toiling among the great number of indentured servants in America at the time. People were so poor in Europe, particularly in Ireland, that they would seek passage to the New World even if it meant being bound out to a family for seven years.

In finding Samuel Atkinson's will, we also found proof that Kevin's ancestor owned black slaves in addition to this white indentured servant. "I give and bequeath to my son, Samuel, my mulatto man called Adam," Kevin read from the will. "I give and bequeath to my daughter Rebecca my mulatto boy called Lott. I give and bequeath to my daughter Ruth my two mulatto boys called Noah and Andrew." He paused. "It's kind of nauseating."

Kevin had weighed the possibility of his ancestors owning slaves, but the fact that it was on the Quaker side shocked him. "There's such a disconnect between the idea that you're coming to some place so that you can practice religious freedom; at the same time you think it's OK to own a human being."

That being said, Samuel Atkinson's will suggests his position on slavery was not cut-and-dried. "I desire that all my mulattos may be kept to their reading," it states. "And when each of them attain the age of 35 years, that they have their liberty provided."

Of the many slave owners' wills that I have seen, Atkinson's is one of the few that leaves explicit instructions to his heirs to continue his slaves' education and to free them. Still, Kevin wasn't impressed. "Set 'em free now!" he explained. "What are you waiting for?"

I soon found myself in the strange position of defending the slave owner to Kevin: after all, at least he was concerned about his slaves' welfare. As Christopher Densmore told us, "By trying to keep them until they're in their thirties, he's very far behind the sentiment of Friends. But by offering to free the slaves at all, Atkinson is far advanced of the great bulk of American society." Densmore put Atkinson's actions in perspective using a well-known example: George Washington, the father of the United States, emancipated "his slaves" but only "by his will when he [was] dead."

We have no idea what inspired Samuel Atkinson to free his slaves in his will of 1781. What we do know is one year earlier the Philadelphia Society of Friends outlawed the practice of buying and selling slaves and commanded owners to prepare their own for emancipation.

Keep in mind this was a full eighty-three years before Abraham Lincoln issued the Emancipation Proclamation at the midpoint of the Civil War, a war that would claim the lives of some 750,000 Americans, North and South. Again, Christopher Densmore guided us through the history. "Lincoln's Second Inaugural [in March 1865], when he talks about slavery, he doesn't talk about it as saying that those Confederates our enemies have been supporting. He talks about this as something that we have done—a shared responsibility. If you've all broken something, you've all got some responsibility for helping put it back together."

Down the line from Samuel Atkinson, Kevin's great-grandmother was a part of this effort to help rebuild the nation. Lydia Townsend Atkinson, a Quaker born in 1843, was just twenty-one years old when she heeded the president's call to service. Deep in the stacks of the Friends Library, Densmore discovered Lydia's journals. Inside are vivid accounts of her journey from New Jersey to Washington, D.C., where she taught in a school established to educate newly freed slaves. In 1865 a Quaker organization called the Friends' Association for the Aid and Elevation of the Freedmen hired Lydia as a teacher at Camp Wadsworth, one of the many government camps set up for freed slaves near the close of the war.

"Atkinson in the 1860s is following a tradition that has been going for more than one hundred years," Densmore said. "When Quakers manumitted slaves, there is a concern for what happens to free people. If we dismantle slavery, what happens to that person? Are they simply going to be unemployed, beg from house to house and die in a ditch? So by the 1750s, Quakers have been heavily involved with African American education."

We are fortunate that Lydia not only was committed to change but had the foresight to record her efforts and observations. Kevin read to us from her journal: "I have over forty pupils in all—men, women, and children. We had a visitor a few days since, a Southern lady, and I could not help feeling a gratified pride as I remarked her wondering face, and heard her expressions of surprise, when the little ones pointed out on the map every State from Maine to Texas, repeating accurately, and without prompting, the capital of each. ["There's no way I could do that," Kevin interjected before resuming.] And when she saw the writing and heard the reading of the different classes, she said she had thought the teaching of such a school would be an unpleasant task, but she believed she would quite enjoy it."

Kevin's family had come a long way from his sixth great-grandfather, Samuel Atkinson, who had tried to hold onto his slaves well into their adulthood.

Kevin was touched by the decision his ancestor made. "What a thing to choose to do with your life." It's the other side of the family, but Kevin's mother Ruth certainly shared this commitment to the education of the underserved as well. "Basically my father married his grandmother," Kevin laughed.

Even as Lydia Atkinson toiled away teaching the freed slaves, the nation still had much work to do. In a chilling passage from her journal, Lydia describes the event that single-handedly changed the nature and pace of reconstruction in post–Civil War America, one of the darkest days in our nation's history.

Kevin read the emotional passage: "April 14, 1865. Oh God! The blow has come. It seems as though some horrid dream, some frightful nightmare were binding me in chains—but alas! I know this anguish is not the fantasy of sleep—were to Heaven it were! I know that I am waking and our idolized President is dead! Why must this calamity have fallen upon us—and now, in the midst of our rejoicings . . . to be robbed by the bloody hand of an assassin of our Nation's dearest life—oh God, where is thy mercy?"

Few among us have ancestors who testified as eyewitnesses to history, but here was Kevin's great-grandmother sharing in her personal diary her anguish over this most public—and pivotal—event. "I like history, I find history interesting," Kevin responded, "but I never really think of it as my own family history. It's like other people. And there she is, right where history's happening."

■ Kevin's ancestors, it seems, have always been where history is happening. Lydia Atkinson's husband, Robert Comly, was something of a genealogy buff himself and had traced his family all the way back to Adam and Eve! (Obviously, this could not be confirmed, but we certainly admire his determination.) Suffice it to say that Kevin's great-grandfather was at least on the right track in believing that his line stretches back exceptionally far. Amazingly, we have a confirmed paper trail for Kevin's family that stretches all the way back to Edward I, the king of England. Edward is Kevin's twenty-second great-grandfather, born in the year 1239. In more contemporary royal history, Princess Diana was Kevin's seventh cousin, which makes her sons, William and Harry—William, of course, being the heir to the British throne—seventh cousins once removed. Then there's Hollywood royalty Brad Pitt, who is Kevin's thirteenth cousin twice removed.

The power connection doesn't stop in Hollywood: Kevin and Richard Nixon—born a Quaker—are eighth cousins, and then, on the other side of the coin, as Kevin described it, we find President Barack Obama on Kevin's family tree. They share a common ancestor, Anthony Woolhouse, and are twelfth cousins three times removed.

Kevin laughed. "I knew I wasn't getting enough respect."

Neither was I, it turned out. Kyra couldn't keep a secret. I'd asked her to keep their undiscovered family ties to herself, but the excitement was too great, and she spilled the beans before I got a chance to. Kevin and Kyra are ninth cousins once removed, with common ancestors Richard Willets and Mary Washburn, born in 1618 and 1629, respectively. I think any geneticist would agree that they're distant enough for their marriage to be considered safe. Kevin agreed: "That's all right, because my kids seem fine."

Even a paper trail as extensive as Kevin's has to come to end, but with DNA we can go even further into a person's past. On Kevin's father's side, we were able to trace his direct paternal ancestor all the way back to the year 1626, when his eighth great-grandfather, Samuel Bacon, was born. His paternal haplogroup, R1b1b2a1a1d, is a subgroup of R1b1b2. R1b1b2 emerged twelve thousand years ago. Interestingly, some of the first men who had this genetic signature were residents of a place called Doggerland, a real-life Atlantis that was swallowed by rising seas in the millennium following the Ice Age. Today it's the most popular haplogroup in Western Europe and is found in more than 50 percent of all Western Europeans. This finding is completely in keeping with what we know of Kevin's genealogy. All points go to England. Of our guests, Harry Connick Jr. and Robert Downey Jr. share this same haplogroup, and so do I.

On his mother's side, we were able to trace Kevin's direct maternal line back to Amelia Kammerer, who was born in about 1832 in Pennsylvania. This result is something of a surprise. His maternal haplogroup is H6a1, which is a subgroup of H6. H6 originated not in Europe but in Turkey and Syria some thirty thousand years ago. Subsequent migration carried the two branches of H6 toward the Altai Mountains of Central Asia, which is why Kevin's maternal DNA is common among speakers of the Altaic languages, such as the Mongolians. H6a was carried to Europe about three thousand years ago and has been found in low levels in the Czech Republic, France, Ireland, and Sweden. This is a very, very rare mitochondrial DNA signature for a white man. Kevin has more genetic cousins in the Far East than in Europe on his mother's side.

His admixture will show us his percentages of African, European, and Native American ancestry over the past five hundred years. Apparently any distant genetic cousins he has in the Far East today became family long before then, because his European ancestry is, as he suspected, 100 percent. That's one reading anyway. One of our companies, Family Tree DNA, read his admixture result as almost 95 percent European but 5.13 percent Middle Eastern. Middle Eastern DNA could mean Bedouin, Druze, Iranian, Palestinian, or Jewish. If this is correct, he is connected to his wife in a small way he never expected. Both companies agree that his overwhelmingly European result means that he has distant genetic cousins living in the United Kingdom but also scattered throughout Northern Europe primarily. His European DNA matches most closely with a group called the Orcadians, who largely descended from Norwegian Vikings and Scots and now live in the Orkney Islands off of northern Scotland.

I asked Kevin if he had a fairy godmother who could introduce him to any one of his ancestors, who would it be? "Lydia," he answered, without hesitation—Lydia Atkinson, his great-grandmother who taught the freed slaves in an effort to heal the scars of slavery. "It is affecting, the transformation on the Quaker side from having indentured servants, owning slaves, feeling that you have the right to put them in your will, and just that transformation in a relatively short time on that side of the family to embracing abolition in a new world, starting the schools. That seems like a pretty strong theme and surprising to me, on both sides of it—surprising that there were slave owners and," he says, thinking of his own recent history, "also surprising that one of my great-grandmothers was so much like my mother in that way."

In our journey through Kyra's and Kevin's ancestry, we've added a new and richer perspective on the history of slavery in the North than we had before. We saw similarities between families that on the outside seemed to have little in common. What they share is the prospect of redemption, either within a single ancestor's life, as was the case with Theodore Sedgwick, or across generations, as we saw in the evolution of the Atkinson family from the eighteenth-century slave owner Samuel Atkinson to Lydia Townsend Atkinson, a woman who brought education to the emancipated at the end of the Civil War, the blood and suffering of which involved a much larger story of national reunion and redemption.

"The concept of six degrees existed long before I was even around," Kevin mused about his own place at the center of Hollywood's favorite parlor game. Then he added, "It's a beautiful concept, that we are connected; that we all essentially climbed out of the same swab, and that to me is what makes it fun to be at the forefront of that idea."

CHAPTER FIVE

The Children of Abraham

For millennia, the origins of our rich and various beliefs in God have fascinated scholars and religious thinkers, yet our choice of religions is perhaps most often decided for us by the beliefs that our ancestors embraced. When I was a child, I worshiped at the Walden Methodist Church simply because my mother was raised as a member of her mother's church, back in Piedmont, West Virginia, where I grew up. And when I switched churches as a teenager, it was to join the Episcopal church where my father was a member.

Such was the case with the Reverend Rick Warren, Rabbi Angela Buchdahl, and Sheik Yasir Qadhi. Each inherited his or her religious beliefs from at least one parent, and for all three, their faith turned out to be a call to religious service, study, and leadership when they were still young, a time of life when most Americans are embracing secular lives. Since then, Rick, Angela, and Yasir have risen to the tops of their professions in a nation where religious freedom is trumpeted in theory but divisions across religious lines still run deep. All three also descend from ancestors for whom religious persecution was a crushing, dangerous part of daily life, whose only option was to flee their homelands or face continued oppression at best and brutality and possible death at worst.

By exploring their roots, we unearthed stories about the spiritual foundations of this country and our unrelenting struggle for religious freedom and tolerance, but also the difficulties of holding onto one's faith and still feeling like an "authentic" American.

We also found questions. Did the journeys of their ancestors help shape their faith in God? And could their family's struggles for religious tolerance have influenced their decisions to become spiritual leaders? Whether the influence was direct or indirect, what is clear from Rick's, Angela's, and Yasir's family histories is that they descend from people who were willing to take risks to preserve their religious identities.

Rick Warren (b. 1954)

The Reverend Rick Warren is one of the most influential pastors in America. He leads the Saddleback Church in Orange County, California. Some thirty thousand parishioners worship there each week, making it one of the largest churches in the United States. Rick is the author of numerous self-help books, including *The Purpose Driven Life*, one of the best selling nonfiction books in the world. He's also acted as a spiritual adviser to powerful business leaders and even heads of state. In 2009 he gave the invocation at President Barack Obama's historic inauguration.

As one might expect, Rick peppers his speech with frequent references to God and the Bible; perhaps less expected are the pop-culture references and irrepressible sense of humor. He believes that as individuals, we are a combination of nature, nurture, and environment and that we can surely learn lessons about our future by delving into our past. "Without a doubt," he said, "because the roots go deep, and you can see those traits. Actually, I believe the Bible says that there are multigenerational blessings."

Richard Duane Warren was born on January 28, 1954, in San Jose, California. His father was a preacher, and his mother worked alongside her husband to build churches across the country. Rick told me that the two of them had a profound impact on his decision to establish his own church.

"My dad was an average preacher, but he was an outstanding carpenter," said Rick. "My dad built over 150 churches, literally all around the world—hammer, nails. He built them up in Alaska; he built them in Guatemala; he built them in China; he built them all over Asia, Australia. When Saddam kicked the Kurds up into northern Iraq, it was my father who took a crew of eighteen guys into those refugee camps and dug the eight water wells for the refugees and built a church there for them. Everywhere my dad built, my mom cooked. And in their later years of life, they did a lot of disaster relief. So if there was a Katrina, they would be there. If there was a tsunami, they would be there."

For Rick, the son of a Baptist preacher, the call to embrace the religious life came young. When he was only five, he was baptized of his own volition. "I was raised in a very loving Christian home," he recalled. "My parents were models of unconditional love. They both had a gift for hospitality." Rick said his father kept a record of all the guests they had in their home over the course of one year, and Rick's mother had served more than a thousand guests. "In that environment it was very easy for me as a little boy to say, 'Well, I don't understand it all, but I want what my parents have.' I made my commitment to God as much as I knew how at that age."

When Rick was twelve, he felt called to the ministry. But he wasn't yet ready for his close-up, as it were. "I went to the pastor of a small rural church where I was attending. The pastor was ready for me to start preaching, and it scared me to death . . . so I ran from it."

Politics also called to Rick at this time. He was active in school politics, he said, "president every year from seventh grade through my freshman year in college." For some of this time, his family was living two hours north of San Francisco. "These were the years of the Vietnam War, and there was a lot of political foment and political action, and I just got involved in it." His interest in a political life culminated when, as a high school sophomore, he was appointed to be a page in the U.S. Senate. But he turned it down, having had an epiphany the summer before while working as a counselor at a Christian summer camp in Northern California. "I came to the conclusion that for me, you weren't really going to change people by laws," Rick explained. "You can't force people to not be racist. You can't force people to not be materialistic. It's got to be a heart change inside. So that light turned on in my life."

Instead of going to the Senate the following summer, Rick returned to the summer camp, where, in his words, "one night I went into a cabin and I got down on my knees. I go, 'God, if there is a God, I want to know you.' It was really that simple. And I said, 'I don't understand it all. I don't get it at all, but if you're real, make yourself real to me. Jesus Christ, I want to know you.' That was really it. And you know what happened? Nothing." Rick laughed. "I mean, no thunder, no lightning, no angels came down. My hair didn't turn white like Charlton Heston's. I didn't get emotional; I didn't cry. It was really a pretty matter-of-fact decision. But that was the turning point in my life." At that point, at age sixteen, his religion "moved from my parents' faith to my faith."

By senior year, Rick had founded a Christian club at his high school called Fishers of Men, a phrase from Matthew 4:19 with great meaning in the evangelical community. He approached the school principal to ask if the club could hand out Bibles on campus. "He said, 'No, I don't think you can do that. I think that's illegal.'" Rick was unwilling to accept the principal's decision as the final word. "So with my activism background, we took it to the Supreme Court of California and the attorney general's office and won."

Christian organizations took notice. "I was invited to speak in January of that year at a large Christian conference in the middle part of California, in Fresno," Rick recalled. "I'm just there to tell my story, tell this testimony, and people started coming up and asking me to come speak at their church. In two days I had enough to fill the rest of the year." Rick had enough credits to graduate high school early, so in the fall of 1972, he decided to go on the road speaking primarily to youth groups up and down the West Coast. "It was in that I had this confirmation, this is what you're supposed to be doing."

While it would still be several years before Rick became a pastor, his call to serve God never abated. "When I gave my life to God, I really didn't put any parameters on it." He recalled the advice of a friend of his mother, a woman named Gail David, who was also a seminary professor. "She wrote me a note and said, 'Don't box yourself in.' She said that God can use you in a lot of different ways. It doesn't necessarily mean you're going to be a pastor or a missionary." Rick served as a writer for a Christian organization, taught English in a church in Japan, was a youth pastor, and taught for a year on a college staff. But his calling, ultimately, was to start a church.

There were no megachurches in those days, no televangelists, just churches that catered to their own local communities. "I found that one of the keys of a healthy church was the pastor stays put, that he's been there ten, twenty, thirty, or longer years," he said. "I've now been in this valley thirty-one years, which means I know more about it than any politician ever will, because I've been marrying their families, burying their dead, seeing their babies, talking to, counseling for thirty-one years. I've watched an entire generation grow up."

With the understanding that longevity was key, Rick sat down and prayed: "Lord, I'll go anywhere in the world you'll want me to go if you'll let me spend my entire life in one location." Once he and his wife, Kay, narrowed their choice down to the United States, Rick took out a map and circled every major urban area in the country, not including the South. "I thought, the South's got plenty of churches." Seattle, San Francisco, San Diego, and Orange County, California, were the final four contenders. "Down in the bowels of Texas Christian University Library I discovered that Orange County, California, between 1970 and 1980, was the fastest growing county in America, and the Saddleback Valley was the fastest growing area. I thought, they're going to need churches," Rick said. "Make a long story short, in January 1980, Kay and I packed up everything in a U-Haul truck with our four-month-old baby, and we moved to Southern California."

The beginnings of Saddleback Church have become the stuff of legend. Rick and Kay's first stop was a realtor's office. Rick's first words to the agent, Don Dale, were, "Hi, my name's Rick Warren. I'm twenty-five years old. I'm here to start a church. I don't have any members, I don't have any building, and I don't have any money, and I need a place to live." Within two hours, Don had found them a condo—and Rick had found his first congregant. A week later, he held his first service in the Warrens' new living room, with seven people present, including Don Dale and his wife. In their little condo, he said, "This is Saddleback Church." Today, the church has some thirty thousand members. "I've preached six services every weekend for the last eight years," Rick said. "We went and rented Angel Stadium, and it seats sixty thousand, and I still had to do two services."

I asked him why he chose to call it Saddleback Church and not Saddleback Baptist Church. "Because this is California," he answered. "And also, there are a lot of things done in denominational names you end up having to defend. Methodists do this, Baptists do this, things like this." Rick's goal has always been to attract "people who don't have any faith, any religious background at all; to find out what un-church people think."

When televangelism became part of the landscape in America, Rick chose to keep his preaching off screen. "I didn't want to be a celebrity," he said, then paused. "Well, the book kind of blew that one out of the water."

Phenomenal as his church's success was, the 2004 publication of *The Purpose Driven Life* made Rick a global star. The book, which remained on the *New York Times* best-seller list for four years, brought in millions of dollars, and unbridled attention. "When you write a book, and the first sentence is, 'It's not about you,' then you know the money's not for you," he said.

But Rick's runaway success created crises in its own right. "The easy part was dealing with the stewardship of affluence," he said. "The hard part was the stewardship of influence." Two years ago, Rick stopped taking a salary from Saddleback, and he and his wife live in the same house they've lived in for twenty-two years.

They found guidance in Psalm 72 in the Old Testament, Solomon's prayer for influence. "He says, 'I want you to spread the fame of my name to many countries. I want everybody to know who I am so that the king may support the widow and orphan, care for the sick, defend the defenseless, speak up for the oppressed.' Out of that passage," Rick said, "it was like a light bulb clicked on. The purpose of influence is to speak up for those who have no influence."

Rick and Kay went on to found three charities: Acts of Mercy, which serves people infected with and affected by AIDS; Equipping Leaders, which trains leaders in developing countries; and the PEACE Plan. "The PEACE Plan is promoting reconciliation by planting churches, and we've been doing that in 195 countries." In a sense, Rick is doing exactly what his parents spent their lives doing, planting churches and assisting in communities where they can, only on an extremely large scale. The question was whether that commitment extended back even further in time.

■ Rick's mother, Dorothy Nell "Dot" Armstrong, was born in Vaughn, New Mexico, on December 29, 1922. She and Rick's father, James "Jimmy" Warren, graduated from Oklahoma Baptist University in Norman, Oklahoma, in 1950. "Mom wouldn't have ever called herself a pastor as a Baptist, but she was definitely involved in ministry," Rick said.

Dot's parents, Chester Moody Armstrong and Nellie Maude Gould Armstrong, were married in 1902. C.M. Armstrong, as he was known, was an ordained deacon and a church planter, "somebody," Rick explained, "who helps get a church started. At Saddleback we call them scaffolding people." He feels indebted to his grandmother for what she passed on to him: "My maternal grandmother was great at telling stories, and she loved to read me books."

Even as a child, Rick recognized the importance of those stories, and he had the foresight to preserve them. "When I was twelve years old, I asked for a reel-to-reel player. That was before cassettes and those things. One of the first things I did," he said, "is I recorded some of my grandmother's stories." Rick shared one of his favorites with us. "Her husband, at that time, was working for the Union Pacific Railroad, and they were living in a little town called Vaughn. My mother was actually born there, and it was still a very rural, rural place. Nobody was around, and one lone Indian came up at night, and she was scared to death. You know, she had heard all of these things about the wild Indians of the West and living in the Wild West."

Rick was doing a fine job of painting a picture of what life looked like in the lightly populated places of our country in the early twentieth century. "She tells the story about how frightened she was. And then she found out he just wanted something to eat. So she brought him in, cooked him a meal, had a great time, sent him on his way."

He enjoyed hearing his grandmother's voice again. "She tells some interesting stories as a homesteader and things like that," Rick said. "What was interesting is that I only got about fifteen minutes of it because I had recorded Cream and Jimi Hendrix over it at a later stage." As we know, our priorities are different when we're young.

Rick knew he descended from a long line of deeply religious ancestors and preachers. In fact, a photograph of Rick's great-great-grandfather, the Reverend Ebenezer McCoy Armstrong, hangs in his library. "I keep it in my office because the family lore about this man was that he was a great man. He was a godly man. He was a kind man," Rick said. Several leather-bound books and sermons in Rick's twenty-thousand-volume library belonged to Ebenezer, a circuit preacher who traveled on horseback between rural Baptist churches. "In those days, a lot of these pastors weren't paid any money," Rick said. "In fact, my father's first church, they paid him with potatoes."

In 1862, just one year after the Civil War broke out, Ebenezer enlisted as a corporal in the 86th Illinois Infantry. On November 17 of that same year, he resigned his office as corporal and was detailed as a ward master in the regimental hospital. Through the records we were able to find, which included his muster roll from November–December 1862, we determined that he served for at least one year in the hospital. For months on end, he had to face a constant succession of wounded people, many of whom were going to die. The historian and president of Harvard, Drew Faust, wrote a book about the Civil War called *This Republic of Suffering*, in which she argued that the massive loss of life during the Civil War fundamentally changed the fabric of our country. I wondered if it had changed Rick's great-grandfather.

"Well, it had to. I know how it's changed me," Rick said. "As a pastor,

I couldn't count the hundreds and hundreds of people over the years I've watched take their last breath, and have been there in their moment of pain. And in the last ten years, Kay and I have traveled around the world, dealing with issues like poverty and disease. I've been in villages where nobody is over the age of twenty-five, because everybody in their village died from AIDS. And when you see this kind of pain, and when you see what people live with, it tenderizes you. I will not hire a pastor who has not gone through major pain."

■ Our genealogical research revealed that Rick's ancestors had been connected to the ministry as far back as the founding of this country. In 1630, only ten years after the *Mayflower* carried those famous Pilgrims to Plymouth Rock, a Puritan named Robert Parke wrote a letter to John Winthrop, who was about to become the founder of the Massachusetts Bay Colony. In it, Parke wrote, "I understand by some of my friends that you are suddenly to go to New England. If not be too late for me, I do propose to go with you and all my company, if please God, to permit us life and health." Robert Parke is Rick's tenth great-grandfather on his mother's side. "So he knew Winthrop?" Rick asked, floored. "I have a first edition of one of Winthrop's sermons in my library. And I found a one-hundred-year-old jigsaw puzzle of Winthrop standing and praying as they land in Massachusetts Bay Colony, and I put it together, and I had it glued together and framed in my library."

Not only was Robert Parke literate; he was the wealthiest man in East and West Keal in Lincolnshire, England, yet he was willing to risk his fortune, life, and limb to emigrate to what was still a dangerous wilderness in search of religious freedom. Although we found records of Rick's tenth great-grandfather in New England as of the year 1639, we couldn't find him in the earliest records of the Massachusetts Bay Colony. Historians speculated it might have taken him several years to settle his estate.

Robert may not have been in the earliest records of the colony, but his son William was. Rick's maternal ninth great-grandfather, William Parke, was born on April 21, 1607, in Suffolk, England. In 1630, at the age of twenty-three, he set sail for the New World, possibly in his father's stead, on the *Lyon*. His reasons for going were the same as everyone else's on board: the pursuit of religious freedom. The following year, the charismatic minister John Eliot arrived in America on a subsequent voyage of the same ship. Eliot was one of the original members of the First Church of Roxbury in New England and is credited with printing the first Bible in the New World.

As we continue to learn in genealogical research, church records are often the key to unlocking the past. The arrival of William Parke in America is noted in the First Church of Roxbury Membership Records. In a later document, his name appears on the list of deacons, a position in which he served under Eliot from the church's founding in 1632 until at least 1674. "This is what you call having Puritan props," Rick said, his joking manner not disguising his thrill at discovering how long his family has been in America in the service of religion and religious freedom.

Unlike early settlements in Virginia or New Hampshire, the Massachusetts Bay Colony was explicitly created to be a religious community. In seeking religious freedom for themselves, the Puritans also endeavored to convert the Native American population already living there. John Eliot, in fact, became known as the Indian Apostle, playing a vital role in converting the Massachusetts Native Americans to Christianity. He even translated the entire Bible into the Algonquin language.

We found an interesting document in the Massachusetts Bay Colony Records from 1646, describing a plan to purchase land for the Native Americans. "For the encouragement of the Indians to live in an orderly way amongst us . . . for the good of the Indians," Rick read, "& further, to set down rules for their improvement and enjoying thereof." Listed among the committee members undertaking this effort: Rick's ninth great-grandfather, the deacon William Parke. William helped establish the very first "praying town"—a community for Christian Native Americans—in all of North America.

Parke was not the only one of Rick's ancestors who played a role in spreading the gospel to Native Americans. Isaac McCoy, the first cousin of Rick's maternal great-grandfather Ebenezer McCoy Armstrong, was "a champion of justice for Native Americans." Rick related the story of Isaac McCoy that had been passed down through his mother's family. "I don't even remember what president it was. The president appointed him as an Indian agent. He first, over the Kansas area, was protecting the Indians that were being mistreated as the settlers moved in and were being misplaced. He was the man who championed the Cherokee Strip and the move to Oklahoma to create the space. 'You've got to give them a homeland; this is their place.'

"And so," Rick continued, "he was not only a pastor [but also] planted many churches. . . . By the way, he planted a church whose member was Daniel Boone. Daniel Boone was a charter member, a scaffolding person of Isaac McCoy's church. I have many of his old records, the letters to the president and back and forth, and his vision was of creating a space where the Indians would not continue to be pushed out."

In Rick's lineage we found pastor after pastor, with a common motif emerging: two different strands of his mother's family, both of whom worked with Native Americans. "Speak up for those who can't speak up for themselves," Rick commented.

The dream to pursue religious freedom and make a better life for themselves had brought men like Rick Warren's ancestors to this country more than three hundred years ago. In 1629, the year before William Parke sailed to the New World, John Winthrop explained in his *General Conclusion* why he and his fellow Puritans should leave civilized England to move to the wilderness of the New World: "'All other churches of Europe are brought to desolation, and our sins, for which the Lord begins all ready to frown on us, and who knows but that God hath provided of this place to be a refuge for many whom he means to save.' That is amazing," Rick said. I posed the question to Rick: was the dream of the Puritans made real?

"Well, I think that their desire to build a 'Christian utopia' has not come true. I think God, as I read Scripture, God doesn't intend for us to have heaven on earth," Rick explained. "Heaven is heaven and earth is earth. But the benefit and the blessing of having that kind of foundation created a nation that is unlike any other in the world. In terms of the commitment to justice, the commitment to truth, the commitment to love, no nation is as generous as America.

"I have seen this as I go around the world in relief efforts," he continued. "The Americans are always the ones taking care of the Pakistanis in an earthquake and all these things like this. I think that comes out of our heritage, the heritage of the Puritan idea that everybody has a vocation, that work is valid, that giftedness is to be used for God."

But despite the high-minded ideals of our founding fathers and mothers, there have been all too many dark hours in our nation's history when we, as Americans, have failed to live up to our original Christian values of religious freedom and tolerance. Some of those stories could be found on Rick's father's side of the family tree.

■ James Russell "Jimmy" Warren was born in Cushing, Texas, on September 16, 1919, the eighteenth of twenty children. Jimmy's father, Thomas Warren, was a poor sharecropper on the East Texas–Louisiana border. The last of his children was born when Tom was seventy-six years old. "My dad had an ability to be comfortable with anybody, whether it was a king or a wino on the street. He just treated everybody with respect and got along good," Rick said. "One of the main things he taught me is just how to love everybody."

Rick's paternal great-grandfather was named John Thomas Church. Rick had heard his name before, but never any stories about him. We found an application he filed in Centerville, Alabama, in March 1867: "The application for the relief of Confederate soldiers and sailors." So while one great-grandfather, Ebenezer McCoy, fought for the Union army, another great-grandfather, John Thomas Church, fought for the Confederacy.

John Thomas was not a slave owner himself, so why would he risk his life to defend the South and the institution of slavery? "I clearly obviously believe the Confederacy was wrong. And some people, I'm sure if you didn't have slaves, you still were going to protect your land, and I think there was a patriotism on both sides," Rick reasoned. "I've traveled enough around the world to know that the way you grow up is the way you're going to see the world. If you're raised Hindu, you're going to think like a Hindu. And if you're raised bigoted, you're going to be raised to be a bigot."

Rick's paternal third great-grandfather was a Baptist named Bird Griffin, born in Wilkes County, Georgia, in 1803. In the 1820s, Bird became one of the earliest settlers of Perry County, Alabama. He was a planter and a justice of the peace. He was also a slave owner.

We found the 1860 Slave Schedule for Perry County. Rick read from the schedule: "He had a 45-year-old female slave, a 35-year-old and a 30-year-old male slave, a 30-year-old female slave, a 27-year-old male, a 14-year-old male, a 12-year-old female, 10-year-old-male, 9-year-old female, 6-, 3-, and 1-month-old male. He had a lot of slaves. Twelve slaves," Rick said.

Bird, it seemed, was relatively well-off. Most people in the South didn't own any slaves at all, and if they did, it was generally one or two. "Well, this obviously shows why he could be a judge and a planter, because he wasn't doing any of the planting," Rick said.

So how did Bird manage his land without those twelve slaves to work it after the end of the Civil War set them free? Apprenticeship contracts filed in December 1866 gave us the answer. "The State of Alabama, Perry

County. I Bush Jones, judge probate in aforesaid county hereby certify that I have this day bound and apprenticed Abraham, free, Moses, [free], to Bird Griffin until he shall attain the age of twenty-one years."

By comparing Abraham's and Moses's ages to the ages of those listed in the 1860 Slave Schedule, we guessed that they were probably Rick's ancestor's own former slaves. "The youngest kids stayed on as apprentices. This was common?" Rick asked.

I had never encountered apprentice contracts before. Slavery was, of course, notorious for breaking up families, because slaves could be sold at any time. Perhaps Abraham and Moses's parents had died or been sold off. Could this have been a way for Bird to look after orphaned children?

It seemed unlikely. We found another legal document that seemed to undermine this more benevolent theory. On February 2, 1867, a woman named Sophia took Rick's third great-grandfather to court over one of these apprenticeship contracts involving Adeline. Bird had secured the contract by claiming that Adeline was an orphan. Here was Sophia, presumably her mother, saying she wasn't an orphan at all; she was a freed child. The court sided with Sophia and ordered Bird to let Adeline go.

Bird Griffin appeared to be holding these children in indentured servitude—slavery by another name. "Well, obviously he had something to protect. He had a farm that he wasn't going to be able to keep," Rick said. "It goes back to your view of humanity. If he did not really see these kids as full people because of their color, he probably thought it was just fine."

During the Civil War, men and women across the South used the Bible and their versions of Christianity to support their right to own slaves and often bolstered their arguments by quoting biblical passages from Leviticus, Corinthians, or Ephesians. Confederate president Jefferson Davis even went so far as to suggest that slavery was decreed as a right by God Almighty. I asked Rick if there is a valid Christian justification for slavery before or during the Civil War.

Rick responded passionately. "There is zero biblical justification for slavery. Zero. From the very beginning of time, God says, 'I have created every man in my image.' I've read those arguments, and they're spurious. They are false exegesis. . . . I always say I believe Scripture is infallible; I do not believe my interpretation of it is infallible."

In *The Purpose Driven Life*, Rick writes, "We're the product of our past, but we don't have to be prisoners of it." Does this pertain to a nation as it does to its people?

"Absolutely," Rick answered. "I am responsible for my decisions. I am not responsible for my parents' decisions. Now, responsibility means we are response-able. We are able to respond. I think in situations, for instance, like the Civil War, it is legitimate to admit the sins of the past. In fact, the denomination that my parents grew up in, the Southern Baptist Convention, eventually apologized for their misreading of Scripture. It was about ten years ago, but it was like a hundred years too late. Sometimes people put off what they should have done a long time ago. But I think the value of that is to say we recognized sin as sin, and there's no justification for it."

Even though Rick tells people that we are not responsible for decisions made by our parents—or, by extension, our ancestors—he admitted that he was "embarrassed" to have a Confederate soldier on his family tree. "The Bible does say that the sins of the father are visited upon the sons and the children, and it also says, 'The fathers have eaten sour grapes, and the children's teeth are set on edge.' There's no doubt that there's a guilt factor that has to do with acknowledging it and not denying it."

Rick reflected further. "I have no responsibility for Bird Griffin. But I do have a responsibility as an American to say that enslaving three and a half million people was evil." It sounds like the Confederate soldier and the slave owner won't be making it onto the wall of Rick's library. "Absolutely not," Rick said. "I don't honor blood. I honor character."

We wanted to take Rick back even farther on his father's line—to an ancestor who could be honored for both. Noah Lacy is Rick's fourth great-grandfather. In the Virginia State Records of 1781, we found this: "'Warrant to Noah Lacy for his services in the militia of this state,'" Rick read. "He's a son of the Revolution." Now Rick can be, too—alongside me! My brother and I were inducted into the Sons of the American Revolution when we learned that our ancestor, a free black man named John Redman, fought as a Patriot. I told Rick I would be thrilled to sponsor him for membership as well.

Rick took a moment to read all the names on his father's family tree aloud, as if saying their names made them present. "Here's me and then my parents and then my dad's parents, William Thomas Warren, Gabriel Warren, William M. Osborne and Polly Tiller, which is Mary's father, Randal Tiller and Jane Lacy, who was the daughter of Noah Lacy and Eliza Mary Wilson.

"I had a fourth great-grandfather in the Revolutionary War," Rick mused. "Really, both sides of my family have been in America for a long time. They're not recent immigrants. That is amazing."

Noah, it turns out, was at the beginning of a trend that would run through Rick's family tree, on both sides, for generations: he became a minister. "August 17, 1799, " Rick read from the church notes. "Met in conference and called Noah Lacy to ordination at Bethany Baptist Church." Rick laughed. "I got another one? This is great. He's not only a Patriot; he's a pastor. And he was a Baptist, too."

In 1804 Noah became the pastor of that same Bethany Baptist Church in Oglethorpe County, Georgia, a position he would serve in for twenty-one years. In a book called *This Is the History of Bethany Baptist Church*, a church history from 1788 to 2008, W.H. Foss wrote, "Among Bethany's pastors few have stood higher than Noah Lacy. And yet, like all of us, he had his failings and weak points, one of them being an ultra-Calvinist." This passage made Rick laugh out loud. "That is so funny, because I am not an ultra-Calvinist. In fact, the ultra-Calvinists believed that if God wanted to save people, he would save them, and we didn't need to send missionaries. In the last eight years I have sent 14,869 of my people to other countries as missionaries."

Bethany Baptist, we discovered, was no ordinary church. We found another page of minutes, dated September 15, 1804, that revealed something very interesting. "Grants a letter of dismission to Betty, a black sister." Bethany Baptist Church in Oglethorpe County was an integrated church. "Now, I want *that* guy's picture," Rick laughed. "He's a Patriot, he's a pastor, and he's got an integrated church."

Betty was a slave. She was granted this letter either because her master was moving or because she was sold to someone else outside of the region or out of the community. The letter gave her permission to leave the church and enter another, if she was lucky enough to find one. Rick's fourth great-grandfather's church welcomed slaves and freed people, blacks and whites, under one roof. Integrated churches were not unheard of—nor were they entirely what we would call integrated. For example, in general, black people were made to sit in separate sections, often in the upper balcony. But what is uncommon about this story is that Betty was recognized in a document as a human being.

"In Baptist theology, a letter is a sign of membership," Rick explained. "You're not an associate person. You're in. You're full membership. And when you move to another area, you take your letter of membership with you. It is a document that is saying you are full membership in this church, which means you're a full human being, obviously."

Not long after Betty received this letter, tensions between black and white worshipers in the nation's churches became untenable. The slaves were begging for the right to worship God with white people, but they had to sit in the segregated section, and white churchgoers couldn't pass the cup with black people. Splits were occurring in the denominations, and black churches were forming. "All the denominations were starting," Rick said, "because the slaveholders would not let them in their churches. They wanted them to know the Lord, but they didn't want to worship with them." In 1808 the Abyssinian Baptist Church opened its doors, founded by African American Baptists who didn't want to be relegated to a segregated section of the Baptist church in New York.

Rick's family tree is heavily populated with ministers, people who sought to do good for others, and people whose actions and beliefs were probably determined by the time and place in which they lived. We couldn't test Rick's DNA for any of these traits, but we were certain something from all these relatives was passed down to him.

■ I was curious to know what Rick, as a Christian, feels science can tell us about the nature and origins of humans and life. "Science confirms the magnificent intricacies of the entire universe," he replied. "And the more you see how it is related, the more I could not believe it was accidental."

Now it was time to see what more DNA science could tell us about Rick. We were able to trace his direct paternal ancestors back to his third great-grandfather, Charles Warren, who was born around 1775 in Spartanburg, South Carolina. Rick's paternal haplogroup is R1b1b2a1a2f, a subgroup of R1b1b2. Twelve thousand years ago, the representatives who had this haplogroup were among the first people to repopulate the western part of Europe after the Ice Age. R1b1b2 is most common in Western Europe, and today it is found in more than 50 percent of the men who live there. Rick and I share a common ancestor who lived very long ago, before the Irish king Niall of the Nine Hostages, who lived around the fifth century.

Besides me, Rick shares this paternal haplogroup with Harry Connick Jr. This means that somewhere way back, probably thousands of years, Rick and Harry have a common ancestor. Considering his famous relative, Rick joked, "Well, how come I can't sing better?"

On Rick's mother's side, we were able to trace back his direct maternal line to his fourth great-grandmother, Sara Hunt, born in 1759 in Haverhill, New Hampshire. His maternal haplogroup is V, which originated in Iberia during the Ice Age sixteen thousand years ago. Twelve thousand years ago, it migrated northward along the Atlantic coast, and it also went through Central Europe and Scandinavia. Haplogroup V is found in a wide variety of populations, from the Basque people in Spain to the Sami people in Finland. Today V is most abundant in the United Kingdom and Germany. While Rick is our only guest in this series with this haplogroup, we found some other famous people Rick can call cousin: "One of my good friends, Bono, and Benjamin Franklin." Rick laughed. "This guy was brilliant at writing proverbs. He knew how to tweet. He would have loved to tweet today like I do." Interestingly, Rick has worked extensively with the Irish musician Bono of the band U2 on the ONE Campaign, which is focused on battling extreme poverty and disease in Africa.

Finally, we looked at Rick's admixture, which measures an individual's percentage of African, Asian, and European ancestry. "I think I've got Indian," Rick said. Nearly every American thinks he or she is descended from a Native American ancestor. "I look at my mother. My mother had some Indian-type features. I felt like her cheekbones were high and looked like that." We'll see.

We had two companies analyze Rick's results. 23andMe came back 100 percent European. Family Tree DNA came back with a slightly different reading: 93.95 percent European and 6.05 percent Middle Eastern. The European population Rick most closely matches is Western European, and specifically the Orcadian population. Orcadians reside primarily in the archipelago north of Scotland, and they are descendants of the Iron Age Scots called the Picts, as well as Norwegian Vikings. Orcadians, I pointed out to Rick, generally practice Presbyterianism. "That's exactly right," he laughed. "They weren't Baptists; that's for sure."

Family Tree DNA specializes in Jewish and Middle Eastern genetic ancestry, which is why the reading from this company was more precise than from 23andMe. The Middle Eastern populations that represent 6 percent of Rick's genome are not Jewish. They could be Palestinian, Bedouin, Druze, Iranian, or Mozabite.

Throughout our journey, Rick commented over and over about how deep his American ancestry went. If he had a fairy godmother who could grant him one wish, I asked him, which ancestor would he want to meet? "Robert Parke's son, William Parke. Without a doubt," he answered immediately. "To be at the Massachusetts Bay Colony and to be with John Eliot and John Winthrop in many ways building the moral foundation of America. . . . People who deny the Puritans' impact on this country are revisionist. We have two sets of founders. We have the Founding Fathers, the political Founding Fathers, and we have the spiritual fathers, which are the Puritans and the Pilgrims."

Rick was inspired and intrigued by his ancestors, both the noble and the less so. "To have one relative who had formed an integrated church and another guy who was keeping kids as slaves after the war shows you that we're capable of anything," he reflected. It wasn't hard for me to picture Rick keeping that lesson foremost in his mind by clearing a space on his office wall for his family tree—yet another sign of what we have been learning through this series: our stories are America's story.

Angela Buchdahl (b. 1972)

Her Korean heritage is evident on her face, but Rabbi Angela Buchdahl wears her Jewish heritage just as openly. She is the first Asian American to be invested as a cantor (song leader) and the first Asian American to be ordained as a rabbi in all of North America. In 2011 *Newsweek* named her one of the fifty most influential rabbis in the United States, and her star continues to rise in the Reform Judaism movement.

Born in Seoul, Korea, on July 8, 1972, to a Jewish American Army veteran father and a Korean Buddhist mother, Angela was raised in Tacoma, Washington, from the age of five, when her family moved to the United States. For years she was conflicted about her multiple identities: Was she an American first? A Korean? A Jew? Today, she is comfortable in her own skin and embraces the fact that she can be all three, but it was not always so.

Although Angela has dedicated her life to Judaism, her earliest memories are from Korea. Each is infused with sweetness and warmth. "I remember my grandmother. We called her Halmoni. She lived with me when I was young. She was incredibly loving, and she would carry me around on her back." Angela also recalled a ritual she shared every morning with her American father. "We slept on the floor in a traditional Korean house, and I slept with a woman who took care of me, and my parents slept in a different room. But every morning I woke up, and I would have toast with my father sitting on the floor. Toast with jam. I don't have a lot of memories of that time," she said, "but I have a very warm, fond sense of being Korean. I only spoke Korean. I felt very much Korean."

Six months after her family moved to the United States, Angela entered kindergarten. Even in the diverse student body, where there were many other Asian children, she stood out. "Maybe I just had the clothes of an immigrant or a little bit of an accent, but people would always ask me, 'Where are you from?' I always would say, 'I'm from Korea.' But then I went back to Korea two years later in the summertime, and all the kids in Korea said to me, 'Where are you from?' I said, 'I'm from here.' They said, 'No, you're not.'"

Angela was confused and upset by these remarks. "I remember saying to my mom, 'I don't have a home. I don't feel like I fit in anywhere.' And she said, 'No. Every place is your home. You can take the best of both of these worlds. You belong here; you belong in the States.'" This is a common experience of children of immigrants. Sanjay Gupta and Margaret Cho shared almost identical stories when we met them. Is the home the child identifies with herself the same as the home other children identify with her?

Classmates teased Angela when she first started school. "Kids would say things like Japanese-o, Chinese-o, and they would make schoolyard taunts. It hurt me in the beginning, but I didn't cry." Much more hurtful to Angela was the way she saw her mother treated. "I was very aware of my mom's Asian accent when I was a child. It was embarrassing to me," she admitted. "But even more, it pained me to watch people talk to my mother as if she weren't smart because she had an accent. It has always stuck with me the way that people judge so quickly off of small things."

It was only when Angela moved to the States that Judaism became a part of her life at all. "It was not a part of my consciousness for the first four and a half years of my life. There was no Jewish life in Korea. No challah to be found in Korea," she joked. "But when we got to Tacoma, I started going to synagogue with my father, and I liked going to synagogue with him, so I figured out, wow, he's Jewish, and everybody else is not."

By third or fourth grade, Angela traded one identity crisis for another. "Suddenly," she said, "it wasn't just that I was also Korean. It was that I didn't celebrate Christmas and I didn't sing the Christmas carols when we had to sing them in my school. Suddenly I felt very different that way, too. And then in my Jewish community, I was different because I was the only person who was Korean there."

Tacoma didn't have a large Jewish population; Angela and her sister were two out of only three Jewish children in her school. "My sister and I joked that in Tacoma people thought Jews looked like us." Her synagogue, which included families from within the hundred-mile swath from Seattle to Olympia, was welcoming. But outside of the familiar territory of her home, this wasn't always the case. "My father's family had been there for so many generations that I felt like part of the establishment in my synagogue. And the rabbi I grew up with was a scholar and a mensch, we'd say, a really wonderful person. He never once questioned my Jewish identity," Angela said. "He went to the extreme of never even telling me that there were going to be Jews out there who didn't think I was Jewish. But when I would go out into other parts of the Jewish world, visit a different synagogue or when I went to Jewish camp or to Israel for the first time, there I was confronted with a tremendous amount of prejudice.

"So it was interesting for me," Angela continued. "Being in my elementary school, at a certain point people stopped asking me where I was from, but in the Jewish community, they never stopped asking what I was."

It took Angela several years to realize her ethnicities didn't have to be in competition with each other. "I think I felt very Korean where I was because I couldn't take that off my face. Everyone related to me as a Korean and would say comments to me, even if they weren't necessarily negative, but, 'Oh, you're good at math because you're Asian.' 'That's why you play piano so well.'"

The Jewish part came later. "As I became more and more connected to my Jewish community, it really was a huge part of my working out of my identity to not feel that they were competing," she explained. "I felt that as one identity took priority, in a sense, that it kind of crowded the other one out, and it took a long time for me to finally feel that it's all one. But the Koreanness in me, my mother's Buddhism, that has been a part of the way I approach the world, it's part of the Jew that I am and the rabbi that I've become."

Although raised a Jew, Angela is not considered Jewish by everyone. Reform Judaism, with which Angela is affiliated, accepts patrilineal descent, but the Conservative and Orthodox branches of Judaism maintain that to be truly Jewish, one must be born to a Jewish mother. She took her first trip to Israel when she was sixteen. "When I went to Israel, I felt so deeply connected and rooted to something so much bigger than myself," she said. "On the one hand I felt like I'd come home in a way. And on another level, it was one of the more challenging places I'd ever been. A lot of Israelis—you think it's a Jewish state, but 80 percent of the country are secular, and if you ask them what it means to be Jewish they say, 'Oh, it's just a nationality. It's who I am.' And I remember thinking, well, if it's not about what you know or how you observe Jewish ritual and it's just like what you are in your DNA, then maybe I can never be 100 percent Jewish since part of my DNA is Korean."

When Angela was twenty-one, she traveled to Israel again. What was meant to be a spiritual journey to strengthen her connection to Judaism almost severed it. How could a person who looked like her, someone demanded, be genuinely Jewish? Angela recalled the sting of this question. "I felt so rejected by the larger Jewish community. I'd had a lot of people say to me, 'You're not really Jewish.' I remember I called my mother from Israel. I couldn't even speak for the first few minutes because I was just weeping so hard. And I said, 'That's it. I think I'm going to just not be Jewish anymore. I'm going to stop. I don't have a Jewish name. Look at me; I don't have a Jewish face. I could just stop being Jewish and nobody would ever know.' And my mother said, 'Is that really possible?' And it wasn't until she really pushed me on that that I realized I couldn't shed my Jewish identity any more than I could shed being a woman or being Korean. It might not be as evident on my face, but it was not just a part of my DNA. It was the way I looked at the whole world. It was who I was in every fiber of my being."

Angela chose to undergo a *giyur*, as a conversion is known in Hebrew; instead of using the traditional term, though, she called it a reaffirmation ceremony. "It was in some ways a statement of saying, 'I'm choosing to be a Jew.' I recognize I have this whole part of my family that was not Jewish, but that is part of who I am as a Jew," Angela said. "And it was as much an affirmation of my mother and recognizing her as it was about choosing Judaism."

For centuries, Jews have been persecuted mercilessly because of their religion. Often, the only choice they had was to leave their homeland behind. Angela's father's ancestors were forced to make just such choices at the end of the nineteenth century. Angela had long known her father's family came from Romania, but why her forbears left, and how on earth they ended up in Tacoma, remained mysteries to her.

■ Angela's father, Frederick David Warnick, was born on April 6, 1940, in Tacoma, Washington. A civil engineer in the ROTC program, he went to South Korea to teach English. Angela's mother was a student in the class, and soon they fell in love and decided to get married. Angela's grandmother back in Washington was "very accepting of my mother from the very start," Angela said. But her Korean grandmother took a bit more convincing. "She didn't have a concept of what it meant that he was Jewish. She just saw him as an American. I think that she was worried that the cultural difference was too vast and that it was maybe just a passing thing and that my father would end up going back to the States and leave my mother behind."

But Frederick ultimately won over his future mother-in-law. "He really truly loved not just my mother but Korean culture. He learned how to speak Korean. He was a very, very good eater of Korean food. And I think he also promised that he would never take my mother out of Korea while my grandmother was alive. I don't know if he put that part on," Angela said, "but he did promise he wouldn't take her out. And he kept that promise."

Frederick's family was deeply rooted in Tacoma, yet he was willing to make his home in a foreign country for an indefinite period of time. Angela explained, "There's a way that Jews have wandered a lot over the years, and I think that he found a home there. . . . I also think that it resonated with him as a Jew the deep sense of culture that Koreans have."

Like many American Jewish families, Frederick's family was more culturally Jewish than they were religious. "They were very proud of being Jewish," Angela said of her Warnick grandparents. "It was very much who they were. But they were not particularly observant, although they celebrated all the holidays, and my grandmother, Frieda, really made great gefilte fish and great kugel and mandelbrot."

Frederick's parents were both the children of immigrants. Angela's grandfather, Robert Warnick, was born in Montreal, Canada, on May 25, 1907, to Russian Jewish parents. By the time Angela was born, her grandparents had divorced, and she didn't know her grandfather very well. But she was close with her grandmother, Frieda May Soss, born in Spokane, Washington, on May 14, 1909.

Angela shared a miraculous story Frieda had told her about the endurance of family connections in the most dire of circumstances. "Her older sister had gotten pregnant when she was only about fourteen or fifteen, and at that time, that would have been kind of the end of her life in this town. So her mother took her back to Romania to some relatives, and she finished out her pregnancy there, and they gave up the baby for adoption, to a Jewish family in Vienna."

The adoption remained a secret until sometime around World War II. "When this family wanted to leave when the Holocaust was erupting, they told their daughter, 'You're actually born of an American mother, and we're going to see if she might be able to get us out of Vienna.' And she did. Through visas they got her whole family out." It wasn't until later that the daughter reconnected with the Soss family. "This woman, Lillian was her name, did not want to seek out her biological mother. But when her parents both died, she reconnected with our family. Her biological mother was no longer alive, but Frieda, who was her aunt, connected with her, and she became a part of our family. She came to my wedding."

Angela believes Judaism played a significant role in her grandmother's upbringing. She described her great-grandmother, Clara, as a "connected Jew." Clara Zilberstein and S.H. Soss came to this country as immigrants from Romania. We were fortunate: our genealogists were able to locate the 1871 birth certificate of Angela's great-grandfather, S.H. Soss. "Birth Certificate of Srul Hersch, male," Angela read from the document. "Born on the 21st of October in Moinesti in his parents' house. He's the son of Mr. Moishe, tinsmith, 42 years old, and Mrs. Rose, 39 years old, merchant." Angela looked up from the paper, thrilled to discover this part of her family's history. "I never knew what S.H. Soss stood for," she said.

S.H. grew up at a turning point in Romanian history. Only seven years after Srul's birth, Romania became independent from the Ottoman Empire. With independence came hope for the Jews, and Romania initially promised full political equality to its Jewish population, which numbered around 250,000. For the first time, Jews could apply to become Romanian citizens. Without citizenship, they were considered foreigners in their own country, even if their families had lived in Romania for generations. But between 1879 and 1913 that promise was kept to a mere two thousand individuals. The birth certificate of Angela's granduncle Itsaach, S.H. and Clara's oldest child, revealed that her family was not among the Jews who could now call themselves Romanian citizens; on it, S.H. and Crentza (Clara) are described as "of Mosaic religion and of Israelite nationality."

Angela's family, along with nearly a quarter million other Jews, remained in Romania, stripped of countless rights. One law prohibited them from peddling, thus depriving thousands of Jewish families of their liveli-hood. In 1882 a new law forced Jews to serve in the military, to fight for a country that denied them their most basic freedoms. (Their plight was eerily similar to that of African Americans who served in the U.S. military throughout the early half of the twentieth century to preserve freedoms in Europe yet who were denied the selfsame rights back home. The same could be said of Japanese Americans, among the most decorated of World War II veterans, who fought loyally for a country that confined their par-ents, wives, and children for the duration of the war to internment camps across the American West.)

At the close of the nineteenth century, rabid anti-Semitism swept across Eastern Europe. It was a desperate time for Romanian Jews. They had no choice but to escape. The writing was on the wall—or, literally, on broad-sheets proclaiming a virulent hatred of the Jews and calling for their de-mise. Although the contemporary clippings we presented to Angela did not contain information about her relatives specifically, the words she read in translation were clearly directed at them: "Fear rebellious kikes." "Kikes' lamentation." "Romanians buy nothing from Kikes."

In 1899, the year that her granduncle Itsaach was born, the "Roma-nian Exodus" began, an unparalleled wave of Jewish emigration even for a people that had spent much of their history leaving one homeland for another. Many Jews in Romania actually fled the country on foot to find freedom, walking hundreds of miles across Europe. They became known in Yiddish as *fussgeyers*. The *fussgeyers* were barred from entering any Ro-manian town or city, and Jewish residents along the way would come out to see them as they passed through. As difficult as life was in Romania, it was still home, and their leaving was out of necessity, not desire.

A group of 120 Romanian Jews living in Bacau, not far from Moinesti, put their heartbreak into words. They left a letter for their neighbors as they left the only home they had ever known. "With a saddened heart we have to say goodbye, beloved brothers," Angela read from it. "The painful moment has arrived when we have to separate ourselves from the place of our birth, from our parents and brothers and our family, and from the beautiful landscape dear to our hearts. We did what we could to live hon-estly among our people; we worked without limit and we were content to live modestly. But the times caught up with us. Give, brothers. Give and it will become truth that Jews are a people of *b'nei rachmunim.*" B'nei *rachmunim* is Hebrew for children of mercy, or sons of mercy. This plea to

Jews for compassion for their fellow Jews suggests these migrants couldn't expect help from anyone else on their desperate walk to freedom.

"It's heart-wrenching," Angela said, clearly moved. "It reminds me of the biblical passage where Abraham is asked to leave for the first time, and it says, 'You have to leave your home, your birthplace, your father's house,' and it repeats that. Why do they have to say it in three different ways? It's because he was so tied to it. And to listen to them—'we have to separate ourselves from the place of our birth, from our parents and brothers and our family, and from the beautiful landscape'—it's that same biblical echoing of those three things that just make it so clear how heart-wrenching it was for them to leave this place."

While there is no record of whether Angela's great-grandparents or anyone else in their family was a *fussgeyer*, we do know that they were among the masses that left at that time, booking passage on a ship bound for the United States. In just a few decades, 30 percent of Romania's Jewish population had left for the United States. Like so many other European immigrants, Angela's family arrived in New York City, where her granduncle Joseph had already begun to build a life for himself and, by extension, for his family.

S.H. and Clara arrived in New York City in 1902. They didn't stay, though. The 1910 census told us that they, along with their four children, the youngest of whom was Frieda, were now living in Spokane, Washington. By 1916, S.H. had become the owner of the Star Loan Office, a pawnshop in Spokane. Owning a pawnshop was a dangerous business. We came across several articles about robberies and break-ins at other stores around town, and in one incident S.H. was held up at gunpoint. (According to the article, he "seized the man's revolver and yelled for help.") Even if S.H. had thought about relocating to a safer area, he was, by then, deeply connected to the city. We found eleven Sosses in the city directory. After fleeing anti-Semitism in Romania, most of the Soss family had reunited in Spokane, including Angela's great-great-grandparents, Moishe and Rose.

"You know what's so amazing? My daughter is Rose," Angela said, touched by the coincidence. "She is named for my husband's grandmother. But it's so beautiful to feel like I just found a relative I never knew. I didn't even know her name was Rose." All the names we've told her today were unfamiliar. Among them she has found a deep and meaningful connection. "Beyond Clara, I didn't know anyone's name. I didn't even know S.H.'s name. And I've found a relative, and she's a Rose. I can't even believe that."

The immigrant story is often one of conflict and confusion: I am loyal to my new home, but does it make me any less American to preserve my native tongue, to honor the old traditions? When new citizens become naturalized, it is a secular baptism of sorts, when immigrants of every faith pledge allegiance to their new home, the United States of America. At this pivotal moment, religious differences are put aside in the name of membership in a broader, secular community. We discovered the naturalization application of Angela's great-grandfather, who was forced to flee Romania because he was Jewish. On this frayed, yellowed piece of paper, Angela was able to see her great-grandfather sign away his allegiance to the country that didn't want him and pledge his allegiance to the one that opened its doors to so many like him. "'It is my intention,'" Angela read, "'to become a citizen of the United States and to renounce absolutely and forever all allegiance and fidelity to any foreign prince, state, or sovereignty and particularly to Charles, King of Romania of whom at this time I am a subject'—who wouldn't have me," Angela added, laughing. Srul had filed his intention to naturalize in 1903, shortly after arriving in America, but he didn't apply for citizenship for another nine years, in 1912.

I asked Angela what she thought her ancestors hoped for when they landed on American soil. "I think they hoped they could be in a place in which they could be freely who they wanted to be," she replied, "both in their religion as well as in their ability to have a livelihood, and just the ability to raise a family and have a good life—but I think maybe even more than that, an ability to dream, to be able to do something even more."

We had one last discovery to share with Angela about her Romanian relatives. Incredibly, her granduncle Israel Soss—Itsaach, whose birth certificate we had managed to locate—participated in a Spokane oral history project and left behind, in his own words, the story of his parents' life there. What a wonderful gift to leave for future generations. Angela read her granduncle's words: "My family was accepted in Spokane right away. There was a Jewish butcher and a grocery store catering to Jewish people. They came from all over Europe. My father was very religious. Friday night and Saturday was the big day. We had a little community with a synagogue. My father was a good, fair man. Very fair. He helped those who were coming from Europe and didn't have much money. After starving when he was young, he was very charitable."

From this oral history, we learned about not only S.H. Soss himself but about the community around him, Jewish immigrants who had made a new home in America while bringing much of the Old World with them—Jewish shops, a synagogue. Of course, Soss had also brought with him the concept of *b'nei rachmunim*. "He had obviously benefited from that along the way as he was traveling by foot to get out, and he never forgot that," Angela said.

The persecution of the Jews is a troubling, documented part of history, one that Angela was well aware of. But to have it made relevant to her personally—that only three generations previous, her family left Romania under terribly inhumane conditions—was very powerful. "I've always felt it was important for Judaism to survive not just because Jews have been persecuted, but because it has so much to offer and is so meaningful and beautiful," she reflected. "But I do have to say, learning about the persecution personally in my own family in this direct way really does give me my own sense of needing to carry this on for what they endured to survive for it to be passed on to me."

■ Sometimes interfaith and intercultural marriages force families to choose religious or ethnic identity at the expense of the other. Angela worries that the rich legacies of her Korean cultural heritage are slipping away from her children. "I feel like we know a lot about our Jewish past and our Jewish history and our Jewish family, but I've done a very, very bad job of teaching about Korean history or Korean family," she said. "My children don't really think of themselves as Korean. I remember watching the Olympics, and a Korean had won a medal. My son Eli said, 'Look, Mom, a Korean won a medal. You're Korean.'"

Angela told me that her mother is less concerned. "I said to her, 'I feel like I need to teach them more about being Korean.' She said, 'You do every day. When you are showing them the way that you respect someone who is elderly, when you teach them that striving for the very, very best in everything they do,' she said, 'those are Korean values. That's part of who you are as a Korean.' I feed them Korean food also, and I teach them stories. But really, she said, it's really about the way you live your life. When you teach them that life is not about just being comfortable but about what you can give back and realizing your potential on earth, she said, 'That's a Korean way of looking at things.'"

Angela's Korean ancestors did not leave their homeland en masse for America as her Jewish ancestors did. Her mother made a personal, intimate decision to immigrate to the United States with her Jewish American husband. Yet displacement is a theme that runs through her mother's side of the family as well.

Sulja Lee or Yi was born in Japan on July 18, 1942, during World War II. Simply put, Angela said, "She is a remarkable woman." Sulja was one of seven children, the only girl in the family and the first of her siblings to go to college. She went on scholarship, the only way she could attend, as Angela's grandmother by that point in her life was a single mother with a house full of children. "She probably knew pretty early on that she wasn't going to have a typical Korean life," Angela remarked about her mother. She flouted convention and centuries of tradition by fleeing from her arranged marriage, to a stable Korean doctor. "She married for love, which was really kind of unusual for that time and that culture."

Her love ultimately brought her to the United States, where she had always dreamed of going. Angela said Sulja "had to start 100 percent from scratch," not just in terms of learning a new language but also forging new relationships. She always kept the Korean community close. About thirty years ago, she started the Korean Women's Association, which met in people's living rooms and focused on helping Korean women immigrants tackle daily tasks made difficult by their language barrier. Under the auspices of the KWA, Sulja also launched the first Korean-language library in Tacoma while creating a women's shelter for abused Korean women and feeding and housing programs for elderly Koreans. Since then, the KWA has grown into a large nonprofit agency with more than one thousand employees, with the goal of providing social and health care to in-need populations, regardless of their ethnicity. "It really is a reflection of her Korean values," Angela said, obviously proud of her mother's accomplishments.

I was curious to know how Angela's Korean family came to live in Japan. "The way my mom said it, there was a period of time when Japan occupied Korea, and they took artists and intellectuals out of Korea and basically kidnapped them and brought them to Japan, I guess to feed the brain and cultural power of Japan," she explained. "Apparently my great-grandparents were among them."

Gaeran Hwang was Angela's grandmother, the woman she called Halmoni. She was born around 1915 in Korea. When Gaeran was about five, she was taken out of Korea with her parents to live in Japan. She spent most of her childhood and young adult life in Japan, speaking the language and absorbing the culture. Japan became her true home.

In Japan, Gaeran was a successful businesswoman, and she had no desire to leave even once World War II ended. Apparently she was given no choice. "When they had to leave Japan, she sold the business and had all this Japanese money," Angela said. "My mother said that she strapped Japanese money to each one of the children in case they would ever get separated on their way back to Korea. Then they got to Korea, and they had this pile of Japanese money, and it was worth less than firewood. She really had nothing from an entire business that she had. She had nothing and started over." Her daughter Sulja told us that Gaeran felt like a foreigner in her own land.

Angela found many parallels between the experiences of her Jewish and Korean ancestors. "That sense of wandering and trying to find a home and a place that is yours, and finding strength within your own immediate family and within some sense of faith, because not being welcome where you are certainly was a story that I think both families experienced."

For much of her adult life, Gaeran had to fend for herself and her seven children. Her husband, Samdal Yi, died when he was relatively young. Even when he was alive, Angela said, he was "a dreamer, an idealist, a romantic"—in other words, not much of a breadwinner.

Samdal Yi was born in Hyung Pun, Korea, around 1910, the same time Japan was annexing Korea. "When he got back to Korea, he was one of the few people that was literate in his town," Angela said, repeating an oft-told story from her mother. "So he would read novels, and then people would all gather in the house, and they would bring some sake or some kind of Korean beer, or a sack of rice, and that was sort of payment." For hours Samdal Yi would tell stories. Angela thought this was where her mother developed her love of literature and books. "My mom remembers hiding out in a backroom because kids weren't allowed, and she would just listen to her father weave these stories."

When we traced Samdal Yi's ancestry, we were amazed by what we found. Angela's family's *joakbo* (the genealogical record of all of the males descended from the "founding father" of their family's clan) is extensive, to say the least. We were able to trace her family tree all the way back to the clan's progenitor, Yi Han—her fortieth great-grandfather. Granted, Angela's name will never appear in the *joakbo* because she is a woman, but this is her clan, too—along with about 2.6 million other descendants. "This is stunning," Angela said.

Angela's extraordinarily deep Korean roots reach back nearly seven centuries—to the king of one of the longest Confucian dynasties in Korean history. Angela's twentieth great-grandfather, King Taejo, lived between 1335 and 1408 and was the founder of the Joseon Dynasty, which ruled for five centuries. Angela was dumbfounded. "Oh, my goodness," she laughed, looking at the massive family tree in front of her. "That's crazy."

Angela's Korean family tree was not lacking for drama. Taejo's son, King Taejong, Angela's nineteenth great-grandfather, led a military coup to kill his two half brothers, and he later killed another of his brothers. Taejong, as it happens, was immortalized on Korean TV in a popular series called *Tears of the Dragon*. The conceit of the series was that Angela's ancestor was actually a devoted son who just did what he had to do to maintain stability in the kingdom.

We'll never know. But we do know that the kingdom continued, and so did his line. Taejong's son, King Sejong, Angela's eighteenth great-grandfather, ruled between 1418 and 1450. Korean television didn't pick his story up, but he was greatly admired, considered by Koreans to be the wisest and most gifted ruler in their entire history. Known as Sejong the Great, he was responsible for many innovative technological and military advances. His greatest contribution to Korean culture is still in use today, every day. In 1443, the twenty-fifth year of his reign, King Sejong created an alphabet with which to write the Korean language. Prior to that, educated people wrote in Chinese characters. This phonetic alphabet, called Hangul, was devised by the king for the benefit of the Korean masses unable to read or write Chinese. As he wrote, "Amongst uneducated people there have been many who have been unable to express their feelings in writing. I am greatly distressed by this, and so I have made twenty-eight new letters. Let everyone practice them at their ease, and adapt them to their daily use."

The Hangul language has survived for five hundred years, minus four of its original letters. Of the six thousand languages spoken around the world, only one hundred have their own alphabets. And Hangul is the only alphabet designed by a single individual who laid out his theory and motives for doing so as clearly as Angela's ancestor King Sejong did.

"Oh, I love that this is why he wanted to do it, to bring the potential for people to express themselves and learn out into the wider world." Angela's delight at finding this ancestor was obvious. "I'm going to cry just hearing this. I'll never look at a piece of Korean text again or a Korean newspaper on the street or walk through Koreatown without feeling incredibly connected to that."

As Angela looked at the names and dates on the family tree in front of her, she said, "It doesn't even feel like it's that long ago." She believes that we must incorporate our family histories into our present lives. "The challenge is for this not to feel like just history but feel like it's my memory. It's the memory of my people."

Our investigation helped cast a new light on Angela's relationship to her Korean ancestors. "It is very powerful to feel this sense of rootedness," she said. "I think when we study the Bible we feel a sense of being connected to something, an ancient story. And I don't think I've ever felt connected to an ancient story on my Korean side in the same way. I was always connected to values, but not ancient stories and memory. I feel very differently now just hearing this."

■ Before we started our analysis of Angela's DNA, I asked her the same question I'd put to Rick Warren: what can science tell us about who we are and where our ancestors came from?

Her answer: "Ultimately, my sense of faith leads me to feeling that we're all in some ways really connected to each other, that we're all one people. We might have ended up in different parts of the world, different colors and with different foods, but in some ways that we're all united in a sense of humanity." More personally, though, Angela was curious to know what her DNA would reveal about exactly who populated her history thousands of years ago.

We started with her father's side of the family. We traced her direct paternal ancestor back to her great-great-grandfather, Jacob Warnick, who was from Russia. Unfortunately, we didn't know when or exactly where he was born. We tested her father's Y-DNA to determine her paternal haplogroup. It is E1b1b1a, which originated about fourteen thousand years ago in a population that moved from eastern Africa to the north, expanding into the Near East. In the Bronze Age, men carried this haplogroup to Turkey and then into east Central Europe. Today, men from Ukraine, Hungary, Romania, and Slovakia all carry this haplogroup at levels of nearly 10 percent. Those people would be Angela's distant genetic cousins. In this case, the genetics and genealogy overlap perfectly.

On Angela's mother's side, we traced her earliest direct ancestors back to her Korean great-grandmother, Sang Joong Kim, born sometime in the late eighteenth century. We know nothing about her other than her name, because as we learned, Korean genealogy provides details only for male ancestors. Angela's maternal haplogroup is Y. This haplogroup arose in eastern Asia in the Amur River Basin of southern Siberia approximately twenty-nine thousand years ago. About eight thousand years ago, women carrying the Y haplogroup began to populate the coasts of Siberia, northeastern China, Japan, and Korea. On this side, just like on Angela's father's, genealogy and genetics are in sync.

"It makes you feel very rooted," she commented. "For a story that I've generally felt about my family being a family that wanders and is seeking a home, in some ways, in a deep way, my family has been in homes for a really long, long time."

Again, there were no real surprises in Angela's admixture. "It's kind of what I look like," she said: "50 percent European, 50 percent Asian." Family Tree DNA, a company that specializes in tracing Jewish ancestry, provided us with a more specific breakdown: 44.63 percent Middle Eastern, 3 percent South Asian, and 52.29 percent East Asian. The East Asian DNA, which is considered Mongolian, matches most closely with north Indian and southeastern Indian ancestry. There was a little mixing going on somewhere in the past, but it was statistically insignificant.

"It's so amazing to feel like those ancestors really were from the Middle East, from Israel. I don't think I really knew that in my heart," Angela said. She had told us earlier that when she arrived in Israel she felt like she was home. And in a way she was.

For generations, Jews, for reasons that need no explanation, married within the tribe. This led to a high degree of "cousinness." We found that Angela was distantly related on her father's side to Barbara Walters, Robert Downey Jr., and Kyra Sedgwick. She actually shares long bands of identical DNA with Barbara on three of her chromosomes. This means that they probably share a common ancestor on Angela's father's side going back about three hundred years. If we were able to do complete family trees for both Barbara's and Angela's Jewish families, ideally they would intersect at one ancestor. "Wow," Angela laughed. "She's my *mishpucha*. My family."

■ By the end of our investigation, we had traveled thousands of miles with Angela's ancestors, on foot and by sea. She learned her Jewish and Korean ancestors had both been uprooted from their homelands, yet she came away with a deep sense of rootedness on both sides of her family. To Angela, it is the stories, the memories, that such people carry and tell and retell that have the most profound influence on our sense of ourselves, our identity.

"I think our families choose the stories that we want to tell about ourselves because that is who we want to be," Angela said. "Sometimes they're difficult stories of overcoming something that show the resilience of our families. Sometimes they are dreams that our families have had. Sometimes they're realized, and sometimes they're not. But those stories that we share, I think, more than any DNA or anything else, shape who we are and shape the stories that we want to pass onto our children, who we want them to become, what we want them to become in the world as well."

When I ask Angela whom among her relatives she would most want to meet if her fairy godmother could transport her back in time, she said it would be her grandfather, Yi Samdal, the storyteller. "I never got to meet my grandfather on my mother's side, and I think that his spirit was definitely passed on to my mother. She was the most adventurous and idealistic and connected to story of all his children. I feel like I share so much of that from my mother that really came from him." Angela paused for a moment. "I'll bring my bag of rice and just hear a bunch of his stories. That's what I want to do."

Yasir Qadhi (b. 1975)

Yasir Qadhi is one of the most influential conservative clerics in American Islam. Drawing a tide of young followers to Orthodox Islam, he strictly adheres to traditional interpretations of the Quran and Islamic law. The school of thought he is associated with is called Salafiya, which takes its name from the Arabic word *salaf*, meaning "ancestor." He is a first-generation American, the son of parents who emigrated from Pakistan to the United States.

Since Yasir's father's arrival in America in 1963, the Muslim population has increased roughly twentyfold, and today there are two and a half million practicing Muslims in this country. Eid, which Yasir described as "the largest congregation of Muslims that come together, basically Christmas and Easter and Thanksgiving," is a very different affair now in Houston than it was when his father first observed it there.

"The question that I always ask my father," Yasir said, "is how did he practice the faith as pretty much the only Muslim, or one of two or three people? He tells me the first Eid prayer that they ever prayed, there was a grand total of three people in Houston praying Eid. My father, he's never led the prayer in his life, he told me. But when he showed up and they didn't have an imam, obviously, what are you going to do? Well, you just become an imam. That's what America does to you, you know?"

The growth of Islam in America is evident in the experiences of Yasir and his father. "My father is in the audience as an elderly man now. Here is the son who's trained as a professional and who's become a scholar in the religion, and instead of three people there's a grand total of thirty thousand Muslims." I told Yasir that this had to be one of the proudest days in his father's life. "I was humbled, too. I was very humbled as well."

Yasir Qadhi was born in Houston, Texas, on January 30, 1975. Religion was always a part of his upbringing. Even though he moved away from Houston when he was five, he has vivid memories of the mosque there, Islamic Sunday school, even the imam. His Pakistani parents made a conscious decision to imbue their home with religious and cultural traditions. "My father realized that since he was pretty much one of only a handful of Muslims in all of Houston, if he didn't do something to preserve the religion for his children, it wouldn't be preserved." Yasir also learned Urdu, his parents' native tongue. "He was adamant that we pass the culture down. We were required to speak Urdu at home. He did not want us to lose the language," Yasir said. "So I speak fluent Urdu almost without an accent, and that's pretty rare for the second generation. We celebrated all the holidays and wore the clothes. Of course, cuisine. You can't really be an Indian Pakistani without the cuisine."

Yasir said that the path his parents followed, from being "cultural Muslims" to being religious ones, was typical of Muslim immigrants. "Like most Muslims who have immigrated to America, the bulk of them come culturally Muslim. And then they need to make a choice. Do I want to commit to the faith, or do I just want to be a little bit cultural, if you like? Both my parents were cultural Muslims. But especially when they had kids—my father tells me this—he realized that if he were just a cultural Muslim, then the faith, the religion, the traditions would not really be passed on. And that inspired them to become more committed to the faith."

The decision is easy in a Muslim country, Yasir said. In a sense, there *is* no decision. "Back home you take the faith for granted. Everybody's a Muslim. You're just pushed with the tide." The same holidays are celebrated; religious expectations are understood. "Ramadan, everybody's fasting; everybody's breaking fast together. Over here you could be the only person in your whole school or office or workplace. Friday in Islamic countries, everything is shut. Society goes to the mosque on Friday. Even if you're going to work, you have a two-hour break where everybody just goes to the mosque. Over here, of course, Friday is just like Thursday and Wednesday. You need to make a commitment."

Yasir's father described his own experience to us: "We were born Muslims. When we came to America, we had to make a conscious decision whether or not to assimilate. We decided to be conscious Muslims. We raised our boys to be American Muslims."

Assimilation weighs heavily on every new immigrant's mind: Do I look and sound American enough? Yasir saw this in his own mother. When he was a child in Texas, she did not cover her head. It was only many years later that she began to wear a headscarf. He has noticed a trend among the second generation, the children of the immigrants, where they express themselves much more freely on their own cultural terms. "The immigrant community, by and large, they did have to assert their American identity," Yasir says, "whereas the second generation, they don't have to assert it; they are an American. They're American-born and -raised. They basically are American in every single aspect, so there is no dichotomy; there is no cognitive dissonance. They can assert their Islam without feeling awkward about their Americanness."

Still, many children of immigrants struggle with feelings of isolation, aware that their version of American looks and sounds different from their schoolmates'. Yasir said he didn't experience this as a child in Houston. "Houston is a pretty multicultural city," he said. "It is a metropolis. I knew that we were Muslim. I knew that we spoke a different language at home. I knew that our food was spicier than my neighbor's foods. But I wasn't made to feel awkward or different."

Saudi Arabia was a different story. When Yasir was five, his father completed his Ph.D. and accepted a job in Jeddah. It was there that he felt very much like a foreigner. "Saudi Arabia, and all over that area, they have an expatriate subculture, and if you're not Saudi, you're going to have an expatriate subculture," Yasir said. "I did not speak Arabic because I had a little bubble of a community. I'm going to a British school; it has a British curriculum; my teachers are all British. The people in my classroom basically are either British or American. When you come home, the friends you're associating with are also of a similar background. You don't associate with the locals, as they say," Yasir explained. "I lived in Saudi Arabia, but I never felt Saudi."

Yasir said that he could have done quite well staying in his bubble, but when it came time for college, his father insisted that he return to the United States to study medicine or chemical engineering. Yasir enrolled at the University of Houston. "I guess I, too, was somewhat of an immigrant when I returned back to Houston, even though English was my mother tongue and I am an American and born and raised here. But the culture was still new to me."

Yasir, like the immigrants of his parents' generation, had a decision to make. "Do I want to be committed to the faith or not?" He explained: "My university years were my formative years in making me committed to the faith. I was raised a practicing Muslim by my father . . . but I chose to be a committed Muslim in college." Typically, college is a time of experimentation in lifestyle, when religion is held at arm's length. Not so for Yasir, who said, "I needed religion to save me from those things, because I don't view them as being moral or healthy for the human soul, and I felt an emptiness that only religion was able to fill."

In October 1994 Yasir helped organize an on-campus dialogue between Christians and Muslims. The NBA star Hakeem Olajuwon was the invited guest. This and other similar discussions Yasir organized were not intended to—or needed to—put out fires between religious groups on campus but for the sake of educational exchange. "Pre-9/11, it was a different America," Yasir recalled. "It was a beautiful America. It was an America where you could be whoever you wanted to be and nobody really cared."

During his sophomore year, Yasir announced to his father that he wanted to be an imam. His father's response carried in it an insistence on practicality typical of immigrant parents of all stripes. "'No way,' he said. 'You must be out of your mind. We didn't move back all the way here from Saudi Arabia so that can go and study Islamic studies. You're going to get your engineering degree,'" Yasir said, recounting the conversation. "Then he said something that I really admire him for. He said, 'And then when you're able to stand on your feet, you make up your own mind. But it's my job to make sure that you're independent.'"

Yasir did go on to get his degree in chemical engineering. After graduating from the University of Houston, he worked at Dow Chemical in Freeport, Texas, for a short time. "That experience opened up my eyes to the reality of corporate America, of working in an office environment," Yasir recalled. "I just felt like my life was worth more to me than solving nth-degree quadratic equations, than writing complex computer code to simulate a chemical reaction." He turned down an offer from Dow Chemical to work there permanently and pursued his dream of becoming an Islamic studies scholar. His parents weren't pleased.

Returning to Saudi Arabia to study Islam meant leaving not only a lucrative job but also the woman he had hoped to marry. "My going to Medina basically meant I'm not going to have a job, and that basically meant I'm not going to get married, because according to our culture and our religion," Yasir explained, "you have to have the means to support your wife." He was giving up a lot, but he "hoped and trusted that God would give me better."

A year later, he and Rumana married, and her parents agreed to let her go to Medina. "I daresay that the quality of my life, maybe even monetarily, I am better off than if I had been a chemical engineer," Yasir said. "But definitely qualitatively there is no question. And true happiness is not bought through money. True happiness comes from self-fulfillment. And that is definitely priceless."

At the Islamic University of Medina, Yasir excelled, becoming the "senior-most Western student in all of Saudi Arabia at the time." He was clearly proud of his accomplishments at the seminary, with good reason. "For an American to break the barrier, to get straight As, was unprecedented, because realize, Arabic is not our native tongue, and for us to master the language at the classical level, it was like learning classical Latin," he said. "All of the books are thousand-year-old books. You're competing with people that have already trained in the tradition before coming to Medina. I had trained as a chemical engineer."

Yasir was the first American to be accepted into the master's program, and on the path to becoming the first Westerner to graduate in any Islamic field from Saudi Arabia.

Then 9/11 happened.

Religious texts, like historical events, are constantly being reinterpreted, and one of the most important functions of our religious leaders is to act as our guide. On September 11, 2001, a group of men with their own perverse, radical interpretation of *their* version of their religion perpetrated the largest act of terrorism on American soil in our nation's history. For Americans of every faith, it was a day that would test our principles of democratic rights and religious tolerance. Across the country, many turned to God for understanding, while others unfortunately sought to lay blame upon an entire faith. For Yasir Qadhi, his understanding of what it means to be a Muslim in America would be altered forever. He heard the devastating news while studying Islamic theology as a graduate student in Saudi Arabia.

The World Trade Center had been hit, a friend told him as he was on his way to afternoon prayer, and early reports were saying Muslims were piloting the planes. "I remember I just froze outside the mosque. And this is in Medina, the Holy City of Medina. I had a premonition that this would be bad."

Yasir returned home to his wife, and they rushed to a neighbor who had a television. There they saw the towers collapse. Yasir's long-awaited plans to return home for a short visit in January were put on hold. "Do not come back to America right now. No, it's not the right time. You don't understand what's going on, the paranoia," Yasir recalled his father telling him. "And I didn't understand the paranoia, because I'm still in Medina."

When Yasir, Rumana, and their baby son returned to America the following year, their reception was hostile. "Multiple times people called me bin Laden," he said. "And I remember we were in a shopping center once, and somebody just walked straight up to me, literally face to face, and my wife was next to me, and she was carrying Ammaar, and he said, 'You guys don't belong here,' and then he walked away." Yasir paused, remembering that painful experience. "This was not the America that I remembered."

For the next three years, Yasir pursued his studies in Medina while spending summers in America. Upon completion of his master's, he decided it was time to return to America for good. It was then, in 2005, that air travel became "problematic" for him. He was a rising star on the national lecture circuit. As a result, his name became known outside of the Islamic community—and began appearing on "watch lists." "I was being harassed at the borders every time I traveled, every time I came back." These memories were painful for Yasir to share. "I have too many stories to tell you. Almost all of them involve being met by two armed guards at the door of the plane. An announcement is made inside the flight—sometimes my name, which is so embarrassing. And even if it's not your name, the announcement is made that you need to show your passport as you exit the plane."

These were not announcements directed at all passengers. "As soon as I came along, you know, 'OK, we got him.' And then they escort me, and this of course is very embarrassing, when people sitting next to you think you're a potential terrorist now. You've had a nice conversation with them. All of a sudden . . ." Yasir went on to describe an experience that most of us fortunately will never go through, that he has gone through simply because of his religion. "Then they escort me to a private room, sit me down. And the worst thing of it, you're not being physically tortured, but it's emotional trauma. You have no idea how long you're going to be there, what the charges are, what you've done wrong." He paused. "It is intimidating. You're asked questions that are very intrusive, so much so that I had been told by multiple lawyers that these are unconstitutional questions. I was asked about my religious affiliations, which mosques I pray in, which charities I give to. On one occasion they even asked me to list my friends and their phone numbers. I was like, what? I once said to one of the people who was interviewing me, 'This is not Communist Russia. This is America.'"

It was around this same time, as Yasir's family was relocating from Saudi Arabia to America, that his son experienced the grade-school version of guilt by association—association with a misunderstood religion, not with any one individual. "My son was going to public school. He was seven years old, and he comes home, and he goes, 'Who is bin Laden?' I was like, 'Why? You're just a seven-year-old kid.' He goes, 'One of my friends said, 'You're with the bin Laden guys.' How do you explain to a seven-year-old kid? He was born the year before 9/11; he doesn't have any memories of it. It was an awkward moment, trying to explain to my child what 9/11 was and why some people were mistakenly associating him with that. Of course now all my kids, even my five-year-old girl, knows what Al Qaeda is and 9/11 because of the atmosphere and the environment we're living in."

The incident was a glaring example to Yasir, once again, of how America had changed. "I felt betrayed by society at large, forces beyond my control. This shouldn't be happening here."

Yasir believes "Islamophobia" is something his children will have to contend with for many years to come. "Islamophobia is of course a post-9/11 phenomenon, a trend that is now culturally acceptable, where political candidates are openly vying with one another to see who can give the most Islamophobic comments." While not yet able to envision a time when relations between Muslims and the rest of American society will return to the halcyon days of the 1990s, Yasir said, "Time does heal most wounds." Either that or "a time will come where the Islamophobia that we're currently experiencing will diminish, only to be replaced by something else, because that is the way of society. A new scapegoat will come along."

Interestingly, Yasir told me 9/11 had only bolstered his feelings of American identity instead of marginalizing it. "I never felt more American than I did post-9/11," he said, "because my American identity was being challenged by fellow Americans. Home is Houston, Texas. I consider this land to be my land. And you're presuming that just because of some incident on 9/11 that has nothing to do with me and in my opinion nothing to do with the correct teachings of my faith, it's being extrapolated and then used against me. I have the option to go many places in the world, but I choose to live here because I want to live here."

We have all been changed by 9/11. We need to remove our shoes at the airport and our sunglasses at the bank. Once considered the safest way to travel, planes are now seen as potential weapons. Americans are afraid that violence will visit their families simply if they are in the wrong place at the wrong time. But Yasir says that American Muslims have felt the impact more than anyone else has. "A lot of Americans don't realize that the people who are most scared of another 9/11 are American Muslims, because they have the most to lose. It's not just that they're going to be a part of those who are killed whenever something like that happens; it's the backlash that's going to transpire."

I asked Yasir if he knew what the most frequently asked question in the black community was in 1963, after the news broke that President Kennedy had been shot. "Was he a Negro? Was he colored?" It was for a similar reason: African Americans feared the backlash that would result if a black person had pulled the trigger. "That is the exact same question that every single Muslim asks every time they hear of any crime that is remotely linked with terrorism," Yasir responded. "Was it a Muslim who did it or not? That's why there is no community that would be a greater resource to fight radicalism than American Muslims, because we have everything to lose."

Yasir and I made a pilgrimage to the 9/11 Memorial in lower Manhattan. It was a haunting experience to walk through the memorial with him, reading the names of the people who perished on that terrible day. Yasir admitted to me that the difficulty he experienced after 9/11, and the treatment he witnessed of Muslims across America in general, severely tested his own tolerance for other religions and cultures.

I asked him directly about a statement he made in 2001, after 9/11, in which he questioned whether the Holocaust actually occurred. I, like many others, found the statement very offensive. "I made a mistake," said Yasir. "There's no ambiguity about that. I believed propaganda that was given to me. Unfortunately, the climate that I was in at that time was a different climate, and the place that I was in facilitated such stereotyping. Post-9/11 I've learned firsthand what happens when groups stereotype you." This was a difficult, public learning process for Yasir, but the aftermath of 9/11, and the event itself, profoundly reshaped his sense of tolerance for the beliefs of people of other faiths—and empathy for the persecution they've experienced for those beliefs.

■ The branches of Yasir's father's family tree were heavy with painful stories of his ancestors' persecution for their religious beliefs. His father, Mazharul-Haq Kazi, was born in Jabalpur, India, on August 23, 1936. He has lived in Houston since 1963, when he came to America from Pakistan to study biology at the University of Houston. "It was a monumental event for the family, because nobody had ever gone to America before." According to Yasir, "Many of my father's relatives didn't even know where America was on a map. They had heard of England because England was the colonial power, but they hadn't heard of America."

His father came to America for the same reason that so many people do. "The land of dreams and opportunities. He wanted to give his children a better future," Yasir explained. "It was a difficult decision for my father because my father was the eldest in his family, and traditionally the eldest son has the job of taking care of everybody. So my father financed his younger brother, helped his parents. My father did everything. But they all wanted him to come to America as well."

This wasn't the first time Mazharul-Haq had left his homeland. In 1947 the Partition of India led to the creation of the independent Muslim nation of Pakistan, and millions of Muslims were forced to leave their homes in India. "This is an interesting fact. The largest mass migration of humans in the history of humanity occurred in 1947," Yasir explained. "Over fifteen million people migrated across borders. Hindus, Sikhs, Muslims, they're all crossing all over. A lot of chaos, a lot of terror, a lot of riots took place."

The end of centuries of British colonialism in 1947 led to murderous sectarian violence perpetrated in the name of religious differences. Hindus and Muslims routinely slaughtered each other in the streets. Sometimes entire villages and neighborhoods were wiped out.

In April 1948, Yasir's father and his family left Jabalpur to embark upon the perilous journey to Pakistan. Mazharul-Haq's family was relatively prosperous, with a large home that had been in the family for two or three generations. With just a few suitcases containing whatever of their past lives they could carry, they fled first to Bombay (now Mumbai) and then on to Karachi, where they hoped to find the freedom to practice their Islamic religious beliefs and start a new life.

His father was old enough to remember the trip, but he never talked much about it. "He's just mentioned the journey that he had by ship and being stuffed in cabins with lots of people in them, just lying on the floor sleeping."

Some Muslims chose to stay. I wondered why Yasir's family left. After all, they were leaving a great deal behind—their home, their family, their history.

"They felt that a new land was being created for them, and they felt a sense of hope, a sense of aspirations that there would be a better future for them in that land," Yasir answered. "The sad truth is, I don't know if that dream became a reality for them or not. I don't know. I know for my father it didn't. I know that my father is very disappointed in the current state of affairs in Pakistan, just the chaos, the confusion. The whole area is literally up in arms, literally and metaphorically." Yasir reflected for a moment. "But for sure for him, that dream that Grandfather and Grandmother had has not materialized."

Yasir's grandparents, Qazi Ishaq Ali, born on March 18, 1894, and Razia Begum, born around 1923, hailed from Jabalpur as well. "My grandmother was the one that I lived with when I was growing up, and I really regret not talking to her more," Yasir said, looking back on what he now considers a missed opportunity. "At the time I was a kid. I just viewed her as a nagging grandmother. She'd always sit us down and tell us stories, but they'd be repetitive, over and over again. After a while she would forget. She told me so many stories about my grandfather. One of the things she said was that I was born the month that he died, and they took that as a good omen, that through me his legacy is living on."

Yasir's grandfather's younger brother, Iftikhar Ali, born in November 1898, was an important Muslim warrior and community leader in Jabalpur. He was an elected official and organizer of the Muslim League political party. He established a newspaper and a madrassa and gained renown for his participation in the political and legal battle in the so-called Chandur Biswa case of 1939. Yasir had never heard of this, but it was portentous of the bloody future that awaited Hindu and Muslim relations less than a decade later.

For centuries, Hindus and Muslims had lived together in India. As the desire to end British colonial rule grew stronger in the 1930s, tensions mounted. Some historians say the British helped fan the flames. On March 17, 1939, a riot exploded in the village of Chandur Biswa. In the confusion, a Hindu congressman named Jagdeorao Patel was killed by a Muslim mob. Local officials rounded up the village's entire male Muslim population and detained the men in inhumane conditions, 156 of them in all, including several fourteen-year-old boys.

The verdict came down on February 24, 1940: six men were sentenced to death, and twenty-four others received life sentences. Yasir's granduncle, Iftikhar Ali, an elected official at the time, believed, with many other prominent Muslims involved in the case, that the sentences were excessive. A newspaper account of the judgment seemed designed to inflame the attitudes of Muslims in the Central Provinces. Yasir read the text aloud: "The Judge observed that he had no doubt in coming to the conclusion that there was an assembly of a large number of Muslims, and that they were the aggressors, and that Jagdeorao and his friends in no way provoked them by insulting slogans or by throwing filth on the mosque."

While the villagers could probably tolerate insulting slogans, "throwing filth on the mosque" was an act of utter degradation and, it seemed, provocation. The case stirred powerful sentiments all over India. The premier of India wrote a letter directly to Gandhi on August 28, 1940, six months after the verdict. "Has a single Hindu anywhere in the whole of India expressed his abhorrence at the conduct of those who thus conspired to send innocent Muslims to the gallows? And, Mahatmaji, what have you yourself done about it? You could not be ignorant of the facts. Yet the tragedy of Chandur Biswa has left you unmoved. How are we to interpret your silence? Do not all these facts conclusively prove that Hindus and Muslims are two different peoples, that democracy in the sense of pure and simple majority rule cannot be accepted by Muslims, and that justice cannot be expected from Hindus in power by Muslims?" Gandhi, of course, and his followers, both Hindu and Muslim, wanted to stay together in a united, independent India, but the sentiment that partition was inevitable was growing.

Yasir agreed: "The feeling was that Muslims can never prosper in a Hindu-controlled India. And these events definitely exacerbated that perception."

Throughout the 1940s Yasir's granduncle Iftikhar remained active in the Muslim League party. He was passionately committed to creating an Islamic nation. We found a transcript of something Iftikhar said in the legislative assembly on November 5, 1939, at the midpoint between the Chandur Biswa riot and the reading of the verdict against the Muslims: "A Mussalman"—the Persian word for "Muslim"—"cannot separate his religion and his politics. To him religion and politics are inseparable elements, and the latter is subservient to the former." Did Yasir agree?

He couldn't answer immediately. "Too many footnotes. I can't agree, and I can't disagree." When I pressed him to expand upon some of those footnotes, he responded, "Nobody can separate his religion from his politics. Let's look at people who are actively pro-life. Is not this belief stemming from their religious beliefs? You are who you are, and part of you is religious. Therefore, at one level, every human being's religious convictions will move him, will shape the direction that they're taking, even if it's a political one. Of course, at another level, should you legislate your religious beliefs into policy?

"As an American Muslim to say this phrase," he continued, "I cannot say it without a number of disclaimers, and the primary one being that our constitution has a clear separation of religion and state, and I don't see any problem in being a committed Muslim and an American at the same time. Speaking from his perspective, they were arguing for the creation of Pakistan, and for them, Pakistan was meant to be a state by Muslims, for Muslims."

Yasir's granduncle Iftikhar was the first member of his family to leave India. He moved to Karachi, Pakistan, in 1947.

Yasir's great-grandfather, Qazi Muhibb Ali, was born around 1865, the year the American Civil War ended. It was from Muhibb Ali that the family got its name, Qadhi. I asked Yasir to explain the origin of the name and its different spellings. He said it wasn't a surname originally, but a title that precedes a name. The difference in spelling indicates a difference in pronunciation. The title Qadhi, meaning judge, comes from Arabic, and Qazi, with its softer pronunciation, is its Urdu adaptation. From what Yasir has heard of his great-grandfather, he was an honorary official of some sort, which is how he received the title. He died during the Spanish influenza outbreak in 1918.

Over the millennia, Muslims came to India from Persia, Central Asia, the Arabian Peninsula, and elsewhere. Yasir didn't know the origins of his own family, although his father had told him that it was Yasir's great-great-grandfather, Mawli Hassan Ali, who had converted from Hindu to Islam. According to family oral history, Mawli Hassan Ali lived in Lucknow, the capital of Urdu culture.

On a trip to India in 2009, Yasir visited the village where his great-great-grandfather lived, including the mosque where he prayed. He also met some of his fifth cousins, who are descendants of his great-great-grandfather. "That was one of the most humbling experiences of my life, because these relatives of mine were literally peasants and farmers. They were tilling the land and couldn't read and write." The contrast between Yasir's life and theirs was jarring. "Here I am doing my Ph.D. at Yale, and here are my distant cousins, and they can barely read and write. They didn't have running water, electricity."

Next we looked to the family history of Yasir's mother, Alia Hayat, who was born on November 4, 1944, in Bilaspur, India. Alia was only three years old when her family moved to Karachi, at the time of Partition. Her father, Hayat Khan, a religious man, eagerly grabbed at the opportunity to make his home in the new Muslim country, but her great-grandfather, Mastan Khan, chose to stay in India. "My mother has no memories of India," Yasir said. "She was for all practical purposes completely raised in Pakistan, so she does identify with the land to an extent."

In the mid-1960s, Yasir's parents got married. It was an arranged marriage, as was typical for Pakistani and Indian couples at the time. "My mother and father did not have a single conversation before they got married," Yasir said. "My mother tells me that my father came to her house to propose, and of course the proposal is just a formality, because the parents have already agreed. So the first time she saw father was when he came to propose. That was the way it was, and they've been happily married." Yasir and Rumana didn't have an arranged marriage. "It's difficult even for me to fathom, but culturally it was the norm."

His parents moved to Houston shortly after they married. Yasir said that it was "a huge culture shock" for his mother. "My mother would dress in the sari and the traditional tunics and whatnot. Her English was not fluent," he said. "But the main stories that she tells me of that time, of her initially moving here in '69, '70, '71, was of the financial problems that both my mother and father underwent while they tried to carve out an existence in America. She came from a relatively upper-middle-class family. And they didn't have a car, and they're eking out an existence. The cost of living, for a graduate student, it was very difficult. My father was working three jobs, and my mother had to find a job as well, and she already had a baby, my older brother. She tells me it was quite difficult. You know, she had one bag of groceries, one bag with my brother, walking miles to get home."

As we discussed earlier, Alia's open commitment to Islam developed after Yasir was already grown. He dated it back to their return from Saudi Arabia. "Throughout the '80s and then especially in the '90s, and again as she returned to America for a second time, after our sojourn in Saudi Arabia, she felt the need to express herself," he recalled. "I remember very clearly when we came back from Saudi Arabia, the first thing my parents did was to open up a class for non-Muslims." This is the same class they teach today, begun eighteen years ago, at the Islamic Society of Greater Houston. "Both my mother and my father committed to teaching their faith to others who were interested in it, either those who wanted to convert or those who were just interested to find out about it, with a passion that sometimes made me jealous, because they would be so dedicated to their students. My father calls it his second family."

Unfortunately, we have very little genealogical information available for Alia's family. Yasir told me that he wouldn't be surprised if there were "elements of Persian ancestry in her." Oral history suggested that his mother's father's line may have come from Kyrgyzstan. Where there's no paper trail to confirm these suspicions, DNA can answer our questions.

■ As with Rick and Angela, I asked Yasir what he thinks science can tell us about ourselves and our ancestors and where we came from. "I think that as we study DNA, the chromosome structure more, I think that we will be able to tell more about our ancestors and where they came from," he responded. "Obviously they can only tell us so much. They cannot tell us the stories of the people who had those DNAs, but they can tell rough origins of where they came from, the geographic locations, ethnicities. I think that's something we can benefit from science."

We started with his father's side. We could trace his direct paternal ancestors back to his great-great-grandfather, Mawli Hassan Ali, who we think was born in Sandhila, India, in the 1830s or 1840s. Yasir's paternal haplogroup is J2. J originated in the Near East about twenty thousand years ago. The subgroup J2 arose in Anatolia and the Caucasus about eighteen thousand years ago and then spread from there throughout Europe and the Muslim world. It reached India about six thousand years ago. Today in India, J2 is more common among people of the upper castes than among those in the lower castes or tribal populations.

J2 also happens to be associated with another ethnic group known for its propensity to migrate, whether by choice or not. It reaches levels of about 20 percent in Ashkenazi Jews, particularly in Central Eastern Europe and in their descendants throughout other parts of the world. The results of Yasir's DNA spoke volumes about how difficult it is to make distinctions about people ethnically, based solely on their religious beliefs. I asked Yasir if this shared ancestry of Muslims and Jews was surprising to him.

"In a way, no. Of course Muslims and Jews consider themselves cousins. Biologically, Arabs and Jews are cousins because they consider themselves to be descendants of Abraham. But I firmly believe that all of humanity indeed goes back, and therefore we're related to everybody somehow. We're all the children of one species, one group of people." The proof is in Yasir's genes.

On his mother's side, we were able to trace his oldest direct maternal ancestors to his great-grandmother, Imtiaz Begum. We know little about her, but she was born in India in the early twentieth century and died in Karachi in the 1980s. Yasir's maternal haplogroup is J1b1a, a subgroup of the maternal haplogroup J1b. This sounds similar to his paternal haplogroup, but paternal and maternal haplogroups have nothing to do with each other. J1b1 arose in the Near East about eight thousand years ago, when agriculture developed in that region. Farming women and their families carried the haplogroup to Turkey and the Balkans and then across Central Europe. Today, it can be found broadly across Europe, particularly in Northern and Western European populations.

The Caucasus, where this maternal haplogroup arose, has historically been considered the western boundary of Greater Persia, which once stretched to the Indus River. By 67 B.C., Zoroastrianism had become the region's dominant religion. But other religious transformations followed: first Christianity, then Islam. In the twelfth century, the Muslims were driven from the Caucasus by a Christian king named David the Builder of

Georgia. Islamic rule would return with the Ottomans, the Mongols, and the Persians. Russia took over in the nineteenth century. Populations of the Caucasus have close genetic affinities with people from Uzbekistan.

Yasir's distant lineage may lead back to one of these places, which dovetails with the family's oral history. Yasir was interested to see how the DNA also confirmed his own suspicions. "I've always felt that they looked Persian."

It turned out that Yasir shares this maternal haplogroup with Barbara Walters (the second time she has come up in this chapter). They are matrilineal cousins. "Of all the people on earth I never would have assumed," Yasir laughed. "I hope she invites me on her show."

We had one more test for Yasir: his admixture test. His results showed 90 percent Asian and 10 percent European. The European result surprised him. "Where did that come from? This means that somewhere back there, there must have been maybe one European ancestor of mine." We used the company Family Tree DNA to analyze Yasir's results because it specializes in Jewish genetic ancestry, particularly Ashkenazi. Family Tree DNA explained that Yasir's European DNA matches Russian ancestry, which jibed with our belief that some of his ancestors might have passed through the Caucasus. It made sense in light of his family's oral history as well.

Yasir Qadhi considers himself culturally Indian and Pakistani. He is proudly American and devoutly Muslim. He defines himself by the many parts of his heritage. "The most important variables are the variables we choose to make the most important," Yasir said. "For some, that is one's ancestry and background. For others, it is one's cultural upbringing. For yet others it is one's religion. I believe that I myself have made a choice, and it is a combination of all of those factors. And to each I give the right that is due to it."

I asked Yasir if he were visited by a fairy godmother who could take him back in time, was there one person in particular on his family tree he would like to meet? He narrowed it down more to a time and place than to an individual. "If I had to make a choice, I would want to be alive in the 1850s in India. I think that was one of the most exciting times in India, and one of the most dangerous times—the mutiny of 1857. And in this generation, basically what we've gone back to was alive at that time."

Through the genealogical paper trails of Rick, Angela, and Yasir, we discovered that, despite their differences of religious faith and national origins, the family histories of all three religious leaders reflect a deep and abiding commitment to spirituality, a courageous determination to harness religious freedom, and a deep desire to worship freely and openly. At the same time, the religions our three guests embrace, the religions they nurture and celebrate each day, have been at the heart of historic wars and violence, even exterminations, that have divided humanity as much as they have united it.

Yet when we set the records aside and look into ourselves, our DNA can teach us just how small the world encompassing these various faiths is—that we are, in fact, in the words of Angela Buchdahl, all *mishpucha*, all family. No matter what we look like, no matter the name of the God we worship, DNA shows how fundamentally connected and similar all human beings actually are. And to that I say, Amen!

CHAPTER SIX

From the Old World to the New

The celebrated actors Robert Downey Jr. and Maggie Gyllenhaal have made careers out of playing complex characters who aren't always what they appear to be on the surface. Anyone who has seen Maggie's turn in the 2002 film *Secretary* knows exactly what I mean; so, too, do the legions of fans of Robert's dazzling work in such blockbusters as *Iron Man* and *Sherlock Holmes*, not to mention *Chaplin*, which depicts the silent-film star whose iconic physical play as the Tramp belied the genius mind behind the camera and in the editing room, and who had crossed the Atlantic from London to the United States to revolutionize cinema before being forced to return home. What these vivid characters represent, what they remind us, is that America is, at its best, a dynamic land where one's past does not determine one's future. This is especially true in the case of immigrants, newcomers from foreign lands who, within their own lives, struggled for a chance to rewrite the scripts of their birth.

Like so many Americans, Maggie's and Robert's ancestors came from places all over Europe. Their particular mixtures, it turned out, are also remarkably similar: both have Jewish ancestors from Eastern Europe on one side, and on the other side, non-Jewish ancestors scattered across the Old World and all the deeper into the past. Neither of them had any idea how close to the surface or far down their American roots ran. As with viewing their splendid array of films, the wonder was in the reveal.

Robert Downey Jr. is one of the most respected, most talented actors in Hollywood. Acting was in Robert's blood from the start. His father, Robert Downey Sr., directed avant-garde films, and his mother, Elsie, acted in her husband's projects. One of those films was of tremendous significance to my generation of African Americans. It also happens to be a film I've written extensively about. Released in 1969, *Putney Swope* satirizes the white power structure in the corporate world and its susceptibility to being toppled by the professional advancement of one black man. It was a brilliant, subversive film.

Four years before its debut, Robert was born, on April 4, 1965, in New York City. With two parents on the cutting edge of the film world, Robert acknowledged that his upbringing was less than conventional. "We lived in a loft near Greenwich Village. I knew that we were a little different from my friends in kindergarten." Robert laughed at memories of his childhood. "I'm not saying that my family doesn't have class of a sort, but we're a little more ragamuffiny, to be honest."

Robert describes his father as "very dedicated to his New York lifestyle," and it's true that New York figures prominently in Robert's personal history. He had a rough idea about his ancestry, but knew no details of it—and he wanted to know more. "Off the top of my head, there's Scottish, German. I heard there's some Irish. I know there's some Eastern European—I would say Russia or Poland," he said. "It's important to know as much as you can about where you come from. When you don't ask these questions, you never know who you are."

Robert *did* ask questions when he was a teenager; he just didn't get any straight answers. "I'd just get very vague answers, which led me to believe that, both of my parents being counterculture-artist types, that that was just a 'Who cares?' sort of deal," Robert recalled. "And I, prone to magical thinking, just figured they were kind of a Knights Templar thing, trying to keep it on the down-low, so when I found out about the majesty of my bloodline, it would be like a grail of sorts."

If there was any majesty in Robert's bloodline, we were determined to find it.

■ We started our exploration of his father's side by paying a visit to Robert Downey Sr. at his apartment in Manhattan, where he showed me a wall covered with generations of family photographs. For someone claiming to have little interest in his family tree, I told him, he had an awful lot of pictures going back an awfully long way. When I asked him if he had any idea where his grandparents came from, his answer echoed his son's: "Just that they were Jewish, and I heard the word Russia."

Robert Sr. had heard right. Born on January 20, 1872, Gussie Goldberg—Robert Downey Jr.'s paternal great-grandmother—arrived in New York in 1892, along with her mother, Ida, at the beginning of an enormous wave of Jewish migration. Gussie and Ida disembarked at Castle Garden, the predecessor to Ellis Island. The ship manifest shows Gussie's name, age (listed as eighteen, but her birth date would indicate that she was twenty), and last residence: Pren, a small town of about twenty-five hundred residents, with half of the population at the time Jewish. Today Pren is in Lithuania, but when the Goldbergs left in 1892, it was part of Russia.

The two women settled on Manhattan's Lower East Side, where some 135,000 other Eastern European Jews had already put down roots. Jonathan Sarna, an expert in Jewish history at Brandeis University, painted a picture for us of what Ida and Gussie would have encountered in their new neighborhood. "Chances are that they lived in a rather poor tenement. There were tremendous housing shortages, and the crowding led to innumerable health problems. Per square mile, more people lived on the Lower East Side than anywhere else on the face of the planet."

In the crush of immigration at the turn of the century, the lives of new Americans often proceeded without leaving much of a trace. Sometimes the sole record of an immigrant's existence surfaced only when he or she died. We found just such a record for Ida Goldberg, Gussie's mother. Neither Robert nor his father had ever heard of Ida before. Sadly, she died just ten months after reaching her Promised Land.

In 1897 her daughter Gussie married Joseph Elias in New York City. Elias was Robert's father's surname before he changed it to Downey, the name of his stepfather. Robert actually has the name Elias tattooed on his ankle. "I've always been drawn to that name," Robert explained. "I've always had some kind of intuitive desire to really find out what the skinny's been all along."

The skinny was nothing that Robert could have imagined. Of course Robert Sr. knew that his mother, Betty McLoughlin, wasn't Jewish. At the time this was a rarity; while today Jews marry outside of their faith at a rate of 50 percent, it was far from standard practice in the early twentieth century, when Robert's grandparents would have married. (In the most extreme cases, observant Jewish families might sit *shivah*—the traditional seven-day period of mourning—for a child who married outside of the faith.)

When we looked at Robert's father's mother's line, we uncovered some surprising information. First we found a commencement record for Betty's mother, Eleanor, or Ella, Ormay, who graduated from Normal College, now Hunter College, in 1904. We also found something that went back much earlier: the manifest for the ship *La Gascogne*, which brought two-year-old Ella Ormay, born on March 13, 1885, to America. Her country of origin: Austria, which at the time was part of the Austro-Hungarian Empire. From there we tracked the Ormay family back to what is now Hungary. Robert had heard that he had Hungarian relatives, but again, he knew little about them.

The Ormay family gravestones, which we located in Tata, Hungary, were inscribed in Hebrew. In other words, this side of the family—his mother's mother's—was Jewish as well. According to traditional Jewish law (as observed by the Orthodox and Conservative branches of Judaism), a child born to a Jewish mother is Jewish. Robert Downey Sr., therefore, is technically Jewish. "See, this is what happens when you don't ask these questions," Robert Jr. said when we told him about his father's surprise. Robert, with a non-Jewish mother himself, is not Jewish. But his own wife, Susan Levine, *is* Jewish, and he pointed out that his son, like his grandfather before him, is Jewish according to the Jewish faith. "It skipped a generation."

With the exception of Ida Goldberg, Robert's great-great-grandmother, we couldn't trace his father's family further than his great-grandparents—which, as we've learned, is sadly quite common among Eastern European Jews, given the persecutions they faced. On the other side of Robert's family tree, however, the genealogical records lead all the way back to the Middle Ages. When we first contacted him, Robert said he was interested in participating only if we could take his family back very far, in the ballpark of the fifteenth century. Confronted with this demand, this dare (he insisted that he was joking), we went back even farther.

■ Robert's oldest ancestor—his eighteenth great-grandfather—on his mother's mother's line was born during the *fourteenth* century. His name was Ruolf Guth, and he came of age in Switzerland during the Middle Ages. To be sure, we were lucky to find a record of Ruolf at all, because he was a peasant, the sort of person who tended to live and die without notice. But Switzerland had begun to preserve church records earlier than most other European countries, so on Ruolf's line, the paper trail continued. For almost a century, we discovered, Ruolf and his descendants lived as farmers and artisans in the canton of Zurich, part of the Holy Roman Empire run by a Catholic bishop.

When, in the 1500s, the Reformation took Europe by storm, splitting the Catholic and Protestant churches, Zurich was a hotbed of Protestant activity, prompting a Catholic reaction. As a result of their persecution, many families left and resettled in what is now Germany, then called the Palatinate. We believe Robert's family was part of this migration, given that seven generations after his birth, many of his descendants were living there.

They didn't stay for long, however. An examination of Robert's family tree shows that several of his ancestors from the same generation were born in Prussia and Germany but died in Pennsylvania. Like thousands of others in the early 1700s, Robert's ancestors fled a region that was coming apart at the seams. The Thirty Years' War (1618–48)—one of the longest continuous wars in modern history—started as a conflict between Catholics and Protestants. Where Catholics held power, Protestants found themselves in desperate peril. Fleeing persecution, we suspect that Robert's Protestant ancestors joined what became another exodus, as entire communities picked up and left the German states. Had Robert guessed when his first ancestors arrived in America, he would have said the mid-nineteenth century, or the beginning of the nineteenth century at the earliest. Yet, as it turns out, most of Robert's German ancestors arrived in America well before the American Revolution.

As we learned in our investigation of Kevin Bacon's family history, Pennsylvania beckoned as a religious and economic haven, mostly courtesy of pamphlets widely circulated by the colony's Quaker founder, William Penn, promising land and religious freedom to Europeans. One of those who answered Penn's call was Robert's original immigrant ancestor, his sixth great-grandfather, Johann Heinrich Schucker (who became John Henry Schucker in America). Johann Heinrich was born in Eckartshausen, Germany, in 1695. We don't know exactly when he arrived in America, but it was as early as the 1720s. We surmised this on the basis of his marriage license, which tells us that he and Anna Catharina Klapp were married in Oley, Pennsylvania, in 1728. We also were lucky enough to find Johann Heinrich's will. By the time he had it drawn up, he was calling himself Henry, and we can see at the end of the document his mark, which indicates that he was illiterate.

The promise of America for immigrants like Henry was land. In exchange, the new Pennsylvania colonists were required to swear allegiance to the British king. But in just a generation, that loyalty to the crown would be profoundly tested. Robert was about to learn that the American Revolution was not something that existed merely in history books for his family.

We found an application for the Daughters of the American Revolution, submitted by Robert's maternal grandmother, Fay Schoch Ford. "'Application for membership to the National Society of the Daughters of the American Revolution,'" Robert read. "My gosh. That's thrilling. That's really, really cool."

To be admitted to the DAR, a person must be certified as a direct descendant of someone who served during the American Revolution. Robert, too, would be entitled to become a member of the Sons of the American Revolution, as I am. (My ancestor, John Redman, was a free black who fought in the Continental army. My brother and I have the rare distinction of being African American members of the austere, traditionally white organization.) This application tells us that Robert has a Patriot ancestor as well: Tobias Schucker, Johann Heinrich's son and Robert's fifth great-grandfather. Born in 1747 in Pennsylvania, Tobias joined the Berks County Pennsylvania Militia in 1780 and served as a private, the military's lowest rank.

We found Tobias in the tax records of Berks County. Robert, reading from the transcribed form, commented: "No acres. No Negroes, thank the lord. No horses—could have done better. And one cattle." He shook his head, marveling at the information. "These are the people that I was expecting, nothing but this—one-cow laborers."

But all around Tobias, Pennsylvania was changing, transitioning from a place where subsistence farmers produced only enough for their own families to a booming agricultural economy after the Revolutionary War. In the 1800s, Pennsylvania grew more wheat than anywhere else in America, making it the country's breadbasket.

As Pennsylvania's fortunes changed, so too did Tobias's. By the time he died, Tobias had gone from owning no land as a younger man to being the proud proprietor of one hundred acres—a classic American success story. Yet, however much he prospered in the country whose independence he fought for, Tobias Shucker never abandoned his German roots. In fact, his will, dated 1813, was written in German.

There was another veteran among Robert's ancestors we wanted him to meet: Robert's great-great-grandfather, the lifelong Pennsylvanian James Peightal, who was born on April 26, 1847, in Woodcock Valley and died in 1925 in Huntingdon County. James was a soldier in the Pennsylvania Volunteers during the Civil War. Robert was comforted to learn James fought for the Union. A volume called *History of Pennsylvania Volunteers: 1861–1865* highlighted what James's unit did during the war. "On entering Petersburg," Robert read from the pages, "it was found that the enemy had escaped across the Appomattox and was flying southward. The men now became exceedingly impatient to return home, many of them being farmers and seed time rapidly approaching."

The enemy, of course, was the Confederate general Robert E. Lee and his army. Robert's ancestor James Peightal was near Appomattox in Virginia just before the Civil War ended, though the unit was not present for Lee's surrender. At the end of the day, James Peightal was an ordinary man more concerned about his life at home than that the course of the nation would be determined just after his departure.

■ Sometimes the past can be as mundane as the present, but buried in Robert's family tree was a first for us. On November 20, 1869, four years after the Civil War ended, James's father, Samuel Peightal—Robert's great-great-great-grandfather—received the estate of his brother John and his sister-in-law Sarah. The estate papers were filed at the same time, which means John and his wife must have died at the same time. What unfolded was one of the most dramatic family stories we've encountered in our research over the last five years. I showed Robert an arresting headline: "Triple murder, burglary, and arson. Trial of Gottlieb Bohner and Albert Von Bodenburg for the murder of John Peightal and Sarah Peightal."

The recorded trial testimony, which Robert read aloud, reveals every detail of the grisly crime: "Was at John Peightal's house, and saw the three bodies. The wound in John Peightal's body was in front of ear on the left side, and was made by a bullet, which did not come out. Mrs. Peightal was shot on the right side of the neck; the bullet did not come out. She was also wounded above her right ear; it was knocked in and the skull broken. They were all dead. All the bodies were covered with bed clothing, which has been set on fire." As is often said, truth is stranger than fiction, but the acclaimed actor sitting beside me did not expect such real-life drama in his family tree.

A newspaper account of the trial tells us that it had become known that John Peightal kept thousands of dollars in silver and gold at home, thinking it safer there than in the bank. The article also gives us some insight into the community he lived in and the life he had chosen: "Peightal was highly respected and regarded as a good, kind-hearted man, who was known to many in Huntingdon," Robert read on. "Many of his kin resided in the area—three brothers and their families living within a few miles of this home. These brothers were likewise successful, well-to-do farmers, and were said to have commanded a share of political influence. Samuel was elected director of the poor in 1860." Samuel, of course, was Robert's great-great-great-grandfather, and in his position he would have been in charge of helping indigent neighbors get back on their feet.

Two of the people he might have tried to help were his brother's killers. They were hanged on March 9, 1870, just five months after the crime was committed. From the gallows, the newspaper recorded the last words of one of the men, Albert Von Bodenburg: "I cannot speak English, do not know the laws of this country, have no friend who could do anything in my favor. Neither had I any money wherewith to make friends." Von Bodenburg, a recent immigrant, stood in stark contrast to Robert's ancestors, at this point long established in Pennsylvania. Interethnic tension, or class tension, played itself out in this German community in Pennsylvania in the murders of Robert's great-great-great-grandfather's brother and sister-in-law. "That's tragic for all of them," Robert said. "And it was his brother, too, who was a commissioner of sorts who would have been somebody you would have thought would have helped out his own kind."

What Robert found more shocking than the story itself was the fact that no one in his family had ever spoken of it. "Something as dramatic and noteworthy as that would have been passed down," he said. "I guess it was kept quiet. It sounds like typical, stoic Pennsylvania Germans."

Another way to break the silence: DNA.

■ Robert's father's line dates all the way back to Martin Ustick, who was born in Cornwall, England, in 1632. Robert Downey Jr. has identical Y-DNA to this old English ancestor. Robert's paternal haplogroup is R1b1b2a, which was confined to Mediterranean Europe during the Ice Age. It's a very common paternal haplogroup, and one he shares with two of our other guests, fellow actors Harry Connick Jr. and Kevin Bacon. "Six degrees indeed," Robert quipped.

On Robert's mother's side, we were able to trace his ancestors all the way back to Margaret, last name unknown, born in Pennsylvania in about 1822. His maternal haplogroup is H1e, a subgroup of H1. H1 originated thirteen thousand years ago in a woman living on the Iberian Peninsula. Today, almost 25 percent of the entire Spanish population shares that haplogroup, and occurrences of it remain quite high in the present-day populations of Britain and Ireland, ranging from levels of 15 to 40 percent. Robert shares this maternal haplogroup root with only one other guest in this series: Kyra Sedgwick, Kevin Bacon's wife and Robert's costar in the 1993 film *Hearts and Souls*.

In guessing what his admixture might be, Robert estimated 85 percent white (European), 10 percent black (African), and 5 percent Native American. Turns out, he is 100 percent European—a white man. "That's a pie with no slice missing," Robert observed. At this point, I couldn't help but recall Robert's standout performance in the war comedy *Tropic Thunder*, in which he plays a white method actor who has his skin surgically darkened so he can play a black man. "I have to admit I'm a little bit disappointed," Robert replied, "because I thought I had some African American influence in my blood. But I'll have to take what I can."

Using a different test that can reveal Jewish ancestry, we were able to zero in on one particular aspect of Robert's genome. According to this test, Robert is 79.89 percent European and 20.11 percent Middle Eastern, which is the descriptor for Jews. In Robert's case, the DNA information overlaps with his family tree. The part of Robert's DNA that points to Jewish ancestry was passed down through his father. This test allows us to determine that Robert's Jewish ancestry is Ashkenazi rather than Sephardic, which jibes with his Eastern European heritage. Ashkenazi Jews have a tremendous amount of "cousinness." Through this line, Robert is related, now on both sides of his family, to Harry and Kyra. There's one new addition as well: Barbara Walters. "This will make a very interesting three-subject interview with her," a floored Robert noted. Harry Connick Jr. and Robert share so much exact DNA, in fact, that we can determine that they are fourth cousins.

Robert had started this project with a basic knowledge of his genealogy, but along the way he received more information than he ever imagined. His greatest surprise was his long line of American ancestors. "The very deeply rooted American lineage is really kind of comforting and cool," he said. "I love America, and I'm glad I've been around here one way or another for a long time."

I asked Robert if he thinks these ancestors, from Ruolf in Switzerland to Tobias in Pennsylvania and on down the line, somehow shaped the person he is today. "I don't see how it couldn't. It's nature and nurture, and it's informing you whether you're conscious of it or not. So probably better to be conscious of it," he said. "I think it would be irresponsible not to communicate this down the bloodline from now on. You light up a constellation that wasn't visible before, and then you can navigate that to new places."

What if he could navigate to an old place, perhaps with a fairy godmother who could help him travel back in time to meet one of his ancestors, American or otherwise? Who would it be? He chose the Civil War veteran James Peightal. "Rather than having the personal glory of seeing Lee surrender, he was more interested in getting back to what was important to him," said Robert: his farm and his family. "I appreciate his attitude."

Maggie Gyllenhaal (b. 1977)

As an actress, Maggie Gyllenhaal has become known for her daring and eclectic choices. She became an indie sensation after her raw performance in the film *Secretary*, and she was nominated for an Academy Award for her role in *Crazy Heart* in 2010. Born on November 16, 1977, in New York City, Maggie is the child of filmmakers; her father is a director, her mother a screenwriter. Her brother, Jake, is also a well-known actor. "My parents weren't movie stars," she qualifies. "They were making small movies, so it didn't feel like a kind of fantasy or glamour life. They both had jobs that seemed like they fed them and excited them."

From the time she was about twelve, Maggie knew she wanted to be an actress. Her eyes lit up as she recalled an early experience on one of her parents' sets. "They worked with really interesting actresses. I remember Debra Winger in particular. She has a power about her. . . . I hid down and just watched through all the equipment this actress working. I was really serious about it even when I was little."

Maggie grew up being called Maggie. As far as she knew, that was her name. Recently, while changing her name legally to include her husband's—she has been married to the actor Peter Sarsgaard since 2009—she learned that her given name is actually Marguerite. If something as personal as her own first name could be a mystery to her, we wondered what other secrets might be lurking in Maggie's family tree.

■ Maggie has always described herself as "half Swedish and half Russian Jewish." In terms of her upbringing, she said, "The Jewish, New York side of my family I think played a bigger part in my life, not so much from a spiritual standpoint as a cultural standpoint."

So it was on that side that we started. Maggie's mother, Naomi Achs, was born on March 4, 1946, in New York City. Maggie describes her mother as analytical and intellectual and curious, born into a family of strong women. Both her ancestors and Robert's were part of the same massive exodus from Eastern Europe at the turn of the twentieth century. This was the height of Jewish migration to America. It was then that Maggie's great-grandfather, Benjamin Silbowitz, stepped off the boat at Ellis Island and settled on the Lower East Side.

Like many of his neighbors on the Lower East Side, Benjamin Silbowitz's journey to New York had been long and arduous. Born in what is now Latvia (then Russia), he grew up in a time and place where Jewish ancestry was a distinct disadvantage. Jewish history expert Jonathan Sarna explained: "By the end of the nineteenth century in Russia, there are many laws that severely restrict the kinds of occupations Jews can enter, where Jews can live, whether they can get higher education, and so forth."

At the time, Russia was in the midst of a bitter war against the Japanese, a war that fueled a seemingly insatiable demand for soldiers. "Thousands of Jews are conscripted," Sarna said. "The Russian army tended to treat soldiers like cannon fodder. It's no great surprise that somebody would have decided to escape." Jews in the Russian army were regularly beaten and humiliated, ridiculed for their inability to speak Russian and for their refusal to eat pork. Many were forced to convert to Christianity. Young Jewish men were desperate not to join.

We discovered that Maggie's great-granduncle, Saul Silbowitz, left behind a priceless oral history in which he told the story of her great-grandfather, his brother Benjamin. In it, he explained how some found a way out. Until we brought it to her attention, Maggie never knew this history existed. Now she was reading from a transcribed version of it: "There was a secret way to leave and cross the Russian border into Germany.

There were certain agents who operated for money to help these young men who did not serve the czar to cross into Germany. From there on they were on their own."

The personal history Benjamin had shared with his granddaughter, Naomi, Maggie's mother, corroborated this. "The Jews weren't allowed to own land in my grandfather's time in Russia," Naomi said. "He would tell me stories that they were very badly treated. The young Jewish boys were going to be conscripted into the army. A couple of them cut off their toes and ran away in the middle of the night and did whatever they could to avoid being in the czar's army."

Saul said that Benjamin made plans to come to America when he became draft-eligible at age eighteen; he estimated the year to be 1904 or 1905. We searched for records that might tell us whether Benjamin had actually been called to military service. We found our answer in a document from Russia dated 1906. It was the Conscription Evasion List, a list of families of Jewish men who were forced to pay a three-hundred-ruble fine for evasion of military duty (the equivalent of almost four thousand dollars today). That they were able to pay this fee indicates that Benjamin's family in Russia must have been at least somewhat well-to-do. Maggie had always heard that they had nothing.

He arrived on the *Barcelona* in December 1906. From documentation of his voyage, we know that he had three dollars in his pocket—almost nothing. "When Benjamin was finally let out from Ellis Island," Maggie read from her great-granduncle Saul's account, "he was on his own in a strange land, strange language. So Benjamin had to sink or swim. He landed a job to cut flowers for ladies' hats. Three dollars a week. He slept in a horse-drawn wagon parked on the streets overnight. He persevered hard, and after many jobs he became a cutter in the ladies' garment trade." Maggie recalled a story she had been told by her mother about her great-grandfather's business: "He used to make my mom coats out of leftover scraps from when he worked as a cutter."

After some years living on New York's Lower East Side, Benjamin moved his wife and daughters up to the Bronx, where he opened a small family business. "There was a gas station and a little store on a little corner street," Naomi said, describing it from memory. "My mother and her sisters pumped gas, and they went to school. They did extremely well. They went on to do these things that I don't think anybody dreamed of."

While very few women had professions at this time, Naomi's mother,

Maggie's grandmother, Ruth, graduated from medical school and became a respected pediatrician. (Maggie's grandaunt Frieda, Ruth's sister, was a lawyer.) Naomi said her mother was on call eighteen hours a day, alongside her father, who also worked at the Brooklyn Jewish Hospital as a surgeon. "Being a professional working person and being a mother at that time was really, really difficult."

Maggie has always taken great pride in her grandmother's unlikely accomplishments. "I think for my grandmother to have come from these immigrant parents from Russia, and her father having done what he did, and then to have become a doctor, and to have raised my mother, that was an incredible thing to do."

Ruth Silbowitz Achs made remarkable contributions to the field of medicine. She discovered that the palm prints of babies born to mothers who had German measles early in their pregnancies could reveal birth defects that might otherwise escape detection. This would be an incredible accomplishment for any doctor, but for a Jewish woman of her generation, it was unprecedented. Medical schools at the time had quotas, allowing in only a small number of Jews and a small number of women. Ruth achieved tremendous success in a field that was both anti-Semitic and misogynist.

"This is what I've heard a lot about, this kind of thing," Maggie said, "and these women, my grandmother and my aunt, who were professionals and women such a long time ago. It's such a different time." I asked Maggie where she thought the Silbowitz women got their incredible drive. "I feel like it must have had something to do with their parents," she answered. "But I don't know. Maybe it's in their blood." Perhaps Maggie's middle name, Ruth, wasn't the only thing she inherited from her grandmother, who had died before she was born.

All the accomplishments in the world couldn't restore the lost paper trail of the Silbowitz family. Such is the fate of most European Jews. Centuries of persecution, forced migrations, and destruction have meant that records were lost and destroyed. As a result, on Maggie's Jewish side, we cannot go back further than her great-grandparents.

On the other side of the family tree, however, the paper trail is long and intact—and extremely impressive. Once again, the self-described half-Swedish Maggie Gyllenhaal was in for a surprise.

■ Maggie's family tree stretches back more than a thousand years. When we follow these lines into the past, they travel through some of the most important events in European history, in this case, back to the time of the First Crusade. Maggie, we learned, descends from Henry I of England, born in 1068.

The reason we could trace Maggie's bloodlines back so far was because she descends from royalty—from kings and queens, earls and dukes in England, France, and Sweden, who kept careful records of their existence in order to establish monarchies and determine inheritance.

Outside of Philadelphia, Pennsylvania, we tracked down a member of the Gyllenhaal family who has done extensive research on the family's noble lines. Ed Gyllenhaal is Maggie's cousin, although they've never met. He works in the Glencairn Museum, where we spoke with him and his wife, Kirsten.

"All of the Swedish nobles, whether they live in Sweden or abroad, are listed in the Swedish Peerage Book," Ed explained. "We can see here that Maggie's father, Stephen Gyllenhaal, is listed, as are Maggie and Jake."

Maggie had heard occasional stories about her illustrious Swedish background, but she was never sure how much of it to believe. "I heard the story that I kind of always thought was a myth about Gyllenhaal, that my great-great-great-great somebody or other on my dad's side studied butterflies, and that he had made such a beautiful book about butterflies that the king of Sweden sent all of his minions out to find this poor farmer, or whatever he was, who happened to have made this beautiful book and brought him back to the palace and ended up making him some kind of Swedish royalty and putting him up to live in a golden hall, and that Gyllenhaal meant 'golden hall.'"

We can debunk the myth—at least some of it. The real story behind the Gyllenhaals' elevation to nobility isn't quite what Maggie had heard. Ed Gyllenhaal set the record straight for us. "The Gyllenhaals became noble in 1652 when Nils Gunnesson Haal was knighted by Queen Christina for bravery in the Thirty Years' War. It was the tradition at that time, when a soldier was knighted, that he could change his name. So his last name, which had been Haal, became Gyllenhaal, *gyllen* meaning "golden" in Swedish."

Maggie did have one piece of the family legend almost right. Her fourth great-grandfather, Leonard Gyllenhaal, born on December 3, 1752, in Södra Härene, Älvsborgs County, in the southern Västergötland province, had a particular, peculiar passion: collecting beetles. Leonard's collection of thirteen hundred previously unidentified insect species is still used today at the University of Uppsala in Sweden. Leonard spent thirty years compiling a work called *Insecta Suecica*. Written in Latin, it describes and catalogs all the insects of Sweden and is considered a classic in scientific history.

Leonard holds great significance in Maggie's family for other reasons: he was the grandfather of Anders Gyllenhaal, Maggie's original immigrant ancestor and her great-great-grandfather. Anders Leonard Gyllenhaal was born in the parish of Ramsberg on July 1, 1842. Two days after his twenty-fourth birthday, on July 3, 1866, Anders left the town of Torp, Sweden, for North America. No more specific destination was given than that, but we know that he went to Illinois, where he would eventually connect with an extremely interesting character on Maggie's family tree, her third great-grandfather, Swain Nelson. Like all immigrants, Maggie's ancestors brought with them their own traditions and their own languages. The tension between the New World and the Old, between assimilation and ethnic identity, eventually would become one of the hallmarks of American culture, as newcomers created communities that to them felt like home.

Maggie had never heard of Swain Nelson, but we were lucky in our search to uncover his handwritten memoir, which chronicles his life, in exceptionally colorful language, in Sweden and America. According to his "Moving Out" permit—the Holy Grail for any genealogist hoping to trace someone of Swedish descent—Sven Nilsson was born on January 30, 1828, in Vinslöv, Skäne, the southernmost province of Sweden, and was "known to be of good reputation." He anglicized his name when he arrived in America.

There was more to learn about Swain's life in Sweden before that point, though. In his memoir, which Maggie read aloud, Swain writes of a fateful encounter with a man who would introduce him to the two great passions that would shape his life. "At home nothing particular happened until one day, a blind man named Hoppman and a 12-year-old boy came to sell books and almanacs. The boy led the blind man, who carried on his back a violin in a bag made of fox skins." Mr. Hoppman became a close family friend and Swain's teacher, making a second, crucial appearance in the memoir. "It happened one time during Mr. Hoppman's teaching school at our house that one of his little daughters, Sophie, came to see him. She was the prettiest girl I had ever seen, and I liked to play with her, but she was shy with me." Over time, Swain fell madly in love with Sophie, but her shyness never abated. "She was often in my mind," he wrote, "and after some time, when an opportune moment came, I ventured to tell her that I loved her. She very kindly answered that she could only love me as a friend." Over the years, Swain tried to get Sophie to change her mind, but again and again and again, she turned him down.

Needless to say, Swain was crushed, but as luck would have it, Mr. Hoppman introduced him to something else at around the same time that seemed to fill the void in his broken heart: Swedenborgianism, a fairly obscure branch of Christianity based on the teachings of the eighteenth-century Swedish scientist and philosopher Emanuel Swedenborg. Professor of theology Thane Glenn explained the history of the religion: "Swedenborg himself never intended to start a religious sect. He simply published his theology with the idea that this would bring a new light, a new way of life to Christianity. The heart of his theology is this idea that people of all faiths have pathways to God and to heaven and to a heavenly life. And Swedenborgianism calls us to live lives of service to others." Today only about eight thousand Americans practice Swedenborgianism—in fact, 90 percent of all Swedenborgians are not from Sweden at all.

Fascinated by Swedenborgianism but no less lovelorn, Swain, at age twenty-four, struck out for America. He ended up in a town called Defiance, Ohio, where he tried all manner of hard work, from farm labor to cigar making, all the while battling poverty and disease. Even with an ocean between them, Swain could not forget his heart's desire, Sophie, and one day he had a revelation. "It happened on Sunday in the spring of my second year in America," Maggie read, "while I was walking along the Miami River, at Defiance. A thought came so strongly to my mind, about her whom I so loved, that I kneeled down under one of those large trees, and prayed to the Lord to give me her for a wife." Convinced that God had heard his prayers, Swain wrote to Mr. Hoppman in Sweden and begged him to convey his message to his daughter. "This guy wouldn't give up!" laughed Maggie. "I think that's really true about the Gyllenhaal side."

At last, after years of refusing Swain's proposals, Sophie relented and joined him in Chicago. They married on July 18, 1857, a Friday, which, Swain writes, "was Sophie's favorite day." Swain's luck was changing. He had finally married the girl of his dreams, and after her arrival, his career began to take off. From his "Moving Out" record, we learned Swain was a gardener. In America he established himself as a landscape architect. Despite the barriers of an unfamiliar language and culture, not to mention personal travails, he ultimately found great success. In 1865, the year of

President Lincoln's assassination, he was commissioned to design Lincoln Park, one of Chicago's most beloved public spaces.

Swain continued to adhere to Swedenborgianism in Chicago, and, in the 1890s, when followers of the New Church preferred to live in their own enclaves for self-protection and preservation, Swain and other Swedenborgians founded The Park in Glenview. Among the other residents there were Maggie's great-great-grandfather Anders Gyllenhaal and his wife, Selma Nelson. His grandson, Leonard Gyllenhaal (not to be confused with the beetle collector), brought the family religion with him when he moved to Pennsylvania.

Just north of Philadelphia, in 1899, the second Leonard Gyllenhaal helped build a town called Bryn Athyn. Like their counterparts in Chicago, the founders of Bryn Athyn wanted to create an intentional community based on their shared faith. Their descendants live there to this day—and it's where Maggie's father grew up. Stephen Roark Gyllenhaal was born on October 4, 1949, in Cleveland, Ohio, but he and his family moved to Bryn Athyn when he was in fifth grade.

Ultimately Stephen left Bryn Athyn and the Swedenborgians. His own children were not raised in the faith of his parents and forebears. Maggie described her father as "operatic," a person who feels things intensely with a unique way of seeing things and an unwillingness to be bound by one way of thinking. "I'd be really young, like six or seven, and he used to say to me things like, 'You see that tree outside? What color do you think it is?' And I'd say, 'Um, it's green.' He would say, 'I'd say it's green, too. What if the color that I'm calling green really looks like the color that you call blue? Imagine what the world would look like to me.'" Maggie laughed. "It's pretty cool, but it's also pretty scary if you're six."

◼ Through her paternal grandmother, Virginia Childs, Maggie's family tree stretches back to the Pilgrims of New England, some of the earliest immigrants to America. John Lothropp, Maggie's tenth great-grandfather, was born in England in 1584.

No one had ever spoken of John Lothropp in Maggie's family. Her English ancestor, however, was a noteworthy figure, a preacher in the Independent Church of London, an underground congregation organized in the early 1600s. At that time, the Church of England was the seat of religious power in the country, controlling all religious practice and allowing no dissenters. To the church Lothropp and his followers were heretics, and in 1632 he was arrested and jailed in London's Newgate Prison for two years, where he was subjected to intense pressure and interrogation. Lothropp never relented, however, and for reasons that remain unknown, the authorities eventually released him, possibly because Lothropp's five children had become homeless after his wife, Hannah, died while he was in jail.

A pariah in England, Lothropp, his five children, and some of his followers set sail for the New World in 1634. Among its earliest immigrants, they arrived just a decade and a half after the *Mayflower* and settled on Cape Cod, where the Lothropp name is still well known today. Helen Taber, a ninety-year-old descendant in Barnstable, Massachusetts, is a proud keeper of Lothropp's history. In fact, the house where Helen and I met was built for him. Today, the library houses one of the community's most prized possessions: the Reverend Lothropp's Bible, which he brought from England on the *Griffin*. Helen pointed out some patches on the pages. One night, the story goes, when Lothropp blew out his candle, a spark burned through several pages, and he patched up the holes and rewrote the burned text from memory.

Helen Taber is in awe of her ancestor, the early American minister. "He brought that congregation over here, and they flourished," she said. "He had the courage of his convictions. He was willing to sacrifice his life."

A direct descendant of John Lothropp, Maggie can trace her roots all the way back to the Pilgrims—and to the family lines that would become a significant part of the American establishment. With ancestors in America since 1634, Maggie is about American as American gets.

"That is so interesting, because I so don't identify that way," she responded, almost uncomfortable with this new knowledge. "I definitely go with the other side, like New York, intellectual Jewish culture. It's never how I identified, as part of the roots of America."

■ We had come to the end of the paper trail—but thanks to DNA science, we can search for further clues. Maggie's Jewish ancestry comes from her mother, who is 100 percent Jewish. On this side, we traced her direct maternal line back to her third great-grandmother, Yetta, last name unknown, who was born in Russia in the mid- to late 1830s. By testing Maggie's mitochondrial DNA, we learned that Maggie's maternal haplogroup is K1a1b1a, a subgroup of the haplogroup K, which arose about thirty-five thousand years ago in the Near East. Maggie's particular branch, K1a1b1a, is specific to Jewish populations, especially Ashkenazi Jews whose roots lie in Central and Eastern Europe. This is, of course, Maggie's background.

The Jewish DNA passed down by Maggie's ancestors contains a wealth of unique genetic information. The president of the company Family Tree DNA, Bennett Greenspan, told us why. "For the last thousand, fifteen hundred years, there's been a lot of cultural pressure within the Jewish community to marry within. Especially for the hundreds of years where Jews were living in Europe in the ghettos, the only choice for a Jew to marry was another Jew." This meant that extended cousins were marrying extended cousins. "They all share a restricted common gene pool," Greenspan said, "going back six hundred or seven hundred years."

Maggie is part of this genetically isolated group of Jewish people, and this portion of her DNA unlocks a window to ancient history. Scientists have concluded that 40 percent of Eastern European Jews share genetic lineages that reach back two or three thousand years, remarkably to just four women. Their birthplaces and family names have been lost to time, but their genetic legacy has endured. Today about 3.5 million Jewish people descend from one of these four maternal ancestors. Greenspan confirmed that Maggie is indeed one of these people. "She has something on the order of 150 exact matches in our system. From a genealogical and genetic standpoint, you kind of hit the jackpot."

I told Maggie that she is genetically Jewish all the way back to Judea and the Bible, "as Jewish as Jewish can get." She insisted that she was not surprised. "I feel Jewish. I feel at least half Jewish!" she exclaimed. "Recently I went to this great Russian restaurant, and it just completely appeals to me. I wanted to eat the red caviar and blinis." We laughed, but then she posed a serious question. "I wonder, is it the culture that I'm responding to? Is it just how I was brought up, or is it something in my genes?"

Maggie's ancestors, we learned, came from all over Europe: Latvia, Sweden, England, France. How far back will the DNA on her other side bring us? We traced Maggie's direct paternal line back to her ninth great-grandfather, Gunne Olofsson Haal, born in Härene, Sweden, around 1634. We administered a DNA test to her father, Stephen, to find out where his paternal ancestors originated. Maggie's paternal haplogroup is G2a, a subgroup of the haplogroup G. Haplogroup G arose about sixteen thousand years ago in southwestern Asia or the Caucasus region. With the advent of agriculture in the Near East about ten thousand years ago, haplogroup

G spread into Europe, where it can be found at low levels today. In Sweden, however, it's found at levels of less than 10 percent in the general population. The occurrence of haplogroup G increases slightly—to about 12 percent—in the eastern province of Sweden called Uppsala, where the university housing Leonard Gyllenhaal's beetle collection is. Although the percentages are not high, the results of Maggie's DNA test and her family's exhaustive paper trail are compatible.

Roughly twenty thousand years separate the origin of Maggie's maternal haplogroup and her paternal haplogroup. She viewed the results with some irony, noting the discrepancy between the length of the paper trail on each side and scientific knowledge. "Interesting, because on my mom's side, because they're not the establishment, the paper trail is so much shorter."

The results of Maggie's admixture test are, again, compatible with what we've seen in her genealogy: a whopping 99 percent European, and 1 percent Asian, or Native American. While it's possible that someone of so-called impure blood entered one of Maggie's lines, it's also possible that it is a rounding error indicative of no Native American ancestry. Because of her Ashkenazi background, we had her DNA analyzed by Family Tree DNA, which specializes in the genetics of Jewish people. According to this analysis, Maggie is 60.1 percent European, specifically Northern European, and 39.9 percent Middle Eastern, which is Jewish.

It turns out that, through her mother's DNA, Maggie is related to three of our other guests: Harry Connick Jr., Barbara Walters, and Kyra Sedgwick. These are her distant cousins, people with whom she shares at least one ancestor who lived during the past three hundred years. As we recall, her genealogy revealed relatives whom Maggie never could have dreamed of, among them the Presidents Bush. But if she could go back in time, if her fairy godmother showed up right now and said she would take her anywhere, to meet anyone, Maggie said she would want to pick one ancestor from each side of the family. With such a long lineage, I couldn't possibly refuse.

On her father's side, she went with romance over science and religion and chose Sophie, her great-great-grandmother. "I would like to know what was going on with her, you know, that she said so clearly so many times, 'No, I don't want to marry you, Sven,' and then he prayed under the tree in Defiance and she changed her mind. I would like the feminist revision of history from her point of view." Maggie's confusion over this story hasn't abated. "Or who knows? Maybe she was going to say, 'I had a fantasy of what love was going to be, but when he left I realized I loved him and I missed him, and I wanted to be with him.' Who knows?"

On her mother's side, Maggie didn't go back in time very far at all. "Honestly, I would really like to have met my grandmother, who I'm named after. She was pretty incredible—obviously probably very complicated like everybody else in the world. But to have come from these immigrant parents from Russia and her father having done what he did, and then to become a doctor and to have raised my mother . . ." Maggie trailed off. Whereas her desire to meet Sophie seemed to stem from an intellectual desire to get into the mind of a nineteenth-century immigrant woman, her desire to meet her grandmother, Ruth Silbowitz Achs, seemed motivated by a very deep love. It is that combination of head and heart, curiosity and love, that has driven all of our ancestors forward, made them all willing to take risks, exchange the known for the unknown, and to leave their old homes behind to build new ones.

The search for Robert's and Maggie's ancestral roots took us to Russia, across Europe, and up and down the Eastern Seaboard. It also kept pulling us back to New York City, the place where so many immigrants have come to become American.

We all build on what our ancestors have given us, sometimes by embracing our past and sometimes by rebelling against it. When Maggie's father left Bryn Athyn and the Swedenborgian faith, he was escaping the beliefs and traditions of generations of his ancestors. He was also taking part in a vast social upheaval that would ultimately transform American culture. Maggie is a product of this transition, as is Robert Downey Jr. In the 1950s and 1960s, the ethnic enclaves that had defined this country for centuries began to splinter. In the process, Old World identities began to fade, and people increasingly thought of themselves as American, nothing more.

Well before then, however, the rebels were immigrants like Robert's and Maggie's ancestors—Jews from Russia living alongside people from Ireland and Italy, just as today the city's streets are full of people from Latin America, Asia, Africa, and the Caribbean. Each year, the United States admits 1 million legal immigrants, a number that is roughly the same as it was in 1906, when Benjamin Silbowitz—Maggie's great-grandfather—got off a boat at Ellis Island. And each of them, every day, contributes something new. So, whether your ancestor arrived with the Pilgrims or with the latest wave of new Americans, as an indentured servant, a religious icono-clast, or a slave, at some point, in the near or distant past, your family epic intersected with the nation's—hence, all of us—and we are more vibrant, more diverse, more *American* for it.

CHAPTER SEVEN

Shadows

Samuel L. Jackson, Condoleezza Rice, and Ruth Simmons all share a remarkably similar quest for their lost roots. All three have long heard rumors that at least one white man, a slave owner, fathered one of their enslaved ancestors. Until now, they have never had any way to establish the truth about these suspicions. The absence of a paper trail is what binds African Americans together—stories with middles and endings but rarely a beginning other than vague notions about oceans and rivers crossed from freedom to slavery and back up to freedom. That doesn't mean the search is futile, however. Now, thanks to our ability to interpret clues hidden in plain sight and clues hidden in DNA, we can piece together the knowledge of these three remarkable African Americans' deep family roots that slavery stole for centuries—but not for good.

I have much in common with Sam, Condoleezza, and Ruth. Each of us was born into the segregated world of Jim Crow, not far from the land where our ancestors were once enslaved. I grew up in Piedmont, West Virginia. Out of Piedmont's two thousand residents in 1950—the year I was born—about three hundred were black, and we all lived in one of three segregated neighborhoods. The color of our skin set strict limits on where we could live and go to school, where we could work, and with whom we could socialize. But it also bonded us together culturally in innumerable ways. We created complex and nurturing communities that helped us to survive the stifling inequalities of racial discrimination.

As an actor, his intensity is almost unrivaled. Samuel L. Jackson is that rare Hollywood star who garners both big results at the box office and plaudits from critics. Starting out on stage and then in television, he has since had an enviable, eclectic career in film. Although the role that most people point to as the one that changed his career is that of the extemporizing hit man Jules Winnfield in *Pulp Fiction*, Sam considers his roles as the crack addict Gator in *Jungle Fever* and Zeus Carver in *Die Hard with a Vengeance* to be the pivotal ones. Add to it roles in such blockbusters as *Star Wars* and *The Avengers* and the critically important slave revenge fantasy, *Django Unchained*. For those coming up behind him in Hollywood, Jackson's career has opened doors previously closed.

In 2011 Sam took on an another immense challenge: starring in his first Broadway show, *The Mountaintop*, and portraying none other than Dr. Martin Luther King Jr. I would find it intimidating to play such a larger-than-life figure. Sam agreed that evoking the public King would have been daunting, but the private King was a different story. "We come into a motel room, we close the door, he slumps his shoulders, he takes his coat off," Sam said, describing the man behind the mystique. "Whole other cat."

Sam's connection to Martin Luther King is more than artistic. In 1968, as a freshman at King's alma mater, Morehouse College, in Atlanta, Sam was given the honor of serving as an usher at Dr. King's funeral. Radicalized by the assassination, Sam joined the Black Power movement. "I wasn't a real advocate of this nonviolence and that whole thing," Sam said. "I was hanging around the SNCC—the Student Nonviolent Coordinating Committee—office a lot. I spent more time with guys like Stokely [Carmichael] and [H.] Rap [Brown], and at the time my favorite slogan about the revolution was 'At a certain point caution becomes cowardice.'" Sam and other students led protests against the school itself, opposing the fact that in the late 1960s and early 1970s, when he was a student there, there was no black studies program, no black representation on the board of trustees, and no involvement from the black community, either off campus or on. "It was all manner of things that the students had no voice in," he said. "It was run like a plantation." He still carries some of that righteous anger into his most electrifying screen work.

As a teenager, Sam never thought about being an actor, although he'd been on stage for as long as he could remember. His aunt Edna was a performing arts teacher, and Sam was included in every show she did. But to consider performing as a profession? No, that didn't cross his mind. "I had no idea how Sidney Poitier or Harry Belafonte got to where they were. That wasn't an option," he laughed. "But the one thing I had decided by this age was that I was not going to spend my life in Chattanooga, Tennessee. The world held a lot of interest for me, and I was going to get out there and get some of that."

Sam left Chattanooga to attend Morehouse, but his eighteen years growing up there fundamentally shaped the person he is today. He was born on December 21, 1948, in Washington, D.C., but was raised from the time he was very young in Chattanooga. He described the Chattanooga of his youth as a "quiet, southern town, extremely segregated. There was still Whites Only signs, and I only interacted with white people when I went to town. When the county fair came to town every year, there was one day that was the black day that we could go to the fair, and that was on Friday."

Family was the first line of defense against the sting of segregation. For Sam, that meant his mother, Elizabeth Montgomery Jackson, and his grandparents, Edgar Montgomery Jr. and Pearl Brown Montgomery. Pearl "was pretty much the first person I saw every morning when I got up," Sam said wistfully. "She was a wonderful, wonderful, wonderful, loving person. She was a chastiser. She was an encourager. She hugged me, kissed me a lot, gave me a lot of love. I was in the kitchen with her a lot."

His father had abandoned his family before Sam could walk, but, as he explained, "I didn't have a sense of not having a father, because I had my grandfather there in the house, who was my best friend. He'd tell me stories. We'd listen to radio dramas. He bought me my first knife, tell me we could carve together. We'd just whittle. We weren't making anything, but the fact that I had a knife and he had one was so cool to me." In an interesting way, Sam feels that not having a father actually gave him more stability than he might otherwise have had. "Most of the kids that I knew who had a father weren't real happy that they had one. Dad was either drunk, beating up Mom or beating them up, so I was kind of glad I didn't have one, somebody bothering me like that."

To Sam, his grandfather was larger than life, his hero. But to most of white Chattanooga, he was probably just another Negro janitor pushing a broom. Sam said he wasn't traumatized by the blatant racism he experienced himself growing up, but he was clearly still angry about the disrespectful treatment heaped upon his grandfather—treatment he outwardly accepted. "Those white people my grandfather worked for, they were always Mr. So-and-so-and-so, but he was twice their age, and they were still calling him Ed. I mean, being called 'Boy, boy, boy,' so my grandfather was a boy. He's sixty years old, and he was still a boy."

Many of us who grew up during Jim Crow look back on that time with mixed emotions. Segregation was inhumane and demeaning, yet our communities that arose in spite of it were nurturing and united. "Integration changed a lot," Sam said. "One of the things integration changed in my mind is the quality of education that black kids started to get because of the care of the teachers and who they were. These teachers had to make home visitations for every student that was in their class. They had a very good idea of who I was and where I came from, and the kind of people that were raising me." None of us would want to go back to that era, but there is a sense in our generation that something was lost.

But that was only *within* the black community. Outside was another story. Sam said his grandparents abided by the rules that the white South inflicted upon them, but he recalled the stand his grandmother took against her white employers when they accused her of forgetting her manners, thereby forgetting her place. "Miss Pearl, better known as Big Shorty," he said, warmly recalling the woman he called "loving and spicy," "was a domestic. She was 'the help.' The people she used to work for used to give me presents every year, Christmas and whatever, and she would make me write a thank-you note. I resented that. Apparently she'd forgotten or I didn't remember, and it took too long for that thank-you note to come back, and one day they said something to her about, 'Pearl, did Sam like that gift we gave him?' She's like, 'Yes.' 'Well, we ain't got no thank-you note. Y'all must not be raisin' that boy right.' And she took her apron off and walked out the door and never went back to that job." Her employers begged her to come back, telling Pearl how miserable their daughters were without her—daughters *she* had raised—but Pearl stood her ground. "That's who she was," Sam said.

Still, opposition to white people was rare. The dynamic between the black and white community was immutable, and as Sam was taught by his elders, it was dangerous to challenge it. This imbalance of power was born and perpetuated in slavery, particularly through sexual relations between master and slave. The history of these relations is written on our faces and our features, but few African Americans have ever been able to establish the facts.

■ Two white families figure prominently in Sam's Montgomery family lore: the Troutmans and the Branhams. Branham was actually a family name—Sam's great-grandmother was Lilly Branham Montgomery—but Sam had heard of the Troutmans as well. "They're just names that fly around in family history," Sam said. "I don't even know if I knew that they were white or not. I just knew that they were talking about Mrs. Troutman, and her name comes up in terms of being a family friend."

Mrs. Troutman—Bessie—was indeed white. Her connection to Sam's family is unclear, but it is firmly established in a series of financial transactions from early in the twentieth century.

Sam's family history actually has its roots in northern Georgia. It was in Rome, at his granduncle Arthur's house, that Sam spent every summer with his aunts and uncles and cousins. In the city there was always the threat of a confrontation with a white person, but in the country, Sam was surrounded only by relatives, only by black people. His summers on the farm in Georgia were idyllic—a far cry from the early 1920s, when Sam's grandfather lived there.

His name was Edgar Montgomery, and he was born in Floyd County, Georgia, on July 21, 1902. He didn't move to Chattanooga until he was twenty years old. Edgar had several brothers, some who moved to Detroit, and some who stayed in Georgia, but Edgar and another brother left for Tennessee. I wondered if Sam knew why.

He had heard stories: "He and one of his brothers got into an argument with somebody, and they shot a white person and had to leave town." As we have seen with so many family stories, this one was grounded in the truth, but the details were off. A series of newspaper articles from the local paper helped us piece together what really happened. "Mystery Murder Is Kept Secret in Armuchee County," one headline proclaimed. We learn that "Lloyd Starr, a young Negro, was shot at a Negro frolic late Wednesday night and died of his wounds Friday."

This was 1922, the height of Prohibition, and here was a story involving liquor, a murder, and African Americans at a "Negro frolic" in Rome, Georgia—in other words, trouble. A follow-up article says, "All the Negroes in the community were trying to keep the matter quiet." The reason for their silence was clear to Sam. "Black-on-black crime," he said. "Why wouldn't they?"

But apparently somebody did talk, because there is a third article in the series: "Ten Negroes Held in Jail as a Result of Fatal Shooting." There was a roundup of black men in the community. One of the men identified as being held was Clarence Montgomery—Sam's granduncle Clarence. Sam's aunt Edna told us that his grandfather Edgar was also among the many men arrested, although his name didn't appear in the article. It seems quite possible that their involvement in the crime, whether or not they pulled the trigger, precipitated their departure from Georgia.

This is where we return to Bessie Troutman. Bessie Troutman, according to Edna and other relatives, helped Sam's grandfather and granduncle get out of jail in 1922 and then helped them escape. We wondered what the relationship between Bessie Troutman, a white woman, and the Montgomerys was.

The federal census from 1910 offers some clues. Edgar's father, Miles Montgomery, born in 1873—Sam's great-grandfather—was a self-employed farmer renting the land on which he worked. A mere nine years later, according to a deed we found, Miles Montgomery purchased 160 acres of land near Rome, Georgia, for an astonishing $6,000. That is the equivalent of $75,600 today—not an insubstantial amount, especially for an African American man who had previously been a farmer with no land of his own. A promissory note in the file lists a series of four $500 payments plus a final one of $3,000, due to the lender on January 1, 1925. Before he could take possession of the land, he was required to pay a $1,000 deposit in cash. Sam was able to guess who loaned the $1,000 to Miles. Bessie Troutman's name is on the document. What this means is that a white woman stood for a loan for Sam's great-grandfather in 1919. This is the same Bessie Troutman who three years later would help Miles's sons Edgar and Clarence get out of jail—and out of the state of Georgia.

Bessie Troutman was the matriarch of a prominent landowning family near Rome, both before and after the Civil War. The Troutmans and the Montgomerys had been in the same area for generations. I asked Sam if he had any theories about why she might have helped his family. "Miles could possibly be her brother," Sam said, "because from what I understand, if you stood him next to a white man you couldn't tell the difference."

Relationships between blacks and whites in the South were often confusing and never clear-cut. While we couldn't establish a familial link between the Troutmans and Sam's family, there certainly was a level of familial care and concern that defies explanation. In this case, the balance of power is unclear. Yes, the white person held the money, but she used it in such a way that allowed the black person to be self-sufficient and, presumably, not beholden.

This was not always the case, especially when the white person was a man. Susan O'Donovan studies power dynamics under the institution of slavery at the University of Memphis. "It was a very coercive world in which power was incredibly inequitable," she said, "in which white men, whether they were overseers, strangers on the road, masters, masters' brothers, whoever, had enormous power over enslaved women. So there's endless opportunity for coerced sexual relationships."

As Sam told me earlier, he knew the Troutman name, but didn't know whether the family was black or white. But he had long heard rumors of an actual white ancestor on his mother's side. He knows that these "mixed-race roots" are a common legacy of slavery. "It's just part and parcel of what you expect if you're in the South and you're part of a southern heritage," he said. "I look at my skin tones, I know that there are white people in my family somewhere." He laughed. "I don't have an issue with that. I know that somewhere in the woodpile . . ."

Our search for clues led us to northern Georgia, where Sam's family on his mother's side has lived since the 1800s. Sam's first cousins Emma and Hilda Finley took us to the Mt. Zion Cemetery, where they showed us the graves of several generations of Sam's maternal ancestors, including the family's matriarch, Lilly Branham Montgomery. Grandma Lilly was Sam's great-grandmother.

According to another of Sam's cousins, Arthur Finley, Lilly Branham had fair skin and was the granddaughter of a white man. "I just heard that her grandfather was a Judge Branham who was white. I knew he had to be white if he was a judge."

Sam knows the Branham name very well—but not *just* the name. "Those are the white people that come to our family reunion," he said. One of the white Branhams, Sam said, enjoys having a famous "cousin." "I tell folks when I'm at the movies," Sam quoted the man, "that's my cousin up there." Whatever the relationship between the Branhams and Sam's mother's family, their presence at reunions means it's been acknowledged to some degree. We wanted to find out exactly what the nature of the relationship was.

Lilly's grandmother—Sam's great-great-great-grandmother—was an enslaved woman named Matilda. If the family story is true, then Matilda had a child with this mysterious Judge Branham. We headed to Putnam County, Georgia, where Matilda was enslaved, to see if we could confirm this story.

In the estate papers of local landowners, Putnam County historian Jim Marshall discovered a crucial record: the will of a white man named Henry Branham. It listed all of his slaves by name, including the one we were looking for: "a Negro woman, Matilda, and her two children."

Henry Branham, who owned Matilda, was a wealthy planter, the scion of a prominent local family. It was true that he was a legislator but not a judge. Yet there was a Judge Branham—Henry's nephew, Judge Joel Branham. Could this have been the elusive Judge Branham who was rumored to have fathered Matilda's child?

The town's geography itself held clues. We found that the shortest route from Joel Branham's home to his work led him right past a familiar address. Historian Jim Marshall described the route: "Judge Branham lived here and would walk downtown passing his uncle's home, where Matilda the slave woman lived. And it was evidently in passing at some point that the rest of the story develops."

The circumstantial evidence confirming Sam's family's story was beginning to mount when we discovered another intriguing piece of evidence. Jim Marshall found that a few months after Henry signed his will, he amended one part of it. "Sent my son, William C. Branham," he read from the document, "a Negro woman named Matilda and her two young children."

Henry sent Matilda and her sons away from his estate to be slaves on a relative's farm in the country. Could this have been an attempt to protect his nephew's secret? To Marshall, it seemed plausible. "It would be embarrassing possibly to have a mulatto child suddenly arrive and be part of the homestead, whereas out in the country, where there were plantations that had hundreds of slaves, and there were probably many mulatto children, it wouldn't have been as noticeable."

This trail of clues had finally brought us face to face with the man who we believed was Sam's white ancestor. If Joel Branham was Sam's ancestor, the former Black Power militant has far deeper roots in the history of this country and the white establishment than he probably ever could have imagined. Joel Branham served as a soldier in the Confederate army, a defender of slavery during the Civil War. Going back even farther, we learned that Joel was the grandson of a Spencer Branham, born in 1751 in

Virginia and who fought as a soldier in the Continental army during the Revolutionary War. If descent could be proved, Sam would be eligible to be a member of the Sons of the American Revolution!

Sam laughed at the notion. "I was asking you when I came here, did I get out the *Niña*, the *Pinta*, and the *Santa Maria*? So it's getting close."

■ Sam was raised in the embrace of a big, nurturing family. He can still rattle off the names of countless aunts and uncles and cousins he sees in pictures, and they still gather regularly for family reunions. But what about the other side of Sam's family, the side whose last name he bears? Sam didn't know his father as a child, and his first meeting with him, as an adult, was tumultuous. All he'd known about Roy Jackson was that he was in the army and his mother was working for the government when they met in Washington, D.C. They married, had Sam, and then he left. He had heard that his father had other children here and there.

Throughout Sam's childhood he received birthday cards and Christmas cards from his paternal grandmother, Imer Watts Jackson, who lived in Kansas City. "She was being diligent," Sam said, unsentimentally. About thirty years ago, Sam was doing a play in Kansas, and he decided to pay her a visit. They had never met in person. It turned out that Roy was living there in the house with his mother. The meeting between father and son was unplanned—and unpleasant. Roy badmouthed Sam's mother, accusing her of ruining his career in the army, and then dropped a bomb on Sam, who was holding his baby daughter, Zoe, in his arms. The anger and loathing in Sam's voice escalated as he told the story of their meeting: "'I want to show you something,'" Sam's father said to him. "We get to this house and there's this older woman who's there, and then there's another woman, maybe forties. Then there's a teenage kid like sixteen or something. So I figured he's going to say, 'I want you to meet your sister.' The sixteen-year-old leaves the room and goes upstairs and comes back with a baby smaller than Zoe. She goes, 'This is your sister.' I go, 'Who? Her?' She says, 'No. The baby.' Now, he just had a baby with this sixteen-year-old girl."

The story, both dramatic and traumatic, continued to unfold. "The oldest woman in the house says, 'How long has it been since you've seen your daddy?' I'm like, 'This is the first time we've really had a chance to have a conversation.' She just kind of dropped her head. We left, and he was mad at me. He was like, 'Why you tell her that?' I'm like, 'What was I supposed to tell her? Me and you hang out and that you took care of me. You made sure I'm the man I am today?'"

Sam told his father directly that a blood connection did not ensure respect or love: "You can't tell me I can't talk to you a certain way because you're my daddy. You've got to earn that. You didn't earn it. We're just two guys."

I was struck yet again by what a powerful storyteller Sam is. He recounts stories of joy and pain with a type of cinematic intensity that is incredibly compelling. I hope that one day he will write his memoirs.

I was also struck by Sam's ability to speak with such clear-eyed vitriol toward his father, yet not want to distance himself from that side of his family tree. There was no love lost between father and son, but Sam was still genuinely interested in learning about the people who came before him on his father's line. We turned to census records to get started.

Sam's father, Roy Henry Jackson, was born in 1929 in Kansas City, Missouri. In 1930, according to the census, Roy was living with both of his parents and his grandmother, Allie Johnson, who was the forty-two-year-old head of household, described as a "Negro." She had been married to a man named Henry Watts, Sam's great-grandfather, sometime before this census was taken. Allie's obituary, published in the *Kansas City Times* in 1972, revealed that she was born in Alabama, which brought our search for Sam's roots to an entirely new location.

In 1900, through the Butler County, Alabama, census, we learned that Sam's great-grandfather, Henry Watts, was a teenage farm laborer living with his parents, Willis Watts, a farmer, and his wife, Kizzie Watts. So far this struck us as a typical arrangement for a black family at the turn of the twentieth century. Long bound to work on plantations as slaves, freed blacks worked predominantly as farmers and farm laborers until well into the twentieth century, when they began to move north by the millions and trade their rural life for an urban one.

From their ages, we know that Willis—forty-seven in 1900—and Kizzie —age forty-two—were born into slavery. But the 1880 census from Butler County tells us something we couldn't have guessed from the paper trail: for both of them, their race is listed as white. Was it merely a mistake, a slip of the census taker's pen? Or were they a mixed-race couple, mulattoes, who might have been passing as white? Sam knew nothing about his father's family, and certainly had no idea of whether there were stories of a white ancestor on this side as well as on his mother's.

We tried to fill in the blanks and, once again, were able to find the name of the owner of Sam's slave ancestors. (This is highly unusual for African Americans; the paper trail usually runs out long before we can even come close to this sort of information.) The estate record we found originated in Butler County, Alabama. It was dated 1859 and belonged to A.C. Watts. In it, Willis is one of three slaves listed by name—valued at $465 for all three, about $12,600 today—who was leased by A.C.'s brother Thomas upon A.C.'s death.

Thomas Hill Watts was no ordinary Alabaman. Before the Civil War, he had been a successful planter and lawyer in Montgomery. In 1862 he was appointed attorney general of the Confederacy. A year later, the man who owned Sam's great-great-grandfather also served as Alabama's eighteenth governor.

His distinction stretched far back in his bloodline: the Watts family was descended from King Edward I of England, known as Edward Longshanks, who was born in 1239. King Edward was responsible for defeating the Scottish freedom fighter William Wallace, the hero in blue face paint made famous by Mel Gibson in *Braveheart*.

■ All this circumstantial evidence and speculation that was leading us to white relatives unfortunately remained just that: speculation. The Branham and Watts descendants we tested shared no segments of DNA with Sam, and we were unable to test any Troutman descendants. Painstaking archival research can help us begin to solve family mysteries, but it can only go so far. But stories passed down over the generations often remain powerful even when science disproves them. In my own case, the paper trail couldn't bring me any closer to proving a link between my enslaved great-great-grandmother, Jane Gates, and the white man my family always suspected to be the father of her children, Samuel Brady. To answer the central mystery of my past, we compared my DNA with the DNA of the descendant of Samuel Brady. To my surprise—and, I have to confess, to my disappointment—the test proved that Brady definitely was not my great-great-grandfather, although another test proved that whoever this man was, he was most probably of Irish or Scottish descent.

In Sam's case, we didn't have our man either. Judge Joel Branham was not the father of Lilly Branham, descendants' attendance at family reunions notwithstanding.

But, like my results, Sam's admixture test reveals there is truth to the family stories; they just are focused on the wrong individual. The admixture test shows a person's percentage of African, European, and Native American ancestry. Based on the stories we've shared with him, Sam guesses that his European—in other words, white—ancestry might be as high as 55 percent. The results, however, show that his African ancestry is 77 percent, his European ancestry 21 percent, and Native American ancestry 2 percent (a percentage that low is generally discounted as being irrelevant in terms of ancestry). So although his European ancestry is not greater than his African ancestry, it is still quite significant. He definitely has white ancestors; we just don't know who they are.

The paper trail runs out, and the DNA test for paternity doesn't pan out, but there's still much more we can learn from Sam's DNA. We were able to trace Sam's direct paternal ancestors back to his great-grandfather, Albert Jackson, who was born on an unknown date in Cheyenne, Wyoming. Of all the surprises he's encountered through this journey, this was one of the greatest: "Some brothers in Cheyenne, Wyoming?" he joked. Using Sam's Y-DNA, we can identify his paternal haplogroup. It is E1b1a7a, which originated in West Africa about twenty thousand years ago. It is the most common male haplogroup among African American men today—hovering around 60 percent—because of the slave trade. He shares this haplogroup with four other guests in our series: Newark mayor Cory Booker, musicians Branford Marsalis and John Legend, and former secretary of state Condoleezza Rice. "I know three of them," he said of his newfound genetic cousins. "But I want to play golf with her."

On Sam's mother side, we traced his direct maternal ancestor back to the same generation, his great-grandmother, Mary Thompson, who was born in 1874 in Mississippi. His maternal haplogroup is L3e3b, which originated about forty-five thousand years ago in Central Africa, in present-day Sudan. It then spread south and east into present-day Cameroon during the Bantu Migration four thousand years go. L3 and its branches are found among more than 25 percent of African Americans today. It turns out Sam has a double cousin: once again, it is Condoleezza Rice. This means that on an ideal family tree, we would be able to determine that Sam and Condoleezza descend from the same person on both sides of the family.

There were conflicting findings on his mother's side, however, so we couldn't determine with certainty his maternal ancestry. The company AfricanAncestry.com said that Sam did not descend from an African female at all, but from a female from the Middle East. They reported that his mitochondrial DNA belongs to the N1c haplogroup, which originated in the Middle East. N is a subgroup of a haplogroup called N3, and N is one of two major haplogroups associated with the emergence of humans from Africa when they migrated out fifty thousand years ago. So Sam could be descended from one of those people who migrated out of Africa and went to the Near East either via the Sinai Peninsula or by crossing the Red Sea near its mouth between fifty and sixty-four thousand years ago.

For African Americans, who were brought to this country by force, our past often remains a mystery, and our country of origin is lost to time and the injustices of history. The genetics research company AfricanAncestry .com, however, prides itself on being able to determine the present-day African nation and tribe or ethnic group from which we descend. On his father's side, AfricanAncestry.com has determined that Sam shares ancestry with the Benga people in the modern country of Gabon.

If a fairy godmother could grant him one wish, and he could talk to any one of those people, who would it be? "Grandpa Miles," Sam said quickly—Grandpa Miles, his great-grandfather who went from renter to owner of land in Georgia with help from an unlikely friend. "I would love to meet him," Sam said. "This was a huge business deal he pulled off. I'd like to know more about that relationship." I agreed that I would like to hear more from Miles myself. White people subsidizing black people, helping them escape town—this was amazing. Sam described it for what it was: "Taking care of family."

As befitting of someone who has spent his life surrounded by a huge extended family, Sam feels that it's our family that allows us to nurture all other connections. "Even herds or prides or flocks, there's a reason that there are those things, and we want to become that for our kids." He and his wife, LaTanya, have made every effort to keep their daughter, Zoe, connected to her many cousins and aunts and uncles. "We want to be her herd so that we give her that sense of family that I got. All those things create a person that understands the world is a community, and it's not just me for myself; that we all help each other; that the world is your family, but your immediate family is your immediate family, and exponentially, you give yourself to the world in that particular way because that's what's happening here."

She is a classical pianist. She was the provost of Stanford University and remains a professor there today. She was the first female African American national security adviser—and the first female African American secretary of state. *Forbes* magazine once called her the most powerful woman in the world. Condoleezza Rice—one of the most recognized public figures in America—is also the great-granddaughter of slaves. The title of her first memoir, published in 2010, is *Extraordinary, Ordinary People: A Memoir of Family*; her second, in 2011, *No Higher Honor: A Memoir of My Years in Washington.*

"I guess people find interesting or fascinating the unbelievable journey of somebody who came from slaves and from segregated Birmingham, Alabama, to be secretary of state," Condoleezza said. "But that's not me; that's our history."

In a speech Condoleezza delivered at Stanford in 1999, she also remarked "identity and history are a double-edged sword." Reading it, I could tell Condoleezza has spent a great deal of time contemplating her own relation to history, both her personal history and that of her ancestors.

"It's awfully important to understand where you came from as a human being in order to know where you're going. Human beings are human because they have a remembrance of a past and an expectation of the future, and they are connected," Condoleezza responded, characteristically thoughtful. "But too often, people become prisoners of their past, prisoners of their history. As secretary of state, I came across so many countries and so many nations that were still fighting wars, psychically at least, that had been resolved seven hundred years ago. It was an impediment to moving forward, so the trick is to be able to know your history but not to be prisoner of it."

For African Americans, though, who wear the scars of slavery in their complexions, history may not always feel like a thing of the past. As we are well aware, rape and forced sexual relations between master and slave were commonplace. African Americans carry this painful history with them from generation to generation. Each time a child is born, DNA acquired out of suffering is passed on. It is not always easy for black people in America to separate being aware of their history and feeling imprisoned by it. "I've always thought that this is the unhealed wound in America, that we have trouble talking about what really happened during slavery," Condoleezza said. "We have trouble talking about the scars of that. That's the unspoken and the unfinished business of race in America."

Condoleezza's journey began back in the 1950s in Birmingham, which Martin Luther King Jr. called the most segregated city in America. She was born on November 14, 1954, and grew up in the black middle-class neighborhood of Titusville. When we think of segregation in southern cities, separation of blacks and whites is what comes to mind. But even within the black community, there were distinctions based on profession, education, and skin color. "Everybody in our community taught school, I think," Condoleezza recalled. "There was an upper crust that lived on the other side of town near Smithfield, which was another quite well-to-do part of Birmingham for the black community. That's where people who had perhaps been bluebloods in the former generation would live, college people who had sent their kids to college."

For a middle class to exist, there is necessarily a lower class nearby, too. The black community, historically, is as class conscious as any other, and Condoleezza's parents were no exception. They were protective of their daughter, an only child. "I went to elementary school in a poorer community across town because my uncle taught there, so I could go home with him after school," Condoleezza said. "That community was not quite as well-to-do, and my mother in particular would say, 'Well, your little friends can come visit you here, but you can't go to their house. They live in a rough neighborhood.'"

While many black people drew subtle distinctions between their own families and other African Americans, there was nothing subtle about the lines drawn between blacks and whites. Condoleezza recalled her moment of discovery when she realized that she was black, and that being black meant being different and, in the eyes of many, lesser.

"We went to see Santa Claus when I was five," Condoleezza said, replaying an experience common to most American children, regardless of race or religion. "I was standing in line, and this particular Santa Claus was taking the little white kids and putting them on his knee. He was taking the little black kids, and he was holding them out here. I heard my father say to my mother, 'Angelena, if he does that to Condoleezza, I am going to strip all that stuff off him and show him to be the crapper that he is.'"

Little Condoleezza, of course, didn't relish the thought of a public confrontation between her father and Santa Claus. Fortunately they never came to blows; Santa yielded. "When I got up there," she continued, "I guess

Santa Claus could read my dad's body language, because Daddy was 6'2", a big man, a football player, and he took me and put me on his knees and said, 'Well, little girl, what will you have for Christmas?' That was really the first time that I realized that there was some kind of racial divide. Maybe at five I didn't fully understand it, but you could sure feel it."

Condoleezza's parents stared down segregation head-on. In doing so, they crossed a line, risking their own safety and their child's, knowing that there could be a high price to pay for their stand. Her father, who she says "lionized" Martin Luther King, "was not really attracted to the idea that you meet violence with nonviolence." As a result, he refused to participate in a planned march through Birmingham. "If somebody comes after me with a billy club," Condoleezza overheard him tell her mother, "I'm going to try to kill them." Condoleezza doesn't remember her parents ever sitting down and telling her what to do if she encountered racism; instead they modeled for her what to do. "I watched them when they could, and when it was just not getting in their way, simply ignore it," Condoleezza said. "I watched them confront it when it was necessary. I heard them actually say, 'This is about them, not about you.' I very often tell people that sometimes you have to ignore it in your personal circumstances, because if you're always confronting it, you'll just run your blood pressure up. Sometimes you actually have to confront it. The key is to know the difference."

There came a point in Birmingham where it became impossible to look away. During the civil rights era, Birmingham became a war zone. As civil rights activists challenged the status quo, white terrorists responded with a wave of violence that earned Condoleezza's hometown the nickname of "Bombingham." Despite the turmoil swirling around her, Condoleezza says she was largely protected from the hostilities and the horrors.

"We were a little cocoon within Birmingham, a very loving and kind and nurturing place. Our parents did everything they could to shield us from it," she said. "And because you went to schools that were completely segregated, your classmates were black, your teachers were black, you didn't actually have to encounter the white community that often. In some ways, because it was so segregated, racism was both everything and nothing at all."

The most infamous attack in Birmingham was the bombing in September 1963 of the Sixteenth Street Baptist Church, which killed four young black girls: Denise McNair, who was eleven; and Addie Mae Collins, Carole Robertson, and Cynthia Wesley, all of whom were fourteen. Spike Lee immortalized this tragic, hate-fueled event in his 1997 documentary film *4 Little Girls*. At the time, nine-year-old Condoleezza was at nearby Westminster Presbyterian Church, getting ready for her own services when she felt the ground rumble from the explosion.

"Every person in black Birmingham knew one of those little girls," Condoleezza said, recalling the day. Condoleezza knew Denise McNair particularly well. Her father was the milkman and the community photographer, hired to take pictures at every child's birthday. And Condoleezza's father had taught Denise in his kindergarten class. She even has a picture of her father handing Denise her kindergarten graduation certificate. The violence perpetrated on this community was both physically and emotionally close to home for Condoleezza. "That night, I asked my parents if I could sleep in their bed."

In the face of this violence, black families in Titusville pulled together. Condoleezza says the protective community instilled in her a great deal of confidence. And out of the tragedy and turbulence of the era came positive changes, legislation that finally ensured that blacks would get the freedoms they had been promised a century before, when the Civil War ended. First came the Civil Rights Act of 1964, and one year later the Voting Rights Act of 1965. Affirmative action was introduced during the Nixon administration, which allowed blacks to take advantage of housing, employment, and educational opportunities they had previously been denied. These were all tremendous gains, but as with everything else in life, there was a gray area. Towns like Titusville began to disappear, and the black communities that had thrived in their enclaves in the South ceased to exist. As strange as it seems to ask, were we better off in the closed world of places like Titusville, Alabama, and my hometown of Piedmont, West Virginia?

Condoleezza didn't think this was a strange question at all. "Like anything, when something changes, you gain a lot and lose something, too. I'm quite certain that we gained more than we lost. I wouldn't have made my way to the University of Denver and a Ph.D. and the Stanford faculty and secretary of state if segregation had continued and if we hadn't had the great civil rights revolution that we had.

"But we did lose a little something, and maybe not so little," she continued. "We lost the coherence of the black community. We lost the sense that we were all in it together. Stratification was one thing, but now the black middle class and the black upper classes were separated from the black underclasses. Those of us who were lucky enough to be parts of families who were prepared to take advantage of the great civil rights revolution moved on, but a whole lot of folks got left behind." Condoleezza is well aware how fortunate she was to be a part of a family that was able to move forward.

■ In fact, Condoleezza's family not only left Titusville but Alabama and the South altogether. When Condoleezza was in tenth grade, her father was working toward a degree at the University of Denver, and the family relocated. She went from an all-black school in Titusville to a school that had only three black girls in a class of seventy-two. She didn't face overt racism, but it was there. A guidance counselor told her, "You may not be college material." Condoleezza was two years younger than all the students and didn't test particularly well on standardized tests, but the counselor didn't factor these issues into her opinion. "She immediately jumped to certain conclusions," Condoleezza said. "It did say to me that these rather insidious ways of racism sort of come in. I was fortunate because I had a strong, fundamental background with supportive parents who'd always told me I could do anything, but that message to a kid who didn't have that might have been debilitating."

My mother told me the same thing. I could be whatever I wanted to be—and long as whatever I wanted to be was a doctor, she would be happy!

"Absolutely," Condoleezza said. "You might not be able to have a hamburger at the Woolworth's lunch counter in segregated Birmingham, but you could be president of the United States."

We wondered what factors contributed to Condoleezza becoming the accomplished woman she is. Was it an ancestor in her past? Was it hidden deep in her genes? First we turned to her father's side of the family to see what we could find.

Condoleezza's father, John Wesley Rice Jr., was born in Louisiana in November 1923. Her father was the minister in the church Condoleezza attended as a child. When Condoleezza was in government, the press ate up the fact that she was a diehard football fan. To imagine this serious, stately woman screaming at her television set on a Sunday afternoon was simply too good for the media to pass up. She inherited her love of the sport from her father, and it was something that drew them together.

"I've loved football all my life, thanks to Daddy. He thought I was going to be his all-American linebacker." She laughed at the memory. "I was supposed to be a boy. I was supposed to be named John. And when he had a girl, my grandmother said that when she told him—because he was actually in the pulpit preaching when I was born—my grandmother says to him, 'Johnny, your baby's been born. It's a girl.' And he said, 'A girl?' because he'd already bought the football. So he taught me all about it instead."

Condoleezza said her parents complemented each other beautifully. Her mother was "reserved, a beautiful lady, never picked up a ball or a bat of any kind. She was a musician." Her father, however, was "a very gregarious, outgoing, big man who played football and basketball and tennis in college. Very good athlete, loved people. Together," she said, "they made a terrific team."

Together, they were also completely devoted to their daughter. "They were supportive, and they wanted me to have every opportunity." They were her chief supporters—and sometimes her chief entertainment. "I'll tell one story that I think kind of sums it up. We loved *The Mickey Mouse Club*. After school, we would get together, and we had mouse ears, each of us, and we would sing the Mickey Mouse song. This particular day, the insurance man, Mr. Benham, was in the living room trying to sell insurance, and I was getting agitated because it was time for *The Mickey Mouse Club*. My parents made Mr. Benham sit in the living room while they put on their mouse ears, and we all sang the Mickey Mouse song." Yet another image that might be hard for people to reconcile with the Condoleezza Rice we see in the press today. She was obviously the product of a happy home, surrounded by love and support.

What about her own father's background? Education was clearly a value that was encouraged and aspired to in his childhood home. His father, John Wesley Sr., was born in Alabama in 1894 and graduated from Stillman College in Tuscaloosa. Whereas Condoleezza grew up in middle-class comfort, her grandfather did not.

"Granddaddy was actually a poor kid. His family was a sharecropper family, but he'd been very serious about school. Then he decided he wanted to get book learning in a college, so he asked how a colored man could go to college." He learned about Stillman College, which was about thirty miles away from his family's home in Eutaw, Alabama. He picked cotton to earn enough money to put himself through school, but after a year the money and the cotton both ran out. He was told he would have to leave. But there were other young black men around him staying on. How are they paying for college? he asked. "They said, 'Well, you see, they have what's called a scholarship, and if you wanted to be a Presbyterian minister, then you could have a scholarship, too.' My granddaddy said, 'You know, that's exactly what I had in mind.' So the family's been Presbyterian and college-educated ever since he did that."

Condoleezza describes her grandfather as "a towering figure because of his commitment to education." Alongside his wife, Theresa Hardnett, John Wesley Sr. founded churches and schools side by side throughout Louisiana, Alabama, and Mississippi. These have come to be known as Rice Schools. In the 1980s Condoleezza went to Baton Rouge and met some graduates of the Rice School there. "It was so heartening to listen to people say, 'Without your grandfather I would never have gotten an education, and not just that, but he made sure that I went to college,' because he would walk the neighborhood, and he would say, as my father would later on, 'You know, your daughter's smart, and I'm going to get her a scholarship to Stillman.'" He secured scholarships for students at other black universities as well, including Knoxville College and John C. Smith University in North Carolina.

John Wesley Rice Sr. overcame the many obstacles he faced not only in the segregated society outside of his home, but those within his home as well. In Condoleezza's memoir, she wrote, "Granddaddy Rice was not a favored son because he was dark-skinned. One of the scars of slavery was a deep preoccupation with skin color in the black community." "Yes," she said. "He was a very dark-skinned boy in a very light-skinned family. So even within his family, he was sort of looked down upon. Then he was the one what managed to go and get a college education. I think education was a kind of armor, too; reading was a kind of armor because he was not the favored son."

Not the favored son, yet his mother, Julia Head Rice—Condoleezza's paternal great-grandmother—had bestowed the greatest gift on him. Apparently recognizing that education was the surest path out of poverty, she had taught her son to read. Julia Head Rice occupies an almost legendary status in Condoleezza's family.

Like Sam Jackson and Ruth Simmons and me—and almost any other African American you might speak to—Condoleezza speaks of a rumor of a white patriarch at the heart of her family story, a story that revolves around the mysterious origins of this same Julia Head Rice. Julia Head, Condoleezza told me, was born a slave, but she lived to see emancipation. As a freed person, she learned to read—the first person in her family to do so.

"Julia Head was a gigantic presence. When she was a young girl, maybe nine, ten years old, she theoretically ran the Union soldiers off her property because she was taking care of the horses," Condoleezza said, relating the oft-repeated family tale. "Everybody told a story of her sitting on the back porch with a pipe. She smoked a corncob pipe apparently, and she used to sit with her shotgun quite a lot. She was a pretty tough lady."

Condoleezza's uncle Philip Rice is Julia's grandson, one of the oldest members of the Rice family and one of the last living relatives actually to have met her. Philip described Julia Head, his father's mother, as "a figure of authority in my house, a bright and elegant woman, compared to many her age at that time." Connie Rice, Condoleezza's cousin, said, "She looks very strong, and very stern. That stern Rice culture. If you're having fun, there's something wrong!"

Julia bore an undeniable sign of mixed African and European ancestry: light skin. Condoleezza's own complexion indicates a good deal of white ancestry, as do many relatives' on both sides of her family tree. Connie and Philip had details about Julia's past that might explain why she was so fair. Julia, they said, was the daughter of a white planter in Greene County, Alabama, named Burroughs, or Burr, Head. (Unbelievably, "burrhead" is one of many vile racist names for black people, but here it was the name of a white slave owner.)

The story goes that Burroughs had a daughter with his "Indian mistress," and the daughter was Julia Head. (The Indian mistress story is highly unlikely—albeit part of every African American family's lore—as the child of a Native American woman would have been free, and Julia was a slave.) Shortly after her birth, Burroughs Head, not wanting to raise an illegitimate child in front of his wife, gave Julia as a gift to a relative on a neighboring farm, where she lived as a slave. To investigate, our researcher Frazine Taylor went to the courthouse in Greene County where she found the will of Burr's brother, William Head, who owned an adjoining farm. It shows all of the personal property belonging to the estate of the deceased William Head, and all the slaves are listed by name.

Condoleezza was horrified to see that her great-grandmother Julia, at four years old, was worth $450 to her master, the dehumanization of slavery spelled out in plain English right in front of Condoleezza's eyes. "Just property. It makes me even sorrier that I didn't meet her, because she was somebody that everybody talked about all the time, her strength, and that she lived to be 101," Condoleezza said. "But to think that she started out as somebody that people put a price on of $450."

So Julia was owned by the brother of Burroughs Head. An interesting bit of information about Burroughs Head: he was the descendant of a man named Francis Cooke, who was one of the 102 passengers to sail on the *Mayflower* to Plymouth Rock in 1620. Another descendant of Francis Cooke: Condoleezza's former boss, President George W. Bush. "Maybe that's why we had the same sense of humor," Condoleezza laughed. "But it's America's story, that through all of these generations and all the separation and all the horrors of slavery and then the coming back together, that a president of the United States and a secretary of state might have been related someplace to an ancestor. It's an American story."

Other than Burroughs Head possibly being Julia's father, we wanted to know more about the other Rice ancestors. Julia Head was married to John Wesley Rice. They were both born in 1856, nearly a decade before the end of the Civil War. Following tradition, he should have been John Wesley Rice Sr., his son Jr., and Condoleezza's father III. But there were unanswered questions about whether the first John Wesley was the biological father of the second one, and he treated his son terribly. It was almost as if Julia's son John Wesley Rice Sr. had erased his father from memory by appropriating "Sr." for himself. Interestingly, the name endured through three generations anyway, but the originator of it was essentially struck from the record.

While he disappeared from family lore, John Wesley Rice didn't disappear from the official record. In the 1870 census for Greene County, Alabama, we find fourteen-year-old John, Condoleezza's great-grandfather, living with his four siblings, ranging in age from five to twenty-one, and his mother, Zina Rice, age forty. Zina Rice, given name Sinai—a black single mother, farm laborer, with a personal estate valued at fifty dollars—was Condoleezza's great-great-grandmother, born in Georgia in the year 1830.

Condoleezza had never heard of Zina before. Could we go back even further? To trace African American families back before 1865, we must scour public documents from the area in which they lived for slave owners with the same last name, who would have left a record in the Slave Schedule of the slaves they owned. The Slave Schedule, unlike a will, listed slaves not by name but by age, color, and gender. A slave with a white father would be listed as a mulatto.

In the 1860 Slave Schedule, we got lucky again. A white man named Hopkins Rice owned several slaves, both adults and children, one of whom was listed as a nameless thirty-four-year-old black female (Zina), another of whom was a nameless three-year-old black boy (Zina's son, John Wesley). "It's a little bit eerie to go back and see Hopkins Rice," Condoleezza said. "Was he a cruel slave owner? Was he somebody who took good care of my great-great-grandfather and my great-grandmother? What was he like? And where did he come from?"

Born in Nash County, North Carolina, in 1785, right after the end of the American Revolution, Hopkins Rice was a western pioneer who took advantage of the newly opened lands of Alabama, annexed in 1819 from territory stripped from the Native Americans. The fertile, dark soil of the "black belt" beckoned to southern planters like Hopkins Rice, and in 1823 he traveled from North Carolina to Georgia with 15 slaves—it was in Georgia that he would have ripped Zina from her home—and on to Alabama, where he eventually owned 150 slaves. With the forced labor of Condoleezza's ancestors, Hopkins built up a successful two-thousand-acre corn and cotton farm. He died in 1865, a month after the conclusion of the Civil War.

Western pioneers are icons in American society, but nobody ever talks about the black people they dragged along with them who did the excruciating physical work of building the economy. The greatest economic boom in the history of the United States was between 1830 and 1860, and it was all about cotton, and cotton was built on the backs of Condoleezza Rice's ancestors.

Zina's drive to succeed must have been relentless. It is awe-inspiring to think of the people who came after her: her son, John Wesley Rice, remained a farmer, like she was. We can assume he was illiterate, because his wife, Julia Head Rice, was the first in her family to learn to read. Their son, John Wesley Rice Sr., attended Stillman College and became what Condoleezza describes as an "educational evangelist," the founder of the Rice Schools. Condoleezza's father, John Wesley Rice Jr., himself became a pastor and college administrator. And then there is the culmination of Zina's line: her great-great-granddaughter, Condoleezza Rice, secretary of state of the United States. In a century and a half, her family rose from the degradation of slavery to the halls of power.

■ Condoleezza's mother's side of the family has plenty of its own stories as well. Are they fact or fantasy, or some mixture of the two? Angelena Ray Rice was born in 1924 in Alabama to Albert Robinson Ray III, born in 1892, and Mattie Lula Parham, born in 1899. Condoleezza knew these grandparents very well. Her grandmother taught her to play the piano, and in looks, Condoleezza is her spitting image.

According to family lore, Condoleezza's grandfather ran away from home at thirteen. In a train station late at night, a white man named Mr. Wheeler happened upon the fair-skinned child and took him home to rear him alongside his own sons. When her grandfather died in a Birmingham hospital in 1965, the first thing her grandmother said to her family was, "Call the Wheeler boys."

Where he had run away from was the source of some debate. It was said that his father, Condoleezza's great-grandfather, was an Italian immigrant with the last name of Ray who owned slaves. The family certainly has a propensity for Italian or Italian-sounding names—there is her mother, Angelena; an aunt Genoa; and of course Condoleezza herself, a name that her mother adapted from the musical term for "sweetness," *con dolcezza*. We searched all the records for the counties where Condoleezza's ancestors lived, but unfortunately, there were neither Rays nor Italian American slave owners. Yet Condoleezza's grandfather was fair-skinned, and she describes his sister as having auburn hair and blue-green eyes. Of their unproved or unacknowledged white ancestry, Condoleezza said, "If you had met . . . my aunt Nancy, you would have known for sure."

Condoleezza's grandmother Mattie Lula Parham's parents were both born about a decade after the end of the Civil War: Walter Parham in Georgia in 1876, the year Reconstruction ended, and Emma Killough two years later in Alabama. The paper trail seemed to end with Emma. But Condoleezza's aunt Gee told us that Emma had a sister, Lexie Williams.

Lexie proved to be a break in the case. We found her in the 1900 census for Jefferson County, Alabama, under the name Lexie Jefferson, living with her husband, Arthur Jefferson. And though this record shows no trace of anyone named Killough, the head of the household is one Lucy Keeler, a black female born in May 1846. Condoleezza's great-grandmother was Emma Killough, and it seemed likely that we had just identified her great-great-grandmother, Lucy Keeler. Killough and Keeler are very similar in sound, and name changes like this were common after slavery. In fact, Booker T. Washington said in *Up from Slavery* that there were two things all slaves did after emancipation: walk off the plantation and make some kind of name change, even if it were just to add what they called their "entitlements," a middle initial. (My father had a friend named Hight H. Washington, and he would say, "Hight, what's the 'H' for?" And Hight would say, "'H.,' you damn fool!")

In the 1880 census for Jefferson County, Alabama, we again find Lucy

Keeler, this time listed alongside her husband, Jerry, age thirty-six, and her two-year-old daughter, Emma. Condoleezza knew her aunt Lexie—she lived to be about one hundred—and now she was being introduced to Lexie's parents, her own great-great-grandparents. Jerry Keeler and Lucy Settles were both born in 1844, he in Alabama and she in South Carolina, almost twenty years before the end of slavery. We checked the 1870 census, and Jerry, Condoleezza's great-great-grandfather, is listed as a farmer with no land of his own; in other words, he was a sharecropper. He and Lucy lived with their eight children.

After reviewing the Slave Schedule for 1860, we believe that both Lucy and Jerry were owned by Abner Killough, the sheriff of Jefferson County and the only white man of that name in the area who owned slaves. There are hash marks on the page representing Condoleezza's great-great-grandparents—human beings reduced to a slash on a piece of paper.

The name changes—and then the changes back—are fascinating. After emancipation, Jerry and Lucy changed their master's name ever so slightly to make a name of their own, but then their daughter, Condoleezza's great-grandmother Emma, returned to the original spelling. Without documentation, we can't know the reason why.

With the discovery of Lucy Settles and Jerry Keeler, the paper trail comes to an end. This is where we turn to DNA to tell us with certainty whether our family stories are true.

■ Circumstantial evidence that the white slave owner Burr Head was the father of Condoleezza's maternal great-grandmother was strong, but would her DNA back up the claim? Greene County Courthouse researcher Frazine Taylor tracked down Burr's great-granddaughter, and she agreed to provide us with a DNA sample. Geneticist Joanna Mountain of 23andMe analyzed the results. "If they are truly third cousins," she explained, "we can hope to see some matching DNA, a longer stretch of matching DNA." Unfortunately, with no matches in the two samples, we cannot find any DNA evidence of the relationship. This central mystery of Condoleezza's father's family is only partially solved: Burroughs Head can be ruled *out* as an ancestor. However, there's no way to rule one particular individual *in*.

For Condoleezza, her DNA test couldn't help us identify her white ancestors by name, but it did allow us to establish her deep African roots, all the way back to the motherland. On her father's side, we traced her direct paternal ancestors back to her great-grandfather, the first of the John

Wesley Rices, who was born in Greene County, Alabama, in 1856. By testing her uncle Philip Rice's Y-DNA, we determined Condoleezza's paternal haplogroup. E1b1a7a originated about twenty thousand years ago in western Africa. E1b1a is the most common haplogroup among African American men; about 60 percent of all African American men share it because of the transatlantic slave trade, which drew individuals from West Africa. In Africa itself, this haplogroup is very common in Nigeria and Cameroon—67 percent in Nigeria and 46 percent in Cameroon. We know that 16 percent of the slaves were shipped through the Bight of Biafra, which makes it quite likely that, on Condoleezza's father's side, she is descended from the Igbo people.

What this paternal haplogroup tells us, conclusively, is that on this side of her family, Condoleezza did not descend from a white man; it takes her directly back to Africa. There is an unbroken line of black men in her father's line. In other words, there are no *Mayflower* ancestors on her family tree, and George W. Bush is not her eleventh cousin. She does, however, share this paternal haplogroup with fellow series guests Cory Booker, Samuel L. Jackson, John Legend, and Branford Marsalis.

Condoleezza's earliest direct ancestor on her mother's line goes back one generation further than her father's, to her great-great-grandmother, Lucy Settles, who was born in North Carolina in 1846. Her maternal haplogroup is called L3e3b, a branch of L3e, which originated forty-five thousand years ago in Central Africa, in present-day Sudan. It spread south and east into present-day Cameroon during the migration of Bantu-speaking farmers four thousand years ago. Branches of L3 are found among more than 25 percent of the African American population—including another one of our guests. Once again, Condoleezza meets her genetic double cousin, Samuel L. Jackson.

An analysis by the company AfricanAncestry.com, which specializes in determining the African ethnic groups and countries or tribes of origin of African Americans today, showed that Condoleezza shares maternal genetic ancestry with the Tikar people in Cameroon. In fact, her mitochondrial DNA sequence is 99.7 percent the same as theirs. When she met the prime minister of Cameroon, Ephraim Inoni, in Washington, D.C., in 2005, little did she know she was meeting one of her distant genetic cousins.

On a trip to Ghana while serving in the Bush administration, she met people who performed their own genealogy "research" on her. "The Ghanaians thought that facially, I looked like maybe I'd been some mixture of Ashanti and European." I joked with her that this was about the time Ghana was applying for a loan from President Bush. People will see connections where they want to. But for Condoleezza, learning where her ancestors came from, before they were slaves, was a moving experience. "It makes me want to go to Cameroon," she said, "and meet my people."

Analyses of both her paternal and maternal haplogroups prove that Condoleezza is not descended from a white man on either side of her family. In the case of Burroughs Head, the Rice family had fingered the wrong white man, but her complexion and that of so many of her relatives is proof enough that there is indeed white ancestry in the family's past. To determine how much, we ran another DNA test for Condoleezza, an admixture test, which measures her percentage of African, European, and Native American ancestry.

"It says 51 percent African, 40 percent European," Condoleezza said, stunned. "It's a lot of European ancestry." There were discrepancies in her Native American percentages, with one company reading her results at 9 percent and the other at zero.

Condoleezza's DNA proves that she does indeed have a large proportion of white ancestors, although not directly on her father's line or her mother's line. Whoever these ancestors were, we unfortunately can assume that some of that European percentage came from the most traumatic and painful experiences of slavery. "It's something that I accept as a fact of American life," Condoleezza said. "I think that my female ancestors probably suffered a lot. I have to be grateful that they survived it at all."

One of those females ancestors who certainly struggled, if not suffered, is Zina Rice, and of all the people in her tree, that is whom Condoleezza Rice would talk to if she had a fairy godmother to transport her back in time. Condoleezza feels a strong connection to this woman whose name she never heard before she embarked upon this journey with us. "I want to meet Zina. I want to meet Sinai," she said, referring to her great-great-grandmother by her given name. "She had to do this alone. I don't know who her husband or mate was—or mates—but they didn't stay with her. She was listed as single, and I'd love to sit down and know how she did it. And she left a really amazing legacy, because Julia and John Wesley, her son, married, and they produced strong people all down the line. She had to be an amazing, amazing woman."

Learning about her roots made history personal for Condoleezza.

"These were real people. They weren't names on those slave registries. They were living, breathing human beings who managed to survive and managed to give birth to the next generation that managed to survive and give birth to the next generation, and had they not, I wouldn't be sitting here. So it's a deeply personal story." *Extraordinary, Ordinary People: A Memoir of Family*—I don't think Condoleezza could have come up with a better title for her autobiography than that.

Ruth Simmons (b. 1945)

Ruth Simmons grew up a just a step removed from slavery. No matter that she was born eighty years after the Civil War ended and slavery was abolished in this country. The youngest of twelve children, she was born on July 3, 1945, into extreme poverty in Grapeland, Texas, into a family of sharecroppers. How this desperately poor African American child grew up to become the president of Brown University, the Ivy League school in Providence, Rhode Island, is an inspirational story of hard work and achievement against the odds.

Almost every aspect of Ruth's childhood revolved around the vast cotton plantation where her family and hundreds of others toiled. Sharecropping was the notorious system under which farmers picked cotton and lived on someone else's land in return for a share of the profits. In theory a family could prosper, but not in reality. They had to pay such high charges for food, clothing, and rent to the plantation's commissary that they often fell into a cycle of debt from which they could never escape. "Another form of slavery is really what it was," Ruth said bluntly.

Ruth described Grapeland as a typical rural community of that era. "It was a town that in this part of East Texas was a crossroads, basically, on the way to someplace else. Palestine was a city nearby that was more important. Crockett was nearby, more important." The white people lived in the town, far from where the black tenants lived on the farms. The houses on the land were small, and the families were traditionally large. Ruth and her parents and eleven siblings slept in a three-bedroom house, girls in one bedroom, boys in another, and parents in the third. The older children were given a great deal of responsibility for the younger ones.

"It was a really hardscrabble life when I think about it now," Ruth said. But it was happy, too. "I mean, I was the youngest of twelve. What could be better than that?" she laughed. Her older siblings still rib her about the privileges of being the little one. "Of course everybody went to the field, no matter how young you were. But they claim that when I went to the field, I rode around on the cotton sacks."

Ruth's parents were her earliest teachers and protectors. They were both born in Texas, her mother, Fannie Eula Campbell, on September 19, 1906, and her father, Isaac Henry Stubblefield, on August 5, 1904. "My mother was a saint, of course," she said, laughing. Her father she described as "a short man, but he had a swagger about him."

Still, Ruth and her siblings were bothered by the way he acted around white people. "One thing I will say about my father. He had, like perhaps all men of that generation with families, there was a certain obsequiousness about him when he was around whites. We, as children, hated that. If he was in the village of Grapeland, and he encountered whites, it would be, 'Yes, sir, Mr. This,' and 'Yes, ma'am, Miss That.' We thought that was just horrendous."

Occasionally, though, her father turned his temper on white people. This was daring and dangerous. Ruth recalled a time that her sister was riding a bus when another passenger complained that some money had been stolen. All eyes turned on her. "What did my father do?" Ruth asked. "Did he console and say don't worry about it? No. He got his gun, and he gathered my brothers, and he said, 'Let's go find the bus driver.'" All bus drivers then were white, so this was a full-blown act of defiance. "They got together and they hunted," Ruth continued, "drove down this street until they found this bus, and they stopped the bus, and they boarded the bus. They said, 'Did you say that she stole the money?' and so forth. They didn't do anything to him." Henry and his sons were extremely lucky. They could have been arrested or worse.

There was a duality about her father's personality that Ruth never understood. He could be extremely harsh, yet extremely sentimental. The duality that he displayed in his actions and his emotions was no doubt all part of the survival mechanism that he had cultivated as a black man living in the Jim Crow South.

"From my earliest days, I was aware that there were certain ways of behaving that were essential to surviving in that environment. My mother and father wanted us to know that we were black and what that meant in society, because of course it was very dangerous not to understand that," said Ruth. "On that porch, sitting at her feet when she was shelling peas or doing some other task, she was saying, 'Don't ever talk back to a white person.' OK. 'If you're on the sidewalk and you meet a white person, step off the sidewalk and let them pass.' We had a long list of things that we dared not do for fear of what might happen to us, because violence against blacks in those days was commonplace."

The society was unforgiving, and the lessons were degrading. "The idea was don't react. You would be debased, you'd be called names all the time, you would be mistreated," she said, "but you could never react. So we were in this vise."

Upon entering the town, Ruth and her siblings followed their parents' instructions about the way they needed to behave to the letter. "You knew where to go and where not to go. You knew what to say and what not to say. It was very strict, actually," Ruth recalled. "At the same time, whites had incredible latitude. We had good friends who were whites who could come and go as they wished." She knew her parents had some associations with white people, but she had no idea how they had come about. "One always had this sense that there were connections there that you didn't quite understand." The reverse could never have happened, certainly never in public.

Most of the children on the plantation, including in her own family, didn't go to school regularly because of the demands of the fields. On those occasions when they did, they were forced to confront their poverty. "They used to make fun of us when we were in school because of the way we dressed," she said, describing herself as "just a child of sharecroppers in tatters." Lunch was certainly not a glamorous affair: "A bucket with syrup, a biscuit, and bacon grease in it. Every day."

Living this life, devoid of opportunity and exposure to the wider world, Ruth saw no way out. "I could not have had any aspirations other than to follow in the footsteps of my parents."

But her parents, fortunately, had aspirations of their own—and older children who were desperate for their parents to have a better life. With mechanization in agriculture, there was less and less need—not to mention less work—for sharecroppers. Some of Ruth's older brothers signed up to fight in the Korean War and sent money home to their parents. Others moved to Houston with their own families and built a little community that made it easier for Ruth's parents to relocate. In 1952, when Ruth was seven years old, her family joined the mass migration of African Americans who were moving from farming towns to industrial cities in search of work. For Ruth's family that meant Houston's all-black Fifth Ward. Ruth told me that this was the very same neighborhood where the great civil rights activist Barbara Jordan, the first African American to serve in the Texas legislature since Reconstruction and the first black woman from the South ever elected to the U.S. Congress, grew up.

Ruth didn't notice a difference in race relations when she and her family moved from the country to the city. They conducted their lives pretty much the same way they always had, staying close to home. "The biggest difference was leaving the farming culture behind," she recalled. "We were, after all, still in an all-black neighborhood in Houston. The idea of going downtown, which was really close by, was not something that one contemplated every day. We walked these streets to go to school, to go to church and so forth. That was a sphere that felt very much like what we had experienced in Grapeland in a way." Their living accommodations were still poor and crowded, because landlords didn't tend to the properties black people rented with any regularity.

But one change was unmistakable, and it was a turning point for Ruth. "That move to Houston changed my life, because the city required us to go to school every day," Ruth said. "That saved things for me." It was here that her lifelong passion for education took root.

At Phillis Wheatley High School, called by the *Houston Chronicle* at the time "the finest Negro high school in the entire South," Ruth's African American teachers were deeply committed to their students, particularly Ruth. Her mother died just a month before Ruth turned sixteen. "That only increased the way people took care of me," Ruth recalled, "because in school, knowing that my mother had died, they just took on this parental role."

In spite of her teachers' care and concern, Ruth had a hard time fitting in, and she buried herself in her studies. Looking back, she realizes she was probably overcompensating. "Imagine this country bumpkin who comes to the city," she said. "I was very conscious of the fact, as I was growing up, of how limited our circumstances were. So I felt like a bit of an outsider."

The turning point in high school came when she signed up for a speech class. The teacher, Vernell Lillie, would become her lifelong mentor. She encouraged Ruth, who was still in mourning for her mother, to get involved in drama, speech, and debate. Ruth called Vernell her "paragon, who just made me a part of her family."

But Vernell Lillie did even more for Ruth than embrace her at a time when she was feeling a bit lost. She told Ruth that she should go to college. It simply had never occurred to her. "To understand why it hadn't occurred to me, you'd have to understand our financial situation as a family. How would it be possible for me to go?" Besides financial difficulties, there was another huge obstacle to African Americans even contemplating college: universities had only recently started coming out of segregation; to call them integrated would be overstating it. Vernell decided that Ruth should go to Dillard University, the historically black university that she herself had attended, and she convinced the school to give Ruth a scholarship. "It's through her good offices that I actually ended up going to college."

Other teachers figure into Ruth's memories as well: an English teacher who took Ruth home with her and let her pick clothes out of her closet for college, because she feared that otherwise Ruth wouldn't be able to afford to buy anything; the social studies teacher who hired her as a maid just so she could earn a little bit of money for herself.

Her father was duly unimpressed with her decision to attend college. "He really didn't think it was a good use of my time, because for my father, women weren't supposed to do things like that." By that time, he had become a preacher, and his interpretation of the Bible was a restrictive one that taught that women existed only to be a help to men.

College proved to be a very difficult transition for Ruth. Dillard was in New Orleans. Because of Ruth's religious upbringing, she didn't drink or dance, and New Orleans certainly did. But Ruth persevered and began to make a name for herself on campus.

She was still in a black community, but the students at Dillard had come from all sorts of backgrounds. Also, she was being taught largely by white teachers. "This is the great civil rights era where things were opening up and the teachers came south to teach in black colleges. We had people coming to teach us who were really dedicated to helping African American students in an era where it was still uncertain what was going to happen with the civil rights movement."

She developed a particular fondness for her Spanish teacher. "When he talked about Latin America, I thought, 'There are different worlds out there.'" The young woman who had grown up in the insular world of tenant farming, where blacks were kept in one place while whites roamed freely to their hearts' content, now decided it was time to see the world herself. Summers, she traveled to Mexico and France on scholarships that she sought out. During her junior year, she was chosen by the president of

Dillard, "a fearsome man," to spend the year at Wellesley College in Massachusetts. At Wellesley she learned about graduate school and ultimately became a Fulbright Scholar. "There were these things that just kept happening to me, mostly because of good people, frankly," Ruth said modestly and gratefully.

A distinguished academic career as a student, including a Ph.D. in Romance languages and literatures from Harvard, led to a distinguished academic career as a scholar and administrator at the University of Southern California, Princeton, and Spelman. In 1995 Ruth became president of Smith College, the first African American woman to hold such a position at a major college or university. Six years later, she was asked to be the president of Brown University. An Ivy League institution had never before had an African American president. Both appointments were joyous, historic occasions, but Ruth was deeply conflicted both times.

"I had all kinds of worries about what the job would do to me," she explained. This was not false modesty; these were deep-seated fears. "You see, given the life that I've lived and my story in terms of my family's circumstances, I feared that perhaps the two positions would separate me from family and who I was." Our families, though, provide the backbone of who we become. Even if we seem to stray, even if life provides us with opportunities that they could never have dreamed of, they remain part of us.

When Ruth became the president of Brown University in 2001, she had taken leadership of a school that had benefited from the slave trade. The first president himself was a slave owner, and even after he freed his only slaves, he continued to accept donations from slave owners and traders. One of the four brothers who gave the university its name was a slave trader, and it is believed, according to school records, that the building that housed Ruth's office during her tenure was built by a labor crew that included slaves.

The investigation that Ruth began into Brown's history spread to other university campuses as well as storied financial institutions and various industries. "It's gratifying to know that in all kinds of settings, people are finally saying, 'Let's acknowledge what happened.'" She believes that Brown was the perfect setting to undertake an investigation of this sort. "I would say there is no subject that is off limits for inquiry in a university context," Ruth said. "I just want people to tell the truth. I want people to stand up in the public square and say, 'This is the way it was.'"

Does a history need to stay hidden? Or can the truth, in the words of the Scripture, set us free? What Ruth wanted for her university we hope we can find for her as well: the truth and its acknowledgment.

■ As a child, Ruth witnessed relationships she didn't understand and no one explained—white people associating with her parents in the confines of Ruth's family's home—but they illustrate what we know to be true. The hidden history of southern race relations suggests that the color line was far more difficult to patrol in private than in public.

We began our search for the truth about Ruth's ancestry on her father's side of the family, with her grandmother, Flossie Beasley Stubblefield, who was born in Grapeland in 1883, nearly a generation after the end of the Civil War. "She was quite fair," Ruth said, describing her grandmother's complexion. "The story in the family was that my grandmother was in touch with her white relatives in Grapeland. Of course, this was whispered about." These relatives were the town's white Beasleys.

Ruth was too young to remember much about Flossie, but her older brothers, Clarence and Wilford Stubblefield, shared something quite intriguing with us: at the height of Jim Crow, the Beasleys, this white family that shared its grandmother's maiden name, would visit Flossie at the farm.

"They would come down and have dinner with us," Wilford said.

"We always took it for granted that there was some crossing of the line in our family because of the colors of our skin," Clarence added. "Some of us are pretty much fair-skinned people, and we knew something had to happen."

We suspected that the truth about Ruth's hidden history—and answers about how her father's mother came by her light skin—might be buried in census records for her hometown. We traced Flossie's family back to the 1880 census—just three years before Flossie was born—where we discovered an entry for her father, Ruth's great-grandfather, a former slave named Peter Beazley, with a "z." The census lists Peter as "age 34, male, mulatto." Now we know why Flossie looked the way she did.

Peter was a mulatto, which means that he had white ancestors. But were they the white Beasleys? We went to the courthouse in Houston County, Texas, to search the 1860 Slave Schedule and examined the entries of all the white Beasleys to see if any owned slaves whose ages and genders would match Peter's. In the entry for a white man named Charles Beasley, we found a slave described as "age 15, male, black." Our genealogists believe that this anonymous slave was Ruth's great-grandfather, Peter Beasley.

"It's quite sobering," Ruth says. "To never have known even my grandparents, and to be able to reach back and to touch beyond them, it's quite something."

So Charles Beasley owned Ruth's great-grandfather, but were the two men related by blood? To find out, we tracked down a direct descendant of Charles Beasley, his great-great-granddaughter, Camber Hayman. A lawyer living in Dallas, she agreed to give us a DNA sample. When we spoke with Camber, she told us that she had long heard a family story that one of Charles Beasley's descendants had fathered a black daughter in Houston County. Ruth's brother Wilford had spoken of the white Beasleys visiting his grandmother Flossie. The strangeness of white people visiting a black family at that time in Texas cannot be overstated.

A comparison of their DNA samples gives us the answer we have been looking for, an answer to the question that's been asked in whispers for generations: the white Beasleys are indeed part of Ruth's family tree. The DNA does not tell us the precise generation, but we can determine that Ruth and Camber share an ancestor since 1800. Which Beasley did the deed remains a mystery, I told Ruth, but there is no question that the deed was done by a Beasley. We could trace the Beasley branch of the family tree back to William Beasley, a wealthy tobacco farmer born in Caroline County, Virginia, in 1787, who owned seven hundred acres of land.

We arranged for Ruth and her brothers to meet their white cousin for the first time. "When they approached you about giving the DNA," Clarence Stubblefield asked Camber candidly, "did you have any qualms about it?"

Camber answered Clarence honestly: "Well, yes and no. But I think it's wonderful to have that richness in the history, because I think that the people that actually started the cross, it meant something to them."

That is something we can never know. Were the families of Ruth and Camber joined in love or in suffering? The truth of our families' pasts, even if born in pain and humiliation, can help us understand the real story of who we are and how we got here.

Ruth believes the pain of slavery is still with us. "There are those who believe that African Americans carry a chip on their shoulders, that we ought to get over slavery—you know, why is that still relevant today? They say just move on. How do you move on from who you are?"

■ We turned to Ruth's mother's side of the family to see what else we could learn about Ruth's history and where she came from. Ruth said her mother was a storyteller, but not of family stories. Whereas the men in Ruth's family told stories for entertainment, Ruth says the women told different kinds of stories. "The objective was not humor. It was to impart to us the values that she and her mother and perhaps her grandmother had handed down to her. So yes, there were stories told, stories told about an accident that took place where my mother's brother, for example, was shot; my cousin was in a hunting accident without people ever understanding what really happened," Ruth explained. "In those days, the value of black life, of course, was not too significant, and so people got shot and hurt all the time with relatively little consequence. So these stories hung around as evidence of the pathos of that era."

Ruth's grandmother Emma reportedly came from North Carolina, but no one knew for sure. She was a curiosity among relatives. "We had pictures of my grandmother carrying water on her head," Ruth recalled. "Nobody in those days in Grapeland knew of any African origins of that. They just thought, well, isn't it odd that she's carrying heavy things on her head?" Her dress and speech patterns, too, were fodder for gossip. "They talked about the way she dressed, always in long dresses made of muslin, very reminiscent of the kind of slave cotton in a way that we, of course, know about today. They talk about the odd way she spoke, as if she were a Quaker. Who else was using 'thee' and 'thou' and so forth? We were fascinated by that, but we were not able to trace it."

In discovering Emma's death certificate, we discovered the truth about her birthplace. Emma Johnson was born on April 5, 1875, in Grapeland, Texas, just like her daughter and granddaughter. Ruth could only guess at why people might have fabricated the facts of her origin. "I think perhaps because people did not know much about where she came from, there was this idea that, well, she must have come from someplace else." What struck Ruth as especially odd, though, was that Ruth's mother and aunts and uncles never corrected this misinformation in the family lore.

One of the interesting things about genealogy is that sometimes when we start looking for one thing, we stumble upon something else equally interesting, if not more so. Emma's death certificate contained another vital piece of information: the names of her parents. They were Taylor Johnson and Matilda Johnson, both born in Texas, not long after it had entered the Union as a state (in 1846). Again, not a soul from North Carolina.

Ruth had never heard the names of her great-grandparents before. We hoped to trace them further back in slavery, but with that, the paper trail on Matilda and Taylor ran out. Houston County is what genealogists call a "burnt county." All the local records were housed in the county courthouse, and although it was constructed of brick, it burned down not once but twice in the nineteenth century. What have we as African Americans lost, I asked Ruth, by being cut off from our slave ancestors' identities, sometimes willfully, as was the case of our parents' and grandparents' generations, where people just didn't talk about it, or circumstantially, as in this case?

"It's hard to say for everybody, but I can tell you there is a certain longing that you always have to know where you came from," Ruth answered, "and it is rarely enough when people say, 'Oh, I think it's from someplace in North Carolina,' or 'I think somebody told me that they came down from Oklahoma on horseback.' You never feel that you have really connected to the people who gave you who you are, and some important part of who I am goes back to my great-grandparents."

Ruth was delighted to learn her great-grandparents' names. But we didn't want to give up tracing her roots into slavery. We looked at the family of her grandfather, Richard Campbell, Emma's husband, as well. Richard Campbell, also called Dick, was born in Oakwood, Texas, in June 1866, one year after the end of the Civil War. To learn about his parents, we cross-referenced several census records for Houston County, Texas, starting with the one from 1880, and were able to establish that Dick's mother, Martha Campbell, was born in North Carolina in 1836; her parents were both born there, too. So here at last was the North Carolina connection—on the wrong side of Ruth's mother's family, but we had finally found it.

In the 1880 record, Martha is listed as the head of the household, raising eight children on her own. Ruth had only ever heard of Dick, her grandfather, and his brother Doc; she had no idea there were six other siblings. What struck us as unusual about the siblings was that half are listed as black and half as mulatto, which suggests two different fathers. Ruth's grandfather is one of the siblings listed as black. Everybody, she said, always said he was very fair. As usual, color was in the eye of the census taker.

According to Ruth, her great-grandfather, Martha's husband Andrew Campbell, was born in Texas around 1837, but he was nowhere to be found in any records. He could have changed his name, passed away, left the state, or simply have been left out of the census. Although he seemed to disappear without a trace, we do know, so far, that both Martha and Andrew, Ruth's great-grandparents, are her oldest slave ancestors.

Our challenge was to trace the Campbells farther back into slavery. Once again, the most important document in tracing an African American's family tree is the 1870 census, the first to list former slaves with their legal names. As is so often the case with freed slaves, Martha Campbell in 1870 is listed under a different spelling—as Martha Camel. But because the same children appear with her, with the same birthplace, we can confirm that these two Marthas are one and the same person.

While Andrew Campbell still wasn't present in the 1870 census, Martha is shown to be living with a black farm laborer, born in Virginia, named Harry Rufin. Harry Rufin stays in the picture for many years. It seemed likely that he was the father of the younger children, but all of Martha's children went by the last name Campbell. In the 1900 census for Houston County, we find Doc Campbell—who we know is Dick's brother, only two years old in the 1870 census—listed as the head of household, with Harry Rufin, now spelled Ruffian, as a border.

Again, we hit a dead end. The two fires in the county courthouse that consumed the records we could have used to trace back the other side of Ruth's mother's family destroyed these as well.

DNA had solved a mystery that had haunted Ruth's family for more than a century and introduced her and her brothers to a new, white cousin. Now it seemed we had also helped find the root of the North Carolina question. But there were other questions that were only hinted at that DNA could help us answer.

■ Literally every African American I have interviewed for each of these genealogy series has claimed to have a great-grandmother with high cheekbones and straight black hair. In family lore, that great-grandmother is usually a Cherokee. Ruth, too, had heard "unspecific" rumors in her family that they had some Native American ancestry. Was it true?

It seemed unlikely. One in three African American men descend from a white man. However, 99 percent of us, because we inherit our mitochondrial DNA from our mother, probably descend from a tribe or ethnic group in Africa, for obvious reasons: because most miscegenation, as we used to call it, resulted from either rape or enforced sexuality of a white man upon a black woman.

We turned to Ruth's DNA once again to find out whether this Native

American ancestor was real. Ruth's maternal haplogroup is D1, which arose about forty-five thousand years ago. It's one of two major haplogroups carried into Asia by the first modern humans to live outside of Africa. Twenty thousand to twelve thousand years ago, indigenous groups from northeastern Siberia carrying this haplogroup crossed the Bering Land Bridge and populated the Americas. Today, haplogroup D is found mostly along the Pacific from Alaska to Chile, rarely east of Nevada, and it's found in only about 6 percent of the entire North American population. D1 is a Native American–only haplogroup.

Amazing—Ruth *is* descended directly from a Native American female! "You're the only black person I know," I joked with her, "whose great-great-great-grandmother was a Cherokee princess." We laughed, but the results were significant and stirring. Ruth's mother's line, surprisingly, has been firmly rooted in the Americas for thousands of years.

To determine whether there were any links to Africa in her bloodline, we turned to her father's line. To do so, we tested her brother Clarence's Y-DNA. Using the paper trail, we were able to trace Ruth's direct paternal ancestors back to John Stubblefield, who was born in 1843 in Kentucky. Clarence's DNA reveals Ruth's paternal haplogroup as E1b1a8a, which originated about twenty thousand years ago in Africa. About 60 percent of all African American men share this haplogroup because of the slave trade. The company AfricanAncestry.com specializes in determining tribe and country of origin for African Americans, and Ruth's father's line descends from the Kota people in Gabon. Her brother's Y-DNA sequence is identical to theirs. Ruth has never been to Gabon. She was clearly moved. "I'll be going now, I can tell you. I'll be going home," she said.

Ruth's admixture test, which reveals percentages of European, African, and Native American ancestry is consistent with our other findings: 71 percent African, 25 percent white, and 4 percent Native American.

Ruth was amazed by how much her documented genealogy and bloodlines back up the many stories she has heard her whole life. "To understand the connection between all of those stories that I've been hearing all of my life about the Beasleys and so forth and to know that is now concrete is a gift, and the connection of those stories to our having some Native American ancestry," she said. The specificity of her connection to the African continent meant a lot to Ruth. "The idea that there isn't this mythical huge landmass that I claim in the 71 percent of myself, but a precise place with a culture that can be explored, that's a tremendous gift."

Unlike any other family we've examined, Ruth's got the big things right and the little things wrong. "That's very exciting to know that somehow our family was trying to hold on to all of these pieces, to create the whole and the sense of connection to all that we are," she said. "What's fascinating to me is that the lore in some ways was so rooted in truth."

And if her fairy godmother appeared and gave her a chance to meet one of the many relatives on her family tree—Beasleys included—who would it be? Ruth took her time before answering, then chose her maternal grandmother and great-grandmother, Emma Johnson and Matilda Johnson. "So much of who I am comes really from Emma through my mother, so probably Emma and Matilda would be very important for me to meet." She chose these women in part because she knew her paternal grandmother. "I'm quite unlike her, actually, and I would say that I don't recognize myself so easily in what I got from her," Ruth said. "So more questions would be answered for me by knowing more about my maternal grandmothers, because they were strong women who endured a lot and who passed a lot down to us."

When she was inducted as the president of Brown University, Ruth Simmons said in her acceptance speech, "I would not have thought it possible for a person of my background to become president of Brown University." Out of this background that forced people into a position of powerlessness, Ruth found strength. "Every day I go to work, and I face the painting of the first president of Brown, a slaveholder. I think the power in the fact that I face the slaveholder as a descendant of slaves is just as it ought to be, because in that march of history, all these things happen."

We can't look away from history. What we must do is look into it, and, in doing that, look into ourselves, to see exactly what—and whom—we are made of.

CHAPTER EIGHT

Crossings

Like so many of us, comedian Margaret Cho, CNN medical expert and neurosurgeon Sanjay Gupta, and Martha Stewart haven't been able to piece together the full story of their pasts. No wonder—all three grew up straddling two worlds: the lives they've built for themselves in America and the lives their parents or grandparents left behind. In previous chapters, we confronted obstacles posed by tracing family roots back through immigrants who crossed oceans to embrace new, often different, lives in America. But in this chapter, we learn of the special challenges faced by those with much more recent immigrant ancestors. Though Margaret, Sanjay, and Martha are trailblazers in entertainment with wildly different backgrounds, they share this common experience of the past: of being cut off from their ancestral heritage not only by distance but by relatives who, in crossing over, chose to keep their memories of the "old country" to themselves, either out of privacy, protection, or pain. "Branding" is an overused word in today's marketplace, yet in investigating this trio of fascinating personalities, we learn its true power by reaching back into the past for those who put their hard-earned stamp on names that, perhaps initially awkward to those inheriting them, have become sources of enormous pride and potential.

Margaret Cho has built a successful standup career spanning nearly three decades. She has developed a unique comedic voice based upon what she knows best: her personal history as the child of recent immigrants. At twenty-six, she starred in her own network television show, *All-American Girl*, the first sitcom to have an entirely Asian American cast. One of her stage routines takes aim at all that the name of her sitcom implied: "I'm the only member of my family to have been born in America," Cho quips. "So my mother would always push me forward, like, 'She's white!'"

Margaret's humor illuminates a universal immigrant experience: the restless, challenging search to find the place where you most belong. I asked her whether she thought of herself more as Korean or American while she was growing up. "I really thought of myself as American until I started to recognize myself in photos, and then I would see myself and be shocked that I was not white," she answered. "I was such a television addict as a very young child, and I didn't look like the people on TV." Margaret never shared her confusion or anger with her parents. "I don't think they would have really understood it, because they knew they were foreigners. I did not have a sense of being foreign."

Margaret's parents immigrated to San Francisco from Seoul, South Korea, in 1964. Four years later, on December 5, 1968, their daughter was born. Her parents gave her the name Moran, a traditional Korean name meaning "peony." In Korean lore, Margaret explained, the peony is the flower that continues to bloom even in the harshest conditions. It was certainly not a stretch for an American girl to have a flower name, but what jumped out at her classmates was the sound, not the powerful meaning. "I did not want to be American with a name like Moran, which sounds much like 'moron,' which I really heard a lot as a kid," she recalled. "I may have been about ten or something, and I thought, I needed a white name; I need an American name."

And so Margaret Cho was born. Although Margaret's parents have lived in America for a half century, she says that to this day, they do not consider themselves American. "America was always a temporary thing. It was as if they never really settled in this country. They never had a sense of permanence, even though they wanted me to be American and my brother to be American."

From the outset, Margaret's parents struggled to build a life for themselves in their new home. They had met and fallen in love at Korea University in Seoul, where her father, Seung Hoon Cho, was studying law and her mother, Young Hie Chun, was studying French. They were married in Seoul in 1963. In America, the former law student was forced to support his young family as a waiter and a janitor, a story typical of many immigrants.

Soon after Margaret's birth, her family was wrenched apart. Margaret's father, in the United States on a student visa, was deported for working illegally. He returned to Korea with Margaret—just a month old at the time—while her mother stayed behind in California, where she was working in a factory. It was a horrible time for Young Hie. But one year later, with a lot of luck, Seung Hoon was able to return to the United States, and the family was reunited.

Margaret believes her father's deportation made her parents strive even more to "be as American as we could." "My father had no real discernible Korean accent," she recalled. "My mother held on to hers, but he really had no evidence of his Asianness. One time I spent the night at a white girl's house. Her mother called my house to see if it was OK, and she talked to my dad. Before they had this conversation, the mother had acted weirdly suspicious around me. When she hung up the phone, she had this big smile on her face, and she said, 'I didn't know your dad was white.' I didn't say anything because I was so excited that she thought that I might be adopted by white people."

This was a moment of recognition for Margaret, although she's not sure the meaning was clear to her at such a young age. "That lodged in my mind like, oh, there is privilege to being white," she explained. "I knew that there were certain privileges that went along with being fully American, and to be fully American really meant to be white."

Throughout her childhood, Margaret felt alienated. When she traveled to Korea to visit relatives, she connected with them, but, unable to speak Korean, she stood out. "Even the way I looked before I would speak, there would be a recognition of 'Oh, they're not from here.'" At home in San Francisco, Margaret believes that the tension she recognized between her parents and the rest of the Korean immigrant community affected her relationship with other Korean children. "I was always weird," Margaret said, remembering her feelings of isolation. "Kids sort of naturally will gang up on one kid when there is something different about them. I was different. I was gay, and all this stuff I didn't know how to talk about or realize came out in my behavior. I think that had a lot to do with kids really not liking me."

By the time she was about fourteen, she had already decided she wanted to be an entertainer, and Margaret was far more interested in the world around her than she was in school. She says her real education began in San Francisco's Castro District, the heart of the city's gay community. Here, in 1977, the Chos opened a bookstore called Paperback Traffic, soon to become a destination for San Francisco's counterculture. "It was not just a gay bookstore but really an alternative culture that was emerging," Margaret explained. "I learned from the people there. It affected me forever. That sort of set me up for life, I think." It allowed her father—a deeply religious Christian, conservative immigrant—to display a rebellious streak that he usually hid: he told us that he loved to bring visitors from Korea to his store just to shock them. His daughter's provocative nature, it seems, didn't materialize out of nowhere.

Margaret began doing standup in comedy clubs when she was fifteen or sixteen. Her immigrant background is an essential part of her comedy, evident in any of her routines: "Because I am one of the more prominent Asian Americans, people like to come to me whenever they have an Asian problem, like when they can't finish their Sudoku," she riffs, "or if they need some kind of alteration."

Although her humor relies heavily on her experiences of being a Korean American, Margaret has gaps in her knowledge. She is almost entirely in the dark about why her father had to abandon his ancestral home as a child in 1948. Both of her parents had come to America after living through two wars—World War II and the Korean War—but they spoke little of them. Seeing Francis Ford Coppola's Vietnam War epic *Apocalypse Now* with their daughter, though, triggered feelings and memories that they'd long suppressed. "There are a lot of dark elements in that film, but they were not involved in the soldiers. They were involved in the villagers. They were like, 'That's what it's like.'"

■ Margaret's father, Seung Hoon Cho, was born in 1937 in Cheorwon, Korea. Today Cheorwon is in the Demilitarized Zone (DMZ) separating North and South Korea. In the year of his birth, Japan went to war with China and mobilized Korea to support its war effort. He shared with me stories about his own father that he had protected Margaret from. Myung

Sook Cho—Margaret's grandfather—worked for the Japanese as a station-master during Japan's occupation of Korea, which began in 1905. According to Seung Hoon, when Japan withdrew from Korea at the end of World War II, his father was branded a traitor by North Korea's new communist leadership. At this point, the family fled Cheorwon for South Korea. Margaret's father was only ten when his father, a civil servant, became an enemy of the state.

Her grandparents moved from Korea in the early 1970s to live with Margaret and her family in San Francisco. Even though they lived in America for about twenty years, Margaret never believed they called it home. Margaret knew nothing of her grandfather's activities during the war, yet she was aware of his knowledge of the Japanese language. "I think he was in a way more comfortable reading Japanese somehow, or got more out of it, because there were a lot more Japanese-language books in his library," she said. She didn't view her grandfather through a political lens at all. "He was a good-natured guy. Dapper. He always wore a hat. He was very old-fashioned in his manner of dress, and he was quite popular with women. I knew that."

Margaret described her grandmother as "pretty dour, pretty difficult, just in a bad mood a lot of the time." In a word, her grandmother, fed up with her "playboy" husband, was tired. "She raised a lot of kids. She ended up raising a lot of grandkids. She was kind of over it."

In 1948, three years after the end of World War II, Korea was divided along the Thirty-eighth Parallel into two countries. Today, this 160-mile-long fortified border has cut off the Chos—and countless other Korean families—from any records containing details about their family's history in the North. Ironically, the DMZ cuts directly through the home provinces of both Margaret's grandfather and grandmother. Her grandfather, Myung Sook Cho, was born on August 2, 1910, in Hwanghae province, just three weeks before the Japanese officially annexed Korea. Her grandmother, Im Soon Lee, was born almost exactly two years later, on August 18, 1912, in Gyeonggi province. "It's such a terrible pain to be cut off from your family and to be cut off from what is really your home," said Margaret seriously.

University of Pennsylvania professor Eugene Park, a specialist in Korean social history, shared with me an interesting fact: in Korea, family clans can be traced back hundreds of years to a genealogical point of origin, a progenitor. The progenitor is essentially the "founding father" who gives the clan its name and its status. All of his male descendants are re-corded in a genealogical record called a *joakbo*. Today there are nearly four thousand clans in Korea, each with its own *joakbo*.

We discovered through a family registry kept by the South Korean government that Margaret's father's family probably descends from the Pyongyang Cho clan. The names of Margaret's father, grandfather, and great-grandfather, however, do not appear in their clan's *joakbo*. In the 1880s, Margaret's great-great-grandfather, whose name we couldn't trace, met some traveling Christian missionaries and converted to Christianity. The first Protestants came to Korea in 1884, so Margaret's ancestor must have been one of their earliest converts. Upon his conversion, he severed ties with his clan association because traditional ancestral worship was incompatible with Christianity. The missionaries said such worship was a heathen, pagan practice, and unless he abandoned it, he would not get into heaven. As a result, his descendants have not been recorded in the *joakbo*. The paper trail of Margaret's family was broken by choice. To reestablish a connection with his clan, Margaret's father must prove descent. Unfor-tunately, older documents of her father's family—which would include the name of this missing great-great-grandfather—are buried somewhere in North Korea.

Although her great-great-grandfather's devotion to Christianity forced the exclusion of his descendants from their *joakbo*, his legacy is still with them. Margaret's family is "intensely religious." But there is more flexibility in their practice of Christianity than there was for her ancestor. Incorpo-ration of Korean Buddhist traditions into the practice of Christianity is no longer considered blasphemy. "There was a kind of back-and-forth," Mar-garet explained of her parents' religion. "There was still kind of an under-standing of that ancestor worship. There was still an idea of reincarnation. There was an idea that a lot of the Buddhist traditions were valid."

Our search for more about her clan took us not to Korea but much closer to home: the Family History Library in Salt Lake City, Utah. Admin-istered by the Mormon Church, the library collects, catalogs, and preserves genealogies from all over the world. According to Tamra Stansfield, a re-search expert in the library's International Wing, the library collects any kind of records that reflect "genealogical need": gazetteers, history books, address books—anything that would help someone find his or her ances-tor anywhere in the world. The library contains 150,000 books on site and two and a half million microfilms with billions of images.

The library's specialist in Asian clan genealogies, Ellen Ly, located a microfilm copy of Margaret's family's *joakbo*. The Pyongyang Cho clan has a whopping fifty thousand relatives. Without knowing the name of her great-great-grandfather, we can't determine which family line is Margaret's. Almost unbelievably, however, we can now find the actual name and biography of the Cho family's progenitor, a man named Cho In-gyu, born in the year 1237.

According to the *joakbo*, Cho In-gyu was a man of many accomplishments. Born around the time the Mongols invaded Korea—ten years after the death of Genghis Khan—he was profiled extensively in the Koryosa, a history of the Goryeo Dynasty. Margaret read the text aloud: "When Cho In-gyu's mother was expecting him, she had a dream in which she embraced the son in her arms. From an early age he was very smart, and soon could read and understand all kinds of writing. When he grew up, the government selected talented people to learn the Mongolian language, and he participated in the program." In 1260, when Cho In-gyu was twenty-seven years old, the Goryeo Dynasty and the Mongol Yuan Dynasty signed a peace treaty, and Korea became a tributary client kingdom of the Mongol Empire. Speaking Mongol became a valuable skill, and Cho In-gyu became a translator for the Goryeo king, Chungyol. He was highly praised by the king in a letter written to the Mongolian emperor: "He has never made a mistake in translating royal edicts . . . , and has always been diligent in serving the Princess. Please bestow awards upon him, and give him a high position." The Yuan emperor abided, making Cho In-gyu a Mongol general and rewarding him with gold and a title. He rose so high in royal esteem that he married one of his daughters to the Korean king's oldest son, the future king Chungson. Margaret, it turns out, descends from royalty.

Unfortunately, Cho In-gyu's fall from grace was as spectacular as his rise. At the time, kings had only one official queen, but they could have as many royal consorts as they wanted. Again, Margaret read from the Koryosa: "Someone posted an anonymous notice on the gate of the palace which said, 'Cho In-gyu's wife has had a shaman put a curse on the King so that he loves only her daughter, not the Princess.' Learning this, the princess jailed Cho In-gyu and his wife and interrogated them. Under torture, Cho In-gyu's wife made a false confession. Cho In-gyu and his sons-in-law returned home, and all of their wealth was confiscated. The Mongol Empire ordered that Cho In-gyu be flogged and sent into exile." In a happy twist of fate, the Mongol emperor restored his land and position, and through his service he gave his entire family great prestige for generations.

Cho In-gyu is Margaret's most important, most illustrious ancestor in Korean history, but he was actually the fifth descendant of another ancestor, Cho Chun, who, according to legend, came from China. Margaret never imagined she might have Chinese roots. Of course she also never imagined she would learn the name of an ancestor who lived eight hundred years ago.

Our next challenge was seeing how far back we could go on Margaret's mother's side.

■ Young Hie Chun was born on November 18, 1937, the same year as her husband. She lived through the same turmoil in Korean history: Japanese rule, World War II, the Korean War. Young Hie didn't share much about her childhood with her daughter. Margaret remembered what little she had been told about her grandfather. "He was a political figure, and so her family was always in the crosshairs. They were always being targeted." Margaret believes that her mother's experiences as a child were traumatic.

Young Hie had a hard time adjusting to America. Only one other member of her family migrated; her parents and sisters stayed in Korea. "Her family was really important to her, and that she was separated from them was really tough," Margaret said. "She was really frustrated with being here. I don't know if she liked being poor. I don't think she liked the food. She didn't like the language. She didn't like anything." Margaret's father's temporary deportation didn't help matters. Margaret lauded her mother's creativity and talents—good cook, good seamstress, good guitarist, good singer—but says she didn't have the desire to pursue a career in the way Margaret has. "I imagined a life for myself that was far more independent than she's ever been. I think that's outside of her realm."

Margaret's grandfather, Chun Jin-han, was an important figure in modern Korea. His humble beginnings were legendary. His obituary tells a story Margaret had heard many times before: "When he was seventeen years old, he traveled barefoot to Seoul. He worked delivering rice and doing other menial jobs to pay for his education." He went on to earn his diploma from Waseda University in Japan in 1928, an achievement that would have guaranteed him a relatively comfortable position in the Japanese-run government. But he took a different route—and paid for it. He joined a union and opposed the Japanese government's "taking money out of Korea," as his obituary states. As a result, he was jailed for two years and had to hide out in the mountains for another ten. It was during this time that Margaret's mother was born.

After Korea was liberated from Japan, Chun Jin-han was appointed Korea's first social economic minister. According to his obituary, he learned of his appointment while reading the paper on a bus. In addition to serving in Korea's first postwar government under Syngman Rhee, Chun Jin-han served five terms as a congressman and helped found the Korean labor movement. As Margaret's father told me, "He never had to have a regular job. He was always head of something."

Margaret's grandfather was a beloved statesman. She didn't know that her grandfather had run for president of Korea twice. According to his obituary, his last words were: "To die before I see the reunification of Korea is devastating." Three thousand people attended his state funeral, and thirteen thousand monks prayed for him there. Yet, for some reason, Margaret's mother's family held back the news of his death from their daughter in America. Young Hie was pregnant with Margaret at the time, and it would be close to five years later, when she was pregnant with Margaret's brother, that they mailed her an aerogram with the news. Margaret believes they were trying to protect her, but what they ended up doing was denying her the right to mourn her father when she deserved to, with the rest of her family and her nation.

We searched the Chun family register to see how far back we could trace Margaret's mother's father's line. Her great-grandfather was born in 1879, and his wife was born in 1885. Margaret's great-grandmother holds an unusual place in family lore—a different sort of public figure from her son. "There was a female relative who dressed as a man or lived as a man, but she had a husband also. I'm thinking this is her, that she dressed in men's clothes and smoked a pipe." Margaret went on to tell me a story that sounds like something out of one of her routines: "She was famously regarded as ugly, and her ugliness was kind of this legend, and people would actually come from miles around and see her because she was famous."

Margaret's mother's family belongs to the Mun Kyung Chun clan, which, the *joakbo* tells us, has only around five thousand members. This *joakbo* also helped us trace Margaret's Chun ancestors back in a straight line for centuries, twenty-three generations—all the way to a direct ancestor born in 1331. The clan's progenitor was Margaret's nineteenth great-grandfather, Chun Yoo Kyum. We had a passage translated from the *joakbo* that reveals not just her ancestor's high position but his origin: "Chun Yoo Kyum came to Korea for Yuan dynasty in 1351 at the age of 20 to serve the Mongol princess, Noguk." This would make Chun Yoo Kyum Mongol or Chinese, not Korean.

Like the progenitor of Margaret's father's clan, Margaret's first Chun ancestor was distinguished in Korean history. According to the *joakbo*, Chun Yoo Kyum married the sister of the Goryeo Dynasty general Choi Young and became a naturalized Korean. When the Yi clan took power and established the Joseon Dynasty, Margaret's ancestor defended the vanquished Goryeo king and queen to the end. But when the new government offered him a position, he said he wasn't interested and went off to live as a hermit—a rebellious streak we've seen in Margaret's grandfather and, of course, in Margaret herself.

Would knowing all along that she came from such distinguished ancestors in Korea, I asked Margaret, have helped her get through some of the darker days of her childhood?

"Oh, it would have helped tremendously," she answered without hesitation. "When I was going to school, it seemed like other kids could respond to history in a way that was personal, and I never could, because it was so much about other people and other experiences that were not mine. It would have been very powerful to have a sense of history."

▪ Few Americans can even come close to tracing their family tree back to the thirteenth and fourteenth centuries. Yet, in spite of all we had learned about Margaret, there were still some holes we wanted to fill in. Was her family originally Chinese, or was it Korean, as she had always believed? We turned to DNA to find out.

We accessed Margaret's father's line by testing her father's Y-DNA. We traced her direct paternal ancestors back to her great-grandfather, Cho Dai Hyun, who was probably born in the 1880s in what is now North Korea. Margaret's father's Y-DNA reveals that her paternal haplogroup is O3a4, a subgroup of the haplogroup O, which is the dominant haplogroup in eastern Asia. Haplogroup O originated about thirty-five thousand years ago. The subgroup O3a split off about thirty thousand years ago, when the first humans to occupy southeastern Asia moved north through present-day China. Today, O3a is common among the Han Chinese and can also be found in the Himalayas, Japan, the Philippines, Malaysia, Vietnam, and Korea. About 40 percent of Korean, Manchurian, and Vietnamese men share the O3a haplogroup. From this result it's not possible to tell for sure whether Cho In-gyu was Chinese or Korean.

On Margaret's mother's line, we could trace her direct maternal ancestor back to her great-grandmother, Lee Jung Hie, who was probably born in the 1880s in what is now South Korea. Margaret's test of her mitochondrial DNA reveals that her maternal haplogroup is called D5a2a1b, which is common in southern China. It is a subgroup of the larger haplogroup D, which arose about forty-five thousand years ago, one of the two major haplogroups carried into Asia by some of the first modern human beings to live outside of Africa. Margaret's haplogroup root, D5, is comparable in age to D itself and is common in southern China but rare farther north.

In Korea, Margaret's haplogroup D5a is exceedingly rare. In fact, it appears in only .05 percent of Korean women. While her subgroup is found most commonly among the Nishi of northeastern India, it has also been observed in China and inner Mongolia. This scientific test suggests that Margaret's ancestors on her mother's side weren't originally from Korea, which dovetails with what her *joakbo* told us.

The third DNA test is the admixture test, which reveals a person's ancestry percentages over the past five hundred years, since the time of Columbus. We know from the test of Margaret's mitochondrial DNA that her line came to Korea from elsewhere. As Margaret suspected, her results are 100 percent Asian.

To learn that somewhere long ago she was not Korean came as a tremendous shock to Margaret. "Because of the amount of national pride that my parents both seem to have, that they regard Korea to be the place of their origin—which it is," she said, "it's surprising that they're from other places actually."

Learning of her family's incredibly long history, of their achievements and sorrows, was extremely meaningful to Margaret. "Your specialness sometimes gets lost with your Americanization," Margaret said. "I love this because now I feel like I exist. You can see back where you came from."

If she had a fairy godmother who could take her to visit just one of her many ancestors, Margaret's first choice was someone who didn't live so long ago. "I would like to visit my maternal grandfather. I think maybe he did want to be there for me. He died right before I was born, and it was like he was hanging on."

Margaret compared her life to the lives of those who came before her. "All of these people lived through so many tremendous changes and such

Margaret Cho • Sanjay Gupta • Martha Stewart   **215**

strife. I wonder what they would think of the amazing privilege that I live my life with now. I do whatever I want all the time. They had all of the social upheaval and wars and different sides of the wars, and there are countries gone, the kind of hardship that I can't even imagine. They would really maybe be pretty shocked at the way that I live."

Sanjay Gupta (b. 1969)

Dr. Sanjay Gupta is CNN's chief medical correspondent and a practicing neurosurgeon. His face is recognized by millions of television viewers, and he has covered health-related stories around the globe, from the war in Iraq to floods in Pakistan to the earthquake in Haiti. On air he's skilled at negotiating several different worlds, but in the world in which he grew up—the small town of Novi, Michigan—he, like Margaret Cho, often felt like an outsider.

Sanjay was born in Novi on October 23, 1969, but his parents were from India. "There weren't a lot of people who had names like ours. There weren't a lot of people who looked like me." In this "small, rural, homogeneous town" in Michigan, Sanjay said, "Being Indian was a very novel thing. It was really something unusual—and not fun, I think in some ways, because you're different."

The differences between him and those around him became more evident to him when he enrolled in school. "My name was different; we had a different skin color," he said. "Not everyone pronounced words the way that we did."

While Sanjay remembers his childhood as essentially happy and secure, like many children of immigrants he just wanted to fit in, and changing his name would have been a start. "I wanted to change my name to Steve," Sanjay said, recalling his discomfort. "Now it sounds silly, but I came pretty close to doing this." Today he embraces his distinctive name, but not then. His choice of name—Steve—came from one of the few television shows he was allowed to watch: *The Six-Million-Dollar Man*, whose main character was Steve Austin. "There was some desire for normalcy, and that would be one way to get it."

When Sanjay was about ten, he told his mother of his plans. She said no outright. "When I brought this up, I thought they would say, 'OK, so when do you want to do this?' But she said, 'You can't do that.' And there was a whole story about this: the name was chosen in part by grandparents and all of this. There was a part of her identity, obviously, in her children. Changing the name would have affected me, but also her." His name was a link to his ancestral past that his mother would not allow him to sever.

Sanjay went through some self-described rough patches when he was about twelve or thirteen and was thrown out of school for fighting. After the Iranian hostage crisis in 1979, ethnic taunting reached an all-time high in Novi. "I was born in this country, and my parents chose to live in this country. Despite all that, when that was happening, there was so much backlash against Middle Easterners and Iranians. And I was the only kid who looked like them." Sanjay's fighting, no matter that it was in self-defense, was an affront to his parents' beliefs. "People talk about Gandhi and they talk about nonviolence, and they talk about it in a historical sense," Sanjay said. "My parents, they lived through that. My dad just told me the other day that he saw Gandhi and his spinning wheel, and he said it with such great pride in his voice."

Although Sanjay's violent reaction to the taunting upset his parents, they didn't punish him for it. "They weren't fighters," Sanjay said, "although my dad, I think at some point he had some sense of what life was like."

Sanjay battled his sense of loneliness and isolation by immersing himself in his studies. His high school yearbook shows a teenage boy who was at the top of his game: "Class Brains," "Most Likely to Succeed," "Most Ambitious." "This is a little strange to look at these photographs now," he said, "because in some ways I don't think these pictures were me. I was a guy who just wanted to keep a low profile just by blending in. . . . But the ethnicity was what I felt most acutely."

Attitudes toward Indian Americans changed dramatically in this country in a relatively short period of time. By 1970, the year after Sanjay was born, there were only fifty-one thousand immigrants from India in America. By 2008, that population had grown to 1.5 million. When we look at census categories throughout the twentieth century, it seems the U.S. Census Bureau wasn't sure exactly what to do with this group. In the 1930s and 1940s, it counted Indian Americans as their own category, Hindu. In 1950 and 1960, they were lumped into a category called "Other Race." In 1970 they became white. And since 1980, Indians and all other South

Asians have been classified as Asian. It's no wonder Sanjay experienced conflict internally and externally. His place in America seemed to be constantly changing.

Sanjay describes himself, for the first ten years of his life, as "an only child." It was just he and his parents. During this time, they took him for his first visit to India, where he met his extended family. "All of a sudden, I have this huge brotherhood and sisterhood of cousins," he recalled happily. "These kids come to greet me at the airport, and they're just playing games. They want to immediately teach me Hindi. . . . I still know it now because of them."

But even in India, Sanjay experienced a phenomenon that exists across many immigrant cultures: he was American, and it was obvious. "I don't know what it is," he said, "but I could do everything just as they would. I could use the Brylcreem that they still used, I could put on the same clothing that they're wearing, and they could still tell that I wasn't from there if I was walking down the street. I don't know if it's your gestures, how long you stare at something, but they can always tell. I would sit there and just try and watch people and see what is it about them that makes that person Indian."

In many parts of Africa, the children of the immigrant branch of the family are teased as "been-tos": they'd been to New York, or they'd been to Atlanta. Sanjay said the Indian version of a "been-to" is an "ABCD": "American-born Confused Desi." *Desi* is a colloquial term, derived from the word *des*, meaning "homeland" in both Hindi and Urdu, which came about post-Partition, after India was divided and Pakistan became a nation. In his cousins' eyes, there was no question that Sanjay was an ABCD. He was loved, though, and he always left India realizing how lonely he was in the States—wishing he could bring his relatives back with him, but never once wishing his parents had stayed there. Even as a child, he was aware that his opportunities in America were dramatically different from his cousins' in India.

I was curious to know what made Sanjay want to be a doctor. He laughed. "Part of it was when I was watching *The Six Million Dollar Man*. They created this man, doctors and surgeons, and they built him 'better, stronger, faster' than before. That was the catchphrase at the beginning of the show. . . . I remember there was an operating-room scene with him, and it was the first time I thought, that's a profession I could throw myself into."

There was a more personal inspiration for Sanjay as well. When he was about twelve years old, his maternal grandfather had a stroke. "He and I were very close. He was one of the people who taught me a lot about what happened in India and Pakistan during the Partition. Then when he had this stroke, it was just so scary, because I'd talk to him all the time, and all of a sudden he couldn't speak. And when he did speak, it was all very garbled and nonsensical. That was frightening."

Sanjay was taken with the doctors and neurosurgeons who worked to improve function in his grandfather's brain. "They ended up doing an operation to restore blood flow to his brain, and he did well from that," Sanjay said. "And these doctors also spent a lot of time with this annoying twelve-year-old kid who was asking a lot of questions. They were very charitable." Culturally, medicine was something of a shift for Sanjay's parents. "In my parents' generation, the smartest kids in India became engineers, so when I said I wanted to become a doctor, from my dad in particular there was a little bit of 'You've done well in school; why would you do that?'"

As an undergraduate at the University of Michigan, Sanjay did a lot of writing about health care policy for various magazines. From 1997 to 1998, he was selected as a White House Fellow, a prestigious program designed to give individuals an opportunity to work as special assistants to high-level government officials. This was during the Clinton administration, and Sanjay worked with First Lady Hillary Clinton on health care.

There he met Tom Johnson, the first White House Fellow, by then the CEO of CNN. Johnson wanted to create a medical unit at CNN, and over the years he began to court Sanjay. What Sanjay saw during his first visit to the CNN newsroom in Atlanta blew him away. "You look at a newsroom, and all these smart, young, curious people are bridges to all over the world. They're taking in bits of information and content on the phone, on the computers. And they're basically trying to decide: is something happening in the world, is it important, and how do we convey it to all of our viewers everywhere in the world?"

Sanjay has long recognized the power of storytelling as a way of connecting generations. With the goal of preserving his family's heritage as well as that of other Indian Americans, in 2009 Sanjay and his brother Suneel initiated the Kahani Oral History Project. They recruited their mother to be its first storyteller. "I started to have a real sense of finiteness," Sanjay said. "I'd always felt those stories would be around forever. My parents, every time we got together, they would tell some iteration of the story, forgetting they had told us before, and it would just always be there, part of our lives. At some point you do realize that that wasn't going to be forever." Perhaps in a nod to his relationship with his own grandfather, the Kahani project encourages grandchildren to interview their grandparents.

■ Sanjay's parents came to the United States during the mid-1960s, both in search of educational opportunities. His mother, Damyanti Hingorani, moved to Oklahoma to complete her education in engineering. After she graduated, she moved to Detroit, where the jobs were. On the drive to Detroit, her car broke down in Ann Arbor. Alone and with no one in particular to call, she found a phone booth and began scanning the directory for Indian names, to find someone who would help her. She called the number of an Agrawal, the first Indian name she came across. Mr. Agrawal wasn't home, but his roommate was. "The rest, as they say, is history," Sanjay said. The roommate would become Sanjay's father, Subhash Gupta.

Sanjay's mother, Damyanti, was the first female engineer hired by the Ford Motor Company in 1967. In fact, when she first began to apply for jobs as an engineer, she was sent to the secretarial pool. She held her ground and got the job she had worked for and so richly deserved. When she was told by her employers that her given name, Damyanti, was too difficult for the American engineers to say and she would have to change it, she changed it to Rani—which means "queen" in Hindu. It was a subtle stab at those trying to control her. Sanjay believes that his father experienced workplace discrimination at the Ford Motor Company as well. "I think there was, at that time at least, a belief that someone like him, that hadn't done all their education in this country, that didn't speak perfect English, couldn't rise through the ranks and become a senior executive."

Although Sanjay was aware of an incident here and there, there were many things his parents shielded him from. "In part maybe it was because they didn't talk about anything that was what they would consider a private matter, something that was happening to them and not to us as a family," Sanjay said. This denial of trauma exists in the African American community as well, and in so many other communities that have experienced pain by virtue of their skin color, their religion, or their heritage.

We started our exploration of Sanjay's heritage on his mother's side. Damyanti Hingorani was born on May 10, 1942, in the town of Tharushah in Sindh, a state that had come under British rule a century before. In 1947 the Partition of India divided the country into two nations, including the new Muslim state, Pakistan. In the chaos, more than a million people lost their lives. Fourteen million were displaced, among them five-year-old Damyanti and her family, though they had lived as part of the Hindu minority peacefully with their Muslim neighbors for generations. Sanjay's grandfather, Jairamadas Hingorani, born on February 14, 1914, also in Tharushah, and his grandmother, Gopibai Bhambhani, born on May 1, 1922, in nearby Padidan, were forced to flee their ancestral home in Sindh, which had become part of Pakistan. This was the first Sanjay had ever heard of his grandmother's birthplace.

His mother spoke of pleasant memories she had of Sindh but kept silent on the difficulties. "Her grandfather was a landowner and owned movie theaters and owned all kinds of different stores, including stores that sold sweets and sodas and stuff," Sanjay said. This idyllic memory is in stark contrast with an article we found in the *Hindustan Times* at the time. "'Hindus have no place in Sindh,'" Sanjay read from the paper. "'A need for a regulated exodus.' They were telling them to get out."

But Damyanti rarely spoke to her son about Partition. "I've tried to find out just how violent it was, what she saw," he said, "but she doesn't talk about it that much. There is a cultural thing that I see among Indians, and maybe it's among Indians who immigrated away from India. There is a desire to protect their kids from some of the tougher parts of their lives." Before his grandfather had his stroke, he would speak of his family's old home. "He loved to tell stories," Sanjay said. "But they were always stories that were fiction."

The facts had been harrowing. The Hingoranis were just one family of more than 7 million Hindus, Sikhs, and Jews who fled what had become Pakistan. Another 7 million Muslims left India in the reverse migration. Sanjay's mother shared with us a heart-wrenching story about this time. "I remember that we had to leave very, very early in the middle of the night, so nobody could recognize us. My dad's mother didn't want to even leave. She said, 'I came as a bride, and I'm not leaving this place.' I remember she used to carry a big keychain with several keys, and she knew exactly which key fitted each lock. She had locked everything, and she used to tell me one day she is going to go back and open all that."

Sanjay's grandmother reluctantly left with the rest of the family. They made the perilous journey over land from their home in Sindh to Karachi and then went by boat to Bombay (now Mumbai). Many Sindhi ended up in refugee camps, but the Hingoranis moved south to Bangalore, and then finally settled in Baroda (now called Vadodara) in the state of Gujarat. Sanjay's mother never told him she'd lived in Bangalore. "It's funny that she never mentioned Bangalore to me, because I talk about it all the time," he said, perplexed. "It's a thriving city now, sort of the Silicon Valley of Asia."

Damyanti told us that her grandmother held on to that keychain till her dying day. "That's proof of where they expected their lives to go," Sanjay said. "They want to go back to where their homes were." Even if the home didn't remain there, it's obvious that the heart did.

Today seventeen thousand people live in Tharushah; the houses abandoned after Partition still stand as reminders of the generations that lived there before. Prior to Partition, Hindu families had their names inscribed on the front gates of their homes; after 1947, the new residents of those abandoned homes had the names removed. We found no evidence of the Hingorani name, but we couldn't help wondering if that long-held key would unlock one of those doors.

Forced to leave almost all of their worldly possessions behind, Sanjay's family's ancestral paper trail on his mother's side runs out with Sanjay's great-grandparents. Like Damyanti's father and Damyanti herself, Sanjay's great-grandfather, Danomal Hingorani, was also born in Tharushah, in the late nineteenth century. We know that Sanjay's grandmother Gopibai's parents, Taurmal Bhambhani and Putlibai, surname unknown, were born in Padidan like she was. Beyond that, though, we can find no documentation of them in any public records. The land records for the entire district had been kept in an office in Padidan, the Mukhtiarkar, until as late as 2007. Sadly, in the violence following Benazir Bhutto's assassination that year, the building was destroyed, along with all the records in it.

Literally and figuratively, Damyanti has kept her connection to her homeland at a distance. Sanjay doesn't believe that his mother has a desire ever to return to India again. As a result, he had wondered if his own connection to his ancestral homeland might have been tempered. But when he covered the massive, unprecedented flooding in Pakistan in 2010, he says he felt something just being on the same land where his mother had lived, even though her time there was not by choice but by decree. "You feel a little stirring when you see a little girl and you think, God, my mom maybe walked down a street like this and looked like that little girl."

■ On his father's side, Sanjay can trace his ancestors only back to his grandfather. Sanjay's father, Subhash Gupta, was born on September 30, 1944, in Simla, a city in the Himalayas once known as the "summer capital" of the British Raj. His parents, Lakhmichand Gupta and Indira Jain, were born in the state of Haryana, just outside of Delhi, where Sanjay's paternal ancestors lived for generations.

Sanjay said his grandfather cut an impressive figure. "He was a big guy, very big for an Indian specifically. I think he was close to 6'4". He was a lawyer, and probably the most educated person in his cohort of peers at that time. He wore that as a badge of honor."

Sanjay didn't know his grandmother as well. He believes this was typical in Indian families. "Indian women at that time, especially in India, didn't sit down and have conversations with people like the men did," Sanjay explained. "The men would sit down and talk, but a lot of Indian women—and my grandmother was no exception—she was doing a lot more of the house duties at that time. She was very affectionate, loving toward me, but it wasn't as much of getting to know her or being social with her as it was with my grandfather."

Lakhmichand was the first educated person in his family. After training as a lawyer in Lahore, he became an income tax officer for the finance ministry, one of only fourteen in India to hold this post. Sanjay's granduncle, Rameshwar Dass Gupta, was also a distinguished man, receiving a certificate, dated August 15, 1972, and signed by Prime Minister Indira Gandhi, "on the occasion of the twenty-fifth anniversary of independence, to mark a memorable contribution in the independence movement."

That certificate, we learned, was not given lightly. In the pages of the book *The Freedom Fighters of Haryana*, we learned that Rameshwar Dass Gupta went to jail—twice—for his commitment to India's struggle for freedom, once in 1930 and then again in 1932. Sanjay was understandably stunned by this information—and by the fact that no one had ever breathed a word about it.

What—or who—was behind the tremendous accomplishments of these two brothers? We started with a look at Sanjay's great-grandfather, Molarchand Gupta, who owned a consignment shop and a grain store in Rohtak, in the state of Haryana. The Guptas lived behind the store; it stayed in the family for decades before being sold off ten years ago. Sanjay pored over never-before-seen pictures of the shops where his family had worked and lived. "This is a part of my life I just figured I wasn't ever going to learn about or know about."

A picture, they say, is worth a thousand words, but there was still more to learn of Sanjay's history, long lost to him. Molarchand had come to Rohtak in 1930 from a much smaller village, Doab. Doab is Sanjay's family's ancestral seat. The experts we asked all told us the same thing: in India, genealogy remains an oral tradition. The best thing to do: go to the family home, ask questions, and wait for people to answer.

In India, we tracked down a distant cousin of Sanjay's, Vinod Mittal. Vinod is the family's unofficial genealogist; he has been researching his and Sanjay's family history for years. Vinod took us to Doab in an attempt to locate the home of their shared great-grandfather. Vinod knew him personally, but Sanjay had never even heard his name. Another relative we meet, Rejinder, told us that all the family's ancestors lived in this area, but over time, relatives began to disperse, making their homes in Delhi, Rohtak, or America.

Sanjay's great-grandfather Molarchand occupied a somewhat legendary status in Doab—so strong, one villager said, that he could leap over a buffalo. "My Baba was big and strong," Vinod told us proudly. Villagers were excited to share their stories about him. "He was very healthy," one man said, "because his business was good." Another showed us the family's home. "Here was your well," he pointed out. "There was a place for children to play, and at the back of it there was the well."

Person after person spoke of Molarchand's great size and tremendous presence. He certainly left his mark on Doab. Molarchand built an eighteen-foot-wide, fifty-four-foot-long pond, secured by a brick wall, that served as a bathing hole for the residents of Doab. Today it is used to bathe animals, but it remains an important community resource. Near Doab, Sanjay's great-grandfather owned another home, which he built in the early 1900s.

That building may be gone, but memories of Molarchand linger. In time, he left the village to open his business in Rohtak. Routinely described as generous and religious, he turned over his house to village priests who were still living in it until 2011, when monsoon damage rendered it uninhabitable. "This is completely a collision of my worlds," Sanjay responded.

Sanjay's cousin Vinod also traveled to Hardwar, a holy city on the Ganges River of tremendous genealogical importance to Hindus. The name *Hardwar* means "gateway to the gods." For thousands of years, Hindus have gone there to perform rites for their dead. At the site are thousands of priests, called Brahman Pandits, or Pandas, who keep handwritten records of visitors' *gotras*, the male lineages on their family trees. We arranged for Vinod to meet with the two priests, the brothers Madhusudan and Shyam Sunder, who are the keepers of Sanjay's family's ledger, or *bahi*.

The scrolls are written in a protective code—Devanagari characters, which is the alphabet used to write Hindi, minus the vowels. They contain precious information going back, incredibly, eight generations on Sanjay's father's line. Cousins, grandparents, great-grandparents, and beyond—they're all there, a symbolic gathering of two centuries' worth of ancestors, of family members that Sanjay never even knew he had. Sanjay read some of the names aloud, but the text was too cryptic and unfamiliar to convey much meaning. We had it translated so that we could give Sanjay as rich a picture as possible of his ancestors' lives. What it says is that in July of Samvat 1928 by the Hindu calendar, which is 1871 by our calendar, Sanjay's great-great-grandfather, Patram Dass, went to Hardwar to perform the Kanwar Yatra, a pilgrimage in which the faithful carry holy water from the Ganges back to the temple of Shiva in their town or village.

Although this pilgrimage has become very popular today, back then, only Brahmin priests or spiritual leaders were allowed to take the Kanwar Yatra. Experts told us that this is one of the earliest such records they've ever seen. Patram Dass must have been very pious, or perhaps he was showing his gratitude for a favor granted by Shiva with the gift of holy water. Whatever inspired him to undertake this pilgrimage, he would have used the *kanwar*, or pole, to transport holy water from Hardwar on the Ganges all the way back to Doab on foot—a journey of about 150 miles, a week of walking in the Indian summer heat.

In another entry, we learned Sanjay's fourth great-granduncle, Ram Jas, visited Hardwar in Samvat 1904, which is 1847 by our calendar. "Ram Jas is the son of Nand Lal, who is the son of Bhiku Ram, who is the son of Lala Khiali Ram." Lala Khiali Ram is Sanjay's sixth great-grandfather. The Pandas don't record birth and death dates, but we can estimate that Lala Khiali Ram was born in the late eighteenth century—eight generations back on Sanjay's family tree. Sanjay stared in disbelief at name after unfamiliar name. He even found a few other Sanjays.

Yet he also noticed the absence of any women's names. Scrolls like those we discovered for Sanjay's father's line record only the men in the family; women's names are lost to time, recorded only as "married female," or the like. DNA analysis would not provide us with names either, but it would allow us to go far back into both sides of Sanjay's family history.

■ The paper trail on Sanjay's mother's family went back only as far as her great-grandmother, Putlibai, who lived in Padidan in Sindh. An examination of Sanjay's mitochondrial DNA revealed that his maternal haplogroup, U2c, arose in the Near East about forty-five thousand years ago and appears most often among the Sindhi people of southern Pakistan. It was prevented from spreading to Europe and East Asia, as so many other haplogroups did, by the Himalayas and the deserts of Iran. This gave us a slam dunk between our genealogical research and the genetic evidence in Sanjay's DNA, suggesting that his mother's family may have been in the Sindh region for a very, very long time.

On Sanjay's father's side, we traced Sanjay's paternal ancestors back to his sixth great-grandfather, Lala Khiali Ram, born sometime in the late eighteenth century in Sanjay's paternal ancestral home of Doab. Sanjay's Y-DNA tells us that his paternal haplogroup is H1, a subgroup of H. Haplogroup H arose in India between thirty thousand and forty thousand years ago, most likely in the eastern part of the subcontinent. It may have arisen near present-day Varanasi on the Ganges River, one of the oldest continuously occupied cities in India. Even today, H1 is rarely found outside of South Asia.

To check our scientific information against our cultural history, we found the name of Sanjay's family's *gotra* (as a reminder, the Hindu term for male lineage or patrilineal clan). All members of a *gotra* descend in an unbroken line from a common male ancestor. Sanjay's *gotra* is Mittal, one of the eighteen Agrawal clans. The patriarch of all eighteen clans was Agrasena, a Sun Dynasty king, born in October of 3064 B.C. According to legend, Agrasena had been a member of the Kshatriya, or warrior caste, but chose to become a member of the Vaishya, or trader caste, for the benefit of his people. The database of South Asians isn't yet large enough for us to verify whether men in the Agrawal clans share the same paternal haplogroup, but if they do, this king who lived five thousand years ago would be Sanjay's direct ancestor. Agroha is the legendary capital of King Agrasena's kingdom. A pilgrimage site for all Agrawals, it is located in Haryana, where Sanjay's father's ancestors lived for generations. (In a funny twist, you'll remember that Agrawal was the last name of Sanjay's father's roommate, the man whose Indian name Sanjay's mother had found in a phone book when seeking help for her broken-down car.)

Sanjay's admixture test compares Sanjay's genome to representative samples from Europe, Asia, and sub-Saharan Africa. As he predicts, it is almost entirely South Asian—90 percent—with 9.4 percent Middle Eastern. The category South Asian indicates Indian ancestry, while Middle Eastern could be Palestinian, Bedouin, Druze, Iranian, Jewish, or Mozabite, or it may be a reflection of his Sindhi ancestry, since Sindh is today part of Pakistan.

Sanjay processed all the new information we had shared with him, amazed at how far back we'd been able to trace his roots. "They've been there forever," he said. "We know where home is."

If Sanjay had a fairy godmother who could take him to any time in history, to meet any one of his ancestors, I asked which one it would be. "Part of me wants to meet Lala Khiali Ram," Sanjay said. "That's where it all began. But also my great-uncle, the freedom fighter. I really want to know what made him tick, why he did it, and why he not only went to jail but then did it again." Rameshwar Dass Gupta fought proudly and fearlessly for the independence of the land on which his family—Sanjay's family—had lived for generations.

"I feel more Indian today, and I feel greater pride in my heritage as well," he said, reflecting on his journey through his roots. "I've always been proud to be Indian, but now I feel like I have a real story to tell."

Martha Stewart (b. 1941)

Martha Stewart is so well known that her name has become a brand. Knowing only her public image, you might think that Martha's ancestors came to America on the *Mayflower*. But the truth is, she's the child of second-generation Polish immigrants. Born Martha Kostyra on August 3, 1941, she grew up in the predominantly white suburb of Nutley, New Jersey. With her blonde hair and fair complexion, Martha herself had an easier time "fitting in" than Margaret and Sanjay did. In fact, she says, "I never, ever felt different." But she was keenly aware of her father's feelings of being an outsider.

"My father was brought up in that era when immigrants were kind of like second-class citizens," she said. "He always complained about his bosses looking down on him because he was a Polack. I hated that he would even think of himself as a 'Polack' instead of someone of Polish descent. It was beneath him to think like that. But again, in those days, Polish was not the thing to be. Italian, yes—dashing. French, yes. But Polish was just sort of ordinary immigrant."

Martha's parents, Edward Kostyra, a gym teacher turned pharmaceutical salesman, and Jadwiga Martha Ruszkowski, a teacher turned homemaker, were the children of Polish immigrants who came to America at the turn of the twentieth century. Like most Polish immigrants, the family practiced Catholicism. Martha's memories of holidays revolve around the festive meals her family would have, full of traditional foods like kielbasa and pig's feet in jelly.

Martha has always been deeply curious about—and deeply proud of—her Polish ancestry. The rest of her family, however, didn't outwardly embrace their heritage. Martha learned very little of the Polish language and believes that her parents intentionally didn't teach it to their children because they wanted them to be perceived as Americans. "Being Polish, and having parents who spoke Polish, I was angry that they didn't teach me Polish." As adults, two of Martha's brothers rejected their Polish last name, Kostyra, for something more "American-sounding."

"My brother Eric said that he had to change his name because he wanted to build a very unethnic dental practice," Martha recalled. He changed the spelling of his first name from "Erik" to "Eric" and adopted the last name Scott. "Why he chose Scott I have no idea. There is nothing Scottish in our family. And then my brother George took his wife's name, which is Christiansen."

According to Martha, her parents weren't bothered by their sons' rejection of their family name. Although open about her roots, she admitted that her married name, Stewart, may have been more palatable to the public than Kostyra. "If my magazine were *Martha Kostyra Living*, I don't know if it would have been as popular as *Martha Stewart*, which kind of rolls off your tongue. It's such a great brand name, like Ralph Lauren instead of Ralph Lifshitz," Martha said of the fashion designer who famously shed his last name not because of its "Jewishness," as he told Oprah in an interview, but because "My given name has the word 'shit' in it."

From early on, Martha focused on becoming financially independent. She signed with the Eileen Ford Modeling Agency when she was thirteen. For a young girl, it was an adventure, taking the bus into New York each weekend and working in department stores and fashion shows. While she was modeling, she sewed all her own dresses out of luxurious fabrics using patterns of some of the great designers—Dior, Balenciaga—which she borrowed from a friend who owned a design house. Martha's formidable dressmaking skills combined with her natural beauty and drive sustained a successful career. She found steady, lucrative work modeling throughout high school and college, appearing frequently in print ads and on television for Lifebuoy soap, Breck shampoo, and Clairol, among others. She was able to put herself through Barnard College and support her family with her earnings. "At one point, when my dad lost his job, my paychecks just went home."

When she began to do photography modeling during college, she changed agencies. "Someone told me to go to Stewart Models, spelled the same way as my married name," she explained. Married at nineteen and already known socially as Martha Stewart, she kept her name professionally. "I was always Martha Kostyra. In modeling, the foreign was good. It's mysterious."

Martha couldn't be tied down to one career. During the 1960s she worked on Wall Street as an institutional banker. From there she made what might be considered an unlikely jump—at least for anyone else—into the catering business, and in 1972 she established her own company in Connecticut. After running the company for a decade, Martha wrote a how-to book. It was called *Entertaining*, and it elevated domesticity to an art form. "I didn't know I was going to be an author," she said, recalling her surprise at her own success. "I didn't know I was going to have a really great book that would sell a million copies or more, and it did." She signed her first big retail contract with Kmart around 1987 and since then has been a household name.

Martha has changed the way Americans view entertaining and housekeeping, injecting domestic duties with style and glamour and making them creative endeavors. Today Martha's impact is so deep and pervasive, it's little wonder that many of us feel that we know her personally. But how much do we really know about who Martha Stewart is and where she came from? How much does Martha herself know?

■ First we wanted to explore Martha's father's side of the family. Edward Rudolph Kostyra was born on August 21, 1911, in New York City. Martha sees a lot of her father in herself. "I think I was closest to Dad of all the siblings," she said. "He was really impatient. I think I got that impatience from him. He was very particular. I've been very particular my whole life. He was also very artistic, and I think I'm very artistic." Accomplished both athletically and musically, Martha's father was a gymnast and a violinist. "He could play by ear pretty much anything," Martha said, clearly enamored of her beloved father. "He also encouraged us to study music. We were all terrible, pretty much."

At Ellis Island, the iconic port of arrival for more than 12 million people, we tracked down all four of Martha's grandparents with the help of Stephen Briganti, who runs the Liberty-Ellis Island Foundation. "The United States government, over time, required that manifests be kept," Briganti explained. "Once they got here, the ship's captain simply gave the manifest to the officials of Ellis Island." The manifest—a listing of the ship's passengers—contained typical census information: sex and age of the passenger, occupation. But sometimes it contained other facts as well. "It might have on it how much money you came with, where you were coming from, where you were going to, sometimes right down to an address," Briganti said. "It's a wonderful depository for tracing your heritage."

We found Martha's grandmother, Helena Krukar—known later as Helen— on a ship manifest from 1904. According to the document, Helena was born on February 21, 1890, in Zagorze, Poland. Polish records indicate that she was born in 1888, which would explain why her age was given on the manifest as sixteen. The teenager made the eleven-day journey, in steerage, to New York on the SS *Moltke* all by herself. She arrived with two dollars in her possession. The manifest also told us that her brother Henry, who had settled in New York City the year before, was waiting for her when she got off the ship. Helena never once spoke to Martha of what must have been a terrifying experience.

"I wish I could just wake her up and have her tell me right now," Martha said, starting a thread of thought which she repeated many times during our time together: that she wishes she had asked more questions when she had the chance. "Memories were not as prevalent or spoken about in those days. I wish I had been a little bit more inquisitive."

In 1908 Helena married another recent Polish immigrant, Martha's grandfather, Frank Kostyra, whom she met while working at a restaurant called Child's in lower Manhattan. Born on October 4, 1879, in Kopki, Poland, Frank had immigrated to the United States in 1905, a year after Helen. The manifest for the ship Frank arrived on lists him as an "alien passenger," his nationality Austrian, his race Polish. "Called aliens, treated like aliens, not welcomed the way they should have been," Martha said with disgust.

The distinction between nationality and race speaks to the complexity of the history of the Polish state. For hundreds of years, sections of what we now know as Poland were divided and controlled by various European powers: Prussia, Russia, Austria. At the time Frank Kostyra emigrated, the region he came from was part of the Austrian Empire known as the kingdom of Galicia.

A self-described history buff, Martha was aware that Poland didn't always exist as we know it today. She also had heard her grandfather served in Franz Josef's cavalry. But the manifest revealed something about him Martha didn't know: his occupation. In his homeland, Frank Kostyra was a basket maker. The town that he came from, Kopki, is renowned for its wicker and basket production. "'Basket maker' really encourages us as crafters," Martha commented.

It may come as no surprise that many of her ancestors were highly skilled in the domestic arts. In addition to basket makers, her family tree is populated with butchers, gardeners, shoemakers, decorative iron workers, and seamstresses. Martha has a whole leitmotif running through her family. She is an extension of this concern with sewing and craftsmanship and gardening. On every branch of her family tree, it keeps repeating.

She saw it in her own home as well. During the course of our journey, Martha spoke often of her father's enviable green thumb, which Martha said he inherited from his mother. He also "cared about cloth. He taught me the difference between worsted and twill and gabardine and silk," she said. "And he had those fingers that could just touch pima cotton versus Egyptian cotton versus six-hundred-thread count. He knew all that." In her own generation, Martha described her brother Eric as "the most amazing craftsperson you've ever seen." A dentist, he began with decoys and then went into jewelry making (which, Martha told us, "all dentists do, because they work with gold"), Tiffany lamps, and Chippendale-quality furniture.

"Those inherent interests," she agreed, "did come down from generation to generation pretty strong, strong feelings for living the good life."

Through church records, we learned more about the lives of Martha's grandparents. In the archives of St. Stanislaus Church in the East Village, we found not only the marriage certificate for Helen Krukar and Frank Kostyra from February 23, 1908, but also baptism and death records for several of Martha's Kostyra relatives. One pair was particularly moving: the baptism record for Stanislawa Kostyra from 1909 and the death certificate for the same child, from 1911. Records revealed that the baby, who died of pneumonia at fifteen months, was buried in the children's section of the Holy Trinity Cemetery in Brooklyn, but we couldn't locate a headstone. "That must have been a child I didn't hear about," Martha said. "Grandma never talked about Stanislawa." Martha's father, Edward, was born later that same year. Helen, Martha had heard, was intensely protective of her son. "Of course," she said. "She lost a child and then had another child. She would certainly want it to be healthy and not die." Martha never heard any mention of her aunt Stanislawa from either her grandmother or her father. The loss of a baby followed so rapidly by the birth of another was a testament to how difficult and vulnerable life was for early immigrants.

Thanks to a distant cousin of Martha's whom she had never met, living in Queens, we obtained a letter, handwritten in Polish, by Martha's grandfather, Frank Kostyra, to his brother back in Poland. For the first time, Martha got to read this treasured heirloom: "I am doing quite well here. I do not go to work now. I have a butchery, and I could give two pounds of meat to every farmer in Kopki, and I would still have some. Please write me what is going on in Kopki. I used to think of going to the country and buying a tenant house in some town, but I think it won't be better there than here. You have to work everywhere, no matter."

Martha, in keeping with her character, commented on both the item's aesthetic value and its deeper meaning. "He wrote very nicely. He was very literate," she said, a trait that could not be taken for granted among first-generation immigrants. "And what beautiful handwriting he had." Martha noted with some surprise that her grandfather had contemplated returning to his homeland after making it in America.

Martha was deeply touched by another letter we found, written by her father back to his uncle in Poland: "I greet you uncle although I cannot write well in Polish and only English because I go to an English school. I play violin. I am nine years and four months old. We wish you a Happy New Year."

Still, as we dug more deeply, we discovered troubling gaps in Martha's genealogy, where whole branches of her family tree suddenly came to an abrupt end. For example, we knew Martha's grandmother Helen (Helena) had come to this country alone, at sixteen, but what about her parents, Martha's great-grandparents, Tekla Grosiewicz and Walenty Krukar, who *didn't* leave?

Unfortunately, we couldn't learn much about Tekla, but Walenty Krukar was born on February 14, 1844, well before the American Civil War, in the town of Zagorze, in the Galicia region of the Austrian Empire. Galicia was extremely poor. In fact, more than 80 percent of the population was impoverished. Oral history tells us that Walenty and his brother owned a successful inn in Zagorze, but it was burned down by the Russians in 1915, a decade after Martha's grandmother had gone to America.

Life in what is now Poland was difficult and dangerous at the time. In 1919, less than a year after the end of World War I, bitter fighting had broken out in a war between the newly independent Polish state and Soviet Russia. The town of Zagorze, home to Martha's great-grandparents, was torn apart by the conflict.

Our research unearthed a remarkable letter from Helena's husband, Frank, to his own family that holds clues about his in-laws' fate: "We had a lot of clothes and shoes to send home to my wife's parents, but now Bolsheviks took everything, and they do not have anything. We sent two ship tickets for passage to America to my wife's sister and brother because their parents died and the house burned down, and they do not have anybody there in the country. Now Americans do not want people from the country to come here for the next 2 years but it is not yet known if they will do this." Judging by her grandfather's letter, it seems that Martha's great-grandparents' house was sacked, and they died in 1920 when the fighting reached their town. With no parents or home to return to, six of their eight children ultimately settled in America.

What happened to the brother and sister whom Frank mentioned in his letter? We found a passenger list for a ship that arrived at Ellis Island on Christmas Day, 1920, carrying the siblings, Miezcyslaw and Stanislawa, aged nineteen and sixteen, to their new home. A third brother, who became known as Joe, was on the passenger list as well. Fortunately, Frank was able to get them out of Poland before strict immigration quotas were put in place by the United States four years later.

Martha had known nothing of this dramatic story. Like many immigrants', Martha's family history is colored by a deep sense of loss and leaving, joy and success, in equal parts. Martha lit up when we mentioned her granduncle Miezcyslaw, whom she knew as Uncle Mitchell. "He had the delicious delicatessen in Jersey City," she said. "I would go there and sit in the prep kitchen and eat potato salad and liverwurst sandwiches. Then we were able to have an ice cream or a piece of candy from the candy counter. It was a really nice store, a precursor to Dean & DeLuca." And, perhaps, a precursor to the catering business that set Martha on her path in life.

■ Next we turned to Martha's mother's family. Jadwiga Martha Ruszkowski, known in the family as Big Martha, was born on September 16, 1914, in Buffalo, New York, and died only recently, in 2007, at ninety-three. Big Martha was a frequent guest on her daughter's television show. "I don't think she ever quite got what I did," Martha said. "She was just proud. . . . I was just her girl, which was nice, and it would bring me back down to Earth if she ever thought I was going anywhere else."

I asked Martha if her Polish identity was important to her mother. "It was not unimportant," she answered. "She spoke Polish, wrote voluminous letters in Polish to the relatives overseas. I think her greatest quality was her ability to keep in touch by letter writing with everybody. So I have tons of letters from my mom. She always signed, 'Your mom.'" She also excelled in the domestic arts. "She was a very good seamstress. She made all our clothes and taught us how to make our clothes. She was a very good cook. She was a good mother, a good mother."

Martha's maternal grandfather, Joseph Ruszkowski, was born in Siedlce, Poland, on August 30, 1888, and his wife, Martha's grandmother Frances Albiniak, was born in Janow on March 17, 1890. Martha loved to visit her grandparents in Buffalo during summer vacation. "The first house they lived in on Guilford Street was right across the street from a thread maker, a thread factory," Martha recalled. "I watched those ladies come out with their babushkas from the thread-making factory for the coffee break and the lunch break. I loved going there." She described her grandfather, the iron worker, as "so strong. You never wanted to shake his hand because he hurt when he shook your hand. He could just crush you if he wanted to. He was supposedly the oldest living member of the Ironworkers Guild in Buffalo, and he was honored when he was about ninety-five." Her grandmother was "a homemaker, very stern, a little bit fun-loving but never wanted to show it." As is the case for so many of us, Martha's memories of her grandmother revolve around food. "My grandmother's pantry in her basement was astonishing. She preserved pears and applesauce and string beans and garlic. Everything was preserved for the winter, so we ate very well, the most delicious food."

The manifest for the ship Joseph Ruszkowski arrived on in 1910 provides insight into life in Poland at the turn of the twentieth century. His nationality is listed as Russian, his race Polish. (Remember that on Martha's father's side, records list the nationality as Austrian.) I asked Martha if she ever discerned that her two sets of grandparents were "different types" of Polish people. "Oh, yes," Martha said. She always believed that physically, her grandmother looked different from the other side of the family; her eyes had an Asian cast. "We always imagined that she was Tatar. We always romanticized."

Joseph and Frances were married in Buffalo. We located their marriage record from the Transfiguration Church. From this document Martha learned her grandmother's maiden name, Albiniak, which she had never known, and something else: a skeleton in the closet. The record was dated June 29, 1914. "My mother was born in September. So how could they have been married only in June?" Martha laughed. Martha's immediate family had the same skeleton in its closet: Her own mother was already pregnant when she married Martha's father. "She's rolling in her grave. She doesn't want anybody to know that."

The name Albiniak opened doors to Martha's past. Our research team located her family's baptism records in Poland. The records brought us back two and a half centuries. Martha's great-great-grandfather, Kazimierz Halbiniak, was born on March 14, 1817, in Janow. This document also gave us the names of Martha's third great-grandparents, Maryanna and Krzysztof Albiniak. Krzysztof was also born in Janow around 1768. This is the oldest ancestor we were able to trace on Martha's family tree.

Kazimierz and his father spent their entire lives in Janow, the small southeastern Polish town where much of Martha's mother's family came from. Local historians told us that many Albiniaks in Janow were shoemakers. Once again, artistry seems to be an inherited trait.

These same historians shared another bit of information that would confirm Martha's suspicions about her grandmother's looks: the name Albiniak, in Martha's family for generations, is associated with the ethnic group called the Tatars. The town of Janow has been inhabited by Tatars and their descendants for centuries. Tatars were a nomadic people who lived throughout East and Central Asia and were conquered by Genghis Khan's army in 1202.

While Martha had guessed correctly at her grandmother's Tatar ancestry, she was still in for a surprise. As far as Martha knew, her ancestors in Poland practiced Roman Catholicism for generations, as her own family did growing up. On the basis of what we found, however, there was a good chance that at least some of her ancestors were Muslim. After their conquest by Genghis Khan, most Tatars embraced Islam. Some began to settle in Poland as early as the fifteenth century. Tatars were known for being exceptionally good horsemen and warriors. In the 1600s a group of Crimean Tatars regularly raided the area in Poland where Martha's ancestors settled, including their hometown, Janow. Many of these Tatars were captured during these raids and stayed in the region, intermarrying with the population and ultimately converting to Roman Catholicism.

This was where the paper trail for Martha's mother's family ended, all the way back in 1768. But could we go back even further in time with DNA?

■ Certain DNA tests act like a genetic "global positioning system," providing valuable clues about where our ancestors once lived. We were able to trace Martha's direct paternal ancestors back to her third great-grandfather, Matheusz Kostyra, who was born in Nisko, Poland, in 1771. Of course Martha, being a woman, doesn't have a Y chromosome, but through her brother George, we could trace Martha's paternal haplogroup. It is R1a1a, which arose in the Near East or present-day Pakistan about eighteen thousand years ago. After the Ice Age, about twelve thousand years ago, R1a1a was gradually carried into the territory that is now Eastern Europe. It is most common in a swath from Ukraine and the Balkans north and west into Scandinavia and is today the primary haplogroup of Eastern Europe, reaching levels of almost 50 percent among Ukrainians. This coincides with the paper trail we have for Martha's father's line. Another of our guests, Kyra Sedgwick, who has strong Eastern European roots, is Martha's distant cousin on this side of her family.

On Martha's mother's side, we couldn't test the Albiniak line directly. But working with the genetic testing service 23andMe, we identified the haplogroup, or genetic signature, encoded in Martha's direct maternal line, which we traced back to her great-great-grandmother, Katarzyna

Tomczyk, born in Lubelskie, Poland, in 1831. Martha's maternal haplogroup is W6, a subgroup of haplogroup W. Haplogroup W originated in Central Asia more than thirty-five thousand years ago in the Near East. It then spread to the area around present-day Pakistan. Today, haplogroup W is widespread in the Near East, Europe, and southwestern Asia, lending support to the theory that at least some of Martha's maternal ancestors were Muslim Tatars. Only one in one thousand individuals in the 23andMe database share this haplogroup, so it is extremely rare. To find a distant relative, we would almost certainly have to find an Asian person.

"I wouldn't mind being related to Genghis Khan," Martha joked. I told her that she probably was—we just had yet to prove it! For now she'd have to be content with her dog being the only one named Genghis Khan in the family.

Next we tested Martha's admixture, which came back as 100 percent European, which means her Tatar ancestry dates back to long before the time of Columbus. It also casts new light on research her father had done into the history of *his* family. As a child, Martha spent a lot of time in the New York Public Library, watching her father pore over genealogy records. He believed he had traced his family back to the ninth century, and that the name Kostyra came from the Isle of Kos. "Kos is right on the Turkish coast. It's a Greek island, but it's a stone's throw away from Turkey," Martha explained. "I went to Kos. I had to go. That's the seat of Hippocrates. That's where he supposedly wrote the Hippocratic Oath, under that big sycamore tree." Her father gathered from his research that his ancestors were mercenaries from Greece or Turkey who had traveled up to Poland and settled there. Another possibility is that they were mercenaries who were captured and converted to Catholicism. For now, though, this part of Martha's history is just speculation. We were unable to find any documentation to prove her father's theory at the time of this writing.

Many Polish people can't get much beyond 1900 in their family trees. On both sides of Martha's family we were able to go back to the eighteenth century. Hers is a deep, rich ancestry, more consistent in terms of abilities displayed by her ancestors than any I have seen in the four genealogy series we have done. On every branch of her family tree are craftspeople. At this point we can only wonder if DNA or environment or some combination of the two determined this. Martha was leaning toward the DNA argument.

"I really think DNA has a lot to do with it. You are who you are who you are. But education, the ability to learn, the ability to be taught, that's pretty important to me," she said. "But the strength in the human part, the living part, is really genetics."

I ended my visit with Martha by asking her the same question that I ask all my guests: if your fairy godmother showed up right now and said, "Martha, you can go back in time and you can meet one person you've met today," who would it be? Without hesitation, Martha pointed to her oldest ancestors on her Albiniak grandmother's family tree. "Definitely way back here on Grandma's side," she said. "First of all, I'm very interested in the 1700s. I'd like to see what they were like, and that's the farthest away I can go right now, and see what kind of life they lived, where they lived, how they lived. But anyone really would be interesting to revisit."

The fact is, you don't have to go too far back in time to see that our ancestors have all been constantly on the move, and it can be measured in our genes just as it can in the paper records left behind. And when we find ourselves on new and unfamiliar shores, those deeper connections to our past can help ground us, make all of us who have at times felt like outsiders part of something much larger. This can be especially profound in the lives of new or recent immigrants, who, in an effort to embrace chosen identities in America, can quickly lose—through distance, discomfort, or silence—connections that bind them together across generations with those who planted the seeds for their adventures. Not only can knowledge of their past struggles, even ancient ones, reinfuse descendants with pride of name as they brand their own; it can also gird them for the struggles they so often face fitting in and standing apart.

CHAPTER NINE

Neither Slave nor Free

The stories of Wanda Sykes's, John Legend's, and my dear friend Margarett Cooper's ancestors bring to light a little-known but crucial chapter in the history of the African American people's struggle for freedom, a struggle as old as the nation itself. Remarkably, we were able to trace John's and Wanda's families back hundreds of years and uncover the most unexpected stories. By the age of ninety-eight, Margarett had spent half a century investigating a stunning tale on her own family tree. We were thrilled to join her for part of the journey.

My own fourth paternal great-grandparents, Joe and Sarah Bruce, were held in bondage as slaves on a farm in Williamsport, West Virginia. That's the story most of us expect to find when we search for an African American's deepest family roots. But what's unusual in this case is that we found the will of their master, who set Joe and Sarah Bruce free in 1823, forty-two years before the Thirteenth Amendment ended slavery once and for all.

What's even more unusual is that they were not alone.

The story of the African American people has often been reduced to one-dimensional stereotypes and clichés, especially when it comes to slavery. But the lives of my free ancestors—as well as those of Wanda, John, and Margarett—reveal that the truth about the lives of black people in antebellum America was anything but simple.

Wanda Sykes is one of our most popular—and fearless—comedians, finding humor in even the most controversial topics. She brings her no-holds-barred style with her no matter where she goes. In 2009 she became the first African American female, and the first openly gay comedian, to emcee the White House Correspondents' Dinner. Not even the president could tame Wanda's tongue. "I know you're biracial, but the first black president! You're proud to be able to say that," she said to him at the event. "Well, that's unless you screw up. And then it's gonna be, 'What's up with the half-white guy, huh?' Who voted for the mulatto?'"

No topic is off-limits for Wanda, who openly discusses her personal life, including her biracial relationship with her wife, Alex. In 2008 Wanda took a public stand on same-sex marriage at a rally in Las Vegas. She says that edgy is "the only way I can do it."

Wanda Yvette Sykes was born in Portsmouth, Virginia, on March 7, 1964, and grew up in Gambrills, Maryland, near Fort Meade. She almost began life as Twinkles Kay. "My brother, he actually wanted to name me Twinkles, as my proper name. Twinkles Kay," Wanda recalled. "I have no idea. But thank God my aunt Mildred stepped in and was like, 'Don't name the girl Twinkles Kay.' And she came up with the name Wanda Yvette."

Wanda started turning provocation into an art in her conservative childhood home. "I was an outspoken kid," she says. "I got in trouble a lot just for being outspoken. If a friend would visit my mother, and I would look at her, and I would go, 'You know, your part is crooked,' kids weren't supposed to say things like that."

Racism was something she was always aware of, always prepared for. "We would go to Ocean City, Maryland, during the summers," she recalled. "My brother and I, we're walking down the street, we would get the drive-by 'niggers.' You know, it was like the people would drive by, 'Nigger,' and keep going. Come on, man, really?" She says that still today, she's attuned to racism. "When I go places, you've got the black sense, like Spiderman. . . . Is this place cool? What's going on? You have to be aware."

Wanda attended Hampton Institute, a historically black college in Virginia. She was tired of being one of the only black students in a classroom. As she recalled of her time in first- or second-grade, "My teacher was calling the roll, and then when she gets to my name, Wanda Sykes, I raised my hand. She goes, 'Oh, a little colored girl. I finally get to teach a little colored girl.' It hit me at first, like, 'Oh, woohoo! I'm her first colored girl!'" It didn't take long for the dig to sink in. "What did she mean her first colored girl? That kind of stuck with me."

I was curious to know if Wanda was openly gay in college. Hampton is a black school, and the black community, traditionally, tends to be homophobic. Being black and gay is considered by many to be a double bind. Wanda said she has known she was gay since she was a child, but she did not come out until 1999, after she had been married to a man for seven years. "As soon as that was over and the divorce was going, I said, 'Well, OK. Hey, I tried it. You can't say I didn't try. Now bring on the girls!'"

Wanda didn't step out on the stage immediately after graduation. Instead, she got a desk job at the National Security Agency. "When you say NSA people think, oh, wow, I have a badge and this optical reader that scans and doors open up and you go into a cave. Nothing like that," Wanda joked. "You just pull in the parking lot and go into the building. I worked in the procurement office. Basically I just shopped all day. Nothing exciting. Maybe a piece of spy equipment or something like that every now and then, but nothing exciting." After hours, she began to hone a standup routine at local talent shows. Wanda had found the perfect outlet for her outspokenness: comedy. In the early part of her career, her comedy role models were Richard Pryor, Bill Cosby, George Carlin, and especially Moms Mabley. "She was the first woman—especially the first black woman—that I saw on TV just doing standup." By Wanda's own admission, it would be a while before she gave any of her heroes a run for their money. She said her parents thought she was "nuts," especially after she invited them to a show early in her career. The audience was brutal. "They booed, they took their chairs and turned them all the way around. I think a card game broke out. It was just awful."

But Wanda loved it. She told us, "You just got to get on stage until you have that good show." She thinks that tenacity might be an inherited Sykes family trait, but she's never been able to learn very much about the ancestors who she's convinced passed it on to her.

"I do have a strength and some mechanism that allow me to, when things are bad, that I can see some good and find a purpose for it," she said. "That has to come from somewhere. There's something in these genes."

I asked Wanda if there was anything in particular she wanted to know about her family history. "Well, of course, some Native American is not bad. I can always use a little casino money. Maybe related to Oprah. That will help, too." She laughed and then turned more serious. "I'm open. I just want to know everything. It's incredibly important, because it gives you a sense of why you are the way you are."

■ Wanda's mother, Marion Louise Peoples, was born on September 4, 1937, in Virginia. Wanda has heard almost no family stories from her mother's side, but she was always curious about her grandfather, Allie Peoples. "My grandfather, I used to get in trouble because I would go, 'Why is this white man in our house?'"

Allie was born on May 20, 1895, in Norfolk County, Virginia. Wanda's grandmother, Sarah Jones, also was born there, on August 11, 1901. "I knew my grandmother very well. My grandfather, I just remember him." Wanda laughed. "He was, I don't want to say belligerent, but he was . . . you know, he had rules. Granddad had rules. You know, when he walked in the house, everything just got real quiet."

We found Allie's parents, William Peoples and Emma Howell—Wanda's great-grandparents—in the 1910 census for Norfolk County. Allie, age sixteen, lived with his parents and two sisters, yet William and Emma had been married for only eight years—a discrepancy that led us to believe William Peoples was not his teenage son's actual father.

There was a marriage record for William and Emma from 1900, but when we looked for an earlier record for Allie and his mother, Emma, before the marriage, we couldn't find a thing. We suspected there might have been another discrepancy in the spelling of the name, so we used a Soundex to help us look for different variants of the way the names could have been pronounced. Still, nothing. Ultimately, we had to search the records by first name; Allie was an unusual name for a boy, so there was still hope.

Finally, the 1900 census yielded a result: Emma Harwood, the single mother of Perlie and Allie Harwood, both boys. From these records we could conclude William Peoples was not Allie's biological father, but we were unable to trace Allie or Emma by any surname in earlier records in Virginia or North Carolina, where Emma was born. The oldest ancestors we identified on Wanda's mother's side were two great-great-grandfathers, most likely slaves, named John Jones and Henry Turner. But without further information on Wanda's mother's family, these common names brought us to a dead end—sadly, a relatively typical result in researching African American genealogy.

"It seemed like there was a lot of missing pieces," Wanda said. "Families, especially just from slavery alone, get so spread out, and you don't know. You don't know where you're from. I know my grandfather was extremely light, so we thought maybe he was passing, you know? I hear that a lot when I talk to my friends. They can't go . . . maybe two, three generations, and that's it."

■ Next we turned to Wanda's father's family. Harry Ellsworth Sykes was born on May 21, 1934, in Virginia. A full colonel in the U.S. Army, he didn't talk much about facing discrimination in the military, although Wanda recalls hearing stories. "I know there was some talk of when he was taken to train, when he was going to camp where h1e had to go for training, that they would get to the Mason-Dixon Line, and it was like, 'OK, colored soldiers in the back.'" If he felt or experienced prejudice, he shared very little of it with his daughter—a typical form of denial practiced by blacks of his generation.

"I would not describe us as a military family," Wanda said, "which is odd, because my brother was also ROTC and was in the military. He retired, I think he was a captain. So we were a military family if you say that we were always connected to the military. We shopped at the PX and the commissary and those things, but as far as the travel, we didn't do a lot of traveling. We didn't get shipped around. That was very important to my parents that we didn't do that."

Wanda's grandfather, Luther Luke Sykes, was born on February 16, 1904, in Portsmouth, Virginia, like Wanda. He was a janitor at Virginia Chemical for years, and Wanda had only pleasant memories of him. "He was just a kind man, always a smile on his face. Just quiet, easygoing. Never, never seen him get upset. Just a sweet man."

We found the marriage record of Luther's parents—Wanda's great-grandparents—Henry Sykes and Hattie Harris. Henry was born on July 22, 1880, in Boykins, Virginia, and Hattie was born in 1879 in Tarboro, North Carolina; Hattie is Wanda's first ancestor whom we traced who wasn't born in Virginia. Henry and Hattie's marriage record also gave us the name of Henry's parents, Daniel Sykes and Virginia "Jennie" Baker, Wanda's great-great-grandparents, whom we then found in the 1880 census for Southampton County, Virginia.

In addition to Daniel and Jennie, we saw in their household a son

Davey, a daughter Deanna, and also Charlotte Jones, Wanda's third great-grandmother on her father's father's side. We wanted to learn more about Charlotte, but with a last name like Jones, additional information was necessary to conduct any deeper search.

We looked for the marriage certificate of Daniel and Jennie and, upon finding it, learned they were married in 1874, nine years after the Civil War, and lived in Southampton County. The name Charlotte Sykes was shown for Daniel's mother; no father was named. But even with the far less common last name Sykes, we couldn't find Charlotte in the 1870 census.

We did, however, find another document: a register from the Freedmen's Bureau in Nansemond County, Virginia. Charlotte Sykes's name appeared on the register, along with two children, Patsy and Pleasant Sykes. Daniel's name was not listed, but this register included only children younger than fourteen. Charlotte had applied for rations, but it looks like she didn't get them. The Freedmen's Bureau was short-lived, so many people who needed help were left to struggle on their own.

This application led us to believe that Charlotte had been a slave in the area. After all, the Freedmen's Bureau was established to help freed blacks get on their feet after emancipation. Furthermore, slaves lacked mobility and money, and almost all were illiterate, which also could explain why Charlotte would have applied for rations close to home.

We then tracked down a John Sykes, a white man who lived in Boykins in nearby Southampton County. According to the Slave Schedule of 1860, he owned twenty-two slaves. In it, there were markings for a seven-year-old male (we already knew Daniel was born in 1853) and a woman who would have been around Charlotte's age. John Sykes had also written a will the year before, in 1859, but he had named only sixteen of his twenty-two slaves in it, and Charlotte wasn't one of them. Still, our best guess was that this John Sykes had been Charlotte's owner. Unfortunately, the paper trail ended there.

■ Looking into the other side of Wanda's father's family, his mother's side, provided us with a very different experience and yielded a different story entirely, unlike any we had heard before. Harry Sykes's mother, Magnolia Wilson, was born on November 6, 1905, in Churchland, Virginia. "Grandma Mag was funny," Wanda recalled. "She was really funny. She would take us on bus trips, different parks and stuff, when we were little kids, but as far as stories, no."

Magnolia's father, Junius Wilson, known as "Papa June," was Wanda's great-grandfather. She never knew him, but her uncle William told us that the Wilson family had traced its roots back to Papa June's maternal grandparents, Wanda's great-great-great-grandparents, John Francis and Elizabeth Banks.

Of the roughly half-million African Americans in Virginia in 1860, most were slaves, and they were rarely listed in public documents by name. We searched property records of local slave owners for any clues about Wanda's third great-grandparents with no success. But then our genealogist Johni Cerny discovered something quite surprising: a marriage certificate dated February 17, 1853, bearing the names of John Francis and Elizabeth Banks.

The fact that Wanda's great-great-great-grandparents were legally married revealed an irrefutable detail about their lives: they were free. "Slaves did not have marriages. They were the property of someone else. They had no rights," Cerny told us bluntly. "Marriage was a right. It was a condition of life that was only entered into by free people."

We showed Wanda the record. She was caught off-guard. She had no idea she descended from any free people. Her third great-grandparents, married in 1853, had been free eight years before the Civil War even began.

Once we knew Elizabeth Banks was free, we knew she must have left a paper trail. Free people paid rent, paid taxes, or owned property. (When we're trying to reconstruct a family tree, we look for any scrap of paper with an ancestor's name on it. Obviously for people descended from slaves this is difficult, if not impossible, to do.) Sure enough, we found Elizabeth in the Register of Free Negroes, Surry County, Virginia. The date: July 22, 1850. Wanda read the entry for her great-great-great-grandmother: "Elizabeth Banks, a free Negro of bright complexion, slight stature, and about 21 years has a scar on her left cheek near the corner of the mouth. Was born free as appears by the certificate of Martha W. Davis now on file in my office. Is four-feet-ten-and-a-quarter inches high. Is registered of the above description by order of Surry County court."

For Wanda's ancestors, this apparent paradox—being black and free in America before the Civil War—defined almost every aspect of their lives. Free blacks obviously posed a threat to the status quo, and the commonwealth of Virginia restricted their rights in order to protect the institution of slavery. The state required free African Americans to file with the Register of Free Negroes, which involved getting a respectable white person to vouch for their character and free status. Free blacks had to carry their papers with them wherever they went; if they were challenged in a public space by a white person, their papers would confirm they were legally free. Unregistered free Negroes could be jailed as runaway slaves, and even a free person with the misfortune of coming up against an unscrupulous person could be forced into slavery. All it would take was one person tearing up those precious papers. Free blacks' freedom was always at risk.

Wanda related to this ambiguous freedom as both a black woman and a gay woman. "As a member of the LGBT community, it is nowhere near this extent, but it is something about not having your freedom that I can definitely identify with." When Wanda made her passionate public stance in 2008 against California's Proposition 8, the gay marriage ban, she told the crowd, "If we had equal rights, we shouldn't have to be standing out here demanding something that we automatically should have as citizens of this country." The same could be said for Wanda's ancestor. Elizabeth Banks was free, a citizen, yet she had to carry papers to prove it.

Those free papers also told us something else very important about Wanda's third great-grandmother: she had been *born* free. If she had been a slave freed by her master, it would have said that on the form. Virginia law required free slaves to leave the state within one year of their manumission. Clearly, the state wanted to limit the size of the free black population. Paradoxically, there was no prohibition on a person born to free parents staying in the state. This told us that Elizabeth's parents—Wanda's fourth great-grandparents—were also free.

Reaching back another generation, to the Register of Free Negroes, Surry County, Virginia, for the year 1826, we saw an entry for Fielding Banks. "Fielding Banks," Wanda read, "a mulatto man and son of Benjamin Banks and Nancy, his wife, free mulattos, as certified to the clerk of Surry County Court by James Wilson, a highly respectable resident of Surry County." Elizabeth's father, Fielding Banks, had registered as a free person of color on September 22, 1826. He was born around the year 1800 in Surry County, also the son of free parents.

Wanda was, again, shocked. "So not just her parents? Her parents' parents?" she said. "What the hell they doing staying in Virginia?"

Gaining momentum, we looked for Fielding's father, and found *him*. Benjamin Banks, Wanda's fifth great-grandfather, was born around 1765, almost a decade before the outbreak of the American Revolution. Wanda, we were to find out, comes from a long line of free Negroes, one of a very few African Americans who can trace their ancestors by name back before the American Revolution.

We turned to yet another Register of Free Negroes, yet another entry for a member of the Banks family. "Benjamin Banks, son of John Banks, a resident of this County," Wanda read from the 1798 register, "a mulatto man born of free parents, also residents of the said County, of a pretty bright complexion, aged about 30 years, has bushy hair, about 5′8″ high, pretty well made, by profession a planter, and is registered under foregoing description on this 5th day of September 1798." Although this document said Benjamin was a planter, his estate record suggested he made his living fishing; he fished for sturgeon, trapped for muskrats, and dug for oysters. Benjamin Banks had a modest lifestyle, but he was a free man.

Amazingly, Benjamin's father, John Banks—Wanda's sixth great-grandfather—had also been born free in Surry County around 1735, some forty years before the American Revolution. Even in these earliest days, when America was still a handful of British colonies, debate raged about whether slavery should be allowed in the new, supposedly democratic "city on the hill." When the Revolution finally came, what must it have been like for John Banks, one of the new country's few free black men, to contemplate a future where all blacks would be free?

Wanda recalled the difficulties free people of color faced in Elizabeth Banks's time, nearly a century later. It was hard to comprehend colonial times. "I don't know. Being free, but tomorrow they can decide no," Wanda said. As she does with everything, Wanda injected some humor into the situation. "Did they socialize? Could they socialize with other blacks who weren't free? 'Yeah, I think Leroy's finished with the crops. He's usually off about this time. And feel my shirt. That's cotton. That's nice, huh? Man, I'm telling you, y'all do a good job.' I mean, what is that life?"

This was not the last of the surprises we had for Wanda. Sometimes free blacks incongruously became slave owners themselves, and we obtained evidence that Wanda's family members may have pursued such a path. Personal property tax lists from Surry County in 1788 and 1789 included the full name of the free white or black taxpayer, followed by the first names of any slaves they owned.

"This is where it goes horribly wrong," Wanda said, shaking her head, trying to process this strange information.

John Banks, Wanda's sixth great-grandfather, was indeed listed in the records, and under his name were the names of his slaves, Fanny and Tab. John Banks paid taxes on these two slaves in 1788 and 1789. His oldest son, Jeremiah, owned four slaves in 1789.

We have no way of knowing what motivated Wanda's relatives to own slaves. There are two theories about this among historians: the good-guy theory and the bad-guy theory. The good-guy theory suggests black slave owners used slavery to protect their own family members from the possible brutality of white slave owners. The bad-guy theory posits free blacks had ceased to feel any commonality with black slaves. They had become so invested in the slave society in which they lived that they too exploited other black people for profit; that one was either free or slave, and race didn't matter. A baffled Wanda said, "I'm going to have to go with the good-guy theory."

The surviving evidence can't answer this question. But there was another mystery that we needed to solve. Given how long Wanda's ancestors had been free, we wondered how they had escaped slavery in the first place.

We worked our way up Wanda's family tree, starting with her fifth great-grandfather, Benjamin Banks. We found free papers and census records that, to our astonishment, added generation after generation of free people of color, all the way back to Wanda's eighth great-grandmother, a woman named Mary Banks. Mary was born in Virginia in 1683, a century before the end of the American Revolution.

Genealogist Johni Cerny explained the circumstances under which black people could gain their freedom. "Free persons of color are freed most often by their previous owners," she said. "People leave a will stating that on my death I want these certain slaves freed." But there was no evidence anywhere that Mary had been freed in an owner's will. Cerny offered another suggestion. "If the mother was free, the child was free. If the mother was a slave, the child was a slave, and it stayed that way," she explained. "So if you were one of the few black people who had a white mother in the colonial period, then you were automatically free."

Following up on this hunch, Cerny made a discovery that finally cracked the case. She uncovered court records from 1683 documenting the conviction of a white indentured woman for fornication with a black slave. That indentured woman was Elizabeth Banks, born in 1665, Wanda's ninth great-grandmother.

Wanda read from the document: "Elizabeth Banks, servant to Major James Goodwin, being presented for fornication and bastardy with a

Negro slave. Ordered that the sheriff take her into his custody and give her thirty-nine lashes on the bare back well laid on, and that she serves her said Master according to Act."

In the early colonial era, the line between indentured white servants and black slaves could be quite porous. At a time when slavery was just getting under way, not all slaves had yet been isolated on large plantations. The proximity of black slaves and white indentured servants meant that it was possible for black males and white females to have sexual relations.

"White servants outnumbered black slaves at this period in Virginia," Eva Sheppard Wolf, a leading historian of free people of color, told us. "It was just shifting in the 1680s. It was a period of more racial flexibility. It was a period when the differences were more between the haves and the have-nots than between white and black."

This was the world in which Wanda's anonymous African male ancestor had a sexual relationship with Elizabeth, an indentured white servant. When Elizabeth gave birth out of wedlock to Mary, Wanda's eighth great-grandmother, the mixed-race child followed the condition of the mother, not of the father, and the mother was free. This law was created, obviously, to ensure that mixed-race children would remain slaves, as most sexual liaisons between blacks and whites involved a white man and a black woman. Incredibly, the historian Paul Heinegg, who is the world's expert on free Negroes in the colonial period, told us that there were only 250 court records of white women bearing the children of black men, Negro slaves, on record in all of American colonial history. This means that less than 1 percent of the black people in colonial Virginia would be mulattoes descended from a white woman.

In Elizabeth and Mary Banks's case, though, the law had the opposite effect. By choosing a black partner to father her child, Elizabeth Banks ensured the freedom of Wanda's entire family. But Elizabeth herself paid dearly with her own freedom. In the seventeenth century, fornication was a grievous crime, and giving birth to an illegitimate child was even worse. For two white indentured servants convicted of fornication, a fine of five hundred pounds of tobacco was exacted, or the term of service could be extended by two years. If the so-called crime were committed with a black person, the penalty was doubled.

Free status didn't necessarily confer on its holder prosperity, and Mary Banks's free status wasn't enough to keep her out of servitude herself. And when she herself bore an illegitimate child at age twenty, in 1703, the penalty she had to pay for her "sin" was very steep indeed: her daughter, Elizabeth, was bound into service to Mary's employer "until she became free according to the law and customs of the country for all mulatto bastards to be free." In 1703 the term of indenture for freeborn mulattoes was thirty years—not quite a lifetime but close to it.

Wanda questioned exactly what freedom meant for her long-ago grandmothers. "They were free," she said, "but Mary having to turn her baby over into indentured servitude for thirty years, they had it better than slaves, but they paid a price."

Wanda's ancestors, black and white, have been in Virginia for almost 350 years. We had never traced any African American family back as far. Usually, if we're able to get back any significant number of generations on an African American's family tree, it's by tracing the line of the identified white master who impregnated a black slave. In Wanda's case, however, we journeyed back through people who, with the exception of her ninth great-grandmother, were legally black in the United States.

Together, we had looked at three lines of her family. Two involved guesswork and extrapolation and ended abruptly; the third had names and dates for people who lived during the seventeenth century. Wanda spoke from the heart about what it meant to her to learn about the different lines of her family, both documented and undocumented. "You know, on this side I'm going back to my ninth great-grandmother. And you feel your history. You know where you're from and you can think about what they probably went through. You get the years, and you know where they were and what your family was doing." She motioned to the other side of her family tree. "And you get here, and it's just dead ends and names that you can't place or just numbers, just property. You can see how it was so devastating and why we're still feeling the effects today. This says you're important; you're a person. This, you were once just property. Your history, who cares?"

■ Now we wanted to look at Wanda's DNA, to see what that could tell about her roots back thousands of years. On her mother's side, her maternal haplogroup is L2a1l1a. L2a1l1a is a subgroup of L2a. Haplogroup L2a dates back about fifty-five thousand years and is present in 20 percent or more of both Africans and African Americans. It is extremely common among most Africans south of the Sahara. In fact, it is so widespread and diverse that it has been difficult to pinpoint where in Africa it arose. Current thinking, however, puts the origins of L2a somewhere in Central Africa. At the peak of the last Ice Age twenty thousand years ago, when the Sahara Desert became entirely uninhabitable and began expanding to the south, people bearing haplogroup L2a began to journey in two directions: east toward the cooler climate of the eastern highlands and west toward the Atlantic coast.

But this ancient expansion was not to be the last in the history of L2a. Beginning about four thousand years ago, two sub-branches of L2a—L2a1a and L2a1b—were swept up with the Bantu-speaking people of West Africa. These people, who had been practicing farming for a millennium or more, began to expand their territory and gradually introduced both their language and their way of life to their eastern and southern neighbors. Today, both L2a1a and L2a1b are well represented in southeast Africa, and L2a reaches levels of 36 percent in the southeastern African nation of Mozambique.

While for the most part the barrier of the Sahara Desert prevented L2a from expanding into North Africa, the haplogroup has been found in about 4 percent of Tunisians. This suggests that at least a few people bearing L2a managed to cross the harsh desert.

L2a is the most common haplogroup among African Americans, reaching levels of 20 percent. The high frequency of L2a among African Americans is probably a result of its concentration in West Africa, which was the main supply region for the Atlantic slave trade. Most African Americans bear a type of L2a that is found only in West Africa. L2a also made its way to South America through the slave trade; today a branch of L2a, L2a1, is found in up to 40 percent in some Afro-Brazilian populations.

Although it is extremely rare in Europe, haplogroup L2a has been found among a small number of people there, mostly in the eastern part of the continent. It is most common among Ashkenazi Jews from Poland, but has also been found among Romanian, French, German, and Russian Jews and non-Jewish Slavs in Slovakia and the Czech Republic. The distribution of L2a in Europe makes it very difficult to determine exactly how and when the haplogroup first appeared on the continent, but genetic analyses indicate that a migration from Africa occurred during the Ice Age, more than ten thousand years ago. Had we been able to achieve results with Wanda's paternal haplogroup, it probably would have originated somewhere in Northern Europe.

We looked at Wanda's admixture to test her African, Asian, and European ancestry from the past five hundred years. We have documented proof that there was mixing in her bloodline 350 years ago. The company 23andMe measured her results at 59 percent African, 35 percent European, and 6 percent Asian. Family Tree DNA's results were similar, although they detected no Asian percentage: according to them, her admixture is 65.47 percent African and 34.58 percent European. In both cases, the amount of European is almost identical.

AfricanAncestry.com is a company that specializes in determining African Americans' origins to a present-day country and tribe or ethnic group on the continent of Africa. Wanda's mother's line leads back to the Bubi people in Bioko Island (Equatorial Guinea) and the Tikar, Hausa, and Fulani people in Cameroon.

Our journey through Wanda's family tree was done. To say that this was a profound experience for both of us is putting it mildly. I had one final question for Wanda before she took all this information back to her family: if her fairy godmother could take her back in time to meet any one of these ancestors, who would it be? Without hesitation, she chose Elizabeth Banks, her white ninth great-grandmother. What would she say to the woman whose choice of partner ensured freedom for Wanda's entire family?

"If I sat down and talked to her as me, Wanda Sykes today, I would ask her, you know, 'How'd we do? And I'd like you to meet my white wife and my white babies. I got your back, Elizabeth. Don't worry. I got your back.'"

John Legend (b. 1978)

Born John Roger Stephens, the platinum-selling musician known to the world as John Legend is living up to his stage name. Early in his career, he made the bold decision to use the nickname as his own. "I figured why not? Let's go out there, put my neck on the line, put my name on the line and say, you know, I'm calling myself Legend. Now it's time for me to try to do something with my career to live up to it. It put the challenge out there for me." The talented singer-songwriter has met that challenge. So far, he's won nine Grammys and collaborated with artists like Jay Z, Kanye West, and Alicia Keys.

John's beginnings were modest. He was born in Springfield, Ohio, on December 28, 1978. His father worked in a factory, and his mother was a seamstress. John's earliest exposure to music came when he sang traditional black gospel in his Pentecostal church choir, but he grew up in a family that valued artistry and creativity. His father paints, his brother plays the drums, and both grandmothers played the piano. He was five when he sat for his first piano lesson.

"I think he thought he was Stevie Wonder or Ray Charles or something," John's father, Ron Stephens, laughed, recalling some of his son's performances leading the church choir in singing his own compositions. John had found his calling. "When I got up and sang at church and saw people get up and clap and get excited, I was like, man, this is the life; this is what I want to do. I would sing at school plays, and everyone would tell me I was great. So I believed I was good from the beginning. I thought I had something going on. I wanted to be on *Star Search*. I watched Ed McMahon on television; I was like, I could beat those little kids on *Star Search*, man."

Many of John's earliest memories revolve around schooling. "My parents homeschooled me a bit when I was a kid, and very early on we'd have flashcards to learn our phonics and learn how to read and learn arithmetic. A lot of my early memories are my mom kind of drilling those things into my head." Apparently the drilling worked, because a newspaper clipping we found bears the following headline: "Product of home teaching wins bee." John was in the equivalent of fourth grade at the time. He remembered winning the bee, but not the winning word. How could he forget it? It was "prejudice."

Of course, John knew what "prejudice" meant, but it wasn't something he had experienced firsthand. "I didn't notice racism when I was a kid. There was one story of a girl at Springfield Christian School," John told us, speaking of the school he attended before his parents began to homeschool him. "She said something about how she didn't want any black kids playing with her or something like that. I actually didn't know she said it until my teacher said something about it to me. She punished the girl, and she came and told me later, 'This is why I punished the girl.' Even though I read about the history of the civil rights era and all these things, I didn't think much about the personal experience of racism in my own life."

John's parents chose to homeschool their children because they were concerned about the local public school system and also because of their religion. "They were very religious, very fundamentalist, Pentecostal Christians," John explained. "A lot of folks in that strain of Christianity end up doing home school because they want to control the moral upbringing of their kids in addition to what they learn. They're concerned about what kind of influences come into their kids' lives and concerned about kids learning evolution, God forbid." In retrospect, John realizes the experience was isolating. "I think kids do lose out a little bit on the social aspect of growing up. I would caution parents to be careful about deciding to homeschool your kids and making sure that you account for the fact that they need some social development as well."

John's mother, Phyllis Elaine Lloyd, was born in Springfield, Ohio, on March 4, 1954. "She is charismatic," John said, "kind of a star in my local community. Especially in the black church community, she would sing at a lot of different events. I have my mom's ambition and desire to be a star and to be out there in public." From his father, Ronald LaMar Stephens, also born in Springfield, on September 18, 1949, John said, he got his even temper. "I'm laid-back like my dad. I kind of take life as it comes. I don't get very mad, and I don't get super-ecstatic either." John's father spent most of his life as a factory worker at Navistar International, which had begun as International Harvester. "They built big rigs, eighteen-wheelers. It was one of those union jobs. You worked with the UAW or whatever, and you would get a guaranteed pension and thirty years on the job. Those jobs have disappeared, to a large extent, in the Midwest, but my dad was in a good time for that. He got hired in the right kind of era where you could sustain a family on a factory job with no college education."

To the outside world, John's family seemed to have it all. "People saw us as the perfect family. We'd sing together at church, we were homeschooled a bit, my mother was beautiful, my dad was a great guy, and everybody loved them. Everyone thought we were the perfect family. I think we were about to win some family-of-the-year award, actually, before my parents got divorced." John's parents' marriage, inexplicably at the time, fell apart. Now John believes his mother had a nervous breakdown, brought on by the death of her mother and her own frustrations with her station in life. "In that generation it wasn't uncommon, but as a woman, to get married at eighteen and go straight from your dad to a husband and not go to college and not have a career of your own, I think she was generally stifled in her situation and was thinking that there had to be something better for her out there." She became estranged from her family and spiraled out of control. In 1987 Ron and Phyllis divorced. (They would remarry and divorce for a second time several years later.) John's father won custody of the children, and his mother moved out of the house. For the next ten years, even though they were all still in the small town of Springfield, John rarely saw or spoke with his mother.

John remembers how hard his father worked to care for him and his siblings. "He was kind of the rare instance of a single black father raising four kids. And my mother was out on the streets, basically. She got involved in drugs and really a very tough life. She got arrested a few times. Things just went very, very badly for a while."

Only nine, John attempted to cope with this loss by throwing himself into his music and academics. Over time, his tremendous success has given him an opportunity to help his mother get back on her feet. "She's in a better place than she was back then, thank God," he said.

Music was always John's driving force and dream, but after graduating from the University of Pennsylvania in 1999, he postponed pursuing a career in music to be a management consultant for three years. "It was mostly the money," he admitted. "But I knew a lot of smart people that worked in consulting, and it seemed like they had an interesting life and an interesting job, and it was something that challenged them mentally. I got an offer of $50,000 a year, which was big money for me. My dad made less than that at that age. So to get that offer right out of college, it was hard to turn down. But I always had an eye toward what I wanted to do. I wanted to be a rock star, but I needed a job, and I didn't want to wait tables." He laughed recalling how he would show up for his early collaborations with Kanye West and Alicia Keys "still in my business casual from consulting."

John's upbringing—deeply religious, difficult at times—influenced the artist he has become. But what other influences were in his past? Like many African Americans, John grew up knowing little about it. "Being a black American, people always ask you, especially when you're light-skinned, 'What mix are you? What are you?'" John said. "People always want to know this about us. Most of us don't know it for ourselves, and we don't really know how to answer the question. We're like, we've got a little African, we've got a little Native American, got a little European. We don't know exactly what it is, where it came from."

John believes gaining an understanding of their own genealogy might be even more significant for African Americans than it is for others. "I think it has special significance because of our history being so compromised, not knowing; a lot of records being wiped out, not a lot of care being taken to keep black families together during the slave era, and then a lot of kids being born under duress," John said thoughtfully. "Black Americans, particularly being separated from Africa and then not knowing what country of origin and all these things, it is something, I think, that's a bit more significant for us than perhaps for other people in other cultures where it's a little more clear-cut."

■ John's grandparents on his mother's side were Elmira Bass and Raymond Lloyd. Elmira died of heart disease in her late fifties, but John has many beautiful memories of her. "I loved hanging out with her. I would play piano with her. She was the church organist at the time. After church on Sundays I would want to go to her house and hang out with her and eat dinner at her house instead of going home. I just loved spending time with her."

As for many of us, food played a central role in John's memories of his elders. "She would make chicken. She baked it most of the time. . . . She would make cornbread and greens. I would go to her house and watch football and just chill out. . . . I was so sad when she died. That was really the first time I cried."

Elmira's mother, John's great-grandmother, was also named Elmira, Elmira Mack Bass, and she was very light-skinned. "I didn't speak to her about it," John said, "but I'm told she was the product of rape, from a white guy who raped a black woman. That's what my uncle told me." This is a painful legacy in the families of many African Americans.

John's maternal grandfather, Raymond Lloyd, outlived his wife by many years. "I think he was born in Tennessee," John said, but he wasn't sure. "They moved up from the South to Michigan and Ohio. They spent time in both places." A minister and the pastor of John's church, Raymond was a voracious reader, though he never finished high school as a teenager. "He loved books, particularly when it came to religion and theology. He just loved to soak it in. He would argue about the minutiae of theological doctrine with all the different ministers," John said. "And he decided he would go back to high school when he was a full-grown adult. I think some of his kids were still in high school when he went." We found a photograph of John's grandfather, at age forty, in the Springfield High School yearbook from 1960, surrounded by his fellow teenage graduates. "He would say all these little sayings of all these big words that no one knew. He would just learn a big word, and he would use it in his everyday life. He would flirt with waitresses and flirt with everybody with his expanded vocabulary. He really valued education."

I wondered if John's passion for education was in any way connected to his grandfather. John is not only a brilliant musician but a brilliant student. He excelled in school and attended the University of Pennsylvania. When he was still in high school, he entered the Future Black History Makers of America writing competition, and in his essay he described how he wanted to be a musician and use his success to help his community. He has done exactly that. John is on the board of Teach for America, the Education Equality Project, and the Harlem Village Academies. He even composed the song for the award-winning documentary *Waiting for Superman*, which exposes the problems faced by our nation's public schools and features the education reformer Geoffrey Canada, one of our guests in this series.

"When you grow up in a working-class family in the Midwest and you don't know what kind of options you have in life, education is such a powerful way to build something new for yourself," John said, adding, "especially with kids who grow up poor, to escape that poverty trap, to empower yourself. . . . It's frustrating to me seeing too many kids languishing in schools that aren't working, so I fight to get more opportunities for kids to get into good schools."

■ As John was about to learn, the fight for empowerment started long ago in his family. We looked at his father's side of the family and were amazed at how deeply we could explore his roots. We began with his grandparents, Arthur Benjamin Stephens and Marjorie Smith, both born in Springfield, Ohio, in 1926 and 1930, respectively. "We called him Pa," said John, recalling his colorful grandfather. "He was kind of badass. He would sit there with his beer and his cigarette and his pipe sometimes. He used to watch westerns all the time. And he was stubborn. They used to call him the Bull, Benny the Bull. He was definitely a character."

John's grandmother, Marjorie Smith, was born when her mother was only sixteen. His great-grandmother, Esther Louise Ryder, was born in Springfield, on October 29, 1914. The family called her, sweetly, Dearo.

John assumed his family had been part of the Great Migration, a time when blacks left the rural South by the millions early in the twentieth century for the promise of the industrialized North. But the paper trail revealed more, including a highly unusual story in John's grandmother's family that explained how it came to Ohio in particular. Through census records, birth records, and death records, we were able to trace Esther's family back to her great-grandfather, a man named John Polley, who was born in Kentucky around 1823.

Miraculously, we then went back even further in time, to John Polley's father, Peyton Polley, also born in Kentucky, around 1797. John had never heard of the name Polley. The story we were about to tell him would guarantee the name would never be lost again.

Peyton Polley, John's paternal fifth great-grandfather, was living as a slave in Pike County, Kentucky, working the farm of his master. At the Pike County Courthouse, researcher David Deskins helped us search for clues about Peyton. Because his last name was Polley, Deskins looked through files of wills to find the name of Peyton's owner, who would most likely have the same last name.

We learned that Peyton Polley's master was David Polley, and embedded in his will was a wonderful discovery. In this legal document, David Polley freed John Legend's ancestors. "After my death," John read from it, "I will and direct that my slaves, to wit: Dug, Peyton, William, Jude, Mariah, John and Spencer, be free and liberated from all servitude." David Polley owned three of John's ancestors—Peyton and his son John, and Peyton's brother Douglas—and he freed them twenty-six years before the end of the Civil War.

John was amazed to learn he descends from free Negroes. In 1847, eight years after his will was written and filed, David Polley died, and Peyton Polley became a free man. Also freed were his brother and son. The will contained something even more stunning. David Polley left his estate to his wife, Elizabeth. We saw nothing unusual in that, until we read the next clause: "After death of my said wife, I will and bequeath to my servants as named—and by this will to be liberated at my death—all my estate, both real and personal." Not only did David Polley free his slaves, he gave Peyton land and money with which to start his new life as a free man. Why would David Polley essentially treat these slaves as he would his own children?

John pondered the question. "Even in the depths of this awful institution, these are still human beings," he said thoughtfully. "The owners are still human beings, and I think spending enough time around slaves, you realize that they're human beings, too, even though legally they're not treated as such. I think he grew to love them, probably, so he looked at them as his family."

When David Polley died in 1847, his now-former slaves were given a freedom certificate, which we found. "December, County Court, 1847," John read from it. "On motion of Douglas, Peyton, and John, slaves formerly belonging to David Polley, deceased, who by his last will and testament set them free, they are permitted to obtain a certificate of their freedom."

Ninety percent of all African Americans were *not* freed until the end of the Civil War. Two generations of John's ancestors were freed nearly two decades earlier. John had a complicated response to his ancestors' freedom certificate. "I feel like that is some sort of privilege," he said. "But I also think about the 90 percent that weren't, and I think about the fact that they had to be slaves all that time beforehand, so I don't get a whole lot of satisfaction out of that. But it's still very interesting to know."

Most free people of color left Pike County as soon as they could. In 1850 there were only eighteen free black people and mulattoes in the whole county. Kentucky was a dangerous place, with slave traders coming in to buy slaves they could resell to the big cotton plantations in the lower South. In fact, between 1850 and 1860, about 16 percent of Kentucky's African American slaves were exported to the South. Free people, too, were at risk of being snatched, so they always had to carry their free papers with them as protection.

In 1803 Ohio joined the Union as a free state. As a result, many free blacks made the journey across the Ohio River to a state where their free-dom was protected under the law. John's ancestors Peyton and his son John were free, but seven other sons and daughters of Peyton were still enslaved in Kentucky. We found no trace of their mother. Peyton refused to leave Kentucky without his children.

The next document we found was astounding. It was a bill of sale, dated 1849, for the purchase of the seven Polley children by Peyton's brother, Douglas, from David and Nancy Campbell. "We David Campbell and Nancy, his wife, of the County of Pike and State of Kentucky, do bargain and sell unto Douglas Polley . . . one black boy named Duges—15 years, one black boy named Peyton aged 13 years, one black boy named Harrison aged 10 years, one black boy named Nelson aged 8 years, one named Aaron aged 4 years, one black girl aged 6 years, one black girl aged 2 years, for the sum of five dollars." Susan O'Donovan, a historian who studies antebellum

American history at the University of Memphis, explained to us why a former slave might buy his own relative. "Free people of color sometimes find it in their best interest to own their own families," she said. "For starters, they're living in a system that's structured around the protection of slave property, so you kind of have the law on your side. In buying one's family, you have control over that family. Then you can free them."

Indeed, this was the case here, as proven in the words of a deposition we found from a white resident of Pike County named H.W. Rust, who made plain Douglas's intentions, and possibly David Campbell's: "I heard David Campbell say some weeks after he had sold his negroes to Douglas Polley that he had done what he always intended to do; that he sold them, the negroes, to Douglas for the purpose that he, Douglas, might take them to the state of Ohio and set them free."

Peyton's family was now intact. Because freed slaves were always vulnerable to kidnapping in the South, the most sensible way for Peyton to protect his children was to move to a state where slavery was prohibited. The Polley family embarked on a dangerous journey, traveling one hundred miles north through slaveholding Kentucky across the Ohio River to the free state of Ohio. There Peyton's children were liberated, their rights recognized and protected by the law.

"It must have been amazing," John said. "Free at last."

Peyton and his children settled in Lawrence County, in the town of Ironton, one of the southernmost towns in Ohio. We tracked down a direct descendant of the Polleys, James Hale, who still lives in the area. Peyton Polley was James's great-great-grandfather, which makes him John's fourth cousin. The two have never met.

James is a member of the same church in Ironton that Peyton Polley attended 160 years ago. "They had hit the Lotto," James Hale said. "They were free. They were farmers. They were working their land; they were earning a living; they were keeping their family. And wow . . . what happens?"

What happened next defies imagination. On the night of June 6, 1850, a band of armed white men from Kentucky crossed the Ohio River, made their way to Peyton Polley's home, and broke down the door with an ax. They had been hired by the notorious slave trafficker David Justice. One of the intruders fired a shot at Peyton, "grazing the wooly top of his head," as an account by one of the kidnappers says, and knocking him to the ground. The other white men kidnapped all eight children, ages four to seventeen, dragging them back across the Ohio River, back into the depths of slavery.

Although John had never heard of Peyton Polley, Paul Finkelman, a leading expert on slave-era law, has been studying the case for years. Over the past quarter-century, Paul has collected a veritable library of documentation about the Polleys, recording the unbelievable chapters of the family's painful saga. He had been researching the legal fate of runaway or fugitive slaves when he stumbled across the records detailing the Polley story. "They weren't fugitive slaves," he said. "This is the opposite of fugitive slaves. This is the kidnapping of free people and dragging them back to slavery."

Paul had never seen a case like this, where kidnappers had crossed state lines to abduct a whole family in a free state. "I think the kidnappers have no legal claims, or even pretend to have any legal claims. The reality is, they see these free black people, they think we can kidnap them because they're children, and it is a matter of force and greed."

By February 1851, eight months after the kidnapping, the Polley children remained in slavery. Not only that, they had been separated. The kidnappers sold the children to masters across Kentucky and Virginia. Recently freed himself, Peyton Polley had only one possible option to rescue his family. "He certainly can't go after the kidnappers alone," Finkelman told us. "They outgun him, outnumber him. They're stronger than he is. The only thing he can do is go to the authorities."

Just over a decade before the outbreak of the Civil War, it may have seemed foolhardy for a former slave to put his faith in the law. Yet that's exactly what Peyton did. Finkelman related the story, which sounds more like the basis of a screenplay than it does reality.

"He goes to the local prosecutor, who writes the governor, Reuben Wood. Of course blacks can't vote in Ohio, so he's not worried about the black vote. But the governor is worried about what Ohio would claim to be its state's rights. Ohio does not want ruffians from Kentucky coming into Ohio and kidnapping people and taking them elsewhere. So the governor intervenes and immediately sends somebody to Kentucky and Virginia to investigate this. And this begins a long saga of how do you get the Polleys back?"

Even though Governor Wood believed the Polley children deserved to be free, the problem was that their status had to be proved in the states where they were now living, the dyed-in-the-wool slave states of Kentucky and Virginia. I explained to John that the House, the Senate, and the governor of Ohio all took on his ancestor's case with a vengeance, sending investigators into the hills to track down the kidnappers. They spent thousands of dollars on lawyers, and they did everything they could to try to rescue the children.

But David Justice kept evading them. He separated the four children still in Kentucky, hiding them away in three different counties. Their names were Hilda, Peyton Jr., Mary Jane, and Martha. When we study black history, we learn that slavery ripped families apart, but rarely are we able to see the specificity of that action. We found a letter from the head attorney on the case, dated May 3, 1851. "Many threats have been made, and the persons of whom I am in pursuit are known to be desperadoes, surrounded by a band of like characters—real outlaws. I can only say in response to taking them [. . .]: 'I'll try, Sir!' and, if spared, report the results."

John was stunned. "It's amazing that so many governors and all these important people were involved in trying to rescue my family. It sounds like this would help ignite the Civil War, like 'How dare you?'"

John was right to mention the Civil War. Peyton Polley found himself caught between the pro- and antislavery forces beginning to pull the nation apart. Susan O'Donovan, the historian from University of Memphis, explained the backdrop against which this case was taking place. "Certainly tensions between free states and slaveholding states are on the rise in the 1850s," she said. "Part of that is a result of people like the Polleys, because they're kind of putting these problems on the front burner. Who protects them? Are they really free? The Ohio governor steps in, and he says yes, they are really free. Well, in saying they're really free, he's annoying a bunch of people in Kentucky. The sectional crisis is deepening."

John described it as "a wild goose chase." It was hard for him to imagine justice being served. But in Kentucky, the attorney general made an unexpected decision: he ordered the immediate release of the four illegally enslaved Polley children. In a letter dated October 16, 1851, addressed to Governor Wood, the news of the decision was expressed with great pride: "We take pleasure in informing you of the favorable issue of the suit of Peyton Polley [Jr., one of the sons] for his freedom. The case was decided about one week ago, and today we placed Peyton on board of the Steamboat *Gen. Pike* bound for Cincinnati. We are pleased to be able to give you the further assurance that whilst there may be wretches in Kentucky who would rob men even of their freedom, the courts of this state are ready to do prompt and impartial justice."

The authorities in Kentucky, where slavery was still legal, did the right thing. In the end, all four of the Polley children held in Kentucky were freed from slavery a second time, and Peyton was reunited with half of his family in the free state of Ohio. But this was only Kentucky. Virginia, the largest slave state in the union, dug in its heels. "The Virginia courts stonewall," Paul Finkelman explained. "They do not want these free people to be returned to freedom. Virginia is saying, 'We don't care if they are free. We see them as black people. We think black people should be slaves. We will treat them accordingly.'"

While an article in the *Ironton Register* of February 2, 1860, reported that the four Polley children who had been enslaved in Virginia—Anna, Nelson, Louisa, and Harrison, James Hale's great-great-grandfather—"were declared free by the court of Cabell County," which is in current-day West Virginia, the court judgment was unfortunately overturned on a dispute over jurisdiction, and when the case came up for trial again, it was postponed.

On March 10, 1860, Dick Parsons, the Speaker of the House in Ohio, issued a statement reaffirming the state's commitment to rescuing the Polley children. All told, five different governors, both Democrats and Republicans, took part in the effort. By now, of course, some of those children were adults. All four would remain enslaved until the end of the Civil War, when the Thirteenth Amendment officially ended slavery for good. Sadly, though, only Harrison made his way back to his father's home in Ohio. We don't know what became of the other three.

As unbelievable as the case is, equally unbelievable is that the knowledge of this history-making case had been lost to John and no doubt many of Peyton Polley's descendants. "The fact that my grandparents don't talk about this or my dad and mom don't know about it, it's pretty amazing," John said.

The Polleys' case was exceptional in legal history, but Peyton Polley was not the only member of his family to find resolution and satisfaction in a court of law. We wondered why Peyton's son, John Polley—John Legend's fourth great-grandfather—would opt to stay in Kentucky when the rest of the family moved to Ohio. John Polley was free, and to stay in a slave state seemed to be courting danger.

"Courting" might be the operative word. We know John Polley was married to Arda Slone, but in the 1850 census, there was no entry for John and Arda Polley as a couple. We did find John Polley living next door to a white woman named Mary Slone. Mary "Polly" Slone, it turned out, owned twenty-three slaves, listed on the 1850 Slave Schedule but without names.

Fortunately for us, Mary Slone left a will—one remarkably similar to the one left by David Polley that freed Peyton. "I will and bequeath that my Negro slave Cloe and her children," it reads, "to wit Weston, Hampton, Anna, Betsy, Arty, Polly, Minta, Sam, Sally, Frank, Jefferson are hereby declared free & manumitted forever from and after my death. And all increase of said Cloe and her children are hereby set free at my death." Arty was Arda, John's fourth great-grandmother. "Incredible," John responded. "It's like everybody's getting freed early, too."

We were right to assume that John Polley had stayed behind for love. Just as his father, Peyton, had refused to leave Kentucky without his children, John Polley refused to leave Kentucky without his beloved. Sadly, though, upon Mary Slone's death in 1853, Arda and her mother and all her siblings became embroiled in a protracted legal battle when fourteen of Mary Slone's heirs contested the will. They claimed she was not in her right mind, that there had been a witness to her destroying the will. Nineteen slaves who had been promised their freedom went to court to demand that the will be upheld. The case dragged on for almost two and a half years, but finally a decision was rendered: "The will as presented to this Court is the last will and testament of Polly Slone, and will be admitted to probate." John's fourth and fifth great-grandmothers, Arda and Cloe Slone, were finally free.

It was indeed a storybook ending for John Polley and Arda Slone. The 1860 census for Pike County, Kentucky, shows an entry for "John Polley, Arda Polley, P.E. Polley, Rebecca Polley, Polley Slone, and Samson Slone." One year before the Civil War, the Polleys were living with their family, free in the slave state of Kentucky.

Only one in ten slaves had been manumitted by the year 1860. To have not one set of ancestors but two set free by their masters long before the Civil War erupted is unlikely enough, but then to have these same two sets of ancestors seek help from the legal system that considered them less than human, and to triumph, is almost beyond comprehension.

"I feel blessed now," John said. "For there to be such a vivid and interesting record, and one with some good endings before the eventual emancipation of all the slaves is incredible."

We had a P.S. to the Peyton Polley story to share with John, about the white people who set his relatives free, and the kidnapper who wrested their freedom away from them. David Justice, the slave trafficker who stole the Polley children and eluded the law for years, was the nephew of both David Polley and Mary Slone.

Shared genes do not always make for shared ideals.

■ The company AfricanAncestry.com has collected DNA samples from the ethnic groups throughout West and Central Africa that were most heavily raided during the slave trade. By comparing John's DNA to the samples in this database, we can learn where John's people originated. John hopes that DNA can fill in some details for him. "Were my white ancestors from Ireland, or were they from Germany? Were my black ancestors from Ghana or Nigeria or Ivory Coast? And then do I have Native American in the family, because a lot of black folks either think they did or did."

On his father's side, we traced back his oldest direct ancestor to a man named Bristol Stephens, John's third great-grandfather, born in Georgia sometime between 1809 and 1819. His paternal haplogroup is E1b1a7a, a subgroup of E1b1a, which arose in East Africa about thirty thousand to forty thousand years ago. It was carried from Africa to regions of Europe and the Near East, and today it remains widespread in Africa. About 60 percent of African American men share this paternal haplogroup with John.

The company AfricanAncestry.com is dedicated to tracing the origins of African Americans back to a specific, present-day country and ethnic group on the continent of Africa. John's father's line leads to the Fula people in Guinea-Bissau, on the edge of West Africa. He shares this haplogroup with two other guests in the series: Branford Marsalis and Samuel L. Jackson.

We want to look at where John comes from on his mother's side as well. Her oldest direct ancestor was a woman named Betty, no last name, born in Kentucky in February 1842. John's maternal haplogroup, L3f1b, like his paternal haplogroup, also originated in East Africa, but sixty thousand years ago. Today branches of the haplogroup L3 are found among more than 25 percent of the African American population. AfricanAncestry. com has determined that on his mother's side, John shares ancestry with the Mende people of Sierra Leone. It turns out that Branford Marsalis is John's double cousin, related to him on both his mother's and his father's side—two tremendous musicians linked genetically by a distant ancestor.

The admixture test measures percentages of African, European, and Native American ancestry over the past five hundred years, since the time of Columbus. Though we found no white ancestor in John's family tree, his light skin indicates he may have a significant portion of European ancestry. His numbers come back at 64 percent African, 32 percent European, and 4 percent Asian, which codes for Native American. As is so often the case in African American families, the stories of the Cherokee great-grandmother don't pan out here. One analysis of his admixture indicates that his white ancestors were from southeastern Europe, around Romania, but he also shares genetic material with people living in the United Kingdom, Ireland, and Jamaica. Different readings show different results, but there are no real surprises for John in his DNA tests.

For John, this journey had helped him discover the long-forgotten history of his family's courageous fight for freedom. If he had a fairy godmother who could introduce him to one of these ancestors, I asked him, who would it be? "Oh, I've got to meet Mr. Polley," he said, "the one who got his wooly head shot. I would love to meet him, absolutely. I'm proud of him."

John sang the praises of each of his ancestors as he recalled their determination. "It makes me proud that I had ancestors that had a sense of dignity. When given the opportunity to be free, they not only became free, but also fought for that freedom and didn't take no for an answer. . . . It shows a certain level of tenacity and a certain resolve and power that makes me proud to know that I had ancestors who had that."

Margarett Cooper (b. 1913)

My esteemed friend, Margarett Cooper, a longtime children's librarian in Virginia and Ohio, has spent many of her ninety-eight years attempting to unravel her ancestors' bold and ingenious plan for their own emancipation in the waning years of the American Revolution. Margarett's great-great-great-grandmother, a woman named Susannah Speed, was a slave in Virginia. In 1782 she took the incredible step of suing her master for her freedom.

It was a book that set Margarett on her quest. "It talked about David Greer, who had been brought to this country as a slave, and yet he was never made a slave," she recalled. "And he married a woman who was a free black, and it traced their line. And I said, 'He was my great-great-grandfather!'"

Margarett had heard of Greer before but not this story. "When asked why they didn't enslave him," she said, "they said that he had a mark on him of some kind, and it meant that he had belonged to a certain tribe, and he was a prince in that tribe. I thought, that's pretty fishy. White people don't do things like that," she laughed. "I'm cynical. But I went back and started with David Greer, and then I just got hinged on all of them." It was Margarett's third great-grandmother who really pulled her in. "When I got to Susannah on my mother's side, that was the key thing, because how could a woman who was a slave go to court and say, 'I want to be free'? And I thought, that's my woman."

We all paint pictures in our head of who our ancestors were. In Margarett's imagination, Susannah took the form of an African American icon. "Harriet Tubman is my all-time heroine of all things, and I wanted her to be like that. Harriet was tough. She's brave and courageous. That sums it up." Margarett also said Harriet was "crazy" for going back down South, but she was fighting for what she believed in.

Margarett wanted to know more about Susannah, to fill in the blanks of her past. "I always wanted to know who I was," she said. "Segregation and prejudice sometimes make people feel inferior. I knew I wasn't."

I was curious about what Margarett saw as the relationship between having a sense of self and having a sense of history. "My father was so insistent that you are and you can be whatever you want to be, because you have it in you. And I believed it," she said after a few moments of reflection. "My mother, she knew that her people worked very hard, and that they had really fought. They were in all the wars. They were in everything, and this country they had really taken such a part in, but never got credit for it. So it gave me a lot to think about."

To be bolstered by their history, African Africans first have to know it, and this is easier said than done when so many records of the past were either lost or distorted. "I really think that most blacks are the way they are because they feel inferior, and it makes me so sad," Margarett said. "They don't realize. They don't know about their history. They don't know what's happened. They don't know about all the famous people we've had—and when I say famous, I don't mean the big names, just the little guys. . . . My ancestors were in the Civil War, the French and Indian War, the War of

1812, all of it. We've been part of all of it. They don't ask you what color you are then."

■ Margarett Jane Gillespie was born on October 15, 1913, in Cincinnati, Ohio. Her mother, Ella Bedenbaugh, was born in Oxford, Ohio, in 1883, and her father, Isaac Gillespie, was born in Somerset, Kentucky, in 1879. His parents were slaves. Isaac told Margarett his father had often been beaten as a slave for running away, while his mother was "the master's child." Of her own father, Margarett said, "He had a temper, and he had to get a lot of hate out him."

Many African American and immigrant families prefer to keep the past in the past, painful experiences and entire histories swept under the rug as a form of protection. Margarett agreed that her parents adhered to this practice. "How do you tell a child about such hatred and prejudice?" she asked. "Home was always a haven. It was warm. It was loving." It was lovely to listen to Margarett reminisce about her childhood. "My mother and father were absolutely wonderful. They took good care of us. We had wonderful food. It was an attractive house. It was nice." Margarett paused. "And then you went out in the world, and you had to fight all the time."

Before emancipation, Ohio had been a Promised Land for slaves escaping to freedom. Yet Margarett also described the Buckeye State as less than hospitable to black people in the early part of the twentieth century. "There wasn't much and there probably still isn't a lot of difference in Ohio and some of the southern states," she said. "You know, they had the Copperheads, they had a great Ku Klux Klan and everything else. Ohio is a nasty state, even though it's home for me."

In Pennsylvania and Hamilton, Ohio, the small town where her family moved when she was young, Margarett had the uncommon experience for a woman of her generation of attending only integrated schools. "Educationally, where I grew up, they had good schools. And if you took advantage of it, it was OK," she explained, even if "they didn't like you." Margarett's parents put a high value on education, and she was a curious, engaged student. "I learned a lot, as I say, not because they wanted to teach me. There was always prejudice. There was always a form of segregation if you stood for it." It wasn't until she enrolled at Wilberforce University that she attended an all-black school. She graduated in the middle of the Great Depression, in 1937, and went on to earn a master's degree in library science from Hampton University (she also studied at Columbia University in New

York) before taking up her career as a children's librarian—perfect training for her second career as the family genealogist.

For most African Americans, we have a moment in our lives when we learn that we are black. Margarett's moment came when she was nine or ten, shortly after her family had moved back from Pennsylvania. Pennsylvania held good memories for her. Her father owned a successful barbershop. "It was a wonderful opportunity for me. It made a lot of money, and it was a big shop. He was doing really well, but we had to come back to Ohio because he got sick."

Back in Ohio, Margarett was out with her father one afternoon when she spotted a vendor selling hot dogs. "I had never seen anybody selling Coney Islands, as they called them then, and I asked my father if he would give me the money so I could get a Coney Island. And he did. And I went to this vendor. It was an old Greek, and I'm sure he hadn't been in this country but about two months, and he looked at me and said, 'We don't serve colored.'" Margarett was floored. "As a child, you don't think about that. You're thinking about this Coney Island and I've never seen anything like it; I wanted to taste it." Margarett had no response for the man. Her father tried to explain it to her as best he could. "He pacified me by telling me that there were a lot of people like this, and that the man was ignorant. And he was. He couldn't even speak English well," Margarett said. "But this was the first time I realized that you're going to have to really fend for yourself and get really tough. That's when I learned to be street smart."

She didn't shy away from confrontations. "In high school, I got really vicious," she laughed. "For instance, you'd get on a bus, and there would be a white person sitting in this seat, and this seat is empty." She motioned with her hands. "The bus is crowded. You get on. And I remember one girl saying, 'This seat you can't sit in.' And I said, 'What do you mean I can't sit in it?' And I stepped on her foot. She screamed, but it was fun." Margarett laughed again. "You could do that in Ohio—that was the redeeming feature of Ohio—and you wouldn't get lynched. But it was a nasty place."

Margarett's maternal grandmother, Margarett Proctor, was born free in Oxford, Ohio, in 1844—a rarity, since, according to the 1840 census, only about 380,000 African Americans were free out of a total population of about 3 million. Margarett never met her grandmother, but her mother talked about her frequently. "Evidently she was a rather warm, compassionate woman. She was tall. And she said that she was pretty when she was young, and then as she grew older, she wore her hair up instead of down. She always had advice for her, too, as mothers do. But she was very helpful, and helped with my older brothers and sisters. When they were born, she stayed." Judging by her mother's assessment, Margarett's maternal grandfather, Joel Bedenbaugh, a successful carpenter, didn't share the same generous spirit. "She said, 'I always wanted to take piano lessons, and he wouldn't even come up with the money to do the piano lessons,' and he could have done it."

It is obvious, looking at a photograph of Margarett's grandmother, that she had a lot of mixture in her ancestry. "She had gray eyes," said Margarett, who worked hard to track down details on the source of that color, but "nobody remembered," she said, even if they "remembered my grandmother."

I asked Margarett if she ever wondered what it was like for her grandmother to grow up free when almost everybody else black would have been a slave. "Yes," Margarett answered. "I could just imagine how terrible it was, although they had quite a community in Oxford, and maybe that was a saving grace, too." Additionally, when the Proctors—Margarett Cooper's great-grandparents, William Proctor and Nancy East—came to Ohio in 1818, they were already free. "So she didn't really know anything but freedom, even though it was a segregated, prejudiced freedom."

Margarett had been told her ancestors migrated from Virginia, but her research took her in a different direction. "There weren't too many opportunities for blacks, although my mother's people all had trades," Margarett said. "When I started researching it, I remembered that my great-grandfather, William Proctor, was a blacksmith. Another one was a farmer. There was one who was a boatman. They had these wonderful trades, and it made me a little curious."

She began to read about a town called Satterwhite Village in Virginia, a little town on the North Carolina border where African American tradesmen would be hired out by their masters and eventually buy their freedom with their wages. We don't hear much about these prosperous pockets of African Americans in the South, even in African American history books, but there were others besides Satterwhite, including Wilmington, North Carolina, and Charles City County, Virginia.

"My great-grandfather was a Proctor, and he was the blacksmith," Margarett said. She was never able to establish a connection to Satterwhite Village, but Virginia was part of family lore. Stories said her great-great-grandfather, Elijah East, whom the family called "Grandpap East" and "the rich East," was a prosperous denizen of Halifax County, Virginia. "Elijah East was a most amazing man," Margarett said. He was a veteran of the War of 1812. "He was in the Battle of the Raisin River, which was the worst battle of 1812, and he came out of it whole. I think about thirty-two people came out of the Battle of the Raisin intact, and Elijah was one of them." He was married three times; his third wife was Jane Bedenbaugh, Margarett's grandaunt and great-great-grandmother at the same time. "He owned a lot. He bought a lot, and I kept wondering how did he get the money."

Turns out, Grandpap East wasn't born in Virginia at all. Census records Margarett found herself said he was born in Kentucky. The same census records also gave her the names and birthplaces of Elijah's parents. "That was a real thrill," Margarett said, "because I'm thinking about Elijah, and I thought that would be the stopping point." Margarett looked at a photograph of her great-great-grandfather. "Oh, I became so intrigued with Elijah until I discovered Susannah."

Elijah's mother was Susannah Speed, Margarett's great-great-great-grandmother. No one had ever spoken of Susannah before. "They didn't know anything about Susannah, because I think my mother would be thrilled to death if she could hear these stories about her now."

Susannah left a paper trail of property records and business transactions highly unusual for an African American woman of the early nineteenth century—or for any woman, for that matter. Through them, Margarett discovered that Susannah and her husband, Robert Speed, had jobs in the Jessamine County Courthouse in Nicholasville, Kentucky. "With Susannah and Robert, they all seemed to invest and buy. And whether the courthouse gave them information about what was for sale and what was going to be cheap, I don't know. But when I went to the courthouse, I was amazed at what they bought, what they sold."

According to records Margarett found, by 1823 Susannah's husband had died, as had a son, James, who, like Grandpap East, had fought in the War of 1812. "It had been a bitter war, and he evidently had problems. He died with no family, just his immediate family, but no children or anything of his own." It was at this time that Susannah and Elijah started selling property in Nicholasville at an alarming rate. But then Susannah disappeared from Nicholasville. Elijah, it seems, took his mother to Oxford, Ohio, which is where she died.

Margarett also found a deed for a land purchase, "Robert and Susannah East's 1821 Gift of Land to Elijah East." They gave a gift of land to their son James as well. Another major find was a grant for a tavern from 1814.

"Oh, boy, she got the grant for that tavern in 1814, yeah," Margarett said, dazzled all over again by the documents she'd unearthed. "That was the earliest record I had of the tavern. And then Bob evidently became quite a caterer." According to an article we found in the *Jessamine Journal*, dated September 30, 1887, the tavern was still drawing business more than seventy years after Susannah purchased it. Margarett read from the article. "This tavern was run by a colored man named Bob Speed, a native of Hanover County, Virginia, and for many years, the friend and trusted servant of Henry Clay, who together with the great lawyers of that day, made it a rule to stop with Bob Speed.'"

"I've been calling Henry Clay everything but a child of God," Margarett said of the nineteenth century's most nimble legislator who had represented Kentucky in the House and Senate while also serving as secretary of state. Known as the "Great Compromiser," Clay brokered a series of infamous deals between slave and free state interests in order to absorb the nation's vast western territories into the Union. Personally, Margarett said, "Henry Clay is the one who had taken Indians as slaves. They all protested at different times and said, 'We are not to be enslaved because we're Indians.' Bob was one who protested." Margarett paused on that detail about her ancestor. "Now, maybe that's the way his friendship with Clay started."

Together, these various records showed that Margarett's ancestors were not just free but prosperous in Kentucky, a slave state, decades before the Civil War—a remarkable discovery in any African American family. But Margarett found additional documents that revealed even more about Susannah.

I pictured Margarett sitting in the New York Public Library poring over pages and pages of paper-thin records. She told me her research wasn't confined to any one room. "It seems to me that you always have wonderful people that you can call on and help," she said. "I didn't know anybody, and when you would ask about a genealogist who might help you do things, when I started, they kind of look at you and say, 'Black people? What kind of genealogy you looking for with them?'

"But when I went to Nicholasville in Jessamine County, the clerk of courts told me about a man. He said, 'He's not a genealogist, but he loves to come to the courthouse and search records and do things.' I called him, and he sort of sneered, too—you know, 'I don't know what you expect to find.' But he said, 'I'll help you.' And his name was Clyde Bunch."

Clyde Bunch turned out to be an invaluable resource, and an unlikely friend, to Margarett. "He would send me clips of stuff, and he got so excited, and he said to me, 'You know, when I started doing this for you, I thought it was just fun, and you must be out of your mind, because I'm not going to find anything.' And he said, 'I have gotten so excited.' He became so excited over black history. This is a guy who probably never knew any black people. And when I found out about Susannah, I wrote him a long letter, but it came back to me." The memory is painful for Margarett. "I figured that he must not be living anymore. I was so hurt, because he was so excited over Susannah."

It's tragic that Margarett couldn't share her discovery with Bunch. That Susannah was free and prosperous at a time when nearly all black people in America were enslaved was impressive enough. But how she came by that freedom was almost incomprehensible: in 1782 she sued her master for her freedom. And she *won*! The crucial documents Margarett found tell a story that would be hard to believe without concrete proof.

The first of the two documents was filed in November 1782, two years before the end of the Revolutionary War. The Halifax County Court Order says, "On the complaintiff, Susannah Speed, and William Rowlette, her master for freedom, setting forth that the sheriff of this county do summon the said William to appear at the next court held for this county when and where to answer the said complaint."

In just one month's time, the court granted Susannah her freedom. The reason is unknown, but Margarett holds the evidence in her hands. "On the complaint of Susannah Speed, a mulatto woman, and William Rowlette, her master for her freedom in the court, hearing the matter fully, it is ordered that the said Susannah, together with her two children, be henceforth released from all bondage and servitude to the said William. And that she together with her said children be forever henceforth free." She won.

Margarett was beside herself when she obtained these documents. "I flipped," she said. "As a black woman who had grown up in a very, very nasty democratic society, I've thought first, she was the bravest woman I know to go to Halifax County, in the courthouse. I can just see all those tobacco-hugging kids sitting around the courthouse. To have the nerve to go in and protest and then to win. But it was absolutely astounding."

It's hard enough to imagine a male slave undertaking this endeavor, but a female slave? How in the world did Susannah Speed bring such a case against her master to court? I asked Margarett to give us her best guess.

After dismissing the thought that she might have been an indentured servant, she arrived at a compelling theory.

"The Indian part intrigued me a little bit," she said. "If you were descended from an Indian squaw, you were to be free. And people like Henry Clay did enslave a lot of Indians. He knew darn well they were Indians, but he didn't care." Margarett stopped to consider her ancestor. "Still, you know, you look around, and you see people now who are too timid to do anything. She was a terrific woman."

We consulted with several historians about this perplexing question. The historian Eva Sheppard Wolf explained the contortions the legal system put itself through to appear fair and just to all Americans, even black ones. "It was always legal for people who were held in bondage to sue for freedom," Wolf said, "because you can't think you have any kind of decent legal system if you don't give people the chance to prove that they're free."

Ira Berlin, a great friend of mine and an expert on slavery and the free Negro community, reminded me of something very important that happened in Virginia in the year 1782. A manumission law was passed, allowing individual owners to free their slaves by will or by deed. Before that, the decision for freedom could be made only by the Virginia legislature. Needless to say, that almost never happened.

Something was in the air; there was an awareness of the hypocrisy of so many of the Founding Fathers—the author and the signers of the Declaration of Independence—who owned slaves themselves. The passage of Virginia's manumission law was part of a larger trend taking place during the Revolutionary War, for just one year before Susannah filed her suit in the Old Dominion, in 1781, another black slave, whom we met through our investigation of Kyra Sedgwick's roots, did the same thing in Massachusetts. Her name was Mum Bett, and, after listening to a reading of the Declaration of Independence, she walked into the law office of Theodore Sedgwick in Sheffield, Massachusetts, and said, "I heard that paper read yesterday that says all men are born equal and that every man has a right to freedom. Won't the law give me my freedom?" Mum Bett won her case, too, and soon after changed her name to Elizabeth Freeman, a beloved figure in the annals of the Sedgwick family—and of the commonwealth, after her case led to the abolition of slavery throughout Massachusetts two years later.

I have an example to share from my own family. In 1794, a little over a decade later, my fourth great-grandfather, a free Negro named Isaac Clifford, filed suit in Hardy County, Virginia, to be freed from false imprison-ment, which is a euphemism for being reenslaved. A white man named James Ryan who lived down the road on an adjacent farm had tried to put him back in bondage. White men testified on Isaac Clifford's behalf that he was indeed free, and he was released. The court fined James Ryan.

Susannah Speed had perfect timing. She took advantage of the change in the law immediately and made it through before the law changed back in 1806. When it did, it slammed the door on this mode of manumission. She was part of a small wave of slaves who demanded their freedom and went to court to get it. She may have the first woman to do this in the com-monwealth of Virginia. We know she was the only person in her household to sue her master, because we found a Halifax County Tax Listing for Wil-liam Rowlette from 1782 that showed he owned a total of six slaves (Su-sannah plus five others).

As we dug deeper, we found that Susannah's stunning victory also presented her with difficult choices. For example, four years later, court records from February 2, 1786, reveal that Susannah, upon gaining her freedom, made a surprising decision to consign her own children into in-dentured servitude. "The said Susannah Speed," the document reads, "has put out and bound to the said William Scott her son, Samuel Speed, until he shall attain the age of 21 years." There was an identical document for her son James. Her sons traveled to South Carolina with William Scott. The paper trail ran dry on Sam after this, and Margarett wasn't able to trace him after his release from servitude. (Margarett speculated that James and Samuel were the sons of either William Scott or William Rowlette, Mar-garett's master. "Robert was not the father of Sam and James, I'm sure," she said.)

We consulted with experts on slavery, free Negroes, and Virginia and Kentucky to help sort this out. They confirmed that free people of color often indentured their children so that they could learn a trade. William Scott was a shoemaker. At the same time, given the ever-present danger of free people of color being snatched back into slavery, it made sense that Susannah would willingly curtail her own children's freedom in order to protect them.

In bringing Susannah Speed's remarkable story to light, Margarett has brought to the fore a part of the slavery story not often told. "Most blacks, especially, think their history is all one thing," Margarett said. "We were all out picking cotton or were picking tobacco, and you didn't do anything else. And you get this harsh picture of slavery. Now, slavery was harsh, and I'm not trying to soften it up. But there were many different facets, and there were some slaves who had different opportunities." She recalled some of the people who populate her own family tree. "One of my ancestors was a boatman, and as I say, the blacksmith and so forth and so on. They learned trades. They did other things. And to me it's exciting to know that it wasn't all one set thing." In a sense, it could be said that Susannah started that vocational training process by indenturing her sons.

I think about the class differences within the black community quite a lot, and I asked Margarett if she thought that there are differences between those black people who are descended from slaves who were freed early, well before the Civil War, and those black people whose ancestors weren't. "I don't know, to be perfectly honest," she answered. "Sometimes I think in terms of people, your DNA, do you have ambition? Do you want to get out of a situation? Do you fight to do that? A lot of people don't. And that's true of slaves or anybody else." She laughed. "Of course there was a lot to keep you from fighting in slave days." Margarett continued. "I don't know whether it was better to be freed at a certain time or not, because damn it, I'm going to fight."

■ Even with DNA, we can't test for the fighting gene, although it's certainly something Margarett shares with Susannah Speed. We were able to trace Margarett's maternal line directly back to Sylvia Fry, Elijah East's first wife, who was born in Kentucky in about the year 1800. Margarett's maternal haplogroup is L2c. Her ancestors come from West Africa on her mother's line. This particular maternal haplogroup is especially common among the Mandinka people of Sierra Leone, who carry this genetic signature at very high levels, around 40 percent. It is also found in Mali and Guinea-Bissau. The Mandinkas, of course, were brought to the United States as slaves. Interestingly, L2c is found in only 5 percent of the African American population. "Sierra Leone," Margarett said, looking at the results. "I was looking for my roots, and here I have them."

It's clear from Margarett's own complexion, as well as that of some of her ancestors that we've seen in pictures, that there has been significant mixing in her genes. When I asked her to guess her admixture percentages, she guessed 60 percent African and 40 percent European. "I have to admit that when you get to Sylvia Fry, it's funny, because Sylvia Fry's father was white. So I have to go along with that. I can't defy nature." I laughed, because she may well be the only black person I've ever tested who doesn't claim to be 50 percent Native American, even though her third great-grandfather Robert Speed purportedly hinted at a Native American relative in his relationship with Henry Clay.

Her admixture results are 48 percent African, 44 percent European, and 8 percent Native American. "That must be Bob," she said. Less than half of Margarett's ancestry is African, and the 44 percent European is much higher than the averages of African Americans in any region of the United States, which are about 20 to 25 percent white. "Well, it's a mix, and I know that," she said. "But I didn't want to admit it." Her percentage of Native American ancestry means that she has a Native American great-great-grandparent. "I've got some more work to do, haven't I?" she said.

Margarett's genealogical sleuthing turned up a story that had sadly been lost over time. At least six of her ancestors were free for many generations before the Emancipation Proclamation. "It shows that somebody said, 'I'm not going to take this. I'm going to do something about it,' which makes me terribly proud."

I sensed Margarett felt as if she already knew her third great-grandmother, Susannah Speed, so I asked her whom she'd like to meet, out of all the people on her family tree, if her fairy godmother showed up and carried her back in time. There were many names to choose from. "It might be Sylvia Fry, Susannah's daughter-in-law," Margarett answered. She then told us a fascinating story about Sylvia, Elijah East's first wife, who died young but was the mother of Margarett's great-grandmother, Nancy East Proctor. "Sylvia grew up on this plantation on which lived William Adam Fry and a slave woman named Thena. They had seven children. There were no other women around, no nothing but the seven children and William Adam Fry and Thena. Sylvia was his daughter. And when Elijah wanted to marry Sylvia, the bond was made with Fry. He and his father made the bond with William Fry to marry her, and he gave permission. They paid fifty dollars for that bond in pounds at that time. Anyway," Margarett said, "when William Adam Fry died, he left a will, and he named each child by name, each grandchild by name, so that his white ancestors couldn't break the will. He left them all the money. In 1835, that's very amazing."

Margarett also was curious about Sylvia's father. "So I traced William Adam Fry back a little bit, and his father was a friend of Thomas Jefferson's, which didn't endear him to me at all. But anyway, I would like to meet Sylvia, to see why she died so young and if Elijah was a bore or if he was fun to be with."

In Margarett Cooper's long life, she has been witness to nearly a century of African American history. She lived through Jim Crow, desegregation, the civil rights movement, and the once-incomprehensible election of a black president. Now she had met ancestors who lived through another period of American history, the colonial period, when freedom was taken for granted by no one.

■ Postscript: As a follow-up to our investigation, I grieve to note Margarett Cooper went home to her ancestors on September 20, 2013, less than a month shy of her 100th birthday. A world-class genealogist to the end, she was a beloved member of the Harlem, New York, scene since she moved there from Ohio after the death of her husband, George Clinton Cooper, a distinguished navy veteran of World War II, in 2002. Our only solace is that, perhaps in crossing over, Margarett has learned all the details of every branch of her family tree—and met those who planted and nurtured its roots over centuries. Like her great-great-great-grandmother Susannah Speed, Margarett is now forever free. In homage to her life's work pursuing the paper trail of those who went before, you can read Margarett Cooper's full obituary from the *New York Times* by searching for her name online at www.legacy.com.

For Wanda Sykes, John Legend, and Margarett Cooper, the discovery of their free ancestors was quite a revelation. But these surprising stories accounted for only a fraction of the branches on their family trees. Most of their other ancestral lines consist of relatives who were slaves until the end of the Civil War, just like the other 90 percent of the African American people. Whether these ancestors arrived at freedom through an accident of birth, a legal document, or a lawsuit, they opened our eyes to a world of free people of color that few realize existed—a world in which even fewer had the opportunity to live.

CHAPTER TEN

In the Footsteps of Conquistadors

Actress Michelle Rodriguez, political commentator Linda Chavez, and actor Adrian Grenier all have Hispanic roots, but each has a very different sense of what those roots means. Michelle describes herself as something of a citizen of the world; Linda sees herself as a mix of European cultures; and Adrian is most comfortable with "other." Their family trees are filled with people who settled in North America long before the Pilgrims did, flying Spanish flags, not English ones.

"I feel very strongly that America is a country that has open doors and welcomes people, that all we ask is that you want to come here and do your best. I think that's been the great building block of America, and I don't want to see it end," said Linda, a strong supporter of federal immigration reform, adding, "I think that some who are trying to rewrite the history of America, who somehow think that previous groups of immigrants were OK, but this new group, well, we're not quite sure of them, don't understand that every group that's come here has faced difficulties, discrimination, prejudice. They've overcome it, and they've succeeded."

In this chapter, we explore these difficulties within the less familiar, yet all the more fascinating, history of Spanish colonization of the New World. The stories of Michelle's, Linda's, and Adrian's ancestors took us across the Atlantic Ocean from Europe to the Caribbean, across Mexico and through the American Southwest, where, in the unfolding drama, we once again encountered the critical—and, at times, painful, even brutal—role that race, color, and religion have played in definitions of self and society. While hierarchies change, it seems, the architecture of hierarchy has long persisted, within groups and across continents, sometimes even to the point of obsession.

As diverse as our three subjects' histories and lives are, my journey to understand each began in three surprisingly similar places: troubled childhood homes.

Michelle Rodriguez (b. 1978)

Michelle Rodriguez is famous for playing tough characters, and if you spend just a few minutes with her, you realize that toughness isn't an act. "I recall looking at a camera, being about eight or nine years old, and it was Pick Your Career Day, and I said I was going to be a boxer," Michelle said. Of course it was her performance as a boxer that established her reputation in Hollywood. I wondered why that was the career she had chosen. "I guess there was a part of me that really wanted to destroy everything that was, because I felt it should be some other way. I was always in warrior mode."

She landed her first role in *Girlfight* with no acting credits to her name. I asked her if she feels she's been typecast, offered certain roles because of her ethnic background. Her answer surprised me. "I think that when anybody offers me anything else, I say no *because* of my ethnic background." Infuriated by what she considers the "machismo" of Latin culture, she has turned down roles as the maid and the girlfriend. "I feel like we got it all wrong. It's always one side. It's either masculine, or with the feminists it's feminine. It's like no, honey, it's the chemical balance between the two."

Mayte Michelle Rodriguez was born in San Antonio, Texas, on July 12, 1978, to a Puerto Rican father and a Dominican mother. Her warrior spirit was forged in a home that had more than its share of conflict. "My dad was so clouded and miserable a lot of the time, he just hit the bottle hard," she said. "And my mom, she's not about all that stuff."

She never heard many family stories growing up. "With my mom's side, the storytelling really didn't occur much because they were so conservative. I know there was a lot of suffering. My grandmother lived under Trujillo's dictatorship in Dominican Republic, and they lost land to the dictatorship. My grandmother, just out of dignity and pride, didn't want to talk about it. It was just like, 'We only talk about things that are necessary,'" she said. "And my dad's side, you know, I was always in and out with him. He was all about reading books and doing your research and not listening to religion. I grew up living a pretty big dichotomy between religion on my mom's side and this quest for knowledge on my father's side."

From her earliest years in San Antonio, Michelle has clear memories of her mother teaching her brothers to dance to "Mexican music" and singing with a band in local parks. Most of her other memories of that period are vague. "I remember playing with the kids across the street who were slightly racist. That used to hurt me sometimes—name calling and asking me to play with them and then doing stupid, mean things. I grew some tough skin because of that kind of stuff."

She didn't pick up on distinctions within the Latino population, even though in San Antonio most Latinos were Mexican and her family was not. She primarily spoke English as a child, but the Spanish language cut across divisions between the communities. "I didn't really feel different from all the other Latinos, because we speak the same language. We're pretty much in the same boat."

When Michelle was five, her parents' fragile marriage collapsed, and her mother became very ill. The family moved to the Dominican Republic, where her grandmother, Sarah Espinal, took custody of Michelle and her two brothers. They lived in a small house in Santo Domingo, supporting themselves by running a local market.

While her family had been among the working poor in Texas, Michelle said that the poverty in the Dominican Republic was shocking. "I recall very, very, very powerful memories of stopping my dancing and my jumping up and down because I see a naked boy walking down the street with his mom, walking with no shoes. You could see the difference in the poverty. That culture shock really hit me hard."

It was in the Dominican Republic that Michelle was first exposed to her grandmother's Jehovah's Witness culture. "It was bye-bye, Santa; bye-bye, Tooth Fairy; bye-bye, imagination," she said. "But then at the same time, welcome, imagination, because a lot of these mythological biblical tales are believed verbatim instead of taking it in symbolic terms. . . . I'm like, 'What's this seven-headed dragon in Revelation? You sure it doesn't have to do with seven consciousnesses?' They're like, 'No, we think it's a seven-headed dragon.'"

After two years of struggling to make ends meet, Michelle's grandmother moved the family from her native country back to America. "Grandma just left everything in Dominican Republic, grabbed Mom, me, and the two bros, and we moved to Jersey." The better life she was seeking for the family didn't materialize right away. Michelle relied upon her grandmother's strength as she struggled to adjust to her new home. She had lost all her English language in the Dominican Republic, and the language barrier at first was a difficult one to breach. At the same time, her grandmother's strict religious observance made Michelle an object of ridicule at school. "Kids made fun of me for wearing a dress to school because I'm Jehovah's Witness," she recalled. "Meanwhile, I'm the biggest tomboy on the planet."

She rebelled, but even in her days as a delinquent, her grandmother served as a guiding light for her. "When I did go out there and I did expose myself to crime or I did expose myself to the life in Jersey City, I always maintained a certain moral, ethical standard." She laughed. "It was so strong that I didn't get pregnant, didn't have any abortions. I didn't have to worry about going to jail for murder. I turned out to be a pretty good kid."

Early in Michelle's life, even before her move to the Dominican Republic and then back to the States, she observed a palpable tension between the families of her dark-skinned Dominican mother and her lighter-skinned Puerto Rican father. "Lots of animosity between my dad's family not being accepting of my mom for being the darker-skinned Dominican," Michelle said. She is clearly still wounded by her grandmother's treatment. "It took me a long to time to speak to her because of how she treated my mom when I was younger—just this kind of slight racism."

To be sure, there has been very little historic conflict between Puerto Rico and the Dominican Republic. The two nations have never been at war. They don't even share a border. Instead, the tension in Michelle's family was about skin color—about lighter-skinned people looking down on darker-skinned people. This trend was evident throughout her family tree. Michelle's light-skinned Puerto Rican ancestors married their own relatives at a truly astonishing rate. Their cultural obsession with race was clear.

■ Michelle's father, Rafael Rodriguez, was born on February 27, 1944, in San Sebastian, Puerto Rico. Michelle described her father as passionate, intellectual, knowledge seeking— in a sense, the polar opposite of her devoutly religious mother. He was politically active, even serving time in jail for not wanting to go to Vietnam. Michelle has referred to him in the past as a Puerto Rican "independentista," meaning someone who believes that Puerto Rico should be independent of the United States. Too strong a connection to the United States, Michelle explained, in the eyes of that movement—and of her father—threatened a loss of Puerto Rican identity and culture.

Michelle's family had lived in San Sebastian for generations, as well as in the nearby town of Lares, site of the Revolt of Lares—*El Grito de Lares*—in 1867, in which Puerto Rican nationalists rose up to demand their independence from Spain. When these revolutionaries moved in to claim San Sebastian, then called Pepino, the Spanish military swiftly crushed the rebellion. Leaders were arrested, and many were executed, but the flame of Puerto Rican nationalism was not extinguished. The original lyrics to the national anthem "La Borinqueña" were penned here, capturing the spirit of the failed revolution: "The drum of war says it's time / It's time to unite / *El Grito de Lares* / The Scream of Lares / It's time to repeat it / And then we'll know to win or die." Given Michelle's family's deep roots in Lares, it's no wonder that her father was so dedicated to the spirit of Puerto Rican nationalism that was born there.

Lares was formally founded in 1827, and Michelle's fifth great-grandfather, Hilario Acevedo, is mentioned in the town's first census, taken sometime between 1823 and 1826. It said, "Hilario Acevedo does not appear in records; we only know of his common-law relationship with Candida de Sotomayor from the death certificate of their daughter Maria Acevedo." The record also described Hilario and Candida as *pardos libres*, "free people of color." Most scholars say that *pardos* were a mixture of African, Native American, and Spanish. "Interesting," Michelle commented, "because that side of the family is as white as snow."

And their identity—particularly the "purity" of their white racial identity—was of paramount concern, as evidenced in the birth record for her paternal grandmother, Isaura Santiago Santiago. "At four in the afternoon on the 5th of February, 1926, a girl of the white race was born at home, and given the name Isaura," the document stated. "This baby girl is the daughter of the declared white 28-year-old male Juan Santiago and the white 24-year-old Juana Santiago. The paternal grandparents are Juan Santiago and Juana Rodriguez, and the maternal grandparents are Loreto Santiago and Higinia Santiago. All are white and residents of San Sebastian.'"

Michelle paused in reading the document. "No wonder that side of the family is racist," she said.

The privilege of having white skin has always been important throughout the Caribbean. Even though Puerto Rico had a long history of race mixing among the Taino Indians, the Africans, and the Europeans, white skin remained prized and protected.

Up and down Michelle's family tree, we were struck by how often the same names and birthplaces appeared. As in the case of the birth certificate, the word "white" was rivaled only in number of mentions by the name "Santiago." Her grandmother Isaura was what Michelle called "a double Santiago." Isaura's maternal grandparents were Loreto Santiago Rivera and Maria Higinia Santiago Lopez. Loreto and Higinia, we discovered, were first cousins. Isaura's other grandfather, Michelle's great-great-grandfather—whose name was Juan Santiago Perez—was also their first cousin. This means that three of Michelle's third great-grandfathers were brothers. This persisted across generations. Michelle's great-grand-father, Zenon Rodriguez Vargas, and her great-great-grandmother, Juana Rodriguez Vargas, were brother and sister. The genealogist who traced Michelle's family tree for us called it "a beautiful depiction of the consanguinity and endogamy of nineteenth-century Puerto Rican families."

While Michelle's family tree is certainly unusual, it was not entirely atypical. In generations past, marriage between close relatives was common and accepted. Brides needed dowries, so the practice of marrying daughters to their cousins helped keep land and property in the family. Isolated geography was another contributing factor.

Michelle took the news of her ancestors' mating preferences with good humor and responded to the description of her family tree with characteristic bluntness: "That's an elegant way of saying you guys love to do it in the family!" But rather than dwell on her father's family's attitudes about color, she said she wanted to learn about the other side of her family tree, the Dominican side.

■ Michelle's mother, Carmen Milady Pared Espinal, was born in Haina, just across the river from Santo Domingo. While Michelle's memories of her own childhood there are happy ones—albeit tempered by her awareness of the wretched poverty in which people lived—her mother didn't share these. "My mom despised everything about Dominican Republic, for some strange reason, and I'll never truly understand," Michelle said. "Maybe it was responsibilities that she was given at a young age, because her dad passed away from a heart attack while she was on his lap at a very young age. He was only like forty-five." Memories can play tricks on our perceptions. Carmen's father was actually about sixty-eight years old when he died.

Carmen stayed in the Dominican Republic into adulthood, where she married for the first time. She left her first husband when she got the opportunity to come to America. "When Trujillo, the dictator, lost power," Michelle explained, "they were giving a bunch of passes for Dominicans to leave the country, and she was one of the first to be like, 'Peace, I'm going to America.'"

Michelle's grandmother remained behind at that time. Sarah Espinal was born in the mountain town of Jarabacoa in La Vega province on December 4, 1923. Michelle traveled to Santo Domingo with our researcher, Jaime Reed, to search for stories about her beloved grandmother. Several of Abuelita Sarah's neighbors—including the 102-year-old woman next door—were still living there and welcomed the opportunity to talk about their old friend. People around town described her as beautiful, intelligent, upbeat. They did not, however, think as highly of Michelle's grandfather, Sarah's husband, Alfredo Pared. Alfredo, they said, was "a tall, dark outsider," thirty years her grandmother's senior who swept through town one day and stole Sarah's heart.

Michelle had never heard a word about this. "Talk about love and attraction to her granddaughter?" Michelle laughed. "Are you crazy?" All Michelle had heard was that he was loved and he died too young.

I asked Michelle if she thought that there might be an element of racism in the way neighbors consistently described her grandfather Alfredo as dark. "There's lots of racists all over Dominican Republic. They hate each other," she said. "And it could range from the people with money to the people without money. I have this sense about Third World countries altogether: the classism is predominant."

One of Michelle's uncles told us Alfredo Pared was a man who didn't like to have his picture taken, and indeed, we couldn't find one. But we did find his baptismal record, which was revealing in its own right. Dated July 1893, it said Michelle's grandfather Alfredo Pared, was "the natural son"—which means born out of wedlock—of Victoria Pared. No father's name was given. Our researchers found baptismal records for Victoria Pared's other children as well, all without a father's name. Alfredo went on to become a successful merchant and property owner, and when he died in 1961, he left Sarah the house in San Carlos, where he had once lived.

Michelle Rodriguez • Linda Chavez • Adrian Grenier   **285**

Sarah passed away in 1999. To learn more, Jaime led Michelle to a graveyard, where some of her relatives are buried. There they discovered Michelle's family tomb. It was meaningful for Michelle to visit her grandmother's burial site, but she still hadn't found what she wanted: something new, something she didn't already know about Sarah.

Michelle's grandaunt Ziola, whom she hadn't seen since she was a child, was the person Michelle had been waiting for. Poring over her rich collection of never-before-seen family photos and scrapbooks, Michelle was able to open the pages of her grandmother's past. In one of the pictures of Sarah's parents, Michelle's great-grandparents Raymunda and Hilario, Michelle noticed an odd discrepancy in their surnames: Raymunda's last name was Espinal, but Hilario's was Piña. As far as Michelle knew, the family's last name was Espinal.

This discrepancy sent our researcher, Jaime, on a quest. In Santo Domingo's Central Archives, he found Sarah's birth certificate and uncovered a deep family secret. According to the birth certificate, Sarah was born out of wedlock; just like her husband, she is called "a natural child" of Hilario and Raymunda. Although Hilario and Raymunda never married, they had two children together.

Michelle said she had no idea why her great-grandparents had never married, especially since their relationship lasted for years and years. The obstacle, we found out, had been insurmountable: Hilario's legal wife. Her name was Olimpia Matos de Piña.

Sarah had never discussed her stepmother Olimpia with Michelle or with anyone else as far as Michelle knew. But the evidence suggests that Sarah knew her stepmother very well and was a frequent visitor in their home. There's even evidence that Sarah's stepmother couldn't have children and that she raised Sarah's brother Manuel as her own.

What in Raymunda's life would make her share her lover and child, it appeared willingly, with another woman? Looking deeper into the lives of Michelle's great-grandparents takes us on a journey through the history of the Dominican Republic. Raymunda Espinal died in 1996, so there were still people in Jarabacoa who remembered her. They described her as a kind of religious nomad. She was born on January 4, 1906, and gave birth to Sarah when she was seventeen. At different times in her life, Raymunda was Catholic, then Protestant, and ultimately Jehovah's Witness, probably the first in Michelle's family.

Incidentally, Jehovah's Witnesses came to the Dominican Republic in

1932, but the brutal dictator Rafael Trujillo banned the religion. The ban was enforced until his assassination in 1961.

How did Michelle's family figure into the island's history? Her great-grandfather, Hilario Piña Batista, was born in San Juan de la Maguana around 1882. Known by the nickname of Cun, or Don Cun, he was a journalist and an intellectual and a key figure in Jarabacoa. A brief explanation of the early-twentieth-century Dominican Republic is necessary to explain Michelle's family's relationship to it.

Starting in 1916, U.S. troops occupied the Dominican Republic. Popular resistance helped bring an end to that occupation on July 1, 1924. The new constitutional government, headed by Horacio Vásquez, took office on July 12. On that day, Michelle's great-grandfather Hilario Piña published this vitriolic statement in one of the nation's papers: "The cumulated errors of our past leaders sacrifice our independence, handing it over to the colossus of the North for a handful of vile gold. The governments that shamelessly indebt the nation, they chain the Republic, they tie its hands and feet with the traitorous cords of fateful treaties. For the wolf will be dismembered by greed, for the blond elephant of Yankee-Land tramples."

Digesting these angry words directed against America, I had to wonder what Hilario would think of his granddaughter's decision to leave the Dominican Republic in the latter half of the century for the reviled "colossus of the North," and his great-granddaughter's frequent refrain about how grateful she is to have been born in America. "I love being an American. I wouldn't choose to be any other culture at the moment. As far as being a woman, this is the place to be," Michelle said. But her great-grandfather's position resonated with her, and it addressed a topic she has thought about many times herself. "I just find it interesting when countries occupy other countries. You're in a position where you see how your sugar is wanted by the outside, and then you also see how they're basically trying to swindle your land right out from under you in the name of something that they want without wanting to give you anything in return. It just sounds unfair. I've always had this deep sense of hatred toward injustice. It really gets under my skin and boils it."

Hilario's sister, Lilia Dolores Piña Batista, was Michelle's great-grandaunt, and she had a close connection to the bloody events of the Trujillo regime. Her husband, Rafael Mirabal, known popularly as Fello, was the uncle of the four Mirabal sisters, or Las Mariposas, as they were known. The Mirabal sisters, three of whom were assassinated by the government, have come to symbolize resistance against the Trujillo dictator-ship. In a case of life imitating art, in 2010 Michelle starred as Minerva Mirabal in the film adaptation of the sisters' story in the film *Trópico de Sangre*. "There's just no coincidences, are there?" she exclaimed. The Mirabals were part of the Dominican cultural, intellectual elites who posed a threat to Trujillo. Like many dictators, Trujillo brought infrastructure to the island—roads, schools, buildings—and the majority of the people, impoverished and illiterate, appreciated the development. "He brings all these beautiful things, so we must follow him," Michelle explained. "Minerva was part of that group of people who thought outside of the box, very similar to Diego Rivera and Frida Kahlo in Mexico. But during a dictatorship, there was just no environment for that level of thinking." Many historians believe that the tragic murders of the Mirabal sisters marked the turning point in popular support for Trujillo. He was assassinated six months later.

Michelle's roots in Jarabacoa run very deep. Hilario's parents, Michelle's great-great-grandparents, Placido Piña Abreu, known as Papa Plao or Don Placido, and Maria Dolores Batista Espejo, known as Lola, were born around 1856 and 1861 respectively. Papa Plao was one of the town's most prominent citizens, a councilman for many years and elected mayor when he was already in his eighties.

Through Lola, we found the story of another relation to Michelle, al-though not on her direct line, who played a critical role in the history of the Dominican Republic. Lola's father, Michelle's great-great-great-grandfather, was Hilario Batista Rodriguez, born in Fundación, in the southern province of Barahona, in 1836. His brother, Daniel Batista Rodri-guez, was a war hero who had been persecuted by the Spanish authorities during the annexation of the Dominican Republic in 1861. After fleeing to the remote mountain town of Jarabacoa, Michelle's family's home for the next century, Daniel joined up with the rebel forces and became a hero yet again in the War of Restoration. Daniel and Hilario became leaders of the growing town. Hilario had quite a distinguished civic career, overseeing the establishment of churches and schools and helping to allocate land to the citizens of the town. Later, both brothers opposed American interven-tion in the Dominican Republic, much as they had opposed Spanish inter-vention. It was Carmen, Michelle's mother, who left the homeland that her ancestors had cared so passionately about and fought so hard for. Interestingly, a powerful belief in independent homelands linked her mother's and father's families to each other.

■ Whether a person embraces or rejects his or her ancestry, and all the attendant baggage that goes along with it, that ancestry—that base—is there in our genes, so when the paper trail on Michelle's family ran out, we turned to DNA. On her father's side, we traced her direct ancestors back to her great-great-grandfather, Reyes Rodriguez, who lived in San Sebastian, Puerto Rico, in the middle of the 1800s. To determine Michelle's paternal haplogroup, we tested her brother Omar's Y-DNA. It is E1b1b1b2a, a subgroup of E1b1b, which arose about twenty-five thousand years ago in eastern Africa and spread into the Mediterranean region after the Ice Age. Today it is most common in North Africa and Southern Europe, including Italy, the Balkans, Portugal, and Spain.

Spain seemed like a likely place of origin for Michelle's paternal ancestors. Columbus landed on the island of Puerto Rico on November 19, 1493, on his second voyage to the New World and declared it a colony of Spain. Spanish people and their descendants have lived there ever since.

What about that claim, that Michelle's mother's side is free of European ancestry? We traced Michelle's direct maternal line back to her great-great-grandmother, Josefa Espinal, who was born around 1860 in La Vega, Dominican Republic. Her maternal haplogroup is A2, a subgroup of A, one of the four major Native American haplogroups that crossed the Bering Land Bridge into North America more than twelve thousand years ago. Michelle is indeed descended from a Native American on her mother's side and a white man on her father's side.

Like African Americans, most Dominicans believe that they have Taino ancestry, but because of the sharp decrease in the Taino population as of 1550, rarely do they. Michelle is in a rare group of Dominicans that actually does.

In her admixture test, Michelle's percentage of European ancestry was evidence that the period of mixing between Native Americans and Spaniards came early in the colonial era and was short-lived. Her Native American percentage is low, only 6.3 percent. Michelle had a hard time accepting the news that she is 72.4 percent European. "That's insane. I'm sorry. I'm so not impressed. I'm European—ew. I wanted to be Native American."

Though disappointed at first, Michelle was intrigued to learn that her

DNA results actually pointed to great genetic diversity. She is 21.3 percent African, a legacy of the fact that throughout the Spanish empire, masters often impregnated their African slaves. While African ancestry was once considered shameful by Michelle's family, she eagerly embraces it.

No matter the color of our skin or the percentages of our admixtures, one thing all Americans have in common is that somewhere along the way, our people came from somewhere else. I was curious to know what Michelle, the American-born daughter of immigrants, thought makes someone an American.

She considered the question deeply. "I think the meaning of a real American is a person who wants to innovate, who's here to make a dream come true and thinks outside of the box and who wants to create a new utopia," she said. "It is somebody who takes pride in the possibility of making something new out of an old ancestry."

Michelle's definition of an American could apply to many of her non-American ancestors as well, born generations ago, who exhibited the same traits of independence, pride, and determination that Michelle displays in her every move and mood. In fact, when I asked her, if she had a fairy godmother to take her into the past, which ancestor would she like to meet, she chose one who embodied this spirit: her third great-grandfather, Hilario Batista Rodriguez, the brother of the war hero Daniel Batista, and himself a leader of her family's ancestral home, Jarabacoa.

"He's got that kind of mentality of hope that I see in myself," Michelle remarked, "just that optimism about life and the idea that if you believe in something, you should really fight for it, and that it will be OK if we just get together and fix it."

Linda Chavez (b. 1947)

Linda Chavez says she has always been viewed with some suspicion. As her last name indicates, she descends on one side from a Hispanic family, but growing up in New Mexico, friends and acquaintances weren't sure what to make of her blonde, blue-eyed mother, a daughter of Ireland. Linda was the first Hispanic person nominated for a cabinet position, and she served in the Reagan and Bush White Houses, yet her views on immigration are liberal and not in line with much of the current Republican Party's.

Then there was the matter of that epithet, awarded to her by *Hispanic*

Magazine: "The Most Hated Hispanic in America." The reason: Linda's 1991 book, *Out of the Barrio*, in which she took a controversial look at Hispanic immigration and assimilation patterns. Instead of running from the smear, Linda used it as the subtitle of her next book, *An Unlikely Conservative: The Transformation of an Ex-Liberal, or How I Became the Most Hated Hispanic in America*. Today the self-described "incipient right winger" is a regular commentator on Fox News, known for her fiercely independent spirit and love of a good fight. "I don't like to preach to the choir. I like to get in there and mix it up," she said. "That's probably from my dad, who's pugnacious." If there's a gene for thick skin, maybe Linda inherited it.

■ Linda grew up feeling proud of her family's connection to New Mexico. She was born on June 17, 1947, in Albuquerque. "I was always told we were a land-grant family. It was special. It means you were part of the founding of that area," Linda said, recalling how her grandfather would point out to her all the Albuquerque sites of significance to her family. I wondered if she ever felt "different" from other Hispanics in New Mexico; after all, on one side she descended from the ethnic groups that have become the backbone of the American establishment. "Hispanics in New Mexico were the majority when I was born," Linda said. "That was the majority population. If I felt funny at all it was in having this blonde-haired and blue-eyed, very fair-skinned mother. She was the outsider. I was part of the majority. She was part of the minority."

Intermarriage was far less common—and certainly less accepted—when Linda was coming of age in the 1950s. "Today we make a great deal about intermarriage. But this is a very important part of the story of America, this melting pot, the mixing of different peoples, the final acceptance of a group." Linda didn't think her parents experienced tension in their marriage related to their different backgrounds. (It came from other issues.) "She became the best Mexican cook I have ever known," Linda said of her mother. "She learned right from my grandmother how to make really, really good chile colorado and frijoles. And I'm a pretty darn good Mexican cook myself."

While a student at the University of Colorado at Boulder, Linda was a founding member of UMAS, United Mexican American Students, an organization whose goal was to recruit more Mexican American students to the university. Although the Hispanic population in the area, and certainly in neighboring New Mexico, was large, Hispanics had a low high school graduation rate at the time, and the public schools they attended, according to Linda, were of lesser quality than the schools colleges tended to draw from. Even as an active member of UMAS, Linda said her standing in the community was often questioned. "I didn't speak Spanish. I didn't have an accent. My coloring is lighter. I grew up in the Anglo part of town; I didn't grow up in the Mexican part of town. I married a Jew. I was the product of a marriage that was not entirely Hispanic."

I was curious to know whether Linda considers herself a Latina. She answered, "I don't like boxes for any purpose other than research. I resent being asked what my ethnicity or racial background is. But on the census form, I check Hispanic. On the race form I check white. I guess I've always considered myself Hispanic. As I get older, I call myself Mexican American usually."

And what is the difference, in Linda's opinion, between being Hispanic and being a Latino. "'Latino' I think of as a more political term, as something that was adopted as a kind of solidarity. A Latino to me, it can be any descendant of somebody from twenty-four different countries," she explained. "Hispanic" was a term embraced by the U.S. government in an attempt to consolidate a massive number of Spanish-speaking people into one monolithic group. "Frankly, most people who have strong ethnic identification identify with their particular group. Most Hispanics or Latinos think they're Mexican American, or they're Cuban American, or they're Puerto Rican. A lot of people looking in from the outside think we're all the same."

They also too often equate "Latino" with "immigrant," even though, like many, Linda's family has deep roots in New Mexico. In fact, her ancestors didn't immigrate to the United States. Rather, the United States, as it were, immigrated to her ancestors. The border moved.

Linda's father, Rudolfo Enrique Chavez, known as Rudy, was born on February 6, 1918, in Albuquerque. "A very imposing man," Linda said of her father, whom she "idolized." "He was really somebody who commanded a lot of attention and earned a lot of respect, even though his social class, he was very much working class."

Rudy had been born into a prosperous, established family with roots in what is now the United States of more than three hundred years, but when Linda's grandfather Ambrosio, or Ambrose, Chavez, was arrested three times for bootlegging (he spent a total of eleven years in Leavenworth federal penitentiary), the family's fortunes evaporated. Linda's father dropped out of school in the ninth grade and worked much of his life as a housepainter, barely earning a living and battling alcoholism.

By the time Linda was in third grade, she had changed schools six times across two states. Her mother tried leaving on her own but eventually convinced Rudy to start over in Colorado. They settled in Denver, where Linda had her first realization that Hispanics weren't always welcome. "What happened to me is a little boy that I played with after school all the time invited me over, and his mother said, 'We don't allow Mexicans.'"

This early, painful encounter with racism paradoxically drew Linda closer to her roots. "It was interesting," she said, "because people were always asking me, 'Where are you from?' People to this day ask me where I'm from, or how long has your family been here? When I tell them several hundred years, that usually stops the conversation cold. But I did have a sense that I came from a family that had done important things, and my mother did say, 'You tell people you're American. That's what you are.' So that was her answer: 'I'm an American.'"

■ The obsession with whiteness we have observed in other Hispanic families is as old as the Spanish settlement of the New World, even though the men who began pouring in more than five hundred years ago didn't arrive on an empty continent, and they didn't bring many females with them. Throughout the Americas, many Spanish settlers—through either rape or consensual relationships—had children both with the Native Americans and with their African slaves, filling the colonies with people who didn't *look* particularly "Spanish."

To police the genetic boundaries, the Spaniards constructed class systems based on color, inventing terms like "mulatto" and "mestizo" and creating elaborate anthropological paintings called *castas* to describe these new racial mixtures. Whiteness was so critical to power that people with limited mating choices sometimes married their own relatives rather than risk diluting the "purity" of their bloodline. You can see this very clearly in Linda Chavez's family tree.

Linda's grandfather, Ambrosio Rosendo Chavez, was born on March 1, 1889, in Albuquerque. Ambrosio married an Armijo—Linda's grandmother, Petra, born in Corrales, New Mexico, on May 29, 1894. Ambrosio's father, Eduardo Chavez, married an Armijo, too—Linda's great-grandmother, Maria Feliciana. Looking across the family tree, we observed

Michelle Rodriguez • Linda Chavez • Adrian Grenier   **293**

Armijos marrying Chavezes and other Armijos over and over and over again. In fact, Linda's grandparents Petra and Ambrosio were related long before they were married; they were third cousins once removed.

One of Linda's most illustrious relatives was the son of an Armijo-Chavez union. Manuel Armijo was born in 1793, the son of Linda's fourth great-grandparents, Vicente Ferrer Armijo and Maria Barbara Chavez. Linda's third great-granduncle was the fabled last territorial governor of New Mexico—the man who lost New Mexico—which at the time was part of Mexico. Mexico had gained independence from Spain in 1821. His first job as a public servant was as mayor of Albuquerque, and from there he went on to serve as governor of New Mexico in 1827 and 1828. He left office that year, only to return to public service in less than ten years' time. In 1837 peasants revolted against the Mexican authority as they had against the Spanish years earlier. Linda's great-great-great-granduncle, Manuel Armijo, led the counterrevolution, putting down the rebellion and returning to the position of governor. As someone who stood up for Mexico, he became a hero to many.

Four years later, Manuel won the public's favor again. In 1841, Texas, which was a sovereign nation then, tried to invade New Mexico. Texas sent out what it called a trading expedition to New Mexico—wagons full of goods, accompanied by soldiers—with the goal of seizing control. Manuel saw through the plot and had the army arrest all the Texans. His hero status was still intact.

But in 1846, when Mexico went to war with the United States, Manuel Armijo went from being revered to being reviled. "He did not put up the fight that people expected," said Linda, and he surrendered New Mexico to the United States without a shot. Had he been bribed? Was he a humanitarian? No one knows why, but Manuel was tarred by Mexican Americans and Anglo Americans alike. Linda good-naturedly drew a parallel between herself and her ancestor. "I'm somewhat vilified by some in the Mexican American community, and being tied to Manuel Armijo may burnish that reputation."

Searching the New Mexico Archives, we realized that the impetus for ethnic purity among the Spanish didn't drive *all* of Linda's ancestors. Going back three generations from Manuel Armijo, to the year 1694, we found Linda's sixth great-grandfather, Vicente Ferrer de Armijo, in a document called the Zacatecas Muster, a list of colonists recruited from Zacatecas, Mexico, to settle in New Mexico. Along with ten-year-old Vicente were his three brothers and their widowed mother, Catalina Duran, the first members of the Armijo family to come to New Mexico. Catalina, the Muster revealed, was mestiza, meaning she was of mixed blood, Indian and Spanish—the first documented evidence we found of racial mixing in Linda's family tree. "It's not terribly surprising," she said. "For all the myths and all of the attempts at racial purity that were important in certain eras, people get together."

Nine years after arriving in New Mexico, in 1703, Linda's sixth great-grandfather, Vicente, married a woman named Maria de Apodaca. The marriage record of their union included the names of Vicente's parents, José de Armijo and Catalina Duran, but only Maria's mother, Juana de Apodaca. Her father's name was left blank—a total mystery, except for the clue we discovered in the three-hundred-year-old journal of a Spaniard named Diego de Vargas, a key figure in what is known as the Pueblo Revolt, a bloody uprising in 1680 by Native Americans angered over Spanish efforts to suppress their religion.

"Basically," explained New Mexico state historian Rick Hendricks, "all over the north they rose up. They really were focusing on killing the priests, desecrating the churches. They were trying to get rid of most of the trappings of Spanish culture."

To the Pueblos, it was a tremendous victory. In fact, it was the most successful Native American rebellion in all of American history. For twelve years, the Spanish were banished from New Mexico. Then, in 1692, Diego de Vargas returned, hell-bent on his mission to restore Spanish control and the Catholic Church's dominance. There was no way the Pueblos could fight off the vast number of Spanish troops that descended upon them—or the wave of colonists that followed.

To our surprise, Vargas's journal contained quite a bit of information about some of Linda's ancestors living in New Mexico *before* the Spanish returned. Vargas kept meticulous records about the mixed-Indian children he found and "saved" through baptism. Among the many names in his journals, one caught our eye: Juana de Apodaca—Linda's seventh great-grandmother. Vargas listed Juana as a captive, meaning she had lived among the Pueblos throughout their revolt. During this time she had also given birth to a daughter she named Maria, which led us to an inescapable conclusion: Maria's father was an Indian.

Linda was thrilled at this discovery—and enjoyed the irony of it, considering her family tree. "So all those Chavezes and Armijos trying to marry each other to keep out the Indian blood, the train had already left the station."

■ We weren't done with the Armijos yet. Miraculously, we were able to trace the family all the way back to Linda's tenth great-grandfather, Antonio de Armijo, born around 1540 in Seville, Spain. It was there, in the Old World, that we continued our journey into Linda's roots. We discovered a four-hundred-year-old shipping record found in Seville, Spain, which stated that Linda's ninth great-grandfather, Francisco de Armijo, born around 1565, sailed from Seville to Mexico in 1590, exactly thirty years before the *Mayflower* carried the Pilgrims across the Atlantic to present-day Massachusetts.

Searching for more about Francisco, we learned he had journeyed to the New World not once but twice, returning again in 1597, this time with his wife, Guiomar Orozco, and their four children. "That's a rare story," historian Rick Hendricks said. "Much more typical would have been starting a new family. I can actually only think of very few people, certainly of that social rank, that would ever do that."

We thought the reason might lie in what was happening in Spain at that time. Francisco and Guiomar lived through some of the darkest days of the Spanish Inquisition. Over the previous century, Muslims and Jews had been ordered to convert to Roman Catholicism or face expulsion. Many had converted. But as the church grew stronger, it turned on those suspected of secretly holding on to their old faith, subjecting them to torture and imprisonment, even burning thousands at the stake.

By the time Francisco and Guiomar married, if you weren't from an old Catholic family, Spain wasn't safe. We sent a researcher to comb through the Spanish Archives to figure out if this was why Linda's ancestors fled to the New World. While he found little regarding Francisco's family (laborers and tradesmen who did not appear in any of the lists of notable families in the area), the family of Guiomar Orozco was another story.

In the estate papers of Benita de Orozco—Guiomar Orozco's mother and Linda's tenth great-grandmother—we learned that the Orozco family had considerable wealth. Unbelievably, the slaves listed in her inventory (three adults and two children) were *not* the proof of great wealth—apparently, even the artisan class owned slaves at this time in Spain—but there were luxury items included that only the finest families could have possessed: "a black taffeta dress trimmed with satin, a black velvet petticoat, a crimson damask canopy." We also found records indicating that Benita had a dowry worth roughly $800,000 in today's dollars. Yet, it turns out, this well-established Seville family also harbored a deep secret which had been kept through ten generations.

In 2001, Dr. Juan Gil, a professor at the University of Seville, wrote *Los Conversos y la Inquisición Sevillana* (The Converted and the Inquisition in Seville), documenting the Jewish families that converted to Catholicism to avoid expulsion. We pored over the eight volumes until we found the name Benita de Orozco, leaving no room for doubt: Linda's ancestors were once Spanish Jews. By marrying their daughter to a Catholic man—albeit one of considerably lower social standing—the Orozcos, as wealthy as they had been, were ensuring her safety and saving her life.

The Orozcos, of course, were not alone. Thousands of converted Jews fled Spain for the New World. They formed their own communities, and there are many indications that some of them continued to practice Judaism in secret. In Albuquerque, New Mexico, we visited the historian Stanley Hordes, an expert on these so-called Crypto-Jews.

"There is today in this part of the world some kind of Sephardic Jewish legacy, ranging all the way from folks who do things and don't know why they do them," Hordes explained, "who light candles on Friday night, who observe the Sabbath on Saturday rather than Sunday and have no idea ostensibly about any connection between what they do and how Jews welcome and observe the Sabbath; ranging from them to people who know exactly who they are, whose grandfather might have taken them into the field when they were fourteen and fifteen years old saying to them, 'You must understand, my son, we're really not Christians. We're really Jews.'"

Even today, there are hints and suggestions of these Crypto-Jews all over New Mexico, in churches where altars bear Stars of David, in graveyards dotted with Old Testament names. Though Linda was raised a devout Roman Catholic, she saw evidence of this in her own family when she was growing up, though nothing had been confirmed until now.

"I still have the statue that my grandmother Petra used to turn to the wall," Linda recalled. "And that was supposedly a sign of having historically Jewish roots, that you kept the statues but you turned them to the wall."

Ironically, Linda herself had converted to Judaism as a young woman when she married her husband, Christopher Gersten, in 1967. Her conversion was in name only, done to appease her husband's family. "It didn't really hold," she said. "If I had been able to go to synagogue and feel a connection—but there was no religious connection, and the lack of religion was what I missed." Linda, who during high school had considered becoming a nun and who describes herself as "profoundly religious," ultimately decided she couldn't leave Catholicism. For her ancestors, abandoning their religion was a matter of survival.

■ We also discovered deep American roots on Linda's mother's side—roots set down by immigrants fleeing religious persecution in their home country. Linda's mother, Velma McKenna, was born on July 21, 1921, in Sheridan, Wyoming. Linda knew her mother's father's family originally came from Ireland, but she knew few details. "I have my great-great-grandmother's scrapbook. I have pages out of a family Bible. It seemed to be passed down matrilineally," she said of the cherished heirloom. "It was from daughter to daughter. Very strong women, I think, in my mother's family. That's my impression."

We were fortunate to find the documents we did, because Irish ancestry is among the most difficult to trace for genealogists. From the late 1500s until well into the 1800s, the British Penal Laws gave Irish Catholics almost no rights. The only records left behind by most were parish records in local churches. Of course, after a point, these churches, too, were outlawed because of the clash between Roman Catholicism and the Anglican Church. The only way to find parish records is to know exactly where a particular ancestor lived, and even that isn't failsafe: the church in which that ancestor worshiped would have had to be left intact by the British, the property not seized, the records not destroyed.

Linda's grandparents' names, we knew, were Leo McKenna and Catherine Dolan. Common names both, but at least we had something to start with. We found the manifest of a ship called the *Victoria* that arrived in New York City on June 11, 1874, which listed a passenger named Michael McIna, an obvious phonetic spelling of McKenna. This was Linda's great-grandfather, born in County Mayo, Ireland, in June 1855, and arriving in America when he was nineteen years old.

Michael, it seems, made his way out to Iowa, where a large Irish community had flourished. There he married Catherine Dolan, born in Clinton County, Iowa, also in 1855. That wasn't the only similarity. Catherine's parents, Linda's great-great-grandparents, John Dolan and Catherine Murphy, had emigrated from County Mayo, Ireland, in the mid-1800s.

They say people take secrets to their graves with them, but tombstones can be revealing, and in Clinton County, we found the grave of Bridget McNamee Dolan, the mother of Catherine Murphy Dolan and Linda's great-great-great-grandmother. Etched in stone is her birthplace, County Tyrone, where she was born in 1795. Everyone else in the family, though, hailed from County Mayo. County Tyrone is in what is now Northern Ireland, separated by several counties and many miles from County Mayo, a northwestern county in the Republic of Ireland. How did Bridget end up in County Mayo, where her son John was born? Bridget, it seemed, had already immigrated once by the time she sailed for America.

The lyrics to an old Irish ballad, written in 1796, provided us with our answer.

A lamentable story, dear people, I'll tell you
That happened in Armagh this very last year.
The landlords combined, with others they joined,
To plunder and rob us of all we hold dear.

Arra, Paddy, dear fellow, where is your shillelagh,
That us'd to assist us when in much distress;
The jails they are filled with your nearest relations
Your wives and your children are sorely oppressed.
Your houses are burned, your lands desolated,
By a band of Ruffians with Orange Cockades.
By the south and the north you will be befriended,
Who will stop the proceedings of the those bloody blade.

The clergy and landlords they have oppressed you
Because that poor Ireland they wished to keep slaves
They bribed your own neighbors to ruin your labours,
Says they, "You are Papists, and so must be knaves."

In 1795, right around the time Linda's great-great-great-grandmother was born, there was a punishing outbreak of anti-Catholic violence in linen-manufacturing towns in County Tyrone and in the county southeast of it, Armagh. Gangs roamed the streets, destroying the homes of Catholics, beating them, sometimes even killing them. This religious persecution uprooted eight hundred families, consisting of four thousand individuals, who settled in the town of Westport in County Mayo, where many of Linda's ancestors were born. The McNamees were most certainly among them.

■ The paper trail for Linda's Irish ancestors was far longer than she had ever imagined. "I just always assumed that whatever was there would be lost on the transit to America," she said. Now we would use DNA to trace Linda's family back even further. First we looked at her mitochondrial DNA to determine her maternal haplogroup. It is U5a1a1, a subgroup of U5, one of the oldest haplogroups in Europe. It arose when modern human beings first moved into western Eurasia from the Near East forty thousand years ago. Nine percent of the Europeans who carry U5 today can trace their maternal ancestry directly back to those early colonizers of Europe. The haplogroup had reached Britain some nine thousand years ago, and mitochondrial DNA extracted from an ancient skeleton discovered in the English town of Cheddar reveals the U5a haplogroup. So while we were unable to trace Linda's direct maternal ancestor, Emily Farley Burk, farther than Virginia, our genealogists concluded that her foremothers came from England.

Linda reacted with awe and humor. "English," she said. "So all my people were persecuting each other. The English were persecuting the Irish. The Spanish were persecuting the Jews. They were mixing it up."

On Linda's father's side, we had identified one Jewish ancestor by name on her family tree, but we wondered if there were even more. There were no records to guide us, and just a few years ago, this would have been an unsolvable mystery. But today, science offers us a possible solution. Two of America's top genetic research firms, Family Tree DNA and 23andMe, analyzed Linda's DNA and returned with the same results: Linda's admixture is 73.31 percent European, 5.82 percent Native American, and 20.87 percent Middle Eastern. The Middle Eastern result, the geneticists told us, is strongly suggestive of Semitic or Jewish ancestry. And 21 percent is a substantial number, indicating the Orozcos were not Linda's only Jewish ancestors.

While her European percentage came from both her mother and her father, the Native American percentage came exclusively from her father's side. This went hand in hand with the genealogical story that we established through the paper trail about her earliest Armijo ancestors and her mestizo ancestors in New Mexico. Of the many guests I have spoken with who assumed they had Native American roots—or desperately wanted to believe they did—Linda actually does.

DNA can help us find where we come from and whom we are related to. Linda is distantly related to our other guest with deep roots in the Southwest, Adrian Grenier—not just related, but they descend from the same man! To find relations, we compare segments of DNA to see where they overlap. Linda and Adrian inherited identical stretches of millions of DNA base pairs on their thirteenth chromosome. Usually when we find this kind of overlap, we say if we could create an ideal family tree, we could identify the common ancestor. In this extremely rare case, we actually could: Diego de Montoya, who was born in about 1596 in Tezcoco, Mexico, then called New Spain. Linda and Adrian are ninth cousins.

"He looks like he could be a cousin," Linda said, looking at a picture of her newfound relative. "He looks a lot like my dad."

We had been able to confirm several stories that Linda had grown up hearing from her father's relatives. To learn the name of her Native American ancestor after hearing talk of the Pueblo Revolt in family lore was exciting for her. Most enlightening, though, was our confirmation of her Jewish roots. "It had been hinted at, thought about, speculated about, but no one ever had any way of knowing," Linda said.

And if Linda's fairy godmother appeared and told her to pick an ancestor to visit, who would it be? "I'd like to go back to Seville and meet the Jewish woman who married into the Armijo family to escape religious persecution," Linda said, referring to her ninth great-grandmother Guiomar Orozco. Part of her interest is historic. "I just find that story a very compelling one. First of all, this is one of our oldest cultures and oldest religions, and that whole period of the Inquisition is one that interests me." But mostly, she had a personal question to ask her ancestor. "I would want to know was this a marriage of convenience or was it true love."

Linda, in fact, did make the journey to present-day Seville to meet with our researcher there. He showed her the archives that hold her Jewish ancestors' records and the church where they may—or may not—have converted to Roman Catholicism. Linda was struck by the fact that this ancient city, where her ancestors once faced such terrible oppression, ultimately became a part of her American identity.

"I've always thought that the story of America was the story of peoples coming here from all different parts of the world, some voluntarily, some involuntarily," she said, "and that what made this country such a great country is that we did have this mixing of people, that we bring into our culture bits and pieces of so many different strains of other traditions and cultures, and that's made us stronger."

This is America's story—a nation shaped not only by great events but also by the smallest details of our ancestors' lives.

The star of HBO's *Entourage* and films like *Celebrity* and *The Devil Wears Prada* is something of a contrarian. He spends more time in his home recording studio in Brooklyn than he does in Hollywood. His roots run deep in the American Southwest, but regarding the subject of his Hispanic heritage, Adrian told me it's a side of his ancestry he's never really embraced. "Every time they make you fill out a census form or whatever, and it says are you black, white, Hispanic, other, I always check 'other,'" said Adrian. "I'm a mixture of things."

He began acting in after-school musicals while attending LaGuardia Arts, the performing arts high school in New York better known as the setting of *Fame*. Adrian spent more of his time at LaGuardia playing the guitar than performing on stage. "It took me a while to start taking acting seriously," he said. "I always shied away from it for some reason. I didn't like being vulnerable. . . . I liked to be much more in control of my destiny."

In his acting career, Adrian has never been typecast, but he has gotten the feedback he is "too ethnic." "I didn't know what to do with that information," he said. He has played characters of a variety of backgrounds, probably because of agents' and casting directors' inability to pinpoint exactly "what" Adrian is based on his looks. "In *West Side Story* I played Tony and Bernardo. And then I played someone from the Middle East. I played an Israeli. I've played the boy next door, you know, the white boy next door."

Adrian's sense of "otherness" stems from his parents. His father's roots trace back to Northern Europe, and while his mother had strong ties to her Hispanic community in New Mexico, she distanced herself from those ties when Adrian was a small child. Adrian was born on July 10, 1976, in Albuquerque, New Mexico, but lived there only until he was four.

"When I was growing up, my mom took me from New Mexico, where the majority of my family was living, and brought me to New York," Adrian told us. "I guess she, on some level, was escaping something." He said he was never particularly curious about his past as a result. "I was raised with this idea that you've got to move forward and create the future."

Adrian credits his mother with teaching him to make sense out of past experiences and learn from them, instead of falling into the trap of complacency or fear. "She had great struggles growing up and overcame a lot of adversity," he said. "One of her survival tools was her ability to see the perspective of her situation and know that it didn't define her, but that she could actually change it by either leaving it or overcoming it in some way."

With little interest in her Hispanic roots, Karesse Grenier was drawn to family stories that tied her to the Apache Indians. "For a long time I always referred to myself as 'Native American white boy,'" Adrian laughed. "Come to think of it, growing up, I did identify with the Native American, or at least I liked the idea of being connected to that Native American heritage. You know, I was authentically an American. My lineage came from this soil."

Many, many Americans claim to be descendants of Native Americans. This is a particularly common misconception among African Americans, but white Americans are often just as convinced of—and ultimately mistaken about—their Native American ancestry. I was curious to know the stories that had been passed down to Adrian about his ancestors, and I wanted to learn the truth behind them.

■ Adrian's mother is from a very old Hispanic family. So why wasn't she drawn to her ancestors? It's impossible to know for certain, but one clue may lie in the estranged relationship that she had with her biological father, Adrian's maternal grandfather. Neither Adrian nor his mother knew him.

Karesse, Adrian's mother, is one of twelve children, the oldest child of Priscilla Grenier and a local politician named Junio Lopez. Priscilla was born in Las Vegas, New Mexico, on April 20, 1928. Junio never publicly acknowledged Karesse as his daughter—and indeed he rarely saw her—even though they lived in the same town. In fact, he was the father of three of Karesse's siblings as well. Karesse told us that she remembers meeting her father only twice in her life, once when she was sixteen and another time when she was twenty-eight. Two-and-a-half-year-old Adrian was with her for the second visit.

Adrian doesn't remember that event, but his mother has been open with him about her history. "She told me when she was sixteen she didn't really know he was her father. He was just a nice guy that took her to have ice cream or something, and she was just like, 'Oh, OK, thanks.'"

Junio Lopez died in 1987, taking with him a host of secrets. For Adrian and his mother, he exists only as a set of tantalizing questions. Although

Junio kept his private life just that, he lived in the public eye, serving in 1958 as mayor of Las Vegas, New Mexico, and later as a Republican state senator.

In 1961 the town of Las Vegas was chosen as one of the All-American Cities, and the local newspaper published a spread about Junio's contributions to its development. A woman who had voted for Junio in the mayoral race two years earlier was interviewed for the article. "From a battered piece of paper she read ten campaign promises which the mayor had printed and distributed two years previous," the article said. "'I told him then,' the lady explained, 'that I was going to keep this list and check off each item as he accomplished it. If in two years he wasn't good to his word, I'd throw this paper in his face. If he does these things, I'll vote for him again. I'm back,' she announced, 'to vote for him again.'"

Adrian's mother was eleven years old when her father ran for his second term as mayor and this article was published. The first word out of Adrian's mouth after reading it was "Hypocrisy." Although Adrian suspects that the townspeople must have known about Karesse and her siblings' biological father, the story of Junio's illegitimate children was either kept out of the press or never discovered. "He might have been married," Adrian speculated. "It just was taboo, and shunned. He couldn't recognize his love for her and the kids, because it was politically totally unacceptable. And I guess my grandmother respected that, or not respected it, but allowed that to be the case."

With his personal life kept under the radar, Junio courted the spotlight in his political career. His ambitions went beyond Las Vegas, and in 1962 he ran as a Republican candidate for the U.S. Congress. He lost this race, and in 1970 ran another, unsuccessful campaign to be governor of New Mexico. Despite the defeats, he remained a popular, admired politician, and in 1987, in a posthumous ceremony, he was honored by the governor for his efforts to unite constituents, regardless of their political affiliation, for the benefit of the community. There's some irony in that: a man who was hailed for his abilities to bring people together was apparently content to keep his illegitimate children as far away from him as possible.

The Lopez name, interestingly, was actually that of Junio's stepfather. Adrian's mother told us that like her son, her mother, and herself, Junio also grew up without a father. According to Karesse, Junio's biological father was handsome and charming—and seeing two sisters at the same time, with both bearing his children. One of those children was Junio. This branch of Adrian's family tree ends with Junio, because we were unable to find the names of his biological parents.

Because they never married, Adrian's grandmother didn't take Junio's last name. Had she, Adrian Grenier today would have been Adrian Lopez. I had to wonder what a difference a last name might have made in Adrian's perceptions of himself. Would he have considered himself Latino? Adrian told me he wasn't even sure where the last name Grenier came from, that his mother at some point changed their last name to Grenier. "Really, again, it was my mother's choice, her choosing her destiny and choosing her identity," he said. "I guess it wouldn't have really mattered, because Lopez or Grenier, I could just choose the name I most identified with."

■ As the story goes, Karesse's Native American ancestry began four generations back on her family tree, with Adrian's great-great-grandmother, Maria Sara Gonzales. According to family lore, Sarita, as she was called, was the daughter of a "full-blooded" Apache known as Julianita. Julianita and her family, Adrian's mother explained, had been driven from the hills north of Villa Nuevo, New Mexico, in a violent attack by white marauders. Adrian's third great-grandfather, Juan Gonzales, found the frightened thirteen-year-old orphan hiding in the bushes. They later fell in love and got married.

"It sounds like a movie I probably want to make one day," Adrian joked. "To be honest," he continued, turning serious, "I've never even questioned that reality."

Hollywood ending aside, we wanted to investigate further to see if the story was true. We looked for records on Julianita's daughter, Sarita, born around 1880 in New Mexico. Fortunately, a portrait exists of Sarita and her husband, Rufino Ortiz. Facial features and skin color, of course, are not definitive evidence of one's ethnic ancestry, but Adrian and I both agreed that, judging by her portrait, there wasn't much trace of Apache on her face, despite the claim in the oral history that said Sarita was half Apache. Furthermore, her death certificate listed her as white, not "red," a distinction also found in census records.

To probe further, we looked for more information on her parents, Juan Gonzales and Petra Ramirez, whose names were found on Sarita's death certificate. Right away there was a discrepancy. Sarita's mother, according to the story, was Julianita, but here was the name Petra. In the 1870 census for San Miguel County, New Mexico, Petra was described as white.

She and Juan lived with her parents, Adrian's fourth great-grandparents, José Maria Ramirez and Maria Manuela Montoya, also described as white.

The marriage record for José and Maria Manuela, however, hints at the Apache story, or at least where the kernel of the idea for it might have come from. "In San Miguel on 27 December 1848," the officiant wrote, "I married José Maria Ramirez, native of the province of Coahuila and resident of this jurisdiction. He didn't state his parents, as he was a captive of the Comanche Nation since he was a small boy, with Maria Manuela (no surname), native of this jurisdiction, daughter of unknown parents."

Raids by both the Comanche and the Apaches on white settlements in Mexico were quite common at this time, especially in the 1830s, prior to the Mexican-American War. And here we had a documented story that José Maria Ramirez was held captive and possibly raised by the Comanche Nation. We assumed this meant he was white, not Native American, but we didn't know for sure until we found the baptism record of José Maria Ramirez, born on December 22, 1830, in Coahuila, Mexico. Not only were both of his parents' names listed on the record; so were all four of his grandparents'—and every one of them was Mexican. His wife, Maria, still remained a mystery, however. If the "daughter of unknown parents" with no surname was Native American, we were unable to find the documents to prove it. While there were a lot of other lines on Adrian's family tree that could have Native American roots, unfortunately, we could not solve the mystery of the Apache orphan; there simply wasn't enough documentation to do it.

We then moved to another branch of Adrian's family tree, that of his great-grandmother, Chata Ortiz, and picked up our search two centuries earlier. In 1637—339 years before Adrian was born in New Mexico—Adrian's ninth great-grandfather, Antonio de Montoya, was born there as well. We were now deep into Adrian's European colonial history. Adrian's ancestry puts into perspective a fact that is often overlooked in history books: New Mexico had been a Spanish colonial province for about a hundred years by the time the English Pilgrims arrived in New England.

For those hundred years, Spaniards had been building towns all over the Southwest, among the many Native Americans, mostly Pueblo Indians, already living there. During Antonio's childhood, relations between the Spanish and the Native Americans were relatively peaceful. But by the time he was an adult, they began to fall apart. We learned of the Pueblo Revolt earlier in the context of Linda Chavez's family history. Adrian's ninth great-grandfather Antonio de Montoya survived the slaughter, but he, his wife, and their three children, and two servants fled the place of his birth and became refugees in El Paso, where it was peaceful and safe. This isn't the image that history usually leaves us with, and it's an interesting reversal: the white European driven off his land by Indians.

Adrian experienced a reversal himself in his perception of his own ancestry. He had always believed his deepest roots were in his Native American ancestry, but now we were finding Spanish ancestors who lived in New Mexico centuries ago. "I've been touting the whole Native American thing for my whole life, and I'm just the guy that was chased out by them."

All colonial records from before 1680 were destroyed in the Pueblo Massacre, but later documents enabled us to piece together more of Antonio de Montoya's story. By 1693, the Spanish families that had been run out of New Mexico by the Pueblos returned, but this time the Pueblos didn't resist. Antonio and his family were among the first Spaniards to resettle the Santa Fe region after the colonists' twelve-year absence. Under the control of Governor Diego de Vargas, whose sole mission was to reassert Spanish control and reestablish the Catholic Church, the Spaniards sought revenge against the Pueblos.

Unfortunately for Adrian, Antonio de Montoya didn't distinguish himself as a voice of peace and compassion. As part of the Santa Fe Militia, he took part in a campaign against the Moqui, or Hopi, Indians. A document from 1716 contained the names of all the soldiers who enlisted, Antonio's among them. He "passed muster with all of his weapons, one horse, and a she mule." On this particular expedition, the Santa Fe Militia approached the Moqui people with peaceful overtures. When they were rebuffed, the militia laid siege to the Moqui areas for sixteen days, driving off their livestock and burning their crops. Ultimately, though, the militia ran out of water and had to abandon the siege—one of many campaigns against the Moqui, Ute, and Comanche waged by the Spanish during this era.

What little thought Adrian had given to his Spanish ancestry had been relatively positive. "I never imagined they were here and up to no good. It was always this romantic 'from Spain,'" he said. "I guess there's always been that one line that I've come back to. When the Europeans came and raped and pillaged the Native Americans, that's when I was born. So I guess on some level, I did recognize that there must have been some conflict and bloodshed and cruelty. I mean, there is in all of our histories." Adrian had just never associated it with his own.

As we traveled one more generation up from Antonio de Montoya, we came across an incredible coincidence. Diego de Montoya, Antonio's father, is Adrian's tenth great-grandfather, born in the year 1596 in Tezcoco, New Spain, the original name for Mexico. Diego de Montoya is also Linda Chavez's direct ancestor. Adrian and Linda are ninth cousins. "We're all connected on some level," Adrian said. True, but most of us are connected fifty thousand years ago. Adrian and Linda are connected by a name.

Did these ancestors make him feel any more connected to that heritage, any more likely to think of himself as a Latino? "I've always avoided these definitions," he answered. "I'm always looking to underplay defining who I am, because it is complex and because I could never really get to the true essence, and no one word is going to describe the subtlety." But he told us he would like to go back to New Mexico now and look at it with "new eyes."

Still, the question of Adrian's Native American ancestry lingered. "There weren't very many marriage partners to choose from," New Mexico state historian Rick Hendricks told us during a discussion about the Spanish and Native American populations. "From the beginning, the men made unions—now, not always marriage, but they formed unions with Native American women." We would see this borne out in yet another branch of the tree of Adrian's great-grandmother Chata Ortiz. That branch would lead us all the way back to sixteenth-century Spain.

Adrian's maternal eleventh great-grandfather, Hernán Martín Serrano, was one of the original Spanish settlers in New Mexico. Adrian was astonished. "That's pretty epic!" he exclaimed.

Hernán was born in Zacatecas, Mexico, a silver-mining town discovered by Spanish explorers in 1540. Adrian's ancestor must have been one of the first Spaniards born there in the 1550s. We thought that Hernán might lead us to a Native American ancestor on Adrian's family tree, but he took us in an entirely different direction. We learned from a muster roll written on February 10, 1597, that Hernán was a sergeant in the army of Don Juan de Oñate, who, in 1595, had acquired a royal contract from the Spanish crown to establish a new settlement in the upper Rio Grande Valley, an area known as La Nueva Mexico, or New Mexico. On April 30, 1598, Oñate, leading a crew of about 130 soldiers, including Adrian's ancestor, claimed New Mexico for Spain. Later that summer, they founded Santa Fe de Nuevo Mexico, the very first European settlement west of the Mississippi River. As a result, Oñate and his men are considered the founders of New Mexico.

Oñate has another, more notorious distinction: historians know him today as "the last conquistador," notorious for brutally subduing the Pueblo Indians. The age of the conquistadors had started around 1501. In October of 1598, Oñate's men got into a dispute with one of the Pueblo tribes, the Acoma Indians. Twelve Spaniards were killed. In response, three months later, war broke out in earnest, and Oñate and his soldiers struck back, killing eight hundred Acoma men, women, and children. Then Oñate turned on the five hundred survivors, who were now enslaved, in an almost unimaginable way. He ordered his men to amputate the foot of every man over the age of twenty-five. We don't know if Adrian's eleventh great-grandfather actually participated, but he did come to the region with Oñate.

"I assume that he did a lot of cruel things," Adrian said, pained to learn about his ancestor's proximity to this brutal punishment. "They had different values, absolutely. But I don't identify with that spirit. Interesting how I guess I've identified with the victims more than the aggressors. I'd like to think that I was part of a more peaceful ancestry."

This horrible story led us to a surprising revelation. Remember that Adrian is not a descendant of Oñate but of a sergeant in his army, Hernán Martín Serrano. (I reminded Adrian of that as well.) Hernán lived out the rest of his life in Santa Fe, New Mexico, dying sometime in the early 1600s and leaving behind a wife and several children. While searching the record for those children, we discovered something unusual about his son, Adrian's tenth great-grandfather, Luis.

Adrian was afraid to find out anything more about this branch of his family, but this new information put his mind at rest. We had found the 1663 document "Inquisition Record naming Luis Martín Serrano."

Luis was born in Santa Fe around 1610. The Spanish Inquisition had ended by this time, but religious persecution and its attendant paranoia were still common. Even in distant New Mexico, people were called to testify against one another. These were dark days, but for genealogists, there is a bright side: the founding families of New Mexico were making recorded statements all the time about one another. Searching someone's family tree becomes a lot easier when documents are available.

As we have learned, an elaborate *casta* system was constructed in the Spanish colonies, which allowed the Spaniards to distinguish among race and caste. There was actually an illustrated chart designed to help with the process. The best way to think of it is almost like a cookbook or a guidebook. It showed the different terms used for white, black, Indian, and mixed-race people, in all possible combinations. There were sixteen color categories in all.

The Inquisition Record we uncovered described Hernán's son Luis as "the Mestizo or Indio Luis Martín Serrano." Mestizo, of course, means Indian; specifically, it was the term used to describe people who were half-white and half–Native American. This record proved that even though Adrian's ancestor entered New Mexico as a conquistador and brought his wife and children with him, he stayed behind and had a family with a Native American woman. In other words, Adrian and his mother do indeed have Native American ancestry after all.

"I'm vindicated!" Adrian laughed, but he was clearly relieved to have definitive proof of the ancestry he had always embraced. Luis's story illustrates a basic fact about the history of Spanish settlers and Native Americans: their histories crossed in ways both terrible and joyous, and they often had children with each other. Their descendants have it in their DNA to prove it.

■ How far back would an exploration of Adrian's father's ancestry take us? John Dunbar was born on July 27, 1951, in Marion, Ohio. Adrian was only about four when his parents split up, and for most of Adrian's adult life, he has been estranged from his father. "I saw him once again when I was about eight or nine, briefly," Adrian said, "and then not again until I was twenty-three, and I showed up at his doorstep with a camera to make my documentary about him." Adrian's documentary is called *Shot in the Dark*, and it explores their broken relationship. "I wanted to put up a mirror to the expectations that people have of what a father should be," Adrian explained.

He and his father do see each other occasionally now, but Adrian said that it isn't always easy to find the common ground between them. "We're very, very different, and in a lot of ways we were strangers for most of my life," he said. "It's harder to reconcile those differences when you don't have that strong blood bond from a very young age."

During his childhood, Adrian maintained contact with his father's side of the family through his paternal grandparents, Carl and Esther Dunbar. "Throughout my estrangement with my father they always kept in touch through letters," he recalled. "My grandmother was always the one to send me a birthday or a Christmas card and twenty bucks. I always felt their presence."

We traced Adrian's father's family back for generations in Ohio, and from there to New England and Pennsylvania. They had arrived in America, for the most part, from Germany and Ireland. As in all family trees, there are many stories to tell, but there was one in particular that I wanted to share with Adrian.

Adrian's fifth great-grandfather was a man named Ludwig Bretz, who came to this country from Germany in 1750. German immigrants were not welcomed with open arms in the British colonies, and by 1727 there was a law in place in Philadelphia requiring all men over the age of sixteen who were not British subjects to swear allegiance to the English monarchy as soon as they landed at the port.

We found Ludwig Bretz in the passenger list for a group of Palatine Germans who took that oath of allegiance when a ship called the *Royal Union* arrived in Philadelphia on August 15, 1750. This was more than a decade before the American Revolution. In that time, Ludwig married Adrian's fifth great-grandmother, Susan Margaret Bischoff, a fellow German immigrant. When the war broke out, this man who had sworn allegiance to the English king enlisted to fight against him, and from 1776 until 1781 Ludwig Bretz was a Patriot. He served in Captain Martin Weaver's 6th Company, 4th Battalion of the Lancaster County Militia from Pennsylvania, which distinguished itself by protecting the West Branch Valley in central Pennsylvania from British and Indian troops that were fighting together.

Adrian's people have been in this country since the beginning. He has a claim on American history on both sides of his family that very few people do. "As an American who has been here from the beginning, it maybe gives me a little bit of leverage to speak what I believe about tolerance and allowing the dynamics in this country to flourish," he said, half-jokingly. "The dynamics of this country are all of the people that make it up, all of the immigrants, all of the human beings that come from all walks of life, throughout the world, to contribute their experiences and their vastly nuanced experiences to make it a country as whole and beautiful as America."

■ It was time to turn to DNA. On Adrian's father's side, we could trace his direct paternal ancestors back to his fourth great-grandfather, Robert Dunbar, born on February 1, 1771, in Philadelphia. Using his Y-DNA, we identified his paternal haplogroup as R1b1b2a1a2f. Ancient members of this haplogroup were among the first men to repopulate Western Europe after the Ice Age ended about twelve thousand years ago. Many men with this haplogroup may be direct descendants of an Irish king named Niall of the Nine Hostages, who ruled in what is now Ireland in about 450 A.D. In New York City, about 2 percent of all men share Adrian's paternal haplogroup; that number is at about 8 percent in Dublin. Unlike some haplogroups, which go back sixteen thousand or twenty thousand years to an anonymous ancestor, this one goes back fifteen hundred years to one virile man.

Adrian shares this paternal haplogroup with just one other person I know—me. (I descend from a man of Irish descent who impregnated my great-great-grandmother, Jane Gates, who was a slave.)

On Adrian's mother's side, we'd found what seemed to be incontrovertible evidence that Adrian has at least one Native American ancestor. But the written record is sometimes fallible, and ethnicity is sometimes in the eye of the beholder. So far, we had traced his direct maternal ancestor back to his fourth great-grandmother, Maria Manuela Montoya, born on January 1, 1830, in San Miguel, New Mexico. Now DNA confirmed what our genealogical research had already revealed. Adrian's haplogroup, C1b2, is a subgroup of C, one of the four haplogroups found among Native Americans. Haplogroup C arose in Asia fifty thousand years ago. Compare that to his paternal haplogroup from Niall, which is only fifteen hundred years old. Between twenty thousand and twelve thousand years ago, the Bering Land Bridge allowed all manner of life, including humans, to cross into the Americas. Once here, haplogroup C diversified into subgroups like Adrian's.

For Adrian, this result was confirmation of his long-cherished sense of his family's Native American ancestry. His admixture test reveals his percentage of African, European, and Native American ancestry since the time of Columbus, who we know didn't precede his own ancestors by long. According to Family Tree DNA, Adrian is 62.61 percent European, 8.44 percent Native American, and 28.95 percent Middle Eastern.

The Middle Eastern result struck Adrian as curious. Family Tree DNA says this finding is consistent with a North African group such as the Moors. The Moors figured prominently in Spanish history. They conquered Seville in the year 712 and remained in power through the thirteenth century. In 1391 Seville became ground zero for the Spanish Inquisition. While the Inquisition focused primarily on routing out Jews, many Muslims, including the Moors, converted and intermarried with Christians. Adrian's Spanish ancestors, Martin Serrano and the Montoyas, may have brought this Middle Eastern or Moorish ancestry with them when they came to New Mexico.

The Native American number is small compared to Adrian's other percentages, but it indicates that his most recent Native American ancestor would be one great-grandparent, which is indeed very recent. While this reinforces the identity with which he was raised, he actually has much more Native American DNA than the oral history would indicate. Julianita, the Apache orphan ancestor of lore, would have been his great-great-great-grandmother.

I asked him what makes us who we are: our experiences, our families, our genome, or some combination? Many people I speak to tell me it's their experiences or their family that shape them most, almost reluctant to admit or acknowledge that DNA may play a part in who they are. But Adrian, the creative and sensitive person I came to know through our journey, surprised me with the first part of his answer. "I think they're the concrete facts. There's the genealogy, the articles, the DNA if you want to be really precise," he said. His softer side emerged in the next part of his answer. "But then there's the interpretation as well. And if you look throughout history, at least from what we've been looking at, a lot of people have made their own interpretations about who they are, including myself. And I think that's important to recognize that you can be who you imagine your best self to be, and you can help change the history and make a new one by your choices."

■ I've enjoyed going so deeply into Adrian's past, and America's past. I ended our time together by asking him the question I ask all our guests: if a fairy godmother said he could meet any ancestor of all those he's met today, which one would it be? "Perhaps our mutual Irish king"—Niall of the Nine Hostages—"because he was the first mutation, and that's pretty interesting to be the first of the entire lineage of mutations." The second person was someone much closer to home: his grandfather, Junio Lopez. Adrian said he just wanted to know what Junio was thinking. "I mean, if he fulfilled that list of promises on that woman's checklist, what about all the other promises or all the other checklists that he never got to, especially with regard to my grandmother and his illegitimate kids?" The idea of what it means to be a father—and is it enough to be a biological father—clearly weighs heavily on Adrian.

In the end, my journey through Michelle, Linda, and Adrian's family trees has helped me understand a significant part of American history in the most personal ways. Some of their ancestors were the original, indigenous Americans, while others were among the first Europeans and Africans to settle in the New World. These two streams met on this continent long ago. And though their experiences were extraordinarily difficult, and often brutal, they shaped the course of American history just as profoundly as the Pilgrims did.

■　■　■　■　■

Mark Twain famously is reported to have said, "History doesn't repeat itself, but it does rhyme." As we grapple with issues of immigration reform in our own time, we would do well to look for—and heed—the warnings in these rhymes, not least in confronting the subtle and not so subtle hierarchies of race, color, and religion that continue to impact the way many discuss—and determine—what it means to be "American," despite the illusion (and dangers) of any "pure" definition.

If we have learned anything from these remarkable and ceaselessly surprising investigations, it is that truth, for our nation and for ourselves, is in the search, while freedom—and empowerment—are found in choosing what to do with truths, once revealed. The form of this book is prose, but there have been plenty of rhymes to go around. My hope is that we will listen and learn from them before drawing any fateful, and too often repeated and regretted, lines between "us" and the next "new group" of dreamers to come to our shores. Isn't five centuries of obsessing enough?

ACKNOWLEDGMENTS

If it's true that it takes a village to raise a child, it takes a regiment to make our weekly documentary television series, *Finding Your Roots*. This book is the companion text to that series, consisting of a much fuller version of the stories of each of our guests' family trees than time allows us to tell on the television show. So I want to start my acknowledgements by thanking our stellar production team, under the leadership of Rachel Dretzin, series senior producer, and Leslie Asako Gladsjo, senior story editor. Our team is composed of the following extraordinarily creative individuals: Michael Bacon, original score; Seth Bomse, R.A. Fedde, Ben Howard, Ken Levis, Peter Livingston Jr., Nancy Novack, and Lisa Shreve, editors; John Maggio, Julia Marchesi, Caitlin McNally, Sabin Streeter, Jesse Sweet, and Jack Youngelson, directors/producers; Hazel Gurland-Pooler and Titi Yu, co-producers; Tom Denison, Josh Gleason, and Sandra McDaniel, associate producers; and Stephen Altobello, Nicole Bozorgmir, Rebecca Brillhart, Greg Brutus, Emily Singer Chapman, Stef Gordon, Stephen McCarthy, Brian Oakes, Stephen Robinson, Sam Russell, Holly Siegel, Danielle Varga, and David Yim.

Genealogy is an art as well as a science, and in a field that seems to be growing exponentially every year, there is no genealogist more outstanding than Johni Cerny, our chief genealogist for *Finding Your Roots*. Johni's capacity to make the archives yield their secrets still astonishes me, even after working closely with her for the past decade. In addition to undertaking the main research tasks herself, she coordinates the work of a large team of genealogical researchers spread around our country and throughout Europe, Latin America, India, and East Asia, each of whom made a major contribution to finding our guests' long-lost ancestors. These researchers include Avani Batra, Christopher Child, Henrietta Christmas,

José Antonio Esquibel, Norma Feliberti, Matthew Hovious, Summer Bomi Kim, Dorothy Leivers, Rhonda McClure, Ronaldo Miera, Jaime Read, Megan Smolenyak, Zbigniew Stettner, Frazine Taylor, Debbie Parker Wayne, Pamela Weisberger, and Jim Yarin. For their additional research I'd like to thank Jane Ailes, Sung Baik, John Caknipe, Alta Cannaday, Sandra Chappell, Patrice Dabrowski, Lauren DeFilippo, Paul Finkelman, Alberto Forero, Carolyn Goudie, Art Green, Ernestine Hamm, Paul Heinegg, TaeYoung Kim, Kelley Kroecker, Nivi Kumar, Suneel Kumar, Ellen Ly, Laurence Martin, Magdalena Mazurek-Nuovo, Angel M. Nieves-Rivera, Greg Osborn, Eugene Park, Oleh Pavlyshyn, Phil Pendleton, Denyce Peyton, Jan Piña, James Pritchard, Judy Riffel, Phillip Smith, Rebecca Snedeker, Barbara Trevigne, Addy Tymczyszyn and The Kosciuszko Foundation, Lyubomyr Vorobiy, Tim Wales, Ewa Wiatr, and Troy Wiley; and interns Megan Abell, Raymond Chiu, Matthew Herzfeld, Madeleine Johnson, Andrew Lobashevsky, Derric Meister, Hannah Olson, Nathifa Perez, Mike Smedes, Chelsea Villareal, and Jesse Weissman.

I would like to thank the following scientists for their generous advice and tutelage about the wonders of the use of DNA analysis to track ancestry: David Altshuler, Mark Daly, and Eric Lander at the Broad Institute; Ken Chahine at Ancestry DNA; George Church at the Harvard Medical School; Bennett Greenspan at Family Tree DNA; Rick Kittles at African Ancestry; Joanna Mountain at 23andMe; Nathaniel Pearson at Ingenuity; and the forty participants of the Genealogy and Genetics Working Group that I coordinate with my colleague, Evelynn Hammonds.

Funding for the series was generously provided by the following corporations and foundations: The Coca-Cola Company, Johnson & Johnson, McDonald's, American Express, Carnegie Corporation of New York, The Atlantic Philanthropies, the Ford Foundation, Pew Charitable Trusts, the Corporation for Public Broadcasting (CPB), and PBS. I would especially like to thank Brian Perkins at Johnson & Johnson and Ingrid Saunders Jones, the former chair of The Coca-Cola Foundation, for supporting each of our five genealogical series since the airing of *African American Lives* in 2006, and Vartan Gregorian at Carnegie, Gara LaMarche at The Atlantic Philanthropies, Rebecca Rimel at Pew, and Darren Walker at the Ford Foundation, for understanding the enormous potential of the series to educate a broad audience about biology, genetics, immigration, and the full sweep of the settlement of America and the history of its remarkable people.

I'd like to thank my co-executive producers and partners, Peter W. Kunhardt and Dyllan McGee, and Stephen Segaller from Channel 13 in New York. At McGee Kunhardt Productions, thanks go to Jill Cowan, Mary Farley, George T. Kunhardt, Teddy Kunhardt, Drew Patrick, and Jaime Sukonnik. Thanks also to Bill Gardner, Beth Hoppe, Paula Kerger, Tammy Robinson, and John Wilson at PBS; Patricia Harrison and Jennifer Lawson at the Corporation for Public Broadcasting; and Julie Anderson, Jon Berman, Lindsey Bernstein, Stephanie Carter, Rachel Hartman, Roberta Lee, Rekha Menon, Julie Schapiro-Thorman, Neal Shapiro, Kellie Specter, Michael Weingrad, and Donna Williams at Channel 13.

The families and friends of the participants in our show were tremendously helpful to us, and I'd like to thank Carolyn and Cary Booker, Seung Hoon Cho, Robert Downey Sr. and Elsie Ford, Dolores and Ellis Marsalis, Yvette Marsalis, Connie Rice, Ron Stephens and James Hale, and Fred and Sulja Warnick for the assistance they gave us tracking down their distant and more recent relatives.

Members of our guests' staffs were particularly gracious in coordinating very busy schedules, including Chris Bailey, Susie Mieras, and Lisa Serra (Kyra Sedgwick and Kevin Bacon); Frank Baker, Jeremy Elder, Steve Komanapalli, and Anne Krumm (Rick Warren); Esther Chen, Deb Dowling, Melany Lynch, Katherine Nash, Jackie Noble, and Daisy Schwartzberg (Martha Stewart); Tia Chester (Sanjay Gupta); Geneva Farrell (Ruth Simmons); Tiffany Fountain (Geoffrey Canada); Allison Garman (Robert Downey Jr.); Robin Garvick (Adrian Grenier); Brenda Jones (John Lewis); Courtney Kivowitz (Maggie Gyllenhaal); Lori Klein, Monique Medina, and Bryant Renfroe (Barbara Walters); Sharon Macklin (Cory Booker); Sarah Martin (Margaret Cho); Volney McFarlin (Samuel L. Jackson); Melissa Mittereder (Harry Connick Jr.); Greg Nishimura-Seese, Hassan K. Smith, and Chris Stinebrink (John Legend); Tiffany Raith (Wanda Sykes); Marilyn Stanley (Condoleezza Rice); and Anne-Marie Wilkins (Branford Marsalis).

In addition, I would like to thank family members and a few dear friends whose love and support nourish and sustain me, including my partner, Marial Iglesias Utset; my daughters, Maggie and Liza Gates; and my son-in-law, Aaron Hatley; as well as Bennett Ashley; Larry Bobo and Marcyliena Morgan; Kevin Matthew Burke; Virgis Colbert; Charlie Davidson; Brenda Kimmel Davy; Driss Elghannaz; Dean Laura Fisher; my astonishingly energetic and well-organized executive assistant, Amy Gosdanian;

Evelyn Brooks Higginbotham; Glenn H. Hutchins; Elaine Walker Johnson; Joanne Kendall; Debora Kilroy; Cindy Francis Leatherman; Connie Butler Lechliter; Brenda Junkins Long; Paul Lucas; Mike Munsie; Deborah Wilson Pamepinto; Steve Rattner; Thelma Rankin Rhodes; Adrienne Sands; Teresa Lupis Savage; Brian Siberell; Steve Simmons; William Julius Wilson; the very able executive director of the Hutchins Center, Abby Wolf; and Julie Wolf, whose expert copyediting and attention to textual and factual detail are marvels to behold.

INDEX

Canada, Henry Richard (Kennedy), 60, 61, 62

Canada, Jerry, 58

Canada, Joyce, 58

Canada, McAllister "Mac," 56–57, 59–60, 62

Canada, Pearl, 59

Canada, Peter (Cannaday/Kennedy), 60, 61, 62

Canada, Reuben, 58

Canada, Sarah Smothers (Kennedy), 60, 61, 62

Canada, Winifred Jackson, 60, 61

Cannaday, Alta, 64

Cannaday, Benjamin, 62, 64

Cannaday, Charles (black man), 62

Cannaday, Charles (white man), 64–65, 67, 69

Cannaday, Julia, 62, 63

Cannaday, Thomas, 62, 63–65, 69, 70

Carlin, George, 241

Carmichael, Stokely, 166

Carson, Ben, 82

Carter, Ben, 10

Carter, Betsy Shipman, 25–26

Carter, Dink, 25

Carter, Elizabeth "Betty," 27–29, 33

Carter, Frank, 25

Carter, Joel, 28–29

Carter, Tobias, 27–30, 31, 33, 43

Cerny, Johni, 245, 248

Chandur Biswa case of 1939, 136–37

Chavez, Ambrosio Rosendo, 292–94

Chavez, Eduardo, 293

Chavez, Linda: Hispanic roots of, 279–80; maternal ancestors of, 290, 291, 298–300; birth of, 291; childhood of, 291, 292–93; education of, 291–92, 293; paternal ancestors of, 292–97, 300, 308; maternal ancestors of, 298–300; DNA profile of, 300–301

Chavez, Maria Feliciana Armijo, 293

Chavez, Petra Armijo, 293–94, 297

Chavez, Rudolfo Enrique, 292–93, 300

Chavez, Velma McKenna, 291, 293, 298

Childs, Virginia, 159

Cho, Margaret: and identity, 112, 205, 206, 207; career of, 205, 206; birth of, 206; childhood of, 206–8, 214, 216; paternal ancestors of, 208–12, 214–15; maternal ancestors of, 212–14, 215; DNA profile of, 214–16

Cho, Myung Sook, 208–10

Cho, Seung Hoon, 206, 207, 208–9, 210, 214

Cho, Young Hie Chun, 206, 207, 208, 212, 213

Cho Chun, 212

Cho Dai Hyun, 214

Cho In-gyu, 211–12, 215

Christiansen, George, 228, 236

Christina (queen of Sweden), 156

Chungson (king of Korea), 211

Chungyol (Goryeo king), 211

Chun Jin-han, 212–13, 215

Chun Yoo Kyum, 213–14

Church, John Thomas, 105

Civil Rights Act of 1964, 31, 181

Civil rights movement: effect on black institutions, 9; and John Lewis, 21, 22, 23–24, 29, 30–31, 44; and Cory Booker, 33, 35, 44; and Condoleezza Rice, 180–82; and Ruth Simmons, 196

Civil Rights Walk of Fame, 21

Civil War, 14, 106, 149, 262

Clark, Jim, 30–31

Clarke, Michael, 88

Clay, Henry, 272, 274, 277

Clifford, Isaac, 274–75

Clinton, Hillary, 219

Collins, Addie Mae, 180

Collins, Alfred H., 41–42

Collins, Henrietta Stamper, 41–43

Collins, Windsor, 41

Comly, Henry, 87

Comly, Robert, 91

Connick, Anita Frances Livingston (Levy), 13, 17

Connick, Harry (Joseph Harry Fowler), Jr.: career of, 2, 12–14, 17, 20; Ellis Marsalis as teacher of, 2, 19; paternal ancestors of, 14–17, 18; maternal ancestors of, 17–18, 19; DNA profile of, 18–19, 69, 92, 109, 151, 162; and Hurricane Katrina, 19

Connick, Harry (Joseph Harry Fowler), Sr., 13, 14–16

Connick, James Paul (1835), 15–17, 18

Connick, James Paul (1902), 14, 15

Connick, John Joseph, 14

Connick, Margaret White, 15, 18